D0212875

BT
119
.C37
1983

BEITRÄGE ZUR
GESCHICHTE DER BIBLISCHEN EXEGESE

Herausgegeben von

OSCAR CULLMANN, BASEL/PARIS · NILS A. DAHL, NEW HAVEN
ERNST KÄSEMANN, TÜBINGEN · HANS-JOACHIM KRAUS, GÖTTINGEN
HEIKO A. OBERMAN, TÜBINGEN · HARALD RIESENFELD, UPPSALA
KARL HERMANN SCHELKLE, TÜBINGEN

25

The Johannine Paraclete
in the Church Fathers

A Study in the History
of Exegesis

by

ANTHONY CASURELLA

SALZMANN LIBRARY
St. Francis Seminary
3257 South Lake Drive
St. Francis, Wis. 53235

1 9 8 3

J. C. B. MOHR (PAUL SIEBECK) TÜBINGEN

66318

CIP-Kurztitelaufnahme der Deutschen Bibliothek

Casurella, Anthony:
The Johannine Paraclete in the Church Fathers: a study in the history of exegesis /
by Anthony Casurella. — Tübingen: Mohr, 1983.
  (Beiträge zur Geschichte der biblischen Exegese; 25)
  ISBN 3-16-144648-8

NE: GT

© Anthony Casurella / J. C. B. Mohr (Paul Siebeck) Tübingen 1983.
Alle Rechte vorbehalten. Ohne ausdrückliche Genehmigung des Verlags ist es auch nicht
gestattet, das Buch oder Teile daraus auf photomechanischem Wege (Photokopie,
Mikrokopie) zu vervielfältigen.
Printed in Germany. Offsetdruck: Gulde-Druck GmbH, Tübingen. Einband: Heinrich
Koch, Großbuchbinderei, Tübingen.

This book is my doctoral thesis, submitted to the Faculty of
Divinity of the University of Durham late in 1980 under the title
'Patristic Interpretations of the Paraclete Passages in John's Gospel.
An Account and Critical Evaluation'. As the title suggests, it is a
critical survey of the use made by the early Church fathers of that
group of sayings in the Fourth Gospel which promise the coming and
describe the activity of ἄλλον παράκλητον (Jo. 14,15-17.25-26; 15,26-
27; 16,4b-15). It is my intention in these pages to describe and,
insofar as I am able, to assess patristic exegesis of the paraclete
passages. This means that I have not been concerned merely to turn
up every allusion or quotation. What we look at here are examples of
ancient writing wherein exegesis of our verses is explicitly (or even
implicitly) to be found.

There are, as will become plain, scores of such passages in
the fathers. This is perhaps to be expected, as the Johannine teaching on the Paraclete possesses evidential value for certain issues
important to the ancient Church and not unimportant today. On this
account, the limitations of space and method require that we concentrate more or less on main lines of development. This does not mean
that the unique and individual is neglected; it is not. But it is
best to acknowledge at the outset that the attempt to do justice to
the whole of patristic exegesis sometimes makes it impossible to give
the individual exegete the detailed attention he would merit if he
alone were the subject of study.

A word is due about the chronological limits adopted for the
research. In my explorations I accepted that the *terminus a quo*

should be the date of the publication of the Gospel. As a *terminus ad quem*, I arbitrarily chose the death of Isidore of Seville (636) in the West and that of John of Damascus (ca. 750) in the East. In the event these dates proved adequate, as the creative era of the interpretation of the passages by the early Church had come to flower and run its course well within these limits. The search for materials led to an examination of all available literature dating from before A.D. 325. Lack of time made it impossible to consult fathers after that date other than those writing in Latin and Greek. For help in understanding the paraclete passages themselves, I have tried to read all the relevant materials published since 1918, again an arbitrarily set limit. The more important of these are set out in the Bibliography and notes. It has not been possible - or, for that matter, necessary and desirable - to take account here of newly published literature, but I have listed at the end of the Bibliography a selection of helpful books and articles (published before the end of 1981) not available to me at the time of writing.

I must also mention one or two matters of form. The book itself is little changed from the days when it was 'just' a thesis. Cross references have, of course, been altered in line with the new page numbers. And, by the kind allowance of the publishers, there is now an Index. As regards orthography, I have followed current practice in the writing of Greek and Latin when it involves my own work. Where I quote from ancient authors, however, I adopt the conventions of the edition from which the quotation is taken. This, of course, leads to some obvious divergences in the use, for example, of capitalization and accents in Greek and the writing of initial v in Latin. There should be no confusion.

In the immortal phrase of John Donne, 'no man is an island'.

This is as true in the writing of books as it is in any other area of
life, and so I wish to acknowledge here my debt to those who have
helped me along the way. Grateful thanks are particularly due to the
Rev. Dr. A. Morrison, formerly a fellow research student in Durham,
for consultation on points regarding the Johannine text of Theodore of
Mopsuestia as preserved in the Syriac version of his works; to Professor C.K. Barrett for his patience, his careful eye and penetrating
comments, and many suggested improvements, in all of which he has gone
beyond what a research student might reasonably demand of his super-
visor; to Miss A.M. McAulay, Durham University Librarian, for her
kindness in releasing the typescript of my thesis for photo-offset
purposes; to the staff of the Emmanuel Bible College in Birkenhead
who have been willing to do without their Principal at times during
the writing up so that he could get on with the work and have over
and over again cheerfully taken his tasks onto their already overloaded shoulders; and, finally, to my wife Sharon for her patient and
enduring support through the years of research and her willingness to
carry an increasing responsibility for our family of four children
and for the work of the College. All these deserve a share in the
credit for the successful completion of this book.

Birkenhead

Christmas 1982

CONTENTS

ABBREVIATIONS

ANCIENT CHRISTIAN WRITINGS

The Greek Fathers

Only a few abbreviations of Greek fathers and writings are shown
here. For all others see G.W.H. Lampe (ed.), A Patristic Greek
Lexicon (Oxford, 1972), the table of abbreviations.

Amphilochius of Iconium
   (Amph.)
   hom. on Jo. 14,28   Homily on John 14,28 (Moss).

Anastasius of Antioch
   (Anast.Ant.)
   or. 1-5   Orationes 1-5, trans. F. Turrianus (PG
                       89,1309-1362).

Anastasius Sinaita
   (Anast.S.)
   hex.   Anagogicarum contemplationum in Hexaemeron
                       ad Theophilum (PG 89,851-1077).

Apollinaris of Laodicaea
   (Apoll.)
   Jo.   Fragments of the Commentary on John (TU
                       89,3-64).

Apophth.Patr.v.s.   Apophthegmata patrum, verba seniorum, trans.
                       Paschasius (PL 73,1025-1062).

Didymus of Alexandria
   (Didym.)
   Spir.   De Spiritu sancto (PG 39,1033-1086).

Eusebius of Emesa
   (Eus.Em.)
   disc.   Discourses (Buytaert).

Gregory of Nyssa
   (Gr.Nyss.)
   ref.Eun.   Refutatio confessionis Eunomii (Jaeger 2,
                       312-410).

Isaias Abbas
   (Is.Ab.)
   or. 1-29   Orationes 1-29 (PG 40,1105-1206).

Severus of Antioch
  (Sev.Ant.)
  Gram.   Liber contra impium Grammaticum (CSCO 93.
                                 101.111).
  hom.   Homiliae cathedrales (PO 4,1-94; 8,209-396;
                                 12,1-163; 16,761-864; 20,271-434; 22,201-
                                 312; 23,1-176; 25,1-174.621-815; 26,259-
                                 450; 29,1-262).

Theodore of Mopsuestia
  (Thdr.Mops.)
  hom. 1-16   Catechetical Homilies (ST 145).
  Jo.Syr.   Commentary on the Gospel of St. John,
                                 Syriac version (CSCO 115).
  Mac.   Disputatio cum Macedonianis (PO 9,637-667).

Theodoret of Cyrus
  (Thdt.)
  exp.fid.   Expositio rectae fidei (CAC 4,2-66).
  qu.et resp.   Quaestiones et responsiones ad orthodoxos
                                 (CAC 5,2-246).

The Latin Fathers

Ambrose of Milan
  (Ambr.)
  fid.   De fide (CSEL 78).
  i.d.s.   De incarnationis dominicae sacramento (CSEL
                                 79,223-281).
  Lc.   Expositio Evangelii secundum Lucam (CCL 14,
                                 1-400).
  Spir.   De Spiritu sancto (CSEL 79,5-222).

Ambrosiaster
  (Ambrstr.)
  Eph.   Commentaria in Epistolam ad Ephesios (PL
                                 17,371-404).
  Mt.   In Matthaeum 24 fragmenta (PLS 1,655-668).
  quaest.   Quaestiones Veteris et Noui Testamenti
                                 (CSEL 50).

Augustine of Hippo
  (Aug.)
  don.pers.   De dono perseuerantiae (PL 45,993-1034).
  ep. 1-270   Epistulae 1-270 (CSEL 34.44.57. CSEL 58 con-
                                 tains indices, critical notes, etc.).
  Faust.   Contra Faustum (CSEL 25,1,249-797).
  Fel.   Contra Felicem (CSEL 25,2,799-852).
  fid.   De fide et symbolo (CSEL 41,1-32).
  fund.   Contra epistulam quam uocant fundamenti (CSEL
                                 25,1,191-248).
  Jo. 1-124   In Iohannis Euangelium tractatus 1-124 (CCL
                                 36).
  Max.   Collatio cum Maximino Arianorum Episcopo (PL
                                 42,709-742).

Max.haer.	Contra Maximinum haereticum Arianorum Epis-copum (PL 42,743-814).
Parm.	Contra epistulam Parmeniani (CSEL 51,17-142).
pec.	De peccatorum meritis et remissione et de baptismo paruulorum ad Marcellinum (CSEL 60, 1-152).
Pel.	Contra duas epistulas Pelagianorum (CSEL 60,421-571).
Ps. 1-150	Enarrationes in Psalmos 1-150 (CCL 38-40).
quaest.	De diuersis quaestionibus (OSA 10,52-379).
Script.	De diuinis Scripturis siue speculum (CSEL 12,287-700).
serm. 1-183	Sermones de Scripturis Veteris et Noui Testa-menti (PL 38,23-994).
serm.Ar.	Contra sermonem Arianorum (PL 42,683-708).
serm.mont.	De sermone Domini in monte (CCL 35).
serm.V.T. 1-50	Sermones de Vetere Testamento 1-50 (CCL 41).
Trin.	De Trinitate (CCL 50-50A).

Alcimus Ecdicius Avitus
(Av.)

diu.Spir.	Fragmenta libri de diuinitate Spiritus sancti (PL 59,385-386).

Bachiarius
(Bach.)

prof.fid.	Professio fidei (PL 20,1019-1036).

Flauius Magnus Aurelius Cassiodorus
(Cass.)

Ps.	Expositio Psalmorum (CCL 97-98).

Eusebius of Vercelli
(Eus.Ver.)

Trin.	De Trinitate, 1-7 authorship disputed, 8-12 authorship unknown (CCL 9,1-99.111-118.129-205).

Faustus of Riez
(Faust.)

ep. 1-12	Epistulae 1-12 (CSEL 21,159-220).
serm. 1-31	Sermones 1-31 (CSEL 21,221-347).
Spir.	De Spiritu sancto (CSEL 21,99-157).

Fulgentius of Ruspe
(Fulg.)

ep.Don.	Epistula de fide ad Donatum (CCL 91,255-273).
Fab.	Contra Fabianum, fragments (CCL 91A,761-873).
incarn.	Liber ad Scarilam de Incarnatione Filii Dei et vilium animalium auctore (CCL 91,309-356).
Mon.	Ad Monimum (CCL 91,1-64).
resp.	Dicta regis Trasamundi et contra ea respon-sionum (CCL 91,65-94).
Tras.	Ad Trasamundum (CCL 91,95-185).

Gaudentius of Brescia
(Gaud.)

tract. 1-21	Tractatus 1-21 (CSEL 68).

Hilary of Poitiers
  (Hil.)
  Trin.   De Trinitate (PL 10,25-472).

Isaac Iudaeus
  (Isaac I.)
  f.i.   Fides Isatis ex Iudaeo (CCL 9,335-343).

Isidore of Seville
  (Isid.)
  ep. 1-12   Epistolae 1-12 (PL 83,893-914).
  etym.   Etymologiarum (PL 82,73-728).

Jerome
  (Jer.)
  ep. 1-154   Epistulae 1-154 (CSEL 54-56).
  in Matth.   Commentariorum in Matthaeum (CCL 77).
  Is.   Commentariorum in Esaiam (CCL 73-73A).

Leo Magnus
  (Leo)
  ep. 1-173   Epistulae 1-173 (PL 54,593-1218).
  tract. 1-96   Tractatus 1-96 (CCL 138-138A).

Maximus of Turin
  (Max.Tur.)
  epiph.   In sancta Epiphania (JTS 16,163-166).

Novatian
  (Nov.)
  Trin.   De Trinitate (CCL 4,1-78).

Pelagius
  (Pel.)
  Rom.   Expositio in Epistolam ad Romanos (PLS 1,
                               1112-1181).
  Trin.   De Trinitate, fragments (PLS 1,1544-1560).

Phoebadius of Agen
  (Phoeb.)
  Ar.   Liber contra Arianos (PL 20,13-30).

Priscillian Work (Anonymous)
  (Prisc.)
  Trin.   De Trinitate fidei Catholicae (PLS 2,1487-
                               1507).

Rusticus
  (Rust.)
  aceph.   Contra Acephalos disputatio (PL 67,1167-1254).

Tertullian
  (Tert.)
  cor.   De corona (CCL 2,1037-1065).
  fug.   De fuga in persecutione (CCL 2,1133-1155).
  haer.   De praescriptione haereticorum (CCL 1,185-
                               224).

mon.   De monogamia (CCL 2,1227-1253).
Prax.   Aduersus Praxean (CCL 2,1157-1205).
uirg.   De uirginibus uelandis (CCL 2,1207-1226).

Victor of Vita
  (Victor)
  hist.   Historia persecutionis Africanae provinciae
                        (CSEL 7).

Caius Marius Victorinus
  (Vic.)
  Ar.   Aduersus Arium (CSEL 83,54-277).

Vigilius of Thapsus
  (Vig.)
  Ar.   Contra Arianos dialogus (PL 62,155-180).

EDITIONS OF ANCIENT CHRISTIAN WRITINGS

ACO   E.Schwartz, Acta conciliorum oecumenicorum 1-4
            Berlin 1914-1971.

Brooke   A.E. Brooke, The Commentary of Origen on S. John's
            Gospel 1-2, Cambridge 1896.

Buytaert   É.M. Buytaert, Eusèbe d'Émèse. Discours conservés en
            Latin 1-2, Louvain 1953,1957.

CAC   I.C.T. Otto, Corpus apologetarum Christianorum
            saeculi secundi 1-9, Wiesbaden 1969.

CCL   Corpus Christianorum, series Latina, Turnhout 1953-.

CSCO   Corpus scriptorum Christianorum orientalium, Louvain
            1903-.

CSEL   Corpus scriptorum ecclesiasticorum Latinorum, Vienna
            1866-.

Field   F. Field, Sancti Patris nostri Johannis Chrysostomi
            Archiepiscopi Constantinopolitani interpretatio omnium
            Epistolarum Paulinarum per homilias facta 1-7, Oxford
            1845-1862.

GCS   Die griechischen christlichen Schriftsteller der
            ersten drei Jahrhunderte, Berlin 1897-.

Jaeger   W. Jaeger, Gregorii Nysseni opera, Leiden 1952-.

Johnston   C.F.H. Johnston, The Book of Saint Basil the Great . . .
            on the Holy Spirit . . ., Oxford 1892.

JTS   The Journal of Theological Studies, Oxford 1899-.

Loofs	F. Loofs, <u>Nestoriana</u>, Halle 1905.
Mason	A.J. Mason, <u>The Five Theological Orations of Gregory of Nazianzus</u>, Cambridge 1899.
Moss	C. Moss, "S. Amphilochius of Iconium on John 14,28: 'the Father who sent me is greater than I'," <u>Le Muséon</u> 43 (1930) 317-364.
NA	The text of the NT, with its *sigla*, selection of variants, and apparatus, as established by E. Nestle and adapted and edited by K. Aland in <u>Synopsis Quattuor Evangeliorum</u>, editio quinta, Stuttgart 1968.
Opitz	H.G. Opitz, <u>Athanasius Werke</u> 1-3, Berlin 1934-1941.
OSA	<u>Oeuvres de Saint Augustin</u> (Bibliothèque Augustinienne), Paris 1939-.
PG	J.P. Migne, <u>Patrologiae cursus completus, series Graeca</u> 1-161, Paris 1857-1866.
PL	J.P. Migne, <u>Patrologiae cursus completus, series Latina</u> 1-221, Paris 1844-1855.
PLS	A. Hamman, <u>Patrologiae cursus completus, series Latina, supplementum</u> 1-5, Paris 1958-1974.
PO	<u>Patrologia orientalis</u>, Turnhout 1903-.
PTS	<u>Patristische Texte und Studien</u>, Berlin 1964-.
Pusey	P.E. Pusey, <u>Sancti Patris nostri Cyrilli Archiepiscopi Alexandrini in D. Joannis Evangelium . . .</u> 1-3, Oxford 1872.
Pusey proph.	P.E. Pusey, <u>Sancti Patris nostri Cyrilli Archiepiscopi Alexandrini in XII Prophetas</u> 1-2, Oxford 1868.
Rupp	J. Rupp, <u>S. Patris nostri Cyrilli Hierosolymorum Archiepiscopi opera quae supersunt omnia</u> vol. 2, Munich 1860.
SCH	<u>Sources Chrétiennes</u>, Paris 1955-.
Scheindler	A. Scheindler, <u>Nonni Panopolitani paraphrasis S. Evangelii Ioannei</u>, Leipzig 1881.
ST	<u>Studi e Testi</u>, Città del Vaticano 1900-.
Staab	K. Staab, <u>Pauluskommentare aus der griechischen Kirche</u>, Münster 1933.
TU	<u>Texte und Untersuchungen zur Geschichte der alt-christlichen Literatur</u>, Berlin 1882-.

PATRISTIC INTERPRETATIONS OF THE PARACLETE

PASSAGES IN JOHN'S GOSPEL

AN ACCOUNT AND CRITICAL EVALUATION

Chapter 1

ANTE-NICENE EXEGESIS

THE GREEK FATHERS: ORIGEN

Origen is neither the first extra-Biblical writer to have
used the term παράκλητος[1] nor the earliest to have referred to the
paraclete passages themselves.[2] He is neither the first writer
known to have written a commentary on the Fourth Gospel[3] nor the
first to have made wide use of it.[4] But he is the earliest ante-
Nicene Greek father of whose paraclete exegesis we still have
examples.[5] So it is with him that this survey must begin. But
the exegesis of Origen is logically, as well as historically, a
good starting place. Not only did his understandings of the nature
of Scripture and its meanings deeply influence later generations of
exegetes, but, as we shall see, more than one development in the
exegesis of paraclete passages began with him.

Basic to Origen's exegesis is his understanding of who
and what the Paraclete is: the Paraclete is the Holy Spirit. More
than that, we learn from princ. 2,7[6] that the Holy Spirit whom our
Lord names Paraclete in John's Gospel is the same Holy Spirit who
was in both apostles and prophets.[7] It is the same Spirit whose
chief advent was given after the ascension of Christ with the
glorious result that now multitudes, and not just the few, are able
to see beyond the merely corporeal meaning of the Old Testament
writings.[8] The Paraclete is divine and is the enlightener of men.[9]
At one point in his homilies on St. Luke's Gospel, Origen notes

that there are those who consider the Paraclete of Jo. 14,16-17 to
be the Apostle Paul; this clearly will not do. Whatever else the
Paraclete is or is not, he must at least be seen as the third
divine person, distinct from both Father and Son.[10] He is even
more explicit in a piece of spiritual exegesis[11] on Num. 21,16
where he quotes 14,16-17 precisely for the purpose of underlining
the unique individuality of the Spirit within the one Trinity.[12]
He places stress on the adjective ἄλλος used to describe the
Paraclete, yet, though the Spirit is ἄλλος, he still takes his
place within the one substance of the Trinity. Origen is in no
doubt that he comes from within the inmost being of God, and he
quotes more than once the clause from Jo.15,26 which reads ὃ παρὰ
τοῦ πατρὸς ἐκπορεύεται, a clause destined to become important in
Churchly confession later on. It is because the Spirit proceeds
from the Father that he can know and can bestow knowledge of the
great love,[13] wisdom, and planning of God.[14] Origen further stresses
his holiness and divine source by contrasting the origin of his
message in Christ (see Jo. 16,14) with that of the 'lying spirit',
who ὅταν λαλῇ, ἐκ τῶν ἰδίων λαλεῖ. The Spirit, by contrast, οὐκ ἐκ
τῶν ἰδίων λαλεῖ.[15]

At princ. 2,7,4[16] Origen considers the meaning of the term
παράκλητος and the basis of its application to the Holy Spirit. He
gives παράκλητος, passive in form, an active meaning, presumably on
the ground that it is formed from παράκλησις which he takes to be
the equivalent of the Latin consolatio.[17] It is in this light that
Origen tells us that the Holy Spirit is called Paraclete because
of his work of consolation.[18] The Spirit's work, as he has already
expressed at the beginning of 2,7,4, is the teaching of truths beyond
utterance. But the result of his teaching is to produce undoubted

comfort and joy in those who learn of him; for, when they learn from

him the reasons of all things which happen, how and why they occur,

they can no longer be troubled but rest in the wisdom of God and

the Lordship of Christ.[19] Origen recognises that this exegesis of

παράκλητος in the Gospel would strain the exegesis of 1 Jo. 2,1-2

where Jesus is spoken of as a paraclete and where παράκλητος would

seem to require the meaning *deprecator*, intercessor. Are we then

to take παράκλητος to mean 'intercessor' when applied to Jesus in

1 Jo.? For Origen the answer is yes; for the context of propitiation

which follows its occurrence in the Epistle seems to require the

sense of *deprecator*. In the case of the Spirit, however, it must

be understood to mean *consolator*[20] inasmuch as the result of his

revelation of spiritual knowledge is comfort and consolation.[21] It

must be observed that Origen's conclusions about the meaning of

παράκλητος in the Epistle, arising as they do from a valid appeal

to context, seem to be based on sound exegetical methodology. But

when he applies the term to the Holy Spirit, he seems to decide for

consolator not so much on textual grounds as on either his obser-

vation of what does happen or his assumption of what must happen in

the minds and hearts of those within whom the Spirit operates. In

any case, it is clear that the Spirit is called consoler not so much

because of what he does directly (viz., he imparts 'unutterable'

knowledge) as on the results that follow from his working. Of major

importance for this history, surely, is the fact that Origen knew a

sense of παράκλητος more or less equivalent to *consolator* and

applied it in his exegesis of the paraclete passages.

Among Origen's exegetical thoughts are those highly inter-

esting ones which, arising principally from Jo. 16,12-13, relate to

the nature and content of the Spirit's mission. The obvious questions

to be asked by the exegete of passages like 14,26 and 16,12 concern the specific content of the Spirit's teaching. What, for
example, are the πολλά which the disciples are not able to bear
now but which the Spirit will declare; what is the ἀλήθεια πᾶσα
into which he is to lead those to whom he has been given? That
Origen considered these questions during the decade following
220 A.D. is clear from the use he makes of the paraclete materials
in his great dogmatic work De principis. In general, Origen makes
it plain that the many things which Jesus at 16,12 et al.[22] reserves
for the Spirit to teach have to do with the divine and profounder
parts of his own teaching and with the deep things of God which
the Spirit alone searches.[23] Specifically, he says that the Spirit
gives knowledge concerning the Father; for, all knowledge of the
Father comes by revelation of the Son through the Holy Spirit.[24]
This is not, he cautions, to suggest that the Spirit derives his
knowledge by revelation from the Son. To do so would be to allow
that he passes from ignorance to knowledge and would make it impossible for him to be reckoned one with the unchangeable Father and
Son in the Trinity. It is, says Origen, both impious and foolish to
confess the Spirit and yet to ascribe to him ignorance.[25] Later in
the same work he contradicts those who underestimate the majesty of
the Spirit by declaring that he is of such power that, pouring himself into their souls, he could instruct them concerning the Trinity.[26] But it is not just the power of the Spirit which equips him
to teach concerning the Trinity. In Origen's eyes the teaching concerning the Trinity is among the things reserved for the Spirit
precisely because he is in himself the perfection and consummation
of the Trinity. Not even the total incarnation event, from birth
to resurrection, gives a complete revelation of the Trinity since

the fulfillment of that revelation does not lie within the province

of the Son.[27] Part, then, of the teaching which the Spirit gives

is concerned with the revelation of the Trinity.

In his great apologetic against Celsus, Origen, writing

late in life, approaches from a different direction the πολλά

of 16,12 and the related question why the disciples were not yet

able to endure them. Because of the needs of the specific context,[28]

the expression of his exegesis takes a form slightly different

from that which we have just considered. Having quoted Jo. 16,12-

13, he raises the question τίνα ἦν τὰ 'πολλὰ,' ἃ εἶχε μὲν 'λέγειν'

ὁ 'Ιησοῦς τοῖς μαθηταῖς ἑαυτοῦ, οὐκ ἐδύναντο δὲ αὐτὰ 'βαστάζειν'

τότε;[29] He gives his view that, perhaps because the disciples were

Jews and had been brought up in the literal understanding of the

Mosaic Law, he had to tell them what was the true law and to show

them the heavenly things patterned and foreshadowed by the Jewish

ceremonies; these were the πολλά which he had to share with them.[30]

The reason he considered them unable to bear the teaching now was

because he knew that, Jews born and bred as they were, it would have

been difficult to convince them that things Jewish are as nothing

compared to the knowledge that is in Christ. Moreover, Jesus

knew that it was not the right psychological moment to bring this

teaching to men not yet able to accept it because it might have

destroyed their precarious impression that he really was the Christ.

Therefore, he postponed the teaching about these things until after

his death and resurrection had prepared them to receive them. For

Origen, then, the πολλά represent the spiritual exegesis of the Law

which the disciples, as Jews, were not ready to accept.[31] The

ceremonies of Jewish worship were, as Peter discovered later at

Joppa, merely a type of the ultimate realities concerning which the

Spirit would teach.[32]

Although we have already covered essentially all Origen's
important exegesis of the paraclete passages, perhaps it will not be
amiss to take up three remaining individual points of interpretation
in bringing our consideration of Origen to a close. The first
relates to his understanding of Jo. 14,15. In his exposition of
Ps. 118(119),45 he concludes from Jo. 14,15 that love toward God
is synonymous with the seeking and execution of the commandments.[33]
He makes a similar pronouncement in Cant. 1 (on 1,4): since he
who loves Christ keeps his commandments, and since there is no
iniquity but only *aequitas* in him who keeps the commandments, then
aequitas has as its twin foci the keeping of the commandments and
the love of Christ.[34] But for Origen this sort of thinking cuts
both ways; if he who loves keeps the commandments, then it is also
true that those who keep Jesus' commandments love him.[35] Con-
versely, insofar as there is in us any iniquity, so far are we from
loving Christ and from keeping his commandments.[36]

The second incidental piece of exegesis comes from Origen's
great work on prayer (written in the years A.D. 233-234) in his
exposition of the words 'Our Father which art in heaven'. It is
simply this: such passages as Jo. 16,5 are, like the Lord's prayer,
not to be taken as in any sense locating the Father; for, far from
being contained by anything, the Father himself encompasses all
things. His justification is that if this were not the way to
exegete these verses, then we must take 14,23 locally, as well, which
is (it is implied) absurd.[37]

Finally, Origen also considers the question of the identity
of the prince of this world of Jo. 16,11 (cf. 12,31; 14,30). He
answers the question in two different ways. In princ. 1,5,2, where
he discusses (without referring specifically to Jo. 16,11) the titles

of the rational infernal beings in the court of Satan, he tells us

that the identity of the *princeps huius mundi* is not yet apparent.[38]

In the same chapter, however, he very clearly identifies the *princeps*

huius mundi, again without referring to Jo. 16,11, with the fallen

angel Lucifer, that is, Satan.[39]   In <u>Cels.</u> he clearly does refer the

term to Jo. 16,11 and he leaves no doubt that to his mind it means

the devil (διάβολος).[40]

THE LATIN WEST: TERTULLIAN AND NOVATIAN

Two figures of the ante-Nicene Latin West make use of the

paraclete passages: viz., Origen's older contemporary Quintus Sep-

timius Florens Tertullianus of Carthage (who is in some real sense

both the first Latin father and, through his pioneer treatment of

Trinitarian dogma, the father of Nicene Orthodoxy[41]) and Novatianus

the Roman priest. The contrast between the sober and practical

theology of the West and the wide range and richness of Alexan-

drian speculation has often been noted; it is a difference which

is not absent in the handling of paraclete materials. But between

the writings of Novatian and Tertullian in the West and those of

Origen in the East another dissimilarity may be noted, as well.

Whereas Origen's mind is constantly preoccupied with exegetical

questions with respect to the Biblical materials he uses, Tertullian

and Novatian are more concerned to impress the passages they cite

into controversial or dogmatic service, and therefore they often

presuppose or even ignore strictly exegetical considerations. They

use the paraclete materials, often in the manner of proof texts,

rather than exegeting them.[42]   Nevertheless, though their purposes

are primarily dogmatic and though neither man ever wrote a strictly

exegetical work, both cite paraclete passages in such a way that

it is often possible from their usage to understand something of
their exegesis.

They defend the deity of both Son and Spirit and expound
the relationships within the divine Economy. It is to be expected,
therefore, that they, as does Origen,[43] equate the Paraclete with
that Spirit who is of equal Godhead with Father and Son,[44] though
subordinate to them.[45] Near the end of his great Trinitarian
book against the patripassian Praxeas, Tertullian alludes to the
promised gift from the Father and identifies him specifically as
the Holy Spirit. In a series of appositives he further specifies
his position and role within the divine Trinity; the promised
Paraclete is

> *Spiritum sanctum, tertium nomen diuinitatis et tertium gradum
> maiestatis, unius praedicatorem monarchiae sed et oikonomiae
> interpretatorem, si quis sermones nouae prophetiae eius ad-
> miserit et deductorem omnis ueritatis quae est in Patre et
> Filio et Spiritu sancto secundum Christianum sacramentum.* /46/

Note the implication in this passage that in Tertullian's understanding knowledge of the Trinity itself, both in unity and in
Economy, is (part of) the *omnis ueritas* into which the Spirit leads
the Church. In Chapter 29 of De Trinitate,[47] his exposition of
the Old Roman Symbol of faith, Novatian also equates the Paraclete
with the Holy Spirit. His exposition of the identity is similar to
Origen's at princ. 2,7.[48] We are admonished, says Novatian, to
believe on the Holy Spirit, he who is called both Paraclete and
Spirit of truth by Jesus.[49] This same Holy Spirit was he who accused
the people in the prophets and who was given to the Church by Christ.
His claim that the Spirit was only partial and occasional in the
prophets but was bestowed liberally on the apostles he supports by
quoting the words of promise found in Jo. 14,16-17; 15,26; 16,7;
16,13.[50]

Novatian and Tertullian have in their Trinitarian writings
the double purpose of establishing the deity of Christ and underlining the distinction of the divine persons.[51] With respect to
the former purpose, both appeal, but in different ways, to the
materials in Jo. 16,14-15. Tertullian does so in the context of
Prax. 17.[52] By his account, Praxeas (and his followers) held that
the divine names applied only to the Father and not also to the
Son. Not so, argues Tertullian. The Father's titles - titles
such as *Deus omnipotens, Altissimus, Dominus uirtutum, Rex Israhelis,*
Qui est - belong, according to the Scripture, to the Son as well
as to the Father; for, the Son has always come under and acted in
them. For proof he appeals to Jo. 16,15: if the Son possesses all
that is the Father's, then he possesses as his own the divine titles,
as well.[53] This exegesis of 16,15 is to be put forward again and
again by later Fathers, East and West, in the controversies of
the Fourth and Fifth Centuries.

Novatian also takes evidence for the deity of Christ from
Jo. 16, but he appeals to 16,14 rather than to 16,15. How, he
argues, can Christ say that the Spirit receives what he declares from
Christ's own things if he be only a man? For, the Paraclete, far
from receiving anything from man, himself gives knowledge to man
and instruction in things future. Either, therefore, the Paraclete
receives nothing from Christ, and Christ is a mere man, deceiving
and deceived, or else (what Novatian says is in fact the case)
Christ was telling the truth and the Paraclete has received of his.
Therefore, Christ is greater than the Paraclete, who would not have
received from him had he been inferior. And, since he is greater,
he must be God.[54] One may note here Novatian's oblique glance at
the Paraclete's work: the impartation of knowledge and instruction

concerning the future. One may also note that his argument implies,
despite its subordinationism, an assumption of the deity of the
Spirit.

Yet another glimpse of the paraclete exegesis of Tertullian
and Novatian is to be found in certain Trinitarian passages which
forward their second major purpose, the stressing of the Trinity of
persons within the Economy. At *Prax.* 9 Tertullian cites Jo. 14,16
in support of the distinction (though not division) of the three
persons. He has just said with respect to Father and Son that the
begetter is one person (*alius*), the begotten another (*alius*); the
sender one (*alius*) and the sent another (*alius*).[55] Then he points
for corroboration for this reasoning to the fact that our Lord himself uses this language (in 14,16), and so shows the Paraclete to be
a person distinct from himself.[56] Tertullian's main exegetical
stress seems to be on the force of *alius* in distinguishing the
persons of Son and Paraclete. But he goes on to suggest, what surely
applies as well to passages other than Jo. 14,16 in this context,
that the very fact of the distinction in names for Father and Son
amounts to a declaration of the distinction of their persons.[57]
He appeals to Jo. 14,16 again in a similar way at *Prax.* 25,1. There,
however, he also introduces a reference to 16,14, *de meo sumet*: the
Spirit receives from the Son just as the Son receives from the
Father. In this he sees three separate yet coherent persons.[58] For
Tertullian, therefore, these passages support the distinction of the
three divine persons who are yet one and undivided in substance.
Novatian takes a similar line. In combatting the monarchian ex-
position of Philip's question and the Lord's answer in Jo. 14,8ff,
he quotes 14,15.16.26, along with other passages, for proof that
Father and Son are not one and the same person; the Son is not the

Father, and Jesus never taught it so. His exegesis is based on the juxtaposition of the names *Father* and *Son* in the Biblical text.[59]

Tertullian's understanding of Jo. 16,12-13 is important to his justification of Churchly faith and practice. In his early controversial treatise, De praescriptione haereticorum (ca. 200 A.D.), he cites these verses to establish that the Spirit is the source (together with the earthly Jesus) and the preserver of the *regula fidei*. Some heretics sought, apparently, to invalidate the rule of faith on the ground that the apostles did not know all things and cannot therefore have delivered a complete faith. Jesus did say, admits Tertullian, that he had things to tell the disciples that they were not yet ready to receive (Jo. 16,12), but he immediately went on to declare that the Spirit of truth would lead them into all truth. In Tertullian's exegesis this means that there was nothing of which the apostles were later ignorant, especially as the Acts of the Apostles shows us that Jesus' promise was fulfilled.[60] It was the work of the Paraclete, therefore, to inform the true Catholic faith as delivered by the apostles.[61] In haer. (perhaps because of the nature of its argument) the Spirit's work of instructing the apostles is perhaps more important to Tertullian's mind than his continued teaching in the Church of the Third Century concerning the *regula fidei*. This second, continuing part of the Spirit's task looms larger, however, in his Montanist writings. At Prax. 2,1 he appeals for his teaching equally to the ancient belief of the Church and to the present illumination of the Paraclete who leads into all truth, an obvious allusion to the matter of Jo. 16,13. In the same place he indicates that, to his mind, the Spirit is specifically the revealer and explainer of the divine Economy, i.e., of the one God as he shows himself in the divine Trinity of Father, Son, and Spirit.[62]

In addition to guaranteeing the accurate transmission of
the *regula fidei*, the Spirit, says Tertullian, gives continuous
instruction concerning discipline and conduct. More than once he
invokes Jo. 16,13, either directly or by allusion, for support for
some of his less popular teachings concerning Christian practice.
With an appeal to 16,13 he explains his general position in the
opening chapter of De uirginibus uelandis (written before the break
in A.D. 207) between Montanists and Catholics in Carthage). The
regula fidei, he explains, *una omnino est, sola immobilis et ir-
reformabilis*.[63] But, this being so, the other points of discipline
are open to correction and improvement; for, the grace of God
operates and progresses to the end just as the devil is also
perpetually busy. The active agent of grace in disciplinary matters is, as Tertullian sees it, the Paraclete. For our Lord sent
the Paraclete for just this reason, that he might carry weak human
nature, which could not endure all things at once, into perfection.[64]
He quotes Jo. 16,12-13 and then, making what for him seems to be
an unusually direct exegetical comment, suggests that the Spirit's
administrative office is nothing other than the direction of
discipline, the exposition of Scripture, the reconstruction of the
understanding, and the advance toward the better things.[65] The point
of this discussion of the Paraclete's mission, however, is the laying
of the foundation for Tertullian's teaching on the veiling of virgins. And he quite forthrightly declares at the end of Chapter 1
that those who are tuned in to the Spirit's prophesying in the
present time hear his instruction that virgins be wholly covered.[66]
As one would expect, Tertullian makes a similar appeal to the
Spirit's guidance in matters of discipline in his Montanist writings.
In De corona (A.D. 211), he intimates that the possession of this

Paraclete, guide to all truth, has made those practical counsels of

St. Paul which had no specific authorization from the Lord never-

theless equivalent to divine command.[67] And in his tract De fuga

in persecutione (A.D. 212) he superciliously appeals to the same

Paraclete-guide for his admonition to Fabian that flight in the

face of persecution is sinful.[68]

Finally, in De monogamia (ca. A.D. 217) Tertullian again

appeals to Jo. 16,12-14 to defend his stringent teaching against

second marriage for Christians and again reveals something of his

exegesis of these verses. His opponents, he says, have complained

that the Paraclete is the instituter of novel and harsh teachings.

He quotes from Jo. 16,12-13 and admits that the Lord himself has

said that the Paraclete is to bring teachings which may be esteemed

alike novel and burdensome.[69] But he denies the charge that he as-

cribes anything he pleases which is novel and burdensome to the

teaching of the Paraclete, even though it comes from the adversary

Spirit. For, the teaching of the adversary is recognisable in that

it would always work to undermine first the regula fidei and then

the orders of discipline. But when the Paraclete comes to complete

the teaching of Jesus he first bears witness to, calls to remem-

brance, and glorifies Christ. Then, when he has been recognised

as the true Spirit by these characteristic activities, he goes on to

reveal things necessary concerning discipline, notwithstanding that

they appear novel or even burdensome.[70] Later, near the end of the

same book, Tertullian urges that it is also part of the work of the

Spirit to enable the Christian to bear the things which were un-

endurable before he was given:[71] this removes all excuse from those

who resist the Spirit's discipline (and therefore from those who

resist Tertullian's teaching!). The points of exegesis to be

noticed in this application of Jo. 16,12-14 are, firstly, that it
is a hallmark of the Paraclete by which he may always be recognised
that he points to and glorifies Christ in complete conformity with
the *regula fidei*, and, secondly, that (as we have already seen in
the paragraphs above) he is both the source of an ongoing revelation
of discipline and practice and the one who enables the Christian to
endure his teachings.

NOTES

1. παράκλητος appears in its forensic sense at 2 Clem. 6 (PG 1,
337) in the middle of the Second Century, though it was surely
in use before that. (It is just possible that Simon Magus may have
used it. Jer. in Matth. 24,5 (CCL 77,223), at any rate, knew
writings which ascribed to Simon the claim that he was the
Paraclete: *haec quoque inter cetera in suis uoluminibus scripta
dimittens: Ego sum sermo Dei, ego sum speciosus, ego paraclitus,
ego omnipotens, ego omnia Dei.*)

2. There are glimpses of earlier appeals to the passages in extant
writings of the fathers. Origen himself, for example, tells us
(hom. 25 in Lc. (GCS 35,162)) that certain followers of Marcion
identified the 'other Paraclete' of Jo. 14,16 with St. Paul; cf.
H.B. Swete, The Holy Spirit in the Ancient Church (London, 1912),
65-66. The adherents of Montanism seem to have believed that when
Montanus appeared in Phrygia around 156 A.D. he brought in the age
promised by the Saviour and that the Paraclete spoke in him; see R.
Seeberg, Lehrbuch der Dogmengeschichte, I (5. Aufl.; Stuttgart,
1960), 323. Irenaeus twice refers to the promise of the Paraclete
in John, once at haer. 3,11,9 (PG 7,890-891) and once at 3,17,2
(PG 7,930). In the former he attacks those who rejected the Fourth
Gospel, apparently either the same group of extreme anti-montanists
whom Epiphanius (haer. 51,3 (GCS 31,250)) names Alogi or a group
which shared their views; see Seeberg, 328 n.2. (According to
Epiph. the Alogi had a second reason, unknown to Irenaeus, for
rejecting the Fourth Gospel: viz., their dislike of its Logos
doctrine; they refused to recognise the identity of Word and Son,
refused, like the Noetians, to recognise the divine economy; see
J. Moingt, Théologie trinitaire de Tertullien, I (Paris, 1966),
109-110. Swete (H.B. Swete, On the History of the Doctrine of the
Procession of the Holy Spirit (Cambridge, 1876), 43) says that
"whether this sect was one and the same with the Epiphanian Alogi
. . . the fact remains that in the second half of the Second Century,
the Fourth Gospel was attacked on two grounds; for its doctrine of
the Eternal Word, and for its doctrine of the Holy Ghost." In this
double attack on the growing Christology of the Church and the
emphasis placed on the person and office of the Paraclete by

Montanism, we see the first expressions of what would result in
the reactionary Monarchianism of the Third Century.) The inference
may be drawn from this passage that in Irenaeus' exegesis the promised Paraclete is the Spirit of prophecy and the source of a
legitimate grace of prophecy within the Church. From the second
passage, 3,17,2, we learn that for Irenaeus the Paraclete was
sent to fit men for God, to bring them into union and fellowship
with him and with one another. (Cf. haer. 5,1,1 (PG 7,1121) and
5,9,2 (PG 7,1144).) In neither of these passages, however, do
we find anything of real value for the history of ante-Nicene
exegesis.

3. Credit must go to the gnostics for the invention of the commentary. It was the Valentinian gnostic Heracleon who wrote
the earliest known commentary on John somewhere near the end of
the Second Century. Clement of Alexandria cites him, but we know
him best from Origen who, in his commentary on John, includes
fragments in order to refute and reply; see G. Bardy, "Commentaires
patristiques de la Bible," Dictionnaire de la Bible Supplément,
II (Paris, 1934), 77. From Origen's references we gather that
the commentary was extensive, and from his observation of
Heracleon's lack of comment on 4,32, we infer that the gnostic
usually commented verse by verse; see M.F. Wiles, The Spiritual
Gospel (Cambridge,1960), 3. For fuller discussion of gnostic
exegesis of the Fourth Gospel generally, see Wiles, 96-111; W.
von Loewenich, Das Johannes-Verständnis im zweiten Jahrhundert,
Beihefte zur Zeitschrift für die neutestamentliche Wissenschaft
und die Kunde der älteren Kirche, Beih. 13, Hrsg. Prof. D. Hans
Lietzmann (Berlin, 1932), 60-115; and E.H. Pagels, The Johannine
Gospel in Gnostic Exegesis: Heracleon's Commentary on John,
Society of Biblical Literature Monograph Series No. 17, ed. L.
Keck (Nashville, 1973).

4. It is, among orthodox writers, Irenaeus who first makes wide
use of the Fourth Gospel and accepts it as fully authoritative.
John and its proper exegesis are at the heart of Irenaeus' battle
with gnosticism, a battle in which he may fairly be said to have
turned against the gnostics their own chief authority. In his
writings he freely quotes and refers to the Gospel; it deeply
influences his thinking; from it he derives his regula veritatis.
See J.N. Sanders, The Fourth Gospel in the Early Church: Its Origin
And Influence on Christian Theology up to Irenaeus (Cambridge,
1943), 83-87 and the foregoing discussion; cf. von Loewenich, 115-
141. He it is to whom the Church owes both the foundation of
its exegesis of John (von Loewenich, 4) and the establishment of
that form of the kerygma found in it as normative for the
Catholic theology (Sanders, 84). For evidence of the knowledge
and use of the Fourth Gospel by Christian writers of the Second
Century, see (for the Apostolic Fathers) The Oxford Society of
Historical Theology (ed.), The New Testament in the Apostolic
Fathers (Oxford, 1905) and (for the period from the Apostolic
Fathers to Irenaeus, inclusive) Sanders and von Loewenich. Sanders
speaks of a gradual growth of understanding and appreciation of the
apologetic value of the Fourth Gospel in the Apologists (p.21).
It is here that indisputable traces of the use of John first appear,
traces clearer in Justin than in Diognetus, in Tatian than in Justin,
and quite certain in Theophilus (p.20). Justin illustrates "the

first tentative use . . . of the Fourth Gospel by an orthodox writer"
(p.31; cf. von Loewenich, 39-50, who supports a much closer connexion
between the Gospel and the Apologist); Athenagoras knew the Gospel but
was not in a position to treat it as Scripture (pp.34-35; cf. von
Loewenich, 53); Tatian has begun to use it as a source for his
theology, as opposed to a text merely to be quoted and alluded to
incidentally (p.34; cf. von Loewenich, 52-53); Theophilus of Antioch
first ascribes it to John, one of the 'inspired men' through whom
the Scriptures come (p.35; cf. von Loewenich, 54-55).

5. Unfortunately, the books of Origen's commentary covering the
paraclete passages, if indeed he ever wrote them, are lost. For
purposes of this study we look, therefore, to references in the
extant works.

6. Or. princ. 2,7 (GCS 22,147-152). Or. also discusses the Spirit
at princ. 1,3 (GCS 22,48-63). In princ. he measures his words and
keeps within the bounds of ecclesiastical tradition respecting the
Spirit. Elsewhere, however, notably in Jo. 2,10 on 1,3 (GCS 10,64-
65; Brooke 1,69), he speculates about the origin of the Spirit in
such a way as to open himself up to the often repeated charge of
subordinationism. The discrepancy between the discussion in princ.
and that in Jo. tends to disappear, however, when we realize that
even in princ. Or. regards the mode of the Spirit's existence as one
left open by the apostolic tradition; see princ. 1, praef. 4 (GCS
22,11), *Tum deinde honore ac dignitate patri ac filio sociatum
tradiderunt spiritum sanctum. In hoc non iam manifeste discernitur,
utrum natus aut innatus, vel filius etiam ipse dei habendus sit.*
Though the controversies over the Spirit were to continue for long
decades, Or. does the Church the favour early on in the discussion
of asking this question and questions like it.

7. Or. princ. 2,7,1 (GCS 22,148), *Sicut enim idem ipse deus atque
idem ipse Christus, ita idem ipse et spiritus sanctus est, qui et
in prophetis et in apostolis fuit.*

8. Or. princ. 2,7,2 (GCS 22,149). Notice that for Or. the promise
of the Paraclete includes more than just the people to whom Jesus
was speaking in the Farewell Discourses. Here he speaks of the
Spirit's ministry to multitudes (*multitudines*). At comm. in Mt.
15,30 (on 20,1-16) he says outright that the promise is to the
apostles and to whoever is παραπλήσιος with them (GCS 40,441).

9. Or princ. 2,7,3 (GCS 22,150).

10. Or. hom. 25 in Lc. (GCS 35,162), *Porro alii, legentes: 'mittam
vobis advocatum, Spiritum veritatis', nolunt intellegere tertiam
personam a Patre et Filio diversam et divinam sublimemque naturam,
sed apostolum Paulum. Nonne tibi hi omnes videntur plus amasse,
quam expedit, et dum virtutem uniuscujusque mirantur, dilectionis
perdidisse mensuram?* Cf. n.2 above. Swete, Holy Spirit, 66, thinks
they probably meant that the promise of the Paraclete was primarily
fulfilled in and through Paul.

11. Two characteristic attitudes toward Scripture informed Origen's
exegetical methodology. First, he believed profoundly that all of
Scripture is a unity and is to be interpreted spiritually in terms of

the revelation of Christ in the NT. Since Scripture is one and
unchanging, he cannot allow that it ever contradicts itself; there
can be no discrepancies, and the role of the exegete is to reconcile
apparent contradictions. This principle of the unity of Scripture
makes it both possible and necessary for Or. to practice the
allegorical exegesis for which he is so famous. It also makes possible his favorite device of gathering parallels, close and remote,
and (as in the context at present under discussion) to interpret
Scripture by Scripture. The second characteristic attitude concerns
inspiration. All Scripture is inspired by God, and it is its
divine inspiration which informs the unity of Scripture and which
makes it possible for Or. to see meaning in every detail, right
down to the very letters of the LXX text. See H.J. Mumm, "A
Critical Appreciation of Origen as an Exegete of the Fourth Gospel"
(unpublished Doctor's dissertation, Hartford Seminary Foundation,
1952), 57-65.

12. Or. hom. 12,1 in Num. on Num. 21,16ff (GCS 30,95), *Et rursus
tertium puto videri puteum posse cognitionem Spiritus sancti.
Alius enim et ipse est a patre et filio, sicut et de ipso nihilominus
in evangeliis dicitur: 'Mittet vobis pater alium paracletum, spiritum
veritatis'. Est ergo haec trium distinctio personarum in Patre et
Filio et Spiritu sancto, quae ad pluralem puteorum numerum revocatur.
Sed horum puteorum unus est fons; una enim substantia est et natura
Trinitatis.* This Trinitarian passage is set in the context of
Origin's exposition of the Song of the Well in Numbers where he
appeals to an allegorical interpretation of the LXX (!) of Prov. 5,
15 (πῖνε ὕδατα . . . ἀπὸ σῶν φρεάτων πηγῆς) to help explain the
Song. *Spring (fons)* he takes to be representative of the Trinity;
wells (putei) he takes as representative of the individual persons
of the Trinity.

13. Or. Cant. Prologus (GCS 33,74), *Etiam secundum hoc, quod 'caritas'
dicitur, solus autem sanctus Spiritus est, qui 'ex patre procedit',
et ideo scit, quae in Deo sunt, sicut 'spiritus hominis scit, quae
in homine sunt'.* The wider context here is Origen's discussion of
caritas as the theme of the Song of Songs.

14. Or. princ. 3,5,8 (GCS 22,279).

15. Or. Jo.20,29 on 8,44 (GCS 10,366; Brooke 2,80).

16. Or. princ. 2,7,4 (GCS 22,151-152).

17. Or. princ. 2,7,4 (GCS 22,151). Apparently παράκλητος would in
this sense have been coextensive with παρακλήτωρ.

18. Or. princ. 2,7,4 (GCS 22,151), *'Paracletus' vero quod dicitur
spiritus sanctus, a consolatione dicitur* (παράκλησις enim latine
consolatio appellatur.

19. Or. princ. 2,7,4 (GCS 22,151).

20. Lagrange (M.-J. Lagrange, Évangile selon Saint Jean, Études
Bibliques (septième édition; Paris, 1948), 382) holds it probable
that Rufinus and not Or. was responsible for the distinction between
the translation of παράκλητος as *deprecator* at 1 Jo. 2,1 and as

consolator in the FG; in support he cites or.10,2, εὐχόμενος ὑπὲρ
τῶν εὐχομένων καὶ συμπαρακαλῶν τοῖς παρακαλοῦσιν (Cf. R. Schnackenburg, Das Johannesevangelium, III (Freiburg, 1975), 85 n.88). This
judgment is questionable. While it is true that Or. does not seem at
or. 10,2 to know a translation of παράκλητος equivalent to *consolator*,
this is surely due to the fact that he there deals only with 1 Jo. 2,1
where the sense is straightforward. This passage does not necessarily
contradict princ. 2,7,4 which recognises and attempts to resolve a
tension between the use of παράκλητος in the Epistle and its use in
the FG. If Or. was ignorant of a dual possibility for παράκλητος,
this cannot be proved from or. 10,2 alone. As other Greek fathers
did know such a possibility (see Chapter 2 below), and in the absence
of better evidence, it seems preferable to attribute princ. 2,7,4 to
Or. rather than to his translator. Even if, as seems likely, the
words *utrumque enim significat in graeco 'paracletus', et 'consolator'
et 'deprecator'* come from Rufinus, he cannot be held responsible for
the comparative discussion of the meanings of παράκλητος in the
Gospel and in the First Epistle.

21. Or. princ. 2,7,4 (GCS 22,152), *Magis in salvatore nomen 'paracleti'
pro deprecatore intellegendum videtur; deprecari enim patrem 'pro
peccatis nostris' dicitur. De spiritu vero sancto 'paracletus'
'consolator' debet intellegi, pro eo quod consolationem praestat
animabus, quibus aperit et revelat sensum scientiae spiritalis.*

22. Or. gives a composite quotation formed from 16,12; 14,26;
and 15,26; see n.23. He apparently quotes from memory and has in
mind all that the Lord has said concerning the Spirit's ministry of
teaching.

23. Or. princ. 1,3,4 (GCS 22,53), *Sed et rursus in evangelio de
divinis ac profundioribus doctrinis commemorans salvator quae nondum
capere poterant discipuli sui, ita ait ad apostolos: 'Adhuc multa
habeo quae vobis dicam, sed non potestis illa modo capere; cum autem
venerit paracletus spiritus sanctus, qui ex patre procedit, ille
vos docebit omnia, et commonebit vos omnia, quae dixi vobis.'* At
princ. 2,7,4 (GCS 22,151), Or. speaks in a similar vein. The
function of the Spirit is, he says, to teach truths which cannot be
uttered in human language: *Oportet ergo nos scire quia 'paracletus'
est spiritus sanctus, docens maiora quam voce proferri possunt et, ut
ita dixerim, quae 'ineffabilia sunt'.* (Mumm, 91, refers this
discussion in princ. 1,3,4 to Origen's understanding of the divine
guidance which, along with the *regula fidei*, informs, in his view,
the exegete's understanding of the Biblical text. But in doing so
Mumm takes the material right out of context; Or., though surely he
did depend upon divine guidance, does not here have the exegete
primarily in mind.)

24. Or. princ. 1,3,4 (GCS 22,53), *Omnis enim scientia de patre,
'revelante filio', in spiritu sancto cognoscitur.* The context is
that of Origen's explanation of how it is that he, following his
Hebrew master, would understand the two Seraphim in Is. 6,3 and the
two living beings (*animales*) or lives (*vitae*) of Hab. 3,2 as Christ
and the Holy Spirit.

25. Or. princ. 1,3,4 (GCS 22,54), *Neque enim putandum est quod
etiam spiritus 'filio revelante' cognoscit. Si enim 'revelante*

*filio' cognoscit patrem spiritus sanctus, ergo ex ignorantia ad
scientiam venit; quod utique et impium pariter et stultum est, sanctum spiritum confiteri et ignorantiam ei adscribere.* It may be noted
that at Jo. 2,18 (GCS 10,75; Brooke 1,82-83) Or. raises with respect to
Jo. 16,14 the question whether or not the Spirit takes in everything
that the Son himself, who has gazed at the Father from the beginning,
knows. This question he sets aside because he thinks it requires
further consideration.

26. Or. princ. 2,7,3 (GCS 22,150), *Evangelium vero tantae eum
potentiae ac maiestatis ostendit, ut dicat apostolos 'non posse capere'
adhuc ea, quae volebat eos docere salvator, nisi 'cum advenerit
spiritus sanctus', qui se eorum animabus infundens inluminare eos
possit de ratione ac fide trinitatis.*

27. Or. hom.3,2 in Jos. (GCS 30,303), *Vides quia non solum apud
Moysen iste tertius numerus non demonstratur impletus, sed adhuc
et Iesus dicit discipulis suis: 'nondum potestis audire', nisi ille
paracletus veniat, 'spiritus veritatis', quia per ipsum et in ipso
adimpletur perfectio trinitatis.* Or. is giving in this homily a
spiritual explanation for why there were only nine and one-half
tribes west of Jordan (instead of ten) and only two and one-half
(instead of three) east of the River. In short, he concludes that
it is because, though the Israelites were not entirely ignorant
of the Trinity, they were only looking for and had not yet seen the
completion of their faith.

28. Or. Cels. 2,1-2 (GCS 2,126-129). In these pages Or. counters
Celsus' charge that the believing Jews have left the religion of
their fathers: τί παθόντες, ὦ πολῖται, κατελίπετε τὸν πάτριον νόμον
καὶ ὑπ' ἐκείνου πρὸς ὃν ἄρτι διειλέγμεθα, ψυχαγωγηθέντες πάνυ
γελοίως ἐξηπατήθητε καὶ ἀφ' ἡμῶν ἀπηυτομολήσατε εἰς ἄλλο ὄνομα καὶ
εἰς ἄλλον βίον; (2,1; GCS 2,128). He answers that they have not
left it but have transcended it through the Spirit by coming to the
full truth of which the Law was but a foreshadowing.

29. Or. Cels. 2,2 (GCS 2,128).

30. Or. Cels. 2,2 (GCS 2,128), τίς ὁ ἀληθὴς νόμος, καὶ τίνων
'ἐπουρανίων' 'ὑποδείγματι καὶ σκιᾷ' ἡ παρὰ τοῖς 'Ιουδαίοις λατρεία
ἐπετελεῖτο, καὶ τίνων 'μελλόντων ἀγαθῶν' 'σκιάν' περιεῖχεν
ὁ περὶ βρώσεως καὶ πόσεως καὶ ἑορτῶν καὶ νουμηνιῶν καὶ σαββάτων
νόμος. καὶ 'πολλὰ' ἦν ταῦθ', ἃ εἶχεν αὐτοῖς 'λέγειν'.

31. Or. Cels. 2,2 (GCS 2,129), 'πολλὰ' γὰρ τὰ τῆς τοῦ νόμου
κατὰ τὰ πνευματικὰ διηγήσεως καὶ σαφηνείας· καὶ οὐκ ἐδύναντό πως
'βαστάζειν' αὐτὰ οἱ μαθηταί, ἐν 'Ιουδαίοις γεγεννημένοι καὶ
ἀνατεθραμμένοι τότε. An example (cf. p.4 and n.11 above) of just
this sort of spiritual exegesis, and one which involves the paraclete
passages, occurs in Cant. 3 on 1,14 (1,15 vg.) (GCS 33,174). 1,14(15)
reads in part, *oculi tui columbae*. Leaving to one side most of the
allegory, it is enough to say that Or. leads us to understand the two
doves of the eyes to be the Son of God and the Holy Spirit. That he
can see allegory for the Spirit is clear enough; the dove is the clas-
sic Christian symbol for the Holy Spirit. That the other eye and dove
represent the Son becomes apparent for him when he reflects that
both Son and Spirit are called *paraclete* in the NT; therefore both

must be doves: *Et ne mireris, si 'columbae' simul dicantur, cum uter-*
que similiter 'advocatus' dicatur, sicut Iohannes evangelista declarat
'Spiritum' quidem sanctum dicens 'paracletum', quod est advocatus;
et de Iesu Christo nihilominus in epistola sua dicit quia ipse sit
'advocatus apud patrem' pro peccatis nostris. Among these ultimate
realities Or. would undoubtedly have included the Trinitarian teaching
which he assigns the Spirit in princ. 1,3,4; see above pp.6-7.

32.   Or. Cels. 2,2 (GCS 2,129), οἶμαι δ'ὅτι καὶ ἐπεὶ τύπος μὲν ἦν
ἐκεῖνα, ἀλήθεια δὲ ἃ ἔμελλε διδάσκειν αὐτοὺς τὸ ἅγιον πνεῦμα, διὰ
τοῦτο λέλεκται· 'ὅταν ἔλθη ἐκεῖνος . . .'

33.   Or. sel. in Ps. on 118(119),45 (PG 12,1596), Ἡ ἀγάπη δὲ πρὸς τὸν
θεὸν ἡ τῶν ἐντολῶν αὐτοῦ ζήτησις καὶ κατόρθωσις· φησὶ γὰρ ὁ Κύριος·
''Ἐὰν ἀγαπᾶτέ με, τὰς ἐντολάς μου τηρήσατε.' Cf. Jo. 20,17 on 8,42
(GCS 10,348-349; Brooke 2,59).

34.   Or. Cant. 1 (GCS 33,112), *Si ergo qui 'diligit' Christum,*
'mandata' eius 'custodit' et qui 'mandata' eius 'custodit', nulla est
in eo iniquitas, sed aequitas in eo permanet, 'aequitas' ergo est,
quae et 'mandata custodit' et 'diligit' Christum. Or. equates these
twin foci of *aequitas* with the two breasts in v.1,4.

35.   While not stated in so many words, this is clearly implied in
Or. sel. in Ps. on 118(119),45 (PG 12,1596).

36.   Or. Cant. 1 (GCS 33,112), *Erit ergo, ut, quantum iniquitatis in*
nobis est, tantum longe simus a dilectione Christi et tantum 'man-
datorum' eius praevaricatio habetur in nobis.

37.   Or. or. 23,1 (GCS 3,349-350).

38.   Or. princ. 1,5,2 (GCS 22,70), *Necnon et quidam 'angeli diaboli'*
nominantur, sed et 'princeps mundi huius', qui utrum ipse sit
diabolus an alius quis, nondum manifeste declaratum est. Cf. Cels.
4,93 (GCS 2,366) where Or. simply does not indicate his thoughts concerning the identity of the ἄρχων τοῦ αἰῶνος τούτου (a phrase which
seems to conflate the term used in the FG with that used at 2 Cor.
4,4).

39.   Or. princ. 1,5,5 (GCS 22,77). Cf. hom. 30 in Lc. (GCS 35,185)
where *princeps istius saeculi* for the devil is surely the equivalent
of *princeps huius mundi* (see n.38): *Et revera, si miseriam et in-*
felicitatem nostram simpliciter volumus confiteri, pene totius mundi
rex diabolus est; unde et 'princeps istius saeculi' a Salvatore
vocitatur. ἄρχων τοῦ αἰῶνος τούτου, used epexegetically for the evil
one (πονηρός) at Cels. 8,13 (GCS 3,230) is similar: νυνὶ δὲ ὑπηρέτας
νομίζων τοὺς προσκυνουμένους ὑπὸ τῶν ἐθνῶν δαίμονας οὐχ ὑπάγει ἡμᾶς
ἀκολουθίᾳ τῇ περὶ τοῦ θεραπεύειν τοὺς τοιούτους, οὓς ὑπηρέτας τοῦ
πονηροῦ ὁ λόγος ἀποδείκνυσι καὶ ἄρχοντος τοῦ αἰῶνος τούτου, ἀφιστάντος
ἀπὸ τοῦ θεοῦ οὓς ἂν δύνηται.

40.   Or. Cels. 8,54 (GCS 3,270), καὶ ἦλθέ γε ὁ Ἰησοῦς ἐλευθερῶσαι
'πάντας τοὺς καταδυναστευομένους ὑπὸ τοῦ διαβόλου,' καὶ περὶ ἐκείνου
εἰπὼν μετά τινος πρεπούσης αὐτῷ βαθύτητος τό· 'νῦν ὁ ἄρχων τοῦ
κόσμου τούτου κέκριται.'

41. Athanasius is usually associated with the formulary of Nicaea
and Leo the Great with the decree of Chalcedon. But for a lucid
discussion which suggests Tertullian as the real father of the orthodox doctrines of the Trinity and of the person of Christ, see
B.B. Warfield, Studies in Tertullian and Augustine (New York, 1930),
83-109.

42. This approach becomes increasingly important in the Fourth
Century when, East and West, paraclete passages are squeezed for
their dogmatic value with respect to many issues, but especially
with respect to the Trinitarian controversies and to the development of the doctrine of the Holy Spirit.

43. See p. 3 above.

44. Early heresies seem to have identified the Paraclete with various
human individuals (see, e.g., pp.3-4 and n.2 above). After the work
of Or. in the East and Tert. and Nov. in the West this does not
appear ever to have been done by Christian writers in any serious way
again. The person and nature of the Spirit were to come into question,
but that he and the Paraclete are one and the same seems to have been
universally agreed.

45. With respect to their Trinitarian teaching, the work of both men
is marked by a strong subordinationism, though for somewhat different
reasons: Tertullian's is conditioned by the subordinationism inherent
in the Logos Christology upon which he stands and which he transcends
only in part (see Warfield, 19ff. On p.19 he makes the helpful observation that Tertullian's Trinitarianism in Prax. is, at base, little
else than the Biblical teaching concerning Father, Son, and Spirit,
elaborated under the aegis of Logos Christology. In the pages following he maintains that the essential purpose of Prax. is the adaptation of the Logos speculation of the Apologists to fit the new conditions created by the success of the monarchians. Tertullian's contribution to the development of Trinitarian dogma was a result of the
need for such adaptation, and in his work he prepares the way for
transcending the Logos speculation entirely. Nevertheless (see
especially Warfield's five observations on pp.28-30) he falls short of
the Nicene orthodoxy precisely because he fails to shake off the subordinationism intrinsic to the Logos speculation.); Novatian's is the
result of his fear of being accused of ditheism, a fear which causes
his subordinationism to exceed that of his predecessors (see J.
Quasten, Patrology, II (Utrecht, 1953), 229-230).

46. Tert. Prax. 30,5 (CCL 2,1204). (Prax. was probably written ca.
A.D. 213, well after Tertullian's conversion to Montanism; the allusion
to the new prophecy in this passage reflects the author's Montanistic
bent. Note that his subordinationism is also clearly visible in the
quotation.)

47. Nov. Trin. 29 (CCL 4,69ff) contains, in fact, his affirmation of
the third element of the Symbol, faith in the Holy Spirit. In Trin.
as a whole Nov. is primarily concerned to give constructive exposition
of the Rule of Truth; he works very hard at not letting his writing
degenerate into an exposé of heresies. And, unlike Tert., when he does
allow himself to engage in polemic, he attacks not only monarchianism
but tritheism. See Warfield, 95-96.

48. See p.3 above.

49. Nov. <u>Trin</u>. 29,3 (CCL 4,69).

50. Nov. <u>Trin</u>. 29,6-7 (CCL 4,69-70). Novatian ascribes operations
to the Spirit in various parts of Chapter 29 which look as though
they might be based on the paraclete passages. But, since such basis,
if any, is nowhere explicit, we do not consider these operations here.

51. M.Comeau, <u>Saint Augustin, exégète du Quatrième Évangile</u> (Paris,
1930), 35.

52. Tert. <u>Prax</u>. 17 (CCL 2,1182-1183).

53. Tert. <u>Prax</u>. 17,2-3 (CCL 2,1182), *Sed nomen Patris: Deus om-*
nipotens, Altissimus, Dominus uirtutum, Rex Israhelis, Qui est.
Quatenus ita scripturae docent, haec dicimus et in Filium competisse
et in his Filium uenisse et in his semper egisse et sic ea in se
hominibus manifestasse. <u>*Omnia, inquit, Patris mea sunt*</u>*. Cur non*
et nomina?

54. Nov. <u>Trin</u>. 16,2-3 (CCL 4,40), *Si homo tantummodo Christus, quo-*
modo paracletum dicit de suo esse sumpturum quae nuntiaturus sit?
Neque enim paracletus ab homine quicquam accipit, sed homini scientiam
paracletus porrigit . . . . Sed si a Christo accepit quae nuntiet,
maior ergo iam paracleto Christus est, quoniam nec paracletus a
Christo acciperet, nisi minor Christo esset. Minor autem Christo
paracletus Christum etiam Deum esse hoc ipso probat, a quo accepit
quae nuntiat, ut testimonium Christi diuinitatis grande sit, dum minor
Christo paracletus repertus ab illo sumit quae ceteris tradit.

55. Tert. <u>Prax</u>. 9,2 (CCL 2,1168), *Sic et Pater alius a Filio dum*
Filio maior, dum alius qui generat, alius qui generatur, dum alius
qui mittit, alius qui mittitur, dum alius qui facit, alius per quem
fit.

56. Tert. <u>Prax</u>. 9,3 (CCL 2,1168-1169), *Bene quod et Dominus usus hoc*
uerbo in persona Paracleti non diuisionem significauit sed dis-
positionem: <u>*Rogabo, enim, inquit, Patrem et alium aduocatum mittet*</u>
<u>*uobis, Spiritum ueritatis*</u>*. Sic alium a se Paracletum, quomodo et nos*
a Patre alium Filium ut tertium gradum ostenderet in Paracleto,
sicut nos secundum in Filio propter oikonomiae obseruationem. In
<u>Prax</u>. 9 Tert. is arguing for the distinction of persons in the Godhead
against Praxeas who, he indicates, extolls the monarchy at the expense
of the Economy and wants to identify Father with Son with Spirit. (As
elsewhere, he adduces evidence from the Gospel of John which counters
patripassianist exegesis of Jo. 10,30, "I and the Father are one.")
His subordination of Son to Father and Spirit to Son is not invisible
in this Chapter.

57. Tert. <u>Prax</u>. 9,4 (CCL 2,1169), *Ipsum, quod Pater et Filius dicuntur,*
nonne aliud ab alio est?

58. Tert. <u>Prax</u>. 25,1 (CCL 2,1195), *Paracletum quoque a Patre se*
postulaturum cum ascendisset ad Patrem et missurum repromittit, et
quidem alium. Sed iam praemisimus quomodo alium. Ceterum: <u>*De meo*</u>
<u>*sumet, inquit, sicut ipse de Patris*</u>*. Ita connexus Patris in Filio et*
Filii in Paracleto tres efficit cohaerentes, alterum ex altero. In

Chapters 21 through 25 Tert. is again concerned to show from John's
Gospel that Father and Son are, contrary to Praxean exegesis, constantly spoken of as persons distinct as to personal existence but
inseparable as to divine nature. (The reference in the quotation is
to Chapter 13 where he has shown the Paraclete to be like the Son,
distinct in person but of one substance with him.)

59. Nov. Trin. 28,16-19 (CCL 4,67). For Nov., Jesus' words can only
be taken in a sense which rightly recognises that Son and Father are
distinct *personae*.

60. Tert. haer. 22,8-10 (CCL 1,204), *Dixerat plane aliquando:
Multa habeo adhuc loqui uobis, sed non potestis modo ea sustinere,
tamen adiciens: Cum uenerit ille spiritus ueritatis, ipse uos
deducet in omnem ueritatem, ostendit illos nihil ignorasse quos
omnem ueritatem consecuturos per spiritum ueritatis repromiserat. Et
utique impleuit repromissum, probantibus actis apostolorum descensum
spiritus sancti.* It is not clear whether the detractors Tert. has
in mind here actually used Jo. 16,12 to support their disparagement of
the faith delivered by the apostles and claimed by the Church, but
it does seem likely from the context of the passage that they did.

61. Tert. says this in other ways, but still with reference to Jo.
16,13 at haer. 8,14-15 (CCL 1,194) and 28,1 (CCL 1,209). In the
former passage he speaks only of the Spirit's instruction to the apostles who then in turn teach the gentiles; one should not infer from
this that Tert. exegeted the gift of the Spirit as to the apostles
only, because so to do would contradict the impression gathered from
22,8ff and 28,1 as well as from other passages. (The latter passage
is interesting quite apart from paraclete exegesis. In it Tert.
argues that the transmission of the *regula fidei* must have been true
and accurate because of the unlikelihood that so many churches would
otherwise have gone astray into one and the same faith: *Ecquid
uerisimile est ut tot ac tantae in unam fidem errauerint? Nullus inter
multos euentus unus est exitus; uariasse debuerat error doctrinae
ecclesiarum. Ceterum quod apud multos unum inuenitur, non est er-
ratum sed traditum,* haer. 28,1-3 (CCL 1,209).)

62. Tert. Prax. 2,1 (CCL 2,1160), *Nos uero et semper et nunc magis,
ut instructiores per Paracletum, deductorem scilicet omnis ueritatis,
unicum quidem Deum credimus, sub hac tamen dispensatione quam oikonomiam
dicimus, ut unici Dei sit et Filius, sermo ipsius qui ex ipso proces-
serit, per quem omnia facta sunt et sine quo factum est nihil.*
(Warfield, 16, indicates that this has been taken to mean that the
doctrine of the Trinity was peculiar to Montanism and that Tertullian
means to say that "we Montanists" have always so believed. But
surely he is right to insist that *nos uero et semper et nunc magis*
contrasts two periods and can only mean that the doctrine dated from
before his Montanist period. Tert. is affirming that what he teaches
in Prax. is part of the traditional doctrine of the Church.) On the
Spirit's role as revealer of the Trinity see Prax. 30,5 (CCL 2,1204)
where he is called *unius praedicatorem monarchiae sed et oikonomiae
interpretatorem, si quis sermones nouae prophetiae eius admiserit et
deductorem omnis ueritatis quae est in Patre et Filio et Spiritu
sancto secundum Christianum sacramentum.*

63. Tert. uirg. 1,3 (CCL 2,1209).

64. Tert. <u>uirg</u>. 1,4 (CCL 2,1209), *Cum propterea Paracletum miserit Dominus, ut, quoniam humana mediocritas omnia semel capere non poterat, paulatim dirigeretur et ordinaretur et ad perfectum perduceretur disciplina ab illo uicario Domini Spiritu sancto.*

65. Tert. <u>uirg</u>. 1,5 (CCL 2,1209-1210), *Quae est ergo Paracleti administratio, nisi haec, quod disciplina dirigitur, quod scripturae revelantur, quod intellectus reformatur, quod ad meliora proficitur?*

66. Tert. <u>uirg</u>. 1,7 (CCL 2,1210), *Hunc qui audierunt usque, nunc prophetantem, uirgines contegunt.*

67. Tert. <u>cor</u>. 4,6 (CCL 2,1044-1045), Interestingly, Tert. has been discussing the veiling of virgins immediately prior to saying this.

68. Tert. <u>fug</u>. 1,1 (CCL 2,1135). Addressing Fabian he says, *Procuranda autem examinatio penes uos, qui, si forte, Paracletum non recipiendo, deductorem omnis ueritatis, merito adhuc etiam aliis quaestionibus obnoxii estis.* See also <u>fug</u>. 14,3 (CCL 2,1155) where the Paraclete is, with respect to the same question of flight in persecution, described as *deductor omnium ueritatum, exhortator omnium tolerantiarum.*

69. Tert. <u>mon</u>. 2,2 (CCL 2,1230), *Dicens enim: <u>Adhuc multa habeo</u> . . . <u>in omnem ueritatem</u>, satis utique praetendit et docturum illum quae et noua existimari possint, ut nunquam retro edita, et aliquando onerosa, ut idcirco non edita.*

70. Tert. <u>mon</u>. 2,4 (CCL 2,1230), *Paracletus autem multa habens edocere quae in illum distulit Dominus, secundum praefinitionem, ipsum primo Christum contestabitur qualem credimus, cum toto ordine Dei creatoris, et ipsum glorificabit, et de ipso commemorabit, et sic de principali regula agnitus illa multa quae sunt disciplinarum reuelabit, fidem dicente pro eis integritate praedicationis, licet nouis, quia nunc revelantur, licet onerosis, quia nec nunc sustinentur.*

71. Tert. <u>mon</u>. 14,6 (CCL 2,1250), *Tempus eius, donec Paracletus operaretur, fuit, in quem dilata sunt a Domino quae tunc sustineri non porterant, quae iam nemini competit portare non posse, quia per quem datur portare posse non deest.*

Chapter 2

GREEK EXEGESIS BETWEEN THE COUNCILS OF

NICAEA AND CHALCEDON

INTRODUCTION

Aside from one or two unfruitful and indirect allusions, the
extant literature of the Eastern Church contains no citations of the
paraclete passages for some three-quarters of a century after Origen
wrote against Celsus. But from the time of the great Council of
Nicaea there is a profusion of citations witnessing both to the sudden
flowering of the golden age of patristic literature and to the sudden
importance which the paraclete texts assume vis-à-vis the dogmatic
controversies of the era between the landmark councils of Nicaea
(325) and Chalcedon (451).

The official favour which the Church enjoyed after Constan-
tine's victory at the Milvian Bridge marks a turning point in its life.
No longer is it required to devote its talents and energies to the
defense against paganism and to understanding and bearing the rigours
of persecution. It is now free to do two things, both of which
markedly condition the history of paraclete exegesis. Firstly, it
is free to devote itself to the development of the theological
sciences. This means, on the one hand, the development of the main
lines of Churchly dogma. On the other, it involves the necessity
that the Church preserve itself from heresy. A large number of outstanding post-Nicene authors address themselves to the heresies of
Apollinarianism, Arianism, Macedonianism, Nestorianism, Sabellianism,[1]

and varieties of these, heresies which put pressures upon the Church
which encourage continuous theological discussion and contribute to
the formulation of orthodox doctrine. The paraclete passages are
seen by the writers of this period to have a special bearing on the
burning dogmatic and polemical issues of their day. Secondly, it
frees the Church to develop through its great schools at Antioch and
Alexandria the exegetical sciences, the exposition and the interpretation of the Scriptures.[1a] This includes exegesis of the Gospel
of John and, consequently, of Jo. 14-16.

There are in the literature of the Fourth and Fifth Centuries
two basic kinds of writing which make use of paraclete materials,
genres which correspond more or less exactly with these two developments in the Church's task. There are, on the one hand, those
writings which are primarily concerned with doctrine, though it
must not be said that they are unconcerned with exegetical questions.
These dogmatic writings contain by far the largest number of individual
citations of and allusions to our materials. There are, on the other
hand, those fewer writings which are more directly concerned with
exegesis. That is not to say, of course, that their authors are unconcerned with dogma.[2] There are marked differences between these
genres in their handling of paraclete materials, though there are
equally marked similarities. In order to present a picture of
developments within this period which is as unblurred as possible and
which avoids going to the unfruitful length of considering each
author in detail, we consider the dogmatico-polemical and exegetical
opera separately here, looking first at the former and secondly (at
somewhat greater length[3]) at the latter.

DOGMATIC WRITINGS

The Gospel of John seems to have been used to support both heretical and orthodox writing in the years between 325 and 451. Indeed, refutation of heretical exegesis of Johannine passages often precedes the development of catholic dogma in orthodox writers. At best, however, there remain to us few glimpses of heretical paraclete exegesis because of the general condemnation under which the writings of the heresiarchs fell. What examples do remain[4] are generally preserved in catholic fathers who reproduce their arguments in order to repudiate them.

The opposite situation obtains with respect to the catholic writers. In the many works which have survived the vicissitudes of the centuries, citations of the paraclete passages occur in rich and sometimes wasteful profusion. The adherents of the School of Alexandria refer to them almost with abandon. Of these, the blind leader of the School, Didymus, invokes them with the greatest frequency; some sections of Trin. and Spir. contain hardly a page without one or more references. By contrast, the writers under Antiochene influence are much more restrained. The same is true of those neo-Alexandrines, the Cappadocian fathers.

Nevertheless, orthodox or heretical, Antiochene or Alexandrian, writing on the paraclete passages between 325 and 451 is governed by three major dogmatic concerns: the Trinity, Christology, and Pneumatology. We take these concerns as an outline for our discussion.[5]

The Trinity

With respect to the doctrine of the Trinity, paraclete passages are invoked as evidence for distinction (or lack of distinction)

of the persons within the one Godhead. Marcellus of Ancyra, writing
against Asterius the Arian and specifically against his assertion
that there are three hypostases in the Godhead, adduces them as
'proof' for his peculiar Sabellian doctrine of the Trinity. In order
to maintain the unity of God against Asterius, he sees the Godhead
as a single hypostasis with a double extension, Spirit and Word,
which will ultimately be reabsorbed.[6] *In nuce* he argues this way:
if the word proceeds from the Father and the Spirit does, as well
(Jo. 15,26), then the Saviour can only speak Jo. 16,14, ἐκ τοῦ
ἐμοῦ λήμψεται καὶ ἀναγγελεῖ ὑμῖν, if an original divine monad is
extended into a triad while nevertheless remaining undivided.[7] If,
however, Spirit and Son are distinct persons, then 15,26 and 16,13-14
are mutually exclusive; for, either the Spirit does proceed from the
Father (15,26) and consequently has no need for any ministry from
the Son (16,14), since everything coming from the Father is perfect
in itself, or, if the Spirit does receive and minister from the Son,
then by the same logic he cannot proceed from the Father.[8] Therefore, the Godhead does not exist in three hypostases. Given this
understanding, 16,15 does not speak of any supposed total harmony
between the separate persons Father and Son; rather, it speaks of
absolute identity between them. For, if the Son is a separate hypostasis, then he defrauds the Father in this verse. There is neither
agreement nor unity in robbery.[9]

    A little more than a decade after Nicaea, Eusebius of Caesarea
wrote his De ecclesiastica theologia in order to refute Marcellus'
teaching on the Holy Spirit. In it he uses the paraclete passages to
support the distinction of the persons of Spirit and Son in a way
representative of catholic usage even in writers more clearly orthodox than himself. Marcellus, he charges, has asserted that Father,

Son, and Spirit are identical, three names but only one hypostasis.[10]
One of the sources of his error is his misexegesis of Jo. 16,14 which
Eusebius can only understand as portraying Spirit and Son as distinct
persons; in any transaction he who receives something is quite a
different person from him who gives.[11] This he supports from each of
the paraclete passages in turn. In 14,15-17 he sees the Saviour teaching clearly, specifically, and in so many words that the Paraclete-
Spirit is quite distinct (ἕτερος) from himself. Not only are giver
and gift to be separated, in Eusebius' thinking, but he seems to
lay stress on the word ἄλλος, as well.[12] Jesus also speaks of the Holy
Spirit as concerning another person (ἕτερος) at 14,26 when he says
ἐκεῖνος ὑμᾶς διδάξει πάντα,[13] at 15,26,[14] and at 16,7.[15] Finally,
the distinction of the Spirit from the Son is clearly evident in Jo.
16,12-14; for it is great foolishness to contend that Christ was
speaking of himself when he spoke as concerning another (ὡς περὶ
ἑτέρου) the words, ὅταν ἔλθῃ ἐκεῖνος, οὐ γὰρ ἀφ' ἑαυτοῦ λαλήσει,
ἐκεῖνος ἐμὲ δοξάσει, and ὅτι ἐκ τοῦ ἐμοῦ λήψεται.[16] On the contrary,
Jesus is here clearly teaching that the Holy Spirit is, although
subordinate to himself, a quite separate and distinct member of the
Trinity.[17] Eusebius is concerned to demonstrate from the paraclete
passages the distinct personhoods of Spirit and Son. But the same
passages are adduced in analogous ways by writers whose immediate
purposes lead them to stress the triple personality of the Godhead.[18]

        At least three Greek fathers also make some attempt to relate
the paraclete passages to the unique oneness which in catholic doctrine
characterizes the three persons of the Trinity. In summing up his
demonstration of the deity of the Spirit and the indivisibility of the
divine Triad, Athanasius sustains the inseparability from a conflation of Jo. 14,17, 15,26, and (perhaps) 16,7. Specifically, he

reasons that the Spirit of truth, who proceeds from the Father, is
inseparable from the Son who sends him as the Son himself is from the
Father.[19] For Didymus there is proof of the union of the divine nature and the oneness of the will of the three hypostases in the fact
that neither Son nor Spirit speak from themselves; he takes his evidence from, among others, Jo. 16,13-14.[20] Cyril of Alexandria sees
evidence for the oneness of the three hypostases in the fact that their
working is one. He illustrates: both Father and Son have it as their
task to reveal the Son. But, as he concludes from his quotation of
Jo. 16,12-14, the Spirit reveals Christ to us, as well. Since all
three have the same function, their working is one.[21] On the whole,
however, paraclete passages are used for substantiating the oneness of
the three persons only in a very minor way. As we shall see, they are
much more widely adduced for establishing the unity of two divine persons, whether of Father with Son, Spirit with Son, or Spirit with Father.

Christology

        The paraclete passages, particularly Jo. 16,14 and 16,15,
play a part in the Christological controversies of the Fourth and
Fifth Centuries in helping to establish the deity of the Son and his
coessentiality with the the Father. 16,14 sets the Son distinctly
apart from the creatures. They partake of the Spirit, but this verse
clearly states that, far from the Son partaking of the Spirit, the
Spirit (which is from God, it is presumed) partakes of him. The Son,
therefore, partakes of the Father's very essence and is no creature.[22]
16,15 also shows that the Son is God and is one essence with the
Father; for no creature possesses all the qualities and attributes of
the Father.[23] Cyril of Alexandria draws this out most specifically in
two individual passages. On the one hand, he maintains that the Son is

neither something made (ποίημα) nor one of the creatures (κτίσμα); for

if he were a creature and spoke 16,15 truthfully, there would be no-

thing in God and creation not held in common. If this is absurd (there

is no doubt that Cyril thinks it is) then the Son is no creature.[24]

On the other hand, using the method of *reductio ad absurdum*, he con-

tends that the Son is not inferior to the Father but is equal to

him. His argument runs like this: Jesus, because he is speaking

truth in 16,15, cannot be less than equal with the Father. For, if

he were less than God, then divine attributes could be attributed

to him (on the strength of 16,15; 17,10) and less than divine at-

tributes to the Father. Furthermore, if this were the case, then

nothing would hinder our saying truthfully that the Son is greater

than the Father and the Father less than the Son. As this is absurd,

Son and Father must be equals.[25]

Whether 16,15 is cited in proof of Nicene dogma or is used

deductively in building a given Christological construct where the

Nicene doctrine is already established, the most important exegetical

question asked of the verse concerns the content of the term πάντα.

Most, if not all, writers who ask the question would seem to concur

in including in πάντα all the things proper to Godhead, but quite

often the needs of a given context require that this be spelled out

in various specific ways. In some passages Jo. 16,15 is exegeted in

such a way that πάντα is taken to include the possession of the divine

nature of the Father.[26] In others it is taken to include the special

divine prerogatives, properties, and attributes of the Father, at-

tributes such as eternity, immutability, and the like.[27] As one

of the divine attributes is impassibility (ἀπάθεια), Theodoret finds

in 16,15 corroboration of his Nestorian teaching that it is only

the human flesh of Christ that suffers in the crucifixion; πάντα

includes impassibility and, as the Father is impassible, so therefore
is the divine nature of the Son.[28] In yet other patristic passages
πάντα is taken to include the divine honours,[29] all the divine titles
save *Father*,[30] and the divine operations.[31] Cyril of Alexandria contends further that, though the Spirit does proceed from the Father,
he nevertheless belongs also to the Son; for did not the Lord teach
at 16,15 that all the things of the Father belong to the Son? For
Cyril πάντα includes even the Holy Spirit.[32]

One very interesting understanding of πάντα takes 16,15 to
mean that the Son possesses all the knowledge which the Father possesses. It was apparently a mark of Arian dogma that it took Jesus'
self-confessed ignorance of the day and hour of the end in Mk. 13,32
and Mt. 24,36 as proof that the Son is unlike the Father in substance
and subordinate to him in dignity. This was, naturally, felt to be
quite damaging to Nicene orthodoxy, and it is evident from extant
literature that steps were quickly taken to interpret the Markan
and Matthean passages in a more catholic way. The favourite approach seems to have been to reinterpret the damaging passages in the
light of Jo. 16,15 on the (largely Origenic) principle that Scripture is not self-contradictory and that, since one Spirit inspires
all Scriptures, any given passage of Scripture may be interpreted
with the aid of any suitable other passage. Athanasius refers the
ignorance of the day and hour to the human nature of the Son; for it
is proper to human nature to be ignorant. But he maintains that as
Word of God, the Son is not nescient since all that is the Father's
is also the Son's.[33] Other writers, particularly those of Alexandria,
do not separate the natures but simply assert like Athanasius that, in
the light of Jo. 16,15, Mk. 13,32 and Mt. 24,36 cannot mean that the
Son himself really was ignorant at this point.[34] This line of

argument is most fully developed by Basil of Cappadocian Caesarea in a letter of January A.D. 376 to his friend Amphilochius of Iconium.[35] Having urged his friend to a comparison of the two Synoptic texts and having quoted them and noted the important difference between them, Basil suggests that they are not really in disagreement and that the Son is not included with his own servants in this ignorance. Rather, he quotes Jo. 16,15 and says outright that one of the things which the Father has is knowledge of the day and hour.[36] The Son, therefore, because he possesses all that the Father does, must possess the same knowledge. Then, after reexegeting Mt. 24,36 in this light,[37] he goes on to suggest that the words of Mk. 13,32 do not after all indicate any ignorance in the Son. What is meant there is that no one, not even the Son would have known had not the Father known; for the cause of the Son's knowing is the Father.[38] We see, therefore, that for the Greek fathers of the Nicene age πάντα in Jo. 16,15 includes (in addition to the other things discussed above) all the Father's knowledge, even knowledge of the date and time of the final consummation.

Pneumatology

Paraclete passages also play a part in the development of the doctrine of the Holy Spirit in the period between the great councils, most frequently, perhaps, in the writings of Didymus of Alexandria. The Greek fathers seek in them confirmation of the increate deity of the Spirit and of his relationship to the other persons of the divine Trinity, though they seldom invoke these passages without further support from argument or reference to other Scriptures.

That the Holy Spirit is increate is shown preeminently from Jo. 15,26, παρὰ τοῦ πατρὸς ἐκπορεύεται; the Spirit is no creature because he proceeds from the (increate) Father.[39]   Rather, it is shown

that, far from being of the creation, he is of God[40] and indeed is

God.[41] The clause παρὰ τοῦ πατρὸς ἐκπορεύεται is important to the

history of the doctrine of the procession of the Holy Spirit[42] in ways

not strictly germane to a history of exegesis of 15,26. Nevertheless,

it is possible to gather something of patristic understanding of the

manner of the procession of the Spirit from those passages where

15,26 is used to establish his deity. For Didymus 15,26 means that

the Spirit proceeds both unoriginately, consubstantially, and eter-

nally from the Father.[43] For Cyril, who seems to intend much the

same thing, it means that the Spirit proceeds from the Father's very

essence (οὐσία).[44] Theodoret's exposition is quite detailed: in

the paraclete passages (he gives a quotation conflated from 15,26;

16,7.13) the Saviour reveals that the Spirit is from (ἐκ) God and is

divine. More specifically, in saying παρὰ τοῦ πατρὸς ἐκπορεύεται,

the Saviour shows that the Father is the source (πηγή) of the Spirit.

And in using the present (rather than the future) tense of the verb,

he shows (with regard to Father and Spirit) the identity of their

nature (τῆς φύσεως τὴν ταυτότητα), the indivisibility and indistin-

guishableness of their essence (τῆς οὐσίας τὸ ἄτμητον, καὶ ἀδιάφορον),

and the union of their hypostases (τὸ ἡνωμένον τῶν ὑποστάσεων).[45]

          That the Spirit is no creature is further evidenced by the

catholic fathers from Jo. 16,13-14. Arian exegesis seems to have

taken 16,13 to support the assertion that the Spirit is not God be-

cause not perfect in and of himself; if he were self perfect and

self existing he would speak ἀφ' ἑαυτοῦ and would need to be re-

minded of nothing.[46] Further, Arian exegesis understood 16,14 to

reveal the inferiority of the Spirit to the Son and, consequently,

to the Father. The Spirit is holy neither by nature (φύσις) nor essentially (οὐσιωδῶς) but is holy only by partaking of the Father's

holiness and sharing it with the creation.[47] Didymus argues against

this in two ways. In the first place, he points out that the Son does

not speak from himself, either, by quoting from John 12,49. Nothing

different, therefore, is said of the Spirit than is said of the Son;

neither speaks anything but the words of God.[48] His second argument,

which he develops variously, is based on exegesis diametrically op-

posed to the Arian. No creature, says Didymus, consistently speaks

the things of God; even the best of creatures speaks often from its

own will which it must suppress in order to do the will of God. But

16,13 shows that the Spirit always speaks the things of God. Not

only does this prove him increate by nature, but it proves that the

divine nature and will are his by right.[49] For Didymus, this pas-

sage was given precisely so that no one might try to distinguish the

Spirit from the will and society of Father and Son (a Patris et Filii

voluntate et societate). Indeed, 16,13-15 was not written to indicate

that the Spirit receives anything that was not already his own by

nature; for in the Godhead communication is direct rather than by

speech and all knowledge is held in common. Giving among the Three

does not deprive the giver, and receiving does not imply an erstwhile

lack. Rather, far from 16,13 showing the Spirit to be a creature,

it demonstrates above everything else that he is of one substance

(una substantia) with Father and Son and is a member of the blessed

Trinity.[50]

The deity of the Holy Spirit is further evidenced in the fa-

thers by showing that he shares the divine titles, the divine at-

tributes, and the divine operations of Father and Son. Examples of

each of these are taken from the paraclete passages. Included in the

catalogues of divine titles are πνεῦμα τῆς ἀληθείας (Jo. 14,17;

15,26; 16,13)[51] and παράκλητος (Jo. 14,16.26; 15,26; 16,7).[52] Among

the divine attributes possessed by the Spirit of truth and witnessed

from the paraclete passages are those of truthfulness[53] and omni-

presence. That the Spirit is indeed present everywhere both above and

below Didymus infers from a juxtaposition of δώσει ὑμῖν with παρ'

ὑμῖν μένει and ἐν ὑμῖν ἔσται (14,16-17).[54] Among the divine oper-

ations proper to the Spirit are these: with Father and Son the Spirit

judges (16,8);[55] he foreknows and foretells (16,13)[56] he teaches and

inspires men (14,26);[57] and he puts men into remembrance and guides

them into all truth, both of which are considered by at least one

author to be divine operations (14,26; 16,13).[58] The point of all

these demonstrations is, of course, that one who possesses by right

the divine titles, attributes, and operations is no creature but

is very God.

In a slightly different way, though to the same purpose,

various aspects of the catholic pneumatology are deduced by finding

in the paraclete passages evidence for the Spirit's equality with

Christ. At least three evidences are to be found in Jo. 14,16-17.

The first is in the word ἄλλος. According to the Nazianzus Gregory,

we are to conclude from it the equal honour (ὁμοτιμίαν) of Spirit

and Son; for, he says, ἄλλος is a word of joint lordship which is not

said of things not consubstantial.[59] Secondly, the Spirit's equality

(ἰσότητα) and consubstantiality (ὁμοουσιότητα) with Christ are also

demonstrated when the Lord reveals in 14,16 that he, too, is a

Paraclete; he is a Paraclete and the Holy Spirit is his co-Paraclete

(συμπαράκλητος).[60] Thirdly, that the Spirit is one with the Christ

and is, indeed, his own Spirit is further evidenced by the fact that

he is called πνεῦμα τῆς ἀληθείας (14,17; 15,26; 16,13) by the one who

is himself Truth (Jo. 14,6).[61] 14,26 shows that his teaching is in agreement with (σύμφωνος)[62] and the same as[63] Jesus' own. And the

assertion that the Spirit's coming and salvation are the same as

Christ's and equal to them is inferred from 16,7.[64]

Polemical writings

Finally, from certain anti-Montanist and anti-Manichaean

passages we may illustrate two further points of exegesis which do

not strictly fall under the rubrics *Trinity, Christology,* and

Pneumatology. The first, based on Jo. 16,14, suggests that the mark

given by the Saviour by which we may distinguish the true Spirit

is that he will glorify Christ. According to Epiphanius, that the

Apostles did glorify Christ shows that they had received the

Paraclete-Spirit; that Montanus, on the contrary, glorifies himself

disqualifies his claim to the Paraclete.[65] The second point of

exegesis treats of the time of the fulfillment of the paraclete

promises. The univocal opinion among catholic theologians seems

to be that the Paraclete was given and Jesus' promise fulfilled most

completely and magnificently on the day of Pentecost,[66] though

there is some variation in attempts to explain Jo. 20,22 in this

light.[67] Didymus marshals this exegesis against Montanist claims

that the Paraclete came when Montanus came,[68] and Hegemonius scorn-

fully suggests that, while Jesus' promise in the passages was to take

place not long after, Manes, if his claim to be the promised

Paraclete is to be believed, contends that it was not in fact ful-

filled until *post trecentos et eo amplius annos*.[69]

EXEGETICAL WRITINGS

Paraclete exegesis is also preserved for us in three major

expositions of John's Gospel, namely, the commentaries by Cyril of

Alexandria and Theodore of Mopsuestia and the homilies by John
Chrysostom.   In addition, we possess fragments of the commentaries
by Apollinaris of Laodicea and the Arian writer Theodore of Heraclea.
None of these works is devoid of all dogmatic intent.[70] Nevertheless,
because of the peculiar nature of a commentary, it is for our purposes relatively easy to differentiate between what may be broadly
described as dogma and exegesis (though in the final analysis the
two must remain inseparable).   This being so, we are able to arrange
our discussion here rather differently from that of the last section.
There it was necessary to organise around certain doctrines in order
to bring coherence without endless repetition.   Here we examine our
materials, supplemented by occasional relevant passages from other
writings, in just the way they themselves are organised, viz., in
the order of the arrangement of the Gospel text.   We begin with a look
at the verses in Jo. 14,15-17.[71]

14,15-17

The three catholic commentators examine the relationship of
14,15 with 14,14, and, with minor variation in the explication, come
to essentially the same conclusion: viz., 14,15 supplies the qualifying condition which makes 14,14 true. Cyril points out that 14,14
is patently not true for all men and that Jesus, so as not to seem to
speak falsehood, adds 14,15 to show that it is only those who love
him and keep the law who are worthy of its promise.[72] Chrysostom suggests that 14,15 was added to show that mere asking is not sufficient;
the condition of loving the Lord is prior to asking of him.[73]
Theodore teaches more or less the same thing.[74]

The message of 14,15 itself is that love does not exist exclusively in statements; saying that one loves God does not make it so.

Real love is distinguished and recognised in works and actions; it has

ethical content, as it were. This is more or less the express exege-

sis of Chrysostom, Apollinaris, and Cyril.[75] When Chrysostom ex-

amines, in addition, the question of the identification of Christ's

commandments, he seems to give two different but related answers. In

the homilies on John he appears to identify τὰς ἐντολάς with Jesus'

command to the disciples to love one another as he has loved them

(Jo. 13,34).[76] In his homily on Mt. 22,34-36, however, he identifies

them with the commands to love first God and then one's neighbour as

oneself.[77] Cyril considers another exegetical question. How is it,

he asks, that Jesus, having confessed throughout the Gospel that his

words are not his own but come from God the Father,[78] now says that

the commands he has given are, indeed, his own? Both question and

answer are closely related to the dogmatic purpose of the commentary;

for the Son's likeness to the Father is, according to Cyril, so exact

that his manner of speaking was not like that of a minister or servant

but differed not at all from the Father's. It is the identity of

essence (τὸ ἀπαράλλακτον τῆς οὐσίας), the consubstantiality of

Father and Son, which makes it quite true and uncontradictory for the

Truth to speak as he has at 14,15 of his own commandments.[79]

Theodore of Heraclea employs 14,15-16 against the Phrygian

sect (Montanists). Did the disciples love Jesus and keep his com-

mandments, asks Theodore? If the Phrygians say no, they are immedi-

ately confounded by the fact that the disciples continuously showed

their love not only in their living works but also in their martyrdom.

If, on the other hand, the Phrygians are forced by the evidence to ad-

mit that the disciples did love and keep, then, in maintaining that

the Paraclete first came upon themselves after two-to-three hundred

years, they make a liar of Christ who promises in 14,15-16 that he

will send the Paraclete on this condition of loving and keeping.[80]
No, the disciples manifestly did fulfill the condition, and the Paraclete was sent immediately according to promise. The Phrygians are
therefore wrong in their claims.[81]

     The first exegetical consideration with respect to 14,16 con-
cerns the sense of ἐρωτήσω τὸν πατέρα; each of the commentators who
deal with the clause explains it differently. According to Apollinaris, the Lord says he will ask the Father κατὰ τὴν ἀδελφικὴν
πρεσβείαν and not (it is implied) because he does not himself give
the Spirit. For it is he himself who, with respect to lordly authority and operation, bestows according to the Father's purposes.[82]
John Chrysostom, having suggested that Jesus speaks this verse to con-
sole the disciples for their coming bereavement of his physical
presence, wonders why Jesus says he will ask the Father when we see
elsewhere (notably Jo. 20,22) that he has no need to do so but sends
the Spirit himself. He decides that it is said to ensure credibility;
for, had Jesus said at this point in time that he himself was going
to send the Spirit, the disciples would not have believed him.[83]
Down the page, Chrysostom makes the further point that ἐρωτήσω τὸν
πατέρα shows the time of the coming (παρουσία) of the Spirit, viz.,
the Spirit was not to come upon the disciples until after Jesus'
sacrifice had cleansed them and he was no longer with them, i.e., after
the ascension.[84] Cyril takes another tack entirely: in Jo. 14,16-17
as a whole, Jesus speaks neither entirely from his human nor from his
divine nature, but is speaking at the same time as God and man.[85]
Notwithstanding, he necessarily (ἀναγκαίως) introduces the Father
(in 14,16) as a co-supplier of the Paraclete so that in speaking the
words of 14,14 he might not seem to do violence to the person and
power of God the Father and Begetter.[86] When, therefore, Jesus says

ἐρωτήσω, he speaks as man rather than as God, and in so speaking attributes to the divine nature, in the person of God the Father, what belongs distinctly to it.[87] Theodore of Mopsuestia differs yet again. To his mind, ἐρωτήσω is said figuratively for δι' ἐμοῦ δέξεσθαι τὴν χάριν. What it does not mean is that our Lord was about to ask in order that the disciples might receive. This gift was both predestined in the sight of God and fore-promised by our Lord, and, if the gift was promised, then the asking was superfluous. Rather, he has chosen this way to recall to mind the gift of the Spirit.[88]

The second exegetical concern in 14,16 is the phrase ἄλλον παράκλητον which is the name, as Cyril asserts, that Jesus gives to the Spirit who proceeds both from his own essence and that of the Father. This identification of Spirit and Paraclete is usual among the fathers.[89]

῎Αλλον is seen to show two things. First, the Holy Spirit is called *another* Paraclete because Jesus is himself a Paraclete. Thus, in designating the Spirit ἄλλον παράκλητον our Lord is saying, more or less, that he is going to ask the Father to send 'another such as I'.[90] Secondly, ἄλλον reveals that the Spirit-Paraclete possesses his own proper personality within the oneness of the Trinity. For Cyril, indeed, 14,15-18 particularly reveals with regard to the Spirit the balancing moieties of Trinitarian dogma, namely, the three hypostases and the one essence.[91] That the Spirit is distinct from Father and Son in whom he is (ὑπόστασις) is shown above all by this phrase in 14,16.[92] The balancing unity of essence (οὐσία) comes in 14,18.[93] John Chrysostom finds both elements within the one expression ἄλλον παράκλητον: ἄλλον shows the distinction of persons (ὑπόστασις), and παράκλητον the connexion of the substance (οὐσία). To his mind opposing heresies are eliminated by the one fortunate

phrase.[94]   Theodore of Heraclea also sees distinction of persons
(πρόσωπα) in 14,16, but he, like Eusebius,[95] appeals to the whole
verse. He contends that no one both asks himself for a gift and
sends himself as the gift.[96]

The meaning of the term παράκλητος is also discussed.
Theodore of Mopsuestia indicates in his commentary on John that
παράκλητος carries the sense *consolator*. The Saviour mentions the
Paraclete, *id est consolatorem*, as an antidote to the disciples'
distress. For through his gifts the Spirit was to make the evil they
had to bear easier. That this has happened is clear from the
transformation of the disciples' fearfulness to an attitude of
rejoicing in tribulation.[97]   In hom. 10,7 he further maintains the
manner of the consoling to be the giving of teaching necessary to
the comforting of their souls amid the world's trials.[98]   Didymus
also applies this sense of the term to the Spirit,[99] but he also
goes on to discuss the force of ἄλλον. ἄλλον is not, he says, indicative of any separation of nature between our Lord and the Spirit.
Rather, it is spoken because the two have different functions
(*operationes*). Jesus is Paraclete because he is an *intercessor*.
The Spirit is ἄλλον because he, as Paraclete has a different function:
he consoles, though this is not to suggest that he does not also
intercede (as, e.g., at Rom. 8,26).[100]   This dual understanding of
παράκλητος is, it will be noticed, similar to that of Origen at princ.
2,7,4 (GCS 22,151-152). In Trin. Didymus specifically rejects the
interpretation of the heretics who understand the Spirit to be called
Paraclete because he entreats on behalf of the creation rather than
because of his work of consolation. For, he says, the words παράκλησις
and παραμυθίας are synonymous.[101]   Every Greek writer who makes plain
his exegesis of παράκλητος understands it to mean *consoler*.[102]

Chrysostom makes one final exegetical point on 14,16 when he suggests that μεθ' ὑμῶν μένει,[103] while it means the same with respect to the Spirit as the Saviour means when he says ἐγὼ μεθ' ὑμῶν εἰμί, nevertheless indicates a difference between them; for Jesus is to leave the disciples, while the Spirit will not depart from them even after the end (τελευτήν).[104]

There are two expositions of the phrase πνεῦμα τῆς ἀληθείας. Cyril supports from it his claim that the Paraclete is Jesus' Spirit: Jesus not only calls the Paraclete πνεῦμα τῆς ἀληθείας, but in the same context (14,6) has told us that he himself is truth. Therefore, the Paraclete is the Spirit of Jesus.[105] Theodore of Mopsuestia explains that the Paraclete is called πνεῦμα τῆς ἀληθείας because he unchangingly teaches nothing but the truth.[106] (Chrysostom does comment on the phrase in a single cryptic sentence but his meaning is unclear.[107])

The rest of 14,17 is treated as a unity; for a writer's interpretation of κόσμος informs his exegesis of what follows and vice-versa. Several writers understand κόσμος to mean materialistic and flesh-bound men who cannot accept what lies beyond their physical sight. Since the Spirit is incorporeal, materialistic man cannot perceive him; for he cannot get beyond the physical to see with eyes of faith.[108] The disciples can perceive the Spirit's incorporeal parousia because they experience it directly and because they are, through Jesus' teachings, freed from the lusts of the flesh and the encumbering materialistic vision.[109]

Other writers would not contradict this. John Chrysostom, for example, explains that Jesus forestalls any expectation of a visible parousia of the Spirit when he adds these clauses in 14,17. But Chrysostom goes on to suggest that θεωρεῖ does not at all relate to

ocular perception.   Rather, Jesus is speaking of knowledge; it is,
indeed, his habit when speaking of knowledge to represent it by sight
(θεωρία) since sight (ὄψις) is clearer than the other senses.[110]
Cyril also interprets θεωρεῖ to mean spiritual rather than physical
vision.   In his understanding those who are in the world are both under the tyranny of fleshly lusts and antipathetic to the things of God.
For this reason the Spirit is, for them, both invisible (ἀθεώρητον)
and uncontainable or incomprehensible (ἀχώρητον).   To those, however,
who keep themselves free of the evils of the world, the Paraclete is
both containable (χώρητον) and easily visible (εὐκάτοπτον); they perceive him spiritually (νοητῶς θεωροῦσι).[111]   Didymus suggests that
κόσμος means heretics who cannot receive the Paraclete because they
neither perceive him (οὐ θεωροῦσιν) with eyes of faith nor glorify
him as God.   The Spirit dwells in those who confess him to be God.[112]
For Theodore of Mopsuestia 14,17 is spoken to show the magnitude of
the gift to be bestowed.   So great is the Spirit that the whole world
together cannot lay hold of him to snatch him.   Only those upon whom he
descends through the divine will can receive him.[113]   This, says Theodore, is confirmed by ὅτι οὐ θεωρεῖ αὐτὸ οὐδὲ γινώσκει; for it is impossible that the world should know what is above its vision and understanding.   The disciples are to receive him, though incomprehensible, through Christ, but they must not expect to see him with physical
sight.[114]

          In this period ἐν ὑμῖν ἔσται is understood to mean that the
Paraclete, far from coming in another incarnation, is to live within
the disciples in their very souls.[115]

14,25-26

          At first glance there seems to be little unanimity in the in-
terpretation of Jo. 14,25-26; every writer seems to go off on his own

exegetical tangent and to have little in common with others of his
age.[116] There are, nevertheless, similarities which reveal a common
recognition of problems raised by the text and of certain dogmatic implications in it.

        The first similarity involves a recognition of the problem
raised by Arian exegesis, namely, that the words spoken here simply
are not consonant with deity. Both Cyril and Amphilochius defend the
passage, basically, by suggesting that Christ here speaks in a human
way. In Cyril's exegesis Jesus' words in 14,24 are a reflection of
his divine nature. Now he suggests that, corresponding to his human
nature, Jesus' speech also (as here at 14,25-26) possesses true humanity, a humanity which communicates with the minds into which it enters.
Jesus speaks as a man, therefore, a man about to vanish from sight.[117]
Amphilochius also refers these verses to the human nature of Christ
and will not allow that they be applied to the divine nature. For him
they are 'humble words' spoken out of consideration for the disciples'
weakness.[118] Amphilochius also recognises a further and related problem: viz., ὃ πέμψει ὁ πατήρ might be exegeted in such a way as to
demean the Spirit, another Arian foible. But for Amphilochius this is
misexegesis. The Spirit is not really sent, as this is impossible.
Rather, Jesus continues his revelation (still using 'humble words') in
terms of sending so that the Father's part in the dispensation of the
Spirit might not be disguised.[119] Theodore of Mopsuestia sees the same
problem, but he solves it by suggesting that Jesus does not here speak
of the divine nature of the Spirit, which exists apart from the world,
but of the grace and operation of the Spirit to believers.[120]

        A second common exegetical outlook interprets 14,25-26 to
mean that the Spirit has things to reveal that Jesus has not revealed
in his earthly ministry. Cyril's exegesis is, at base, that Jesus'

revelation has been necessarily incomplete and that the most complete
revelation of 'the mystery' is given us through the Paraclete.[121] For
Theodore of Mopsuestia 14,25-26 means that Jesus, while with the
disciples, revealed all the things it was important for them to know;
now he promises that when they have received the grace of the Spirit,
they shall know many signs they do not yet know.[122] Amphilochius
refers the first πάντα of 14,26 to the things Jesus had not said and
the second to those which he had. The Spirit is to teach the things
not said by Jesus and to bring to memory the things which he did
teach.[123]

      Finally, it is inferred from 14,25-26 that the teaching and
mind of the Spirit are not different from those of Jesus. This is
expressed in more than one way. Cyril, for example, says that Jesus
can and does say that the Paraclete shall teach us all things because, as the Spirit of Jesus, he is in reality Christ in us. But
at base it means only one thing: the Paraclete belongs by right
in the Godhead and, in terms of identity of nature, he is what Christ
is and therefore knows and possesses all that is in him.[124] He does
not come by his knowledge of all the things of Christ by being
taught, but possesses it by nature because he is both of and in
Christ.[125]

15,26-27

      There is even greater diversity in the exegesis of Jo. 15,
26-27. Theodore of Mopsuestia, for example, is the only one to comment on the first two clauses of verse 26: ὅταν ἔλθῃ ὁ παράκλητος
ὃν ἐγὼ πέμψω ὑμῖν. He exegetes the passage in a, for him, characteristic way by suggesting that it is not the omnipresent divine substance which Jesus here promises but that grace of the Spirit which

is to be poured out upon the disciples after the ascension.[126] Neither is there unanimity among the three who do comment upon the
title πνεῦμα τῆς ἀληθείας. For John Chrysostom this title shows
that the Spirit, when he comes, shall be worthy of belief precisely
because he is the Spirit of truth.[127] Cyril echoes his earlier
exegesis of 14,17: The πνεῦμα τῆς ἀληθείας is the Spirit of Jesus
who is truth (cf. 14,6).[128] Theodore of Mopsuestia writes that
πνεῦμα τῆς ἀληθείας denotes at once the greatness of the Spirit's
nature and his power to grant to whomever he pleases benefits which
never perish.[129]

The clause ὃ παρὰ τοῦ πατρὸς ἐκπορεύεται is variously con-
strued to be indicative of the coessentiality of the Godhead. According to the two Theodores it shows the consubstantiality of Spirit
with Father; for the Spirit proceeds from the very nature (*ex
natura*)[130] or essence (οὐσία)[131] of the Father. For Cyril, on the
other hand, this clause and verse show the coessentiality of Father
with Son. Here is his argument: Jesus in one breath calls the
Paraclete πνεῦμα τῆς ἀληθείας (i.e., his own Spirit) and says that
he proceeds from the Father. This means that as the Spirit belongs
to the Son, being in and proceeding through him, so also he belongs
to the Father. Therefore, since the Spirit is common to both Father
and Son, the three are not distinct in essence, and they are wrong
who maintain that the Son vouchsafes the Spirit as a mere minister of
the Father.[132]

The exegetes also consider briefly the nature of the witness
to be borne by the Spirit (15,26) and by the disciples (15,27). The
Spirit will testify concerning Jesus by working marvels in the disciples.[133] He is to do his work through them and will not witness
apart from them. The disciples, on the other hand, are qualified

to be witnesses because they have themselves observed all that Jesus
said and did; such is the meaning of ἀπ' ἀρχῆς μετ' ἐμοῦ ἐστε.[134]

16,4b-15

The exegesis of Jo. 16,4-15 tends to cluster around three
groups of verses, corresponding roughly to natural divisions in the
text. The first of these groups concerns the matter in 4b-7. Cyril
explains why these verses are spoken by Jesus in this context: the
disciples were expecting to overcome every obstacle while they had
Jesus with them, as would anyone who had experienced such power.
But Christ has just forewarned them of unexpected perils and he is
compelled, therefore, to explain to them why he had not forewarned
them at first and so allayed their dismay and forestalled their
disappointed hopes.[135] Why, then, did Jesus not previously warn the
disciples? The answer (found in v.4b) is that, so long as he was
with them, he himself was sufficient to meet all their needs for
peace of mind, protection, instruction, assistance; it is only now
that he is going away that it is necessary to explain to them what
is coming.[136] Such is also the interpretation of John Chrysostom[137]
and Theodore of Mopsuestia.[138] In verses 5 and 6 Jesus reveals
that he is aware of their inner suffering.[139] Indeed, the cause of
their speechlessness as in 16,5 is shown by 16,6 to be the paralysis
produced by sorrow and fear.[140]

The one common element in the exegesis of 16,7 seems to be
the observation on the part of several writers that expedience and
truth are of more importance than pleasure. It brings the disciples no pleasure to hear that their Lord is to leave and that they
are to undergo trials and persecutions. But the Lord refuses to
forbear on that account and insists on telling them what is both true
and for their own good.[141]

The fullest discussion of why Jesus' going was expedient comes in a longish passage from Cyril. To begin with, he points out that now that the time has come for Jesus to depart his going would be advantageous to the disciples but his staying would be disadvantageous.[142] The departure is expedient for two reasons: on the one hand, it is vital that Jesus depart into the presence of the Father not for his own sake but for ours; it is a necessary part of his work that he become our forerunner. On the other hand, while all Jesus' work on earth is accomplished, it is still necessary that we become partakers of his divine nature or that, alternatively, we give up our old life for a new one pleasing to God. But the only way to get such life is by participation in and fellowship with the Holy Spirit. And, as it is essential that the Lord should continue to associate by the Spirit with his worshippers so that they might advance in virtue and withstand the assaults of men, the most suitable time for the Spirit's mission is the occasion of his own departure.[143] Further, the Spirit changes all whom he indwells into a new likeness (εἰκών), turning their inclination from things earthly to things heavenly and their cowardice to courage. Indeed, it is unquestionable that the disciples are later steeled by him to indifference toward their assaulters. Therefore, Jesus speaks truth in 16,7; for his going is to be the occasion of the Spirit's coming.[144]

John Chrysostom also comments on 16,7, but his concerns are somewhat different. For one thing, he reveals by a rhetorical question that he sees here evidence against those with too low a view of the Spirit, apparently those who see the Spirit as the servant of the Son. How can it be expedient, he asks, that a master depart in order that his servant might come?[145] But more important to Chrysostom is the question why the Spirit did not come before Jesus departed,

a question to which he gives more than one answer. In his <u>hom. 78,3</u>
<u>in Jo.</u> he suggests that it was because man was still under the curse
which put him at enmity with God; it was necessary that man and God
be reconciled before the gift could be received. It is in this
light that he interprets πέμψω αὐτόν to mean προπαρασκευάσω ὑμᾶς πρὸς
τὴν ὑποδοχήν. It cannot mean what it seems to, for that which is
everywhere cannot be sent.[146] But in the <u>hom. 1,5 in Ac.</u> he suggests
that the Lord had to go first in order both that the disciples might
long for the Spirit sufficiently to receive that grace and that
the consolation (παραμυθία) of the Spirit's coming might be sufficiently great.[147] Their desire was to be increased in the face of
their great need by the lapse of time between Jesus' withdrawal at
the ascension and the Spirit's coming.

   The second unit into which exegesis falls is that pertaining
to 16,8-11. Cyril puts the passage into context: Jesus has just
shown that his departure is the proper occasion for the descent and
mission of the Spirit and has thus sufficiently allayed the fears
of the disciples. Now in 16,8 he shows what the work of the Spirit
will be. Furthermore, he points out what form each of the Spirit's
reproofs will take.[148] Cyril then discusses these verses point by
point and, in the context of his discussion, reveals in two ways his
exegesis of the word κόσμος. In the first place, he defines it as
those ignorant men who persist in unbelief and are in bondage to
their love of wordly pleasure.[149] For Cyril the term (and therefore
the Spirit's reproof) is not limited only to the Jews but applies
generically to the race, to all who cling to that wickedness which
is of the devil.[150] This understanding is made even clearer when
he suggests that those who are not of the world are those true believers who love Christ and are worthy both of him[151] and of the

Paraclete, whom they confess to be both God and creator of the universe.[152]

The Spirit will make his first reproof when he reveals the
sin of the world[153] and condemns (κατακρίνω) it as bound and doomed
under sin.[154] The overarching cause of his reproof and, one would
gather, the underlying basis of the sin is the world's rejection of
and lack of faith in the Saviour, the sinless one.[155]

There are two basic strands in the interpretation of Jo. 16,
10. The first, represented by John Chrysostom, interprets the verse
so that it is the righteousness of Jesus concerning which the Spirit
will convict the world. Though Jesus had led a blameless life, his
opponents constantly urged against him that he was a sinner. The
Spirit is to refute this argument utterly, and his proof will be to
show that Jesus goes to the Father to abide continually, a thing which
no sinner ever does.[156] This understanding of 16,10 ties δικαιοσύνη
most closely with πρὸς τὸν πατέρα ὑπάγω. The second strand of
exegesis ties δικαιοσύνη more closely with the clause οὐκέτι θεωρεῖτέ
με. According to this view it is the righteousness of those who
believe in Christ even though they have never seen him concerning
which the Spirit is to reprove the world. This understanding stresses
the importance of belief in the unseen as an element in the faith of
the righteous. It also points out the unrighteousness of a world
that has refused to rise to belief in the unseen Christ.[157]

There is greater diversity in the understanding and exposition
of 16,11, though there is general agreement that the ἄρχων τοῦ κόσμου
τούτου whose condemnation the Paraclete is to show is identical with
the Devil (διάβολος), Satan (Σάτανας).[158] Chrysostom interprets 16,11
in the light of v.10 as a further proof of the righteousness of
Christ. Had Jesus been a sinner he could not have overthrown his

opponent the Prince of this world. But the proof to the world of his

righteousness is the condemnation through him of his adversary.[159]

Pursuing quite another line of thought, Cyril says that the third re-

proof will be ἡ δικαιοτάτη κατάκρισις τοῦ ἄρχοντος τοῦ κόσμου τούτου.

Specifically, magnifying Christ as Lord of the universe, the Paraclete

is to convict the world of having left off the worship of him who is

by nature God, i.e., Christ, and turned to the worship of Satan, who

is not.[160] Cyril offers proof that Satan is not God: had he been

God by nature, he could not have lost his power; God sits unshaken on

the throne. But Satan *has* lost his power, as is shown by his im-

potence over those sanctified by the Spirit in Christ and by the pow-

er of Spirit-filled Christians over demons.[161] Cyril also offers a

word of exegesis concerning the title ὁ ἄρχων τοῦ κόσμου τούτου. God

(sic) does not call him this because he really is the ruler of this

world, nor because he possesses some inherent authority. Rather, the

title is given because he has stolen his glory by fraud (ἀπάτη) and

covetousness (πλεονεξία) and because he continues to enslave all who

stray through error and wickedness, though they could easily be freed

through conversion to Christ. Satan is, therefore, only a pretender

to the throne of the world.[162]

       Concerning the third unit of the text, 16,12-15, there is

great, though not necessarily conflicting, variety of exposition,

variety arising primarily from the momentary purposes and styles of the

individual writers. There is also, however, an underlying unanimity

among our writers which, while it may not immediately meet the eye, is

nevertheless real. Although it is not always easy to summarise this

material, we do look at certain common elements and at various features

peculiar to given authors which may be important to the later history

of exegesis or to the developments of dogma in this era. We turn

first to 16,12-13.

Several writers, in addition to expounding specific details, discuss the overall message of these verses. For Chrysostom 16,12-13 show that the Spirit is neither greater nor less than Christ, but is precisely equal to him. His greatness and dignity (ἀξίωμα), indeed, his deity, are shown both in the expedience of Jesus' departure, in his miracles and bringing of perfect knowledge, and, most of all, in his foretelling of future things.[163] But, having spoken many things about the Spirit's function (Chrysostom quotes from 14,26; 16,7.12.13), Jesus goes on to say ἐκ τοῦ ἐμοῦ λήμψεται and οὐ γὰρ ἀφ' ἑαυτοῦ λαλήσει lest the disciples fall into the error of thinking the Spirit greater than Christ.[164] Cyril suggests a two-fold reason why Jesus keeps silence concerning the πολλά of v.12: the disciples are alarmed and sorrowful at what he has already said about the future (τὰ ἐσόμενα) and Jesus does not wish to dispirit them further; he refuses to share the deeper mysteries concerning himself because they, not yet illumined by the Spirit, are not prepared to apprehend them. When the Paraclete comes he will both prepare them to receive and deliver to them the deeper mysteries of the faith.[165] Theodore of Mopsuestia says that the disciples are to prove the power of the Spirit in a greater degree, because when he comes they shall not only hear but understand the things which they are unable to bear at the present time.[166]

The explanation why the disciples were unable to bear the πολλά of v.12 is, in the main, the same throughout the Greek fathers, though details of exposition differ slightly. For, with the exception of Theodore of Mopsuestia, who suggests merely that they were unable to bear them because they would not be able to understand them if said,[167] those who deal with the question maintain that the disciples cannot bear the higher and spiritual things because they are still bound by the letter of the Law and their Jewish training.[168]   Origen,

it will be remembered, gave a similar answer at <u>Cels</u>. 2,1.[169]

What, then, are the πολλά which are not now bearable (16,12)

but concerning which the Spirit will conduct the disciples into all

truth (16,13)? Didymus says that 'yet many things (<i>multa</i>)' means

'yet more things (<i>plurima</i>)' in this context. He argues that Jesus'

words are directed not to new disciples, but to old ones who have

heard his words but have not yet attained all things. He has taught

them sufficiently for the present and postpones the rest of his

teaching which is not to be understood apart from the Spirit's in-

struction.[170]   Other writers would not disagree with Didymus' con-

tention that πολλά means 'things additional', but do go on to in-

dicate that the Spirit's curriculum will include the higher things,

the perfect and secret things, the deep mysteries of the faith, the

things to come. He will teach the secrets of the ineffable Trinity and

will guide into all the truth concerning Jesus himself, chiefly the

truth relating to his divine nature.[171]   But, as Theodore of Mopsuestia

cautions, the Spirit's teaching is not to come in words audible to

the ear but is to be communicated directly to the minds (<i>animae</i>) of

the disciples.[172]

It will be useful to look briefly at exegesis of particular

phrases and clauses of 16,13. Cyril gives his usual interpretation of

the phrase πνεῦμα τῆς ἀληθείας: the coming Paraclete is shown by it

to be no lofty stranger but to be Jesus' own Spirit. In promising

the Paraclete, therefore, Jesus promises them his own presence in

the Spirit's, a thing possible because Spirit and Son are of one

essence (οὐσία).[173]   οὐ γὰρ λαλήσει ἀφ' ἑαυτοῦ, ἀλλ' ὅσα ἀκούσει

λαλήσει is taken to mean that the Spirit will speak nothing contrary

to or out of accord with the teachings of Jesus but speaks, rather,

that which the Son, as one with the Father, speaks. The text at this
point shows the perfect coessentiality of the Spirit with Father and
Son[174] and must not be taken in any way to suggest that the Spirit
learns anything that he does not eternally possess with Son and
Father.[175] The final clause of 16,13, καὶ τὰ ἐρχόμενα ἀναγγελεῖ ὑμῖν,
is variously understood to show the Spirit's deity, as it is a divine
prerogative to foretell the future,[176] and to give the sign that the
Spirit of truth is consubstantial with Jesus; for, Jesus himself
foretold the future.[177]

The Greek exegetes consider both the meaning of ἐκεῖνος ἐμὲ
δοξάσει, and how it is to be accomplished. With respect to the former
consideration, Cyril suggests that it is the Spirit's function to
reveal the mystery of Christ's nature and greatness and that, contrary
to the Jews who did him to death, he is more than mere man, that he
is himself God. By so doing he increases the honour in which Christ
is held.[178] But how does the Spirit fulfill this mission of glori-
fying Christ? Chrysostom teaches that he does it by granting his
inner workings, which will be productive of greater miracles than
Jesus' own, in Jesus' own name.[179] Cyril's answer is somewhat
different: he does it by performing his operations omnisciently and
omnipotently and in a thoroughly divine manner. Surely, if his own
Spirit who receives of him is both omniscient, omnipotent, and truly
divine, then Jesus must also possess these attributes.[180] Theodore
of Mopsuestia has a similar argument, but he reasons from the finite
to the infinite, from the disciple to the Lord, rather than from
Spirit to Son: the Spirit shall glorify the Son by placing a small
part of the grace that is in and with him on the disciples so that they
shall perform mighty works. The magnitude of their miracles, healings,
exorcisms, prophecies, and other works which shall come as a result

of the Spirit's grace will point to the Son's much greater power and
honour since he, indeed, possesses the whole of the grace of which
the disciples are to have but a part.[181]

Three observations may be made concerning the exegesis of
16,14b. First, it shows that the Spirit's teaching is identical
with that of Jesus.[182] Secondly, it is to be understood in a way that
is consonant with the consubstantiality of the Trinity. The Spirit
receives nothing he did not already have; he receives no change of
nature; he is not lacking in inherent power and sufficiency.[183]
Rather, as Cyril puts it, it is because of his consubstantiality with
and procession through the Son that Christ says ἐκ τοῦ ἐμοῦ λαμβάνει.[184] Thirdly, several writers consider the meaning of the
phrase ἐκ τοῦ ἐμοῦ,[185] though they explain it in different ways.
Apollinaris, linking it with 16,15, teaches that when Jesus says the
Spirit will receive of his (παρ' ἐμοῦ) he means that he will receive
of the Father's, as well; for the things of Jesus are the things of
the Father.[186] Eusebius of Caesarea refers the question of the τοῦ
ἐμοῦ to Col. 2,3: the things the Spirit receives come out of the
treasures of wisdom and knowledge hidden in Christ.[187] John
Chrysostom, on the other hand, seeing here again the consubstantiality
of Son and Spirit, suggests that ἐκ τοῦ ἐμοῦ means ἐξ ὧν ἐγὼ οἶδα,
ἐκ τῆς ἐμῆς γνώσεως. Μία γὰρ ἐμοῦ καὶ τοῦ Πνεύματος γνῶσις.[188]

Finally, arriving at last at 16,15, we summarise the exposition of Cyril and of Theodore of Mopsuestia. According to Cyril,
this verse reveals the consubstantiality of the three persons of the
Godhead.[189] Indeed, 16,15 makes it plain that Christ and the Father
exist in absolute oneness, that they are, in a word, coessential.[190]
πάντα, then, like the dogmatic writers (above pp.33-34), he refers
to the divine attributes, the things uniquely the Father's own,

including the Spirit.[191] This understanding informs his exegesis of

16,15b, as well: as the Father reveals himself and accomplishes his

purposes through the Spirit, and, since the Son, because consubstantial

with him, does the same, so it is for this reason that Jesus says ὅτι

ἐκ τοῦ ἐμοῦ λαμβάνει καὶ ἀναγγελεῖ ὑμῖν. On this understanding, λαμ-

βάνει is a distinct though unavoidable anthropomorphism. The Spirit

neither derives nor receives anything from Father and Son which he

did not already possess; for absolute wisdom and power are his, not

by participation, but by nature.[192]

In his usual paraphrastic manner Theodore of Mopsuestia gives

an entirely different exposition of the verse. 16,15a is Jesus'

claim to have received universal domination, an understanding

Theodore supports by suggesting that he is a partaker of all the

things which belong to God the Word on account of his union with

him.[193] The disciples (16,15b) are to receive a part of that grace

of universal lordship which is entire in Christ upon themselves,

enough so that they shall also be called lords. Had they been going

to receive all, the Lord would (in Vosté's translation) have used

the generic *meum*; instead he uses the limiting partitive *de meo*.

This shows the great difference between Christ and his disciples.

In all of this, according to Theodore, the greatness and power of

the Spirit is manifest. For it was the mediating gift of the Spirit

which effected Jesus' union with God the Word and delivered to him

his unversal domination. It is also the Spirit who is to place part

of the great dignity of Christ upon the disciples, a mission which

to Theodore's mind also reveals the great power of the Spirit.[194]

NOTES

1. Sabellianism was, it is true, properly a Third Century phenomenon. Nevertheless, continued pressure from varieties of modalism
elicited concern with this heresy (sometimes by name) at councils, in
confessions of faith, and in some of the great treatises about the
Godhead in the whole period from the Fourth to the Sixth Centuries in
the East. Cf. J.N.D. Kelly, The Athanasian Creed (London, 1964), 76-
77. The sophisticated modalism developed by Marcellus of Ancyra was
condemned at Constantinople in 381. Eusebius of Caesarea repudiated
Marcellus' doctrines as being those of the heretics Sabellius and
Paul of Samosata; see below pp.29-31.

1a. It is interesting to note that in theological discussions and
controversies even the Alexandrine school adopts the historical and
grammatical methods of their Antiochene rivals. They have found the
allegorical methods of Or. inadequate to confute the heretical
exegeses of Arius and others and consequently use it only for edifi-
cation. See J. Quasten, Patrology, III (Utrecht, 1960), 2.

2. An outstanding case in point is the commentary on John by Cyril of
Alexandria. It is strongly dogmatic and polemical and seeks to prove
both the consubstantiality of Father and Son and their unique personal subsistence. But, although there is this dogmatic interest in
the commentary, Cyr. is concerned with more than just the doctrinally
interesting aspects of the text. Even when the dogmatic and polemical
features of his commentary are strongest, exegesis may be more or
less easily distinguished from mere doctrine because Cyr. is concerned to interpret the NT text in a way that would be otiose in
works dedicated solely to the development of a particular dogma.

3. The nature of the theological issues in the Fourth and Fifth
Centuries limits the dogmatic use of the paraclete passages to
rather clearly defined categories. The writings which deal primarily
with such questions may therefore be summarised more neatly and with
greater economy of space than those which are primarily concerned
with exegetical questions and have, therefore, less common ground.

4. E.g., nearly all that we know of the thought of Marcellus in his
treatise against Asterius is preserved in Eus. Marcell. and e.th.

5. In the discussion which follows, while no attempt is made to
list all examples of a given line of exegesis, it is hoped that the
clearest and most important examples are included and that only minor
and obscure passages are left out. Because of the highly condensed
nature of this summary, it is neither necessary nor desirable to make
clear the context of every passage cited. It is expected that the
reader will supply these for himself where useful.

6. Marcell. fr. 66 (GCS 14,197), ἀδύνατον γὰρ τρεῖς ὑποστάσεις
οὔσας ἐνοῦσθαι μονάδι, εἰ μὴ πρότερον ἡ τριὰς τὴν ἀρχὴν ἀπὸ μονάδος
ἔχοι.

7. Marcell. fr. 67 (GCS 14,197-198), οὐ σαφῶς καὶ φανερῶς ἐνταῦθα
ἀπορρήτῳ δὲ λόγῳ ἡ μονὰς φαίνεται, πλατυνομένη μὲν εἰς τριάδα,
διαιρεῖσθαι δὲ μηδαμῶς ὑπομένουσα; . . . πῶς γάρ, εἰ μὴ ἡ μονὰς

ἀδιαίρετος οὖσα εἰς τριάδα πλατύνοιτο, ἐγχωρεῖ αὐτὸν περὶ τοῦ πνεύματος ποτὲ μὲν λέγειν ὅτι ἐκ τοῦ πατρὸς ἐκπορεύεται, ποτὲ δὲ λέγειν 'ἐκεῖνος ἐκ τοῦ ἐμοῦ λήψεται καὶ ἀναγγελεῖ ὑμῖν'.

8. Marcell. fr. 67 (GCS 14,198), πῶς γὰρ εἰ ἐκ τοῦ πατρὸς ἐκπορεύεται παρὰ τοῦ υἱοῦ τὴν διακονίαν ταύτην λαμβάνειν ἐπαγγέλλεται; ἀνάγκη γὰρ εἰ δύο διαιρούμενα, ὡς Ἀστέριος ἔφη, πρόσωπα εἴη, ἦ τὸ πνεῦμα ἐκ τοῦ πατρὸς ἐκπορευόμενον μὴ δεῖσθαι τῆς παρὰ τοῦ υἱοῦ διακονίας (πᾶν γὰρ τὸ ἐκ πατρὸς ἐκπορευόμενον τέλειον εἶναι ἀνάγκη, μηδαμῶς προσδεόμενον τῆς παρ' ἑτέρου βοηθείας), ἦ, εἰ παρὰ τοῦ υἱοῦ λαμβάνοι καὶ ἐκ τῆς ἐκείνου δυνάμεως διακονοίη τὴν χάριν, μηκέτι ἐκ τοῦ πατρὸς ἐκπορεύεσθαι.

9. Marcell. fr. 73-74 (GCS 14,198-200).

10. Eus. e.th. 3,4,5 (GCS 14,159), διὰ δὴ τούτων καὶ τῶν τούτοις ὁμοίων ὁ σοφώτατος πειρᾶται κατασκευάζειν ἕνα καὶ τὸν αὐτὸν εἶναι τὸν πατέρα καὶ τὸν υἱὸν καὶ τὸ ἅγιον πνεῦμα, τριῶν· ὀνομάτων κατὰ μιᾶς ὑποστάσεως κειμένων.

11. Eus. e.th. 3,4,9 (GCS 14,159), καὶ τὸ ἅγιον δὲ πνεῦμα ὁμοίως ἕτερον ὑπάρχον παρὰ τὸν υἱόν . . . ἄντιχρυς γὰρ παραστατικὸν ἂν εἴη τούτου τοῦ μὴ εἶναι ἕν καὶ ταὐτὸν τὸν υἱὸν καὶ τὸ ἅγιον πνεῦμα· τὸ γὰρ παρ' ἑτέρου λαμβάνον τι ἕτερον παρὰ τὸν διδόντα νοεῖται.

12. Eus. e.th. 3,5,1 (GCS 14,160), ὁρᾷς ὅπως τὸ πνεῦμα τὸ παράκλητον ἕτερον εἶναί φησιν καὶ ἄλλο παρ' ἑαυτόν; 3,5,6 (GCS 14,160), οὐκοῦν ἕτερος ἦν παρ'αὐτὸν ὁ παράκλητος, περὶ οὗ τὰ τοσαῦτα ἐδίδασκεν. Cf. the First Creed of Sirmium as in Ath. syn. 27,3 (Opitz 2,1,256) which seems to give 14,16 a similar interpretation. All three persons are distinguished in 14,16 by Thdr.Heracl. fr.Jo. 261 (TU 89,134); see below p.44 and n.96.

13. Eus. e.th. 3,5,4-6 (GCS 14,160-161).

14. Eus. e.th. 3,5,8 (GCS 14,161).

15. Eus. e.th. 3,5,9 (GCS 14,161). See also Epiph. anc. 81,9 (GCS 25,102), haer. 57,4,1 (GCS 31,348). Eus. has, at this point in e.th., noticed the apparent discrepancy in the Saviour's words about who really does send the Paraclete in Jo. 14-16; for he goes on to explain that Jesus is not teaching contraries. Since the Son does whatever he sees the Father doing (Jo. 5,19) and judges as he hears (Jo. 5,30), Son and Father work together. Therefore, when the Father in his judgment wills, then the Son sends the Paraclete. 3,5,11 (GCS 14,161).

16. Eus. e.th. 3,5,15-16 (GCS 14,162).

17. Eus. e.th. 3,5,17-18 (GCS 14,162-163). That Jesus does show the Spirit subordinate to himself Eusebius supports from his exegesis of 16,13, οὐ γὰρ ἀφ' ἑαυτοῦ λαλήσει, ἀλλ' ὅσα ἀκούσει λαλήσει, and 16,14, ἐκ τοῦ ἐμοῦ λήψεται καὶ ἀναγγελεῖ ὑμῖν. (With respect to the passages as a whole, Eus. e.th. 3,5,19-21 (GCS 14,163) says that by calling the Spirit παράκλητος Jesus presents his unique character; for the title distinguishes him on the one hand from Father and Son who are both called πνεῦμα, and it distinguishes him on the other hand from the angels who are also sometimes described as πνεύματα but are never called paraclete-spirits and are certainly not included in the Trinity.)

18.   See Bas. hom.24,2 (PG 31,604-605); Didym. Trin. 3,38 (PG 39,974. 976.977), 3,41,1 (PG 39,984); Epiph. anc. 8,4 (GCS 25,15), haer. 57,4,2 (GCS 31,348), 57,4,9 (GCS 31,349), 65,5,8-9 (GCS 37,8); Eus.Em. disc. 3,21 (Buytaert 1,91), 13,29 (Buytaert 1,312).

19.   Ath. ep.Serap. 1,33 (PG 26,608), . . . ὁμολογοῦντες Υἱὸν καὶ ἐν αὐτῷ τὸ Πνεῦμα. Ἀχώριστον γὰρ τοῦ Υἱοῦ τὸ Πνεῦμα, ὡς ἀχώριστος ὁ Υἱὸς τοῦ Πατρός. Αὐτὴ ἡ Ἀλήθεια μαρτυρεῖ ἡ λέγουσα· 'πέμψω ὑμῖν τὸν Παράκλητον, τὸ Πνεῦμα τῆς ἀληθείας, ὃ παρὰ τοῦ Πατρὸς ἐκπορεύεται, ὃ ὁ κόσμος οὐ δύναται λαβεῖν,' τουτέστιν οἱ ἀρνούμενοι αὐτὸ ἐκ τοῦ Πατρὸς ἐν τῷ Υἱῷ. Ath. implies that in his exegesis the κόσμος are those who deny that the Spirit is from (ἐκ) the Father in (ἐν) the Son.

20.   Didym. Trin. 3,19 (PG 39,889-892). Didym. makes an interesting exegetical remark on 16,13 here: he says that Jesus is not suggesting that the Spirit never speaks from himself and by-way of demonstration adduces passages showing the third divine person doing just that. Rather, having pointed out that it is the future tense of λαλέω which is used, he concludes that the Spirit's non-self-speaking refers only to a particular time and occasion. This reasoning allows Didym. to reconcile what seems to him to be contradiction between Jo. 16,13 and certain other texts.

21.   Cyr. Jo. 4,1 (Pusey 1,509).

22.   See Ath. Ar. 1,15 (PG 26,44); cf. 1,50 (PG 26,116) and Cyr. thes. 4 (PG 75,45). This is reminiscent of Novatian's (subordination-ist) argument for the deity of Christ outlined on p.11 above.

23.   See, e.g., Ath. Ar. 2,24 (PG 26,197), ep.Serap.2,5 (PG 26, 616); Cyr. thes. 20 (PG 75,353); Didym. Trin. 2,23 (PG 39,796).

24.   Cyr. thes. 21 (PG 75,357), Εἰ ποίημά ἐστιν ὁ Υἱὸς, λέγει δὲ ἀληθεύων, ὅτι 'Πάντα ὅσα ἔχει ὁ Πατὴρ, ἐμά ἐστιν·' οὐδὲν ἄρα περιττὸν ἐν θεῷ καὶ κτίσμασιν, εἰ πάντα πρόσεστιν αὐτοῖς ὅσα καὶ τῷ Πατρί. Εἰ δὲ τοῦτο ἄτοπον (πολὺ γὰρ τὸ θεῖον τῶν ποιημάτων ἀπῴκισται), οὐκ ἄρα ποίημά ἐστιν ὁ Υἱὸς, ᾧ πάντα πρόσεστι φυσικῶς τὰ τοῦ Πατρὸς ἴδια καὶ ἐξαίρετα.

25.   Cyr. Jo.1,3 (Pusey 1,42). This conclusion simply confirms what it is Cyril's purpose to show in this chapter. The chapter heading reads: Ὅτι καὶ θεὸς κατὰ φύσιν, καὶ κατ' οὐδένα τρόπον ἢ ἐλάττων ἢ ἀνόμοιός ἐστι τοῦ Πατρὸς ὁ Υἱός (Pusey 1,31).

26.   See Cyr. Juln.9 (PG 76,952) and Thdt. ep. 151 (PG 83,1433).

27.   See Ath. Ar.3,4 (PG 26,329), ep.Afr.8 (PG 26,1041-1044); Cyr. thes. 11 (PG 75,156), 14 (PG 75, 240), 32 (PG 75,557.560); Didym. (Pseudo-Ath.) dial.Trin. 3,3 (PG 28,1205); Gr.Nyss. Eun. 2,216 (Jaeger 1,288), ref. Eun. 121 (Jaeger 2,364).

28.   Thdt. eran.suppl. 3,2 (PG 83,329).

29.   See Cyr. Lc. 3,21 (PG 72,521-524) and thes.11 (PG 75,156).

30. See Ath. Ar. 3,4 (PG 26,329), syn. 49,1-2 (Opitz 2,1,273); Cyr.
thes. 12 (PG 75,184); Gr. Nyss. Eun. 1,683 (Jaeger 1,222}, cf. 1,
594 (Jaeger 1,197).

31. See Cyr. thes.16 (PG 75,301); Didym. Trin. 1,26 (PG 39,384);
Gr.Naz. or. 30,11 (PG 36,116; Mason 123).

32. Cyr. ep.Euopt. (ACO 1,1,6,135). Cf. Didym. Spir. 38 (PG 39,
1066).

33. Ath. Ar. 3,44 (PG 26,417), Πάλιν τε εἰ πάντα τὰ τοῦ Πατρὸς
τοῦ Υἱοῦ ἐστι· τοῦτο γὰρ αὐτὸς εἴρηκε· τοῦ δὲ Πατρός ἐστι τὸ
εἰδέναι τὴν ἡμέραν, δῆλον ὅτι καὶ ὁ Υἱὸς οἶδεν, ἴδιον ἔχων καὶ τοῦτο
ἐκ τοῦ Πατρός. (There is no direct quotation of the Gospel in
this passage, but the allusion is rather clearly to Jo. 16,15 and/
or 17,10.)

34. See Cyr. thes. 22 (PG 75,372)   (Just prior to his argument from
16,15 he adds a parallel argument from 16,14 which appears to be
unique to him. The Spirit, he says, must know the day and the hour
as he knows all things, even the deep things of God (an allusion to
1 Cor. 2,10). How then, he asks, can the Son be really ignorant of
day and hour since the Spirit receives from the Son?); also Didym.
Eun.4 (PG 29,696); Epiph. anc. 16,5-6 (GCS 25,24-25).

35. In an extant fragment from a sermon entitled Περὶ τῆς ἡμέρας καὶ
ὥρας, Amph. fr.(PG 39,104) takes precisely the same line as does Bas.
here. In this light and on the ground that Amph. had apparently asked
the great Cappadocian about the Anomoean argument as though it were
new to him (In his letter ep. 236,1 (Johnston 168) Bas. says to Amph.,
τοῦτο νῦν παρὰ τῆς σῆς συνέσεως ἡμῖν ὡς καινὸν προεβλήθη.), it would
appear that the sermon from which the extant fragment is taken was
written after its author had received Basil's letter, after, that
is, January of A.D. 376.

36. Bas. ep. 236,2 (Johnston 170), Ἀψευδὴς γὰρ ὁ εἰπών, ὅτι 'Πάντα
ὅσα ἔχει ὁ Πατὴρ ἐμά ἐστιν.' Ἐν δέ, ὧν ἔχει, καὶ ἡ γνῶσίς ἐστι
τῆς ἡμέρας ἐκείνης καὶ τῆς ὥρας.

37. Basil's text of Mt. 24,36 lacks the words οὐδε ὁ υἱός, which
for him means that it must be handled differently from Mk. 13,32,
though in his eyes the two verses are not contradictory. In Mt.,
the word μόνος distinguishes the Father only from the angels, not from
the Son. The angels of heaven are in ignorance, but by passing over
his own person, the Son implies that the Father's knowledge of day
and hour is also his own since elsewhere (Jo. 10,15; Bas. has already
at this point quoted and explained 16,15) he has said that he and
the Father know each other. In this way Bas. concludes that Mt.
24,36 does not indicate ignorance in the Son, after all. (Had the text
before him contained, on the other hand, the variant οὐδὲ ὁ υἱός,
Basil's exegesis of it would presumably have been analogous to his
exegesis of Mk. 13,32, though the presence of μόνος would surely
have caused him rather special problems.) Bas. ep. 236,2 (Johnston
170).

38. Bas. ep. 236,2 (Johnston 170-171), Τὸ δὲ Μάρκου, . . . οὕτω νοοῦ-
μεν· ὅτι οὐδεὶς οἶδεν, οὔτε οἱ ἄγγελοι τοῦ θεοῦ, ἀλλ' οὐδὲ ὁ Υἱὸς

ἔγνω, εἰ μὴ ὁ Πατήρ· τουτέστιν, ἡ αἰτία τοῦ εἰδέναι τὸν Υἱὸν παρὰ τοῦ Πατρός . . . . Ἔστιν οὖν ὁ νοῦς ὁ παρὰ τῷ Μάρκῳ τοιοῦτος. Περὶ δὲ τῆς ἡμέρας ἐκείνης ἢ ὥρας οὐδεὶς οἶδεν, οὔτε οἱ ἄγγελοι τοῦ θεοῦ, ἀλλ' οὐδ' ἂν ὁ Υἱὸς ἔγνω, εἰ μὴ ὁ Πατήρ· ἐκ γὰρ τοῦ Πατρὸς αὐτῷ ὑπῆρχε δεδομένη ἡ γνῶσις.

39. See, e.g., Cyr. thes. 34 (PG 75,589); Didym. Trin. 2,2 (PG 39, 460); Gr.Naz. or. 31,8 (Mason 154; PG 36,141); Gr.Nys. ref.Eun. 188 (Jaeger 2,392).

40. See Didym. Spir. 25 (PG 39,1055-1056) and Trin. 2,2 (PG 39,460).

41. See Cyr. thes. 34 (PG 75,589); Thdt. haer. 5,3 (PG 83, 453-456).

42. For an older but still helpful history of the doctrine of the procession see H.B. Swete, On The History of the Doctrine of the Procession of the Holy Spirit (Cambridge, 1876).

43. See Didym. Trin. 2,2 (PG 39,460) and 3,38 (PG 39,976).

44. Cyr. thes. 34 (PG 75,589). (Cyr. teaches here that the Spirit is also from (ἐκ) the essence of the Son, a characteristic teaching which in some ways prefigures the filioque of the Latin West.)

45. Thdt. haer. 5,3 (PG 83,453-456).

46. See Cyr. thes. 34 (PG 75,581-584), Εἴπερ οὖν ἦν ἐξ ἑαυτοῦ, τὸ τέλειον ἔχειν δυνάμενον, ἐλάλησεν ἂν καὶ ἐφ' (sic) ἑαυτοῦ, μηδὲν τῆς παρ' ἑτέρου δεηθὲν ὑπομνήσεως. Cyril's purpose here in thes. 34 is precisely to show Ὅτι τέλειον τὸ Πνεῦμα τὸ ἅγιον καὶ οὐδὲν ἀτελὲς ἐν αὐτῷ (PG 75,581). Cf. Didym. Eun. 5 (PG 29,765) and dial.Trin. (Pseudo-Ath.) 1,22 (PG 28,1149.1152).

47. See Cyr. thes. 34 (PG 75,593). (In trying to describe the Arian heresy Cyr. uses, at this point, the simile of an iron cooking pot: the Holy Spirit spreads divine holiness in Arian teaching much as the iron vessel accomplishes the work of fire by taking heat from the fire. Cyril's immediate purpose in this part of thes. 34 is to show Ὅτι οὐκ ἐκ μετοχῆς τῆς τοῦ θεοῦ καὶ πατρὸς ἅγιόν ἐστι τὸ Πνεῦμα, ἀλλὰ φύσει καὶ οὐσιωδῶς ἐξ αὐτοῦ.)

48. Didym. Eun. 5 (PG 29,765), Ἐὰν δὲ λέγωσιν· Οὐ λαλεῖ ἀφ' ἑαυτοῦ τὸ Πνεῦμα, ἀλλ' ὅσα ἂν ἀκούσῃ λαλήσει· λέγομεν αὐτοῖς· Οὐδὲ ὁ Υἱὸς ἀφ' ἑαυτοῦ λαλεῖ· Ἀλλ' ὁ πέμψας ρε (sic), φησι, Πατήρ, ἐκεῖνος μοι εἶπε τί εἴπω (sic) καὶ τί λαλήσω· πάντα γὰρ ὅσα λαλεῖ τὸ Πνεῦμα καὶ ὁ Υἱὸς, τοῦ θεοῦ εἰσι λόγια. Cf. Spir. 36 (PG 39,1065).

49. See Didym.' (Pseudo-Ath.) dial.Trin. 1,22 (PG 28,1149-1152) and 1,23 (PG 28,1152), Eun. 5 (PG 29,765), (Pseudo-Ath.) Maced.dial. 1,16 (PG 28,1316).

50. See Didym. Spir. 36-37 (PG 39,1064-1065).

51. See Didym. Trin. 2,3 (PG 39,473); Gr.Naz. or. 31,29 (Mason 180-181; PG 36,165); cf. Gr.Nyss. ref.Eun. 188 (Jaeger 2,392).

52. Gr.Nyss. ref.Eun. 184-185 (Jaeger 2,390-391). This entire context in Gr.Nyss., ref.Eun. 182-188, contains some interesting exegesis of our passages. A partial summary of his argument will be instructive. Discussing Eunomius' statement of faith, he asserts that the heresiarch has avoided using the term *Holy Spirit* in order to avoid acknowledging that complete unity of the Spirit with the Father and the Son implied in the fact that all three persons are described by the same appellations, ἅγιος and πνεῦμα (182-183 (Jaeger 2,389-390)). Instead of professing faith in the Holy Spirit, Eunomius μετὰ τοῦτον πιστεύομεν, φησίν, εἰς τὸν παράκλητον, τὸ πνεῦμα τῆς ἀληθείας (182 (Jaeger 2,389), 184 (Jaeger 2,390)). But this will not help; for the appellation παράκλητος is likewise ascribed in Scripture to all three persons: Father, Son, and Spirit. John gives the title to the Son in one of his Catholic Epistles (1 Jo. 2,1). David (Ps. 76,17) and Paul (2 Cor. 1,3-4) show by using the verb παρακαλέω that the Father deserves the title; for οὐ . . . δὴ τὸ ἔργον ποιῶν τοῦ παρακλήτου ἀπαξιοῖ τοῦ ἔργου τὸ ὄνομα. And the Lord applies it to both himself and the Spirit in the Gospel when he speaks of the Spirit of truth as ἄλλον παράκλητον (Jo. 14,16), ὁ γὰρ υἱὸς ἐπίσης ἑαυτόν τε καὶ τὸ πνεῦμα τὸ ἅγιον ὀνομάζει παράκλητον· . . . καὶ αὐτὸς δὲ ὁ κύριος δι'ὧν εἶπε καὶ ἄλλον παράκλητον ἡμῖν ἀποσταλήσεσθαι, περὶ τοῦ πνεύματος λέγων, ἐφ'ἑαυτοῦ πάντως τὸ ὄνομα τοῦτο προωμολόγησε (185-186(Jaeger 2,390-391)). But, says Gr., the Scriptures recognise and use two senses of παρακαλεῖν, the first, ῥημάτων τε καὶ σχημάτων, ὑπὲρ ὧν, ἄν τινος δεδμενοι τύχωμεν, εἰς συμπάθειαν αὐτὸν ἐπαγόμεθα, and the second, τῆς θεραπευτικῆς τῶν ψυχικῶν τε καὶ σωματικῶν παθημάτων ἐπινοίας. That the conception *Paraclete* applies to the divine nature in either sense he illustrates from 2 Cor., the former from 2 Cor. 7,6 and the latter from 2 Cor. 5,20 (186 (Jaeger 2,391)). Since he has already made his point, Gregory does not go on to say which of these meanings he thinks the term may bear when applied to the Spirit. He merely asserts that whichever way one takes the term (no doubt implying that there was debate on the matter in his day), Eunomius has not achieved his purpose by substituting παράκλητος for *Holy Spirit* in his creed. He does go on to speculate that by using the further term πνεῦμα τῆς ἀληθείας the heresiarch wished to suggest that the Spirit is a possession and chattel of Christ who is the truth. But this is improper exegesis and would be similar to suggesting that, because we say δικαιοσύνη ὁ θεός, God therefore is a possession of righteousness. No, says Gr., πνεῦμα τῆς ἀληθείας is properly a divine title, for immediately after saying it (at 15,26) the Lord adds παρὰ τοῦ πατρὸς ἐκπορεύεται, a thing never asserted of any created being (187-188, Jaeger 2,391-392)).

53. See Didym. Trin. 2,6,13 (PG 39,540).

54. See Didym. Trin.3,38 (PG 39,976), Τὸ δὲ ἔχειν, 'Δώσει ὑμῖν,' καὶ, 'Παρ'ὑμῖν μένει,' καὶ 'ἐν ὑμῖν ἔσται,' ἐσήμανεν, ὡς καὶ ἄνω καὶ κάτω, ἅτε δὴ θεὸς, πανταχοῦ παρὸν τὸ ἅγιον Πνεῦμά ἐστιν, cf. 2,6,2 (PG 39,509-512).

55. See Didym. Trin. 2,7,9 (PG 39,597). Didym. is here concerned to show that the Spirit is destined to judge all things with Christ. He begins with a conflation of OT texts, then adds Jo. 16,8 as a more telling proof, Ποίαν δὲ ἀπόδειξιν ἄν εἴποι τις ἰσχυροτέραν εἰς τοῦτο, τοῦ καὶ τὸν Σωτῆρα παρ''Ιωάννῃ λέγειν περὶ τοῦ ἁγίου Πνεύματος· ''Ελθὼν ἐκεῖνος ἐλέγξει . . .'

56. See Didym. <u>Trin</u>. 2,7,12 (PG 39,597-600). The assertion concerning the Spirit in this context is ὅτι προγινώσκει, ὡς ὁ Πατὴρ καὶ ὁ
Υἱός· μόνης δὲ θεϊκῆς φύσεώς ἐστιν, ἀκριβῶς εἰδέναι τὰ μέλλοντα.
Jo. 16,13 is cited for support, Καὶ ἐν Εὐαγγελίῳ δὲ ὁ Χριστὸς περὶ
τοῦ Πνεύματός φησιν· 'Καὶ τὰ ἐρχόμενα ἀναγγελεῖ ὑμῖν·' τοῦτ'ἔστι,
τὰ μέλλοντα. Note Didymus' interpretation of τὰ ἐρχόμενα.

57. See Didym. <u>Trin</u>. 2,10 and context (PG 39,444).

58. See Bas. <u>Spir</u>. 19,49 (Johnston 100; SCH 17,202).

59. Gr.Naz. <u>or</u>. 41,12 (PG 36,444-445), Ἄλλος δὲ, ἵνα σὺ τὴν ὁμοτιμίαν
ἐνθυμηθῇς. Τὸ γὰρ, ἄλλος, ἄλλος οἷος ἐγώ, καθίσταται. Τοῦτο δὲ
συνδεσποτείας, ἀλλ' οὐκ ἀτιμίας ὄνομα. Τὸ γὰρ, ἄλλος, οὐκ ἐπὶ τῶν
ἀλλοτρίων, ἀλλ' ἐπὶ τῶν ὁμοουσίων οἶδα λεγόμενον.

60. See Epiph. <u>haer</u>. 74,13,4 (GCS 37,331), καὶ πάλιν, ἵνα δείξῃ τὴν
ἑαυτοῦ ἰσότητα καὶ ὁμοουσιότητα πρὸς τὸ πνεῦμα αὐτοῦ τε καὶ τοῦ
πατρὸς αὐτοῦ τὸ ἅγιον, φησίν 'ἐὰν ἀγαπᾶτέ με . . . ἄλλον παράκλητον
δώσει ὑμῖν', ὡς αὐτοῦ τοῦ κυρίου παρακλήτου ὄντος καὶ τοῦ πνεύματος
τοῦ ἁγίου συμπαρακλήτου ὄντος ὁμοίως. Cf. Bas. <u>Eun</u>. 3,3 (PG 29,
661).

61. See Cyr. <u>Jo</u>. 2,1 (Pusey 1,188), <u>ep</u>. 17 (ACO 1,1,1,39) (Notice
that Cyr. here seems to suggest that the Spirit proceeds from both
Father and Son, πνεῦμα γὰρ ἀληθείας ὠνόμασται καὶ ἔστιν Χριστὸς ἡ
ἀλήθεια καὶ προχεῖται παρ' αὐτοῦ καθάπερ ἀμέλει καὶ ἐκ τοῦ θεοῦ
καὶ πατρός.); Thdt. <u>exp.fid</u>. 5 (CAC 4,20).

62. See Didym. <u>Trin</u>. 2,17 (PG 39,725), Καὶ σύμφωνον δὲ τῇ ἑαυτοῦ
τὴν τοῦ ἁγίου Πνεύματος διδασκαλίαν παριστῶν, ἔφη· ' "Οταν ἔλθῃ τὸ
Πνεῦμα τὸ ἅγιον, ἐκεῖνο ὑμᾶς διδάξει καὶ ἀναμνήσει πάντα, ἃ εἶπον
ὑμῖν.

63. See Cyr.H. <u>catech</u>. 16,14 (Rupp 2,222), ὁ παράκλητος, περὶ οὗ
εἶπεν ὁ σωτήρ, ἐκεῖνος ὑμᾶς διδάξει πάντα καὶ ὑπομνήσει ὑμᾶς πάντα
(οὐκ εἶπε διδάξει μόνον, ἀλλὰ καὶ ὑπομνήσει ὅσα εἶπον ὑμῖν· οὐ
γὰρ ἄλλα Χριστοῦ διδάγματα καὶ ἄλλα ἁγίου πνεύματος, ἀλλὰ τὰ αὐτά),
. . .

64. See Didym. <u>Trin</u>. 2,17 (PG 39,725), Καὶ ἐν Εὐαγγελίῳ τοὺς
ἀποστόλους διδάσκων ὁ Δεσπότης, ὅτι τῆς ἑαυτοῦ ἐπιφανείας οὐχ ἥσσων
ἔσται ἡ παρουσία τοῦ ἁγίου Πνεύματος, καὶ ἡ ἐκεῖθεν περιγινομένη
σωτηρία τῇ κτίσει· ἀλλ' ἴση καὶ ἡ αὐτη, διὰ τὴν μίαν θεότητα καὶ
ἐνέργειαν, λέγει· 'Συμφέρει . . .'

65. Epiph. <u>haer</u>. 48,11,5-10 (GCS 31,234-235), Χριστὸς γὰρ ἡμᾶς
ἐδίδαξε λέγων ὅτι 'τὸ πνεῦμα τὸ παράκλητον ἀποστέλλω ὑμῖν' καὶ τὰ
σημεῖα διδοὺς ἔλεγεν ὅτι 'ἐκεῖνός με δοξάσει' ὡς τὰ ἀληθῆ ἔστιν
ἰδεῖν ὅτι οἱ ἅγιοι ἀπόστολοι τὸ παράκλητον πνεῦμα λαβόντες κύριον
ἐδόξασαν, οὗτος δὲ ὁ Μοντανὸς ἑαυτον δοξάζει (48,11,5-6 (GCS 31,
234)). In Chapter 11 Epiph. combats two claims which he attributes
to Montanus, viz., ἐγὼ κύριος ὁ θεὸς ὁ παντοκράτωρ καταγινόμενος ἐν
ἀνθρώπῳ, and, οὔτε ἄγγελος οὔτε πρέσβυς, ἀλλ'ἐγὼ κύριος ὁ θεὸς
πατὴρ ἦλθον. Cf. Ign.‡Eph. 9 (PG 5,740) where it is similarly argued
that the true Spirit may be distinguished (from the deceiving spirit
in false teachers) because he tells the things of and glorifies Christ.

66. See, e.g., Didym. Trin. 3,41,2 (PG 39,988); Epiph. haer. 66,19,3
(GCS 37,43), 66,61,5-6 (GCS 37,98-99); Gr.Naz. or. 41,12 (PG 36,445).
Also, cf., among others, the personal statement of faith of Theophan-
ius of Tyana subscribed to by the Eusebian council in Antioch (341)
as in Ath. syn. 24,4 (Opitz 2,1,250) which places the fulfillment of
the paraclete promise in Acts, surely meaning at Pentecost. (It also
identifies the Paraclete with the Spirit promised in Joel 2,8, an
identification almost taken for granted among catholic writers.)
That the Paraclete was given (in fullest measure) on the day of
Pentecost seems to be a thing so self-evident among the Greek fathers
that it does not often require direct comment, perhaps because (apart
from Montanists, Manichaeans, and others like them) it was not
heavily disputed by the heretics of the day.

67. For an example of such explanation see below n.147.

68. Didym. Trin. 3,41,2 (PG 39,985.988). Didym. does not mean to
suggest, however, that the Spirit first came at Pentecost; for he is
eternally omnipresent. Christ did not lie at 14,17 when he said,
παρ' ὑμῖν μένει, καὶ ἐν ὑμῖν ἔσται. But the Paraclete appeared, was
received, and was more completely manifest at Pentecost, and this in
fulfillment of Jesus' promise, οὕτω καὶ τὸ ἅγιον Πνεῦμα ἀεὶ μὲν πάντα
ἐπλήρου καὶ συνεῖχεν, μετὰ δὲ τὴν ἐν τῇ Πεντηκοστῇ ἐπιφοίτησιν αὐτοῦ
τελειότερον ἐπεγνώσθη καὶ ἐδοξάσθη (PG 39,988).

69. Hegem. Arch. 31(27),6-9 (GCS 16,44). In the same place Hegem.
imagines the souls of those who died between Jesus' promise and its
supposed fulfillment in Manes making their complaint to God: *Cur
enim, cum promiseris sub Tiberio Caesare missurum te esse paracletum,
qui argueret nos de peccato et de iudicio et de iustitia, sub
Probo demum Romano imperatore misisti?* Later in his book (38(34),5-6
(GCS 16,55-56)), he tries a more dubious argument based upon an
eccentric exegesis of the words *de meo accipiet* (Jo. 16,14) which
seems to take *meo* to mean something like 'my disciples': *Post hunc
[Paul] ergo et post eos qui cum ipso fuerant, id est post dicipulos,
nullum alium venire secundum scripturas sperandum est; ait enim
dominus noster Iesus de paracleto, quia et de meo accipiet . . . .
Et sicut non super omnes homines spiritus habitare poterat, nisi super
eum qui de Maria dei genitrice natus est, ita et in nullum alium
spiritus paracletus venire poterat, nisi super apostolos et super
beatum Paulum.* The more usual catholic exegesis in this period sees
the promise of the Paraclete as applicable to all Christians, though
of necessity it came first upon the disciples; cf., e.g., Gr.Naz. or.
41,13 (PG 36,448) In seeking to deny the Manichaean claim to
possess the Paraclete, Hegem. effectively denies his continuing
presence in the Church.

70. Both Cyr. and Thdr.Mops. are preoccupied in their commentaries
with Arianism and other heresies. Even Chrys., whose primary concern is
the application of Scripture to the needs of the hearers, continually
meets with texts used by Arians (especially Anomoeans) to support
their doctrine that the Son is not even of like substance with the
Father. These he seeks to reclaim for the Church and, to do so,
develops his doctrine of condescension to explain texts relating to
the human weakness of Christ. Moreover, in addition to providing
mere δογματικωτέρα ἐξήγησις which will counter every point of heretical
teaching, Cyr. sees the commentator's task as including a positive

consideration of the doctrinal implications of the text (see M.F. Wiles, The Spiritual Gospel (Cambridge, 1960), 6) and it is his aim in the commentary on John to prove both that the Son is of the same divine substance as the Father and that both have their own individual subsistence. Thdr.Mops. considers it the commentator's primary task to concentrate on the difficult texts, especially those perverted in current heretical preaching (See Wiles, 6). For Thdr., then, as for all the School of Antioch, the task of exegesis is the task of defending orthodoxy and is therefore intimately bound up with dogma. The fragments of the two heresiarchs seem not to include any of the more offensive and heretical dogmas of their authors.

71. In this section we are again concerned primarily with represent-ative exegesis and significant variation. Matters which seem to be largely the result of individual idiosyncracy will be either con-signed to footnotes or left out altogether.

72. Cyr. Jo. 9,1 (Pusey 2,463), ἵνα τοίνυν ἐπιδείξῃ σαφῶς ὁ Κύριος ἡμῶν Ἰησοῦς ὁ Χριστός, πρὸς τίνας αὐτῷ γέγονέ τε καὶ ἔστιν ὁ λόγος, καὶ τίσιν ἡ τῆς ὑποσχέσεως ὀφείλεται χάρις, ἐφ' ᾧ ἔσται καὶ ἀληθῶς, παρεκόμισεν εὐθὺς τῶν ἀγαπώντων τὸ πρόσωπον, καὶ τὸν ἀκριβῆ νομοφύλακα παραζεύγνυσι τῷ λόγῳ, δεικνὺς ὅτι πρὸς αὐτοὺς καὶ οὐχ ἑτέρους ἡ τῆς ἡμερότητος ἐπαγγελία καὶ ἡ τῶν πνευματικῶν ἀγαθῶν ἐπίδοσις δι' αὐτοῦ κρατήσει καὶ γενήσεται.

73. Chrys. hom. 75,1 in Jo. (PG 59,403), ἵνα μὴ νομίσωσιν ἁπλῶς τὴν αἴτησιν ἰσχύειν ἐπήγαγεν· Ἐὰν ἀγαπᾶτέ με· τότε, φησί, ποιήσω. Cf. 76,2 (PG 59,412).

74. Thdr.Mops. Jo. 126 (ST 141,391), Jo.Syr. on 14,15 (CSCO 115, 271-272), Ὑμᾶς μὲν, φησιν, αἰτεῖν προσῆκει πρότερον ἀγαπῶντας καὶ τὴν ἀγάπην δεικνύντας τῇ τηρήσει τῶν ἐντολῶν. (Note: passages from Thdr.Mops. in which the Greek fragments correspond with the Syriac translation will be quoted here in the Greek only. Where helpful, divergences will be quoted both in Greek and in the Latin of Vosté's translation of the Syriac (as in CSCO 116).)

75. See Apoll. Jo. 103 (TU 89,42), ἡμέτερον γὰρ ἡ τήρησις τῶν ἐντολῶν καὶ τοῦτο τῆς πρὸς τὸν κύριον ἀγάπης ἀπόδειξις; Chrys. hom. 75,1 in Jo. (PG 59,403), Τί δήποτε δὲ ταῦτα εἶπον; Ὅτι πολλοὶ νῦν εἰσι λέγοντες φοβεῖσθαι τὸν θεὸν καὶ ἀγαπᾶν, τοῖς δὲ ἔργοις τὰ ἐναντία ἐπιδείκνυνται· ὁ δὲ θεὸς τὴν διὰ τῶν ἔργων ἀγάπην ἐπιζητεῖ . . . Τοῦτό ἐστιν ἀγάπη, τὸ πείθεσθαι τούτοις, καὶ εἴκειν τῷ ποθου-μένῳ; Cyr. Jo. 9,1 (Pusey 2,464-465), οὐ γὰρ ἐν ἀργαῖς ῥημάτων κολακείαις ἡ πίστις, ἀλλ' ἐν ταῖς τῶν δρωμένων ποιότησι δοκιμάζεται . . . οὐκοῦν ἀπόδειξις τῆς ἀγάπης καὶ τελεώτατος τῆς πίστεως ὅρος, τῶν εὐαγγελικῶν δογμάτων ἡ τήρησις καὶ τῶν θείων ἐντολῶν ἡ φυλακή. (Thdr.Mops. hom. 10,3 (ST 145,248-249), taking another line, suggests in his paraphrastic way that it is because of the greatness of the gift to be given the disciples that they ought to keep the com-mandments with perseverance and great diligence.)

76. Chrys. hom. 75,1 in Jo. (PG 59,403), Ἔδωκα ὑμῖν ἐντολήν, ἵνα ἀγαπᾶτε ἀλλήλους· ἵνα οὕτω ποιῆτε ἀλλήλοις, καθὼς καὶ ἐγὼ ὑμῖν ἐποίησα. Τοῦτό ἐστιν ἀγάπη, τὸ πείθεσθαι τούτοις . . .

77. Chrys. <u>hom. 71,1 in Mt.</u> (PG 58,661), Αἱ δὲ ἐντολαὶ αὐτοῦ, καὶ
τὸ κεφάλαιον αὐτῶν· ᾿Αγαπήσεις Κύριον τὸν θεόν σου, καὶ τὸν πλησίον
σου ὡς ἑαυτόν.

78. Cf. Jo. 12,49-50; 14,10.24.

79. Cyr. <u>Jo.</u> 9,1 (Pusey 2,465).

80. Thdr.Heracl. <u>fr.Jo.</u> 260 (TU 89,133-134), εἰ δὲ ἀλήθεια ὑπάρχων
ἀπέστειλεν αὐτοῖς τὸ πνεῦμα τὸ ἅγιον, μάτην πλανώμενοι φαντάζουσι
φάσκοντες διὰ Μοντανοῦ καὶ Πρισκίλλης ἀπεστάλθαι τὸν παράκλητον μετὰ
διακόσιά που καὶ τριάκοντα ἔτη τῆς ἀποστολικῆς χάριτος γενομένων.

81. Thdr. Heracl. <u>fr.Jo.</u> 261 (TU 89,134), ᾿Εξ ὧν πάντα ἐποίησαν
οἱ ἀπόστολοι τὰ τοῦ θεοῦ θελήματα καὶ ὑπεραπέθανον αὐτοῦ δῆλον, ὅτι
ἐτήρησαν αὐτοῦ τὰς ἐντολάς. οὐκοῦν ἠξιώθησαν καὶ τῆς τοῦ ἁγίου πνεύματος ἐνοικήσεως εὐθὺς καὶ διαφεύδονται ἡ τῶν κατὰ Φρύγα αἵρεσις λέγοντες
μετὰ σ'λ' ἔτη διὰ Μοντανοῦ καὶ Πρισκίλλης καὶ Μαξιμίλλης ἀπεστάλθαι
τὸν παράκλητον.

82. Apoll. <u>Jo.</u> 103 (TU 89,42), αἰτεῖν δὲ λέγει τὸν πατέρα κατὰ
τὴν ἀδελφικὴν πρεσβείαν ὑπὲρ ἡμῶν· αὐτὸς γάρ ἐστιν ὁ διδοὺς κατὰ
τὴν δεσποτικὴν ἐξουσίαν καὶ κατὰ τὴν ἐνέργειαν ἁπάντων τῶν πατρικῶν
βουλημάτων.

83. Chrys. hom. 75,1 in Jo. (PG 59,403-404), ἐνταῦθα δέ φησιν
ἐρωτᾶν τὸν Πατέρα, ὥστε ἀξιόπιστον ποιῆσαι αὐτοῖς τὸν λόγον. (Chrys.
follows this with references to various Scriptures to show that not
only had Jesus no need to ask the Father but could himself send, but
also that the Spirit had no need to be sent but could himself de-
scend.) Gr.Naz. or. 31,26 (Mason 178-179; PG 36,161-164) has an
intriguing explanation for Jesus' statement that he will ask the Father and its apparent conflict with 14,26; 15,26; 16,7. The context
for his explanation is his contention that revelation has been and
is progressive or gradual so that, as it were, the human circuit
might not be overloaded. Accordingly, in the OT the Father is revealed clearly, the Son only obscurely. In the NT the Father and the
Son are manifestly revealed, but the Spirit is only suggested. Now
the Spirit dwells with us and supplies a clearer demonstration of
himself. The Spirit himself, for the same reason, only came to
dwell in the disciples gradually at the beginning of the Gospel.
Now Gr. adds to this his rather sophisticated explanation concerning
these verses, suggesting that it was the same divine concern not to
overextend the human capacity that prompted him to a gradual revelation of the Spirit in the Farewell Discourses: καὶ ὑπὸ ᾿Ιησοῦ
κατ' ὀλίγον ἐκφαίνεται, ὡς ἐπιστήσεις καὶ αὐτὸς ἐντυγχάνων ἐπιμελέσ-
τερον· ᾿Ερωτήσω, φησί, τὸν πατέρα, καὶ ἄλλον παράκλητον πέμψει ἡμῖν,
τὸ πνεῦμα τῆς ἀληθείας· ἵνα μὴ ἀντίθεος εἶναι δόξῃ τις, καὶ ὡς
ἀπ' ἄλλης τινὸς ἐξουσίας ποιεῖσθαι τοὺς λόγους. εἶτα, Πέμψει μέν,
ἐν δὲ τῷ ὀνόματί μου. τὸ ᾿Ερωτήσω παρείς, τὸ Πέμψει τετήρηκεν. εἶτα,
Πέμψω, τὸ οἰκεῖον ἀξίωμα· εἶτα, ῞Ηξει, ἡ τοῦ πνεύματος ἐξουσία.
(It is interesting to wonder if Gr. might not also have used a similar
line of argument to explain the separation of the paraclete materials
in John had the implications of their segregation occurred to him.)

84. Chrys. <u>hom.</u> 75,1 in Jo. (PG 59,404), Τί οὖν, φησίν, ἐστιν,
᾿Ερωτήσω τὸν Πατέρα; Δεικνὺς τῆς παρουσίας τὸν καιρόν. Chrysostom's

imaginary interlocutor asks two further questions, the answers to
which are instructive. First, why did the Spirit not come while Jesus
was with the disciples? Chrys. answers that it was because it was
only later, after their sins had been loosed by the not yet accomplished sacrifice of Jesus and they were being sent forth into dangers,
that they had need for the Anointer (ἀλείφοντα). Secondly, to the
question why the Spirit did not come immediately after the resurrection, Chrys. answers that the delay was to increase the disciples'
desire for the Spirit through tribulation and fear so that they might
receive the gift with great joy.

85. Cyr. Jo. 9,1 (Pusey 2,466), λαλεῖ τοιγαροῦν ὡς θεός τε ὁμοῦ καὶ
ἄνθρωπος, οὕτω γὰρ ἦν τηρῆσαι καλῶς τῇ μετὰ σαρκὸς οἰκονομίᾳ τοὺς
πρέποντας λόγους.

86. Cyr. Jo. 9,1 (Pusey 2,466-467), ἵνα μὴ δοκοίη διὰ τούτων τὸ
τοῦ θεοῦ καὶ Πατρὸς παρωθεῖσθαι πρόσωπον, ἤγουν παραιρεῖσθαι τὴν
τοῦ τεκόντος αὐτὸν ἐξουσίαν, τὴν ἐπὶ ταῖς τῶν ἁγίων φιλοτιμίαις
φημί, χρήσιμον αὐτὸν συγχορηγὸν ἔσεσθαι καὶ συνεπιδώσειν ἡμῖν τὸν
παράκλητον ἔφη.

87. Cyr. Jo. 9,1 (Pusey 2,467), τὸ Ἐρωτήσω πάλιν ἐπιὼν, ὡς ἄνθρωπος, ἰδικῶς τε ἀνατιθεὶς ὅλῃ τῇ θείᾳ τε καὶ ἀρρήτῳ φύσει τὸ αὐτῇ
μάλιστα πρέπον, ὡς ἐν προσώπῳ τοῦ θεοῦ καὶ Πατρός.

88. Thdr.Mops. Jo. 126 (ST 141,392), Jo.Syr. on 14,16 (CSCO 115,272),
Κἀκεῖνο δὲ προσεκτέον, ὅτι τὸ ἐρωτήσω σχηματίσας μᾶλλον εἶπεν, ἀντὶ
τοῦ Δι' ἐμοῦ δέξεσθε τὴν χάριν. Οὐ γὰρ δὴ πρεσβεύειν ἔμελλεν ἵνα
λάβωσι, καὶ τοῦτο δῆλον ἐξ ὧν προώριστο οὕτω γενέσθαι παρὰ τοῦ
θεοῦ διὰ τὴν ἡμετέραν χρείαν καὶ προαπήγγελτο, . . . Εἰ δὲ ἐν
ἐπαγγελίᾳ ἔκειτο ἡ δόσις, περιττὴ τῶν ἐπηγγελμένων ἡ αἴτησις.

89. Cyr. Jo. 9,1 (Pusey 2,467), Ἄλλον γεμὴν Παράκλητον τὸ Πνεῦμα
καλεῖ τῆς τοῦ θεοῦ καὶ Πατρὸς οὐσίας, ἤτοι τῆς ἑαυτοῦ.

90. See Chrys. hom. 75,1 in Jo. (PG 59,403); Cyr. Jo. 9,1 (Pusey
2,467); Didym. Trin. 3,38 (PG 39,976); Gr.Nyss. ref.Eun. 184 (Jaeger
2,390-391); Nonn. par.Jo. (Scheindler 159); Thdr.Mops. Jo.Syr.
on 14,16 (CSCO 115,272), cf. Mac. 3 (PO 9,640).

91. See Cyr. Jo. 9,1 (Pusey 2,470-473).

92. Cyr. Jo. 9,1 (Pusey 2,467), ἄλλον τοίνυν παράκλητον τὸ Πνεῦμα
καλεῖ, ἐν ἰδίαις μὲν ὑποστάσεσι νοεῖσθαι θέλων αὐτό.

93. Cyr. Jo. 9,1 (Pusey 2,472), τὸ γεμὴν ἐν ἀπαραλλάκτῳ κεῖσθαι
ταυτότητι τὴν ἁγίαν Τριάδα διακηρύττει σαφῶς.

94. Chrys. hom. 75,1 in Jo. (PT 59,403), Καὶ γὰρ τὸ θαῦμα τοῦ λόγου
τοῦτό ἐστιν, ὅτι τὰς ἐκ διαμέτρου ἑστώσας αἱρέσεις μιᾷ πληγῇ κατήνεγκε.
Τῷ μὲν γὰρ εἰπεῖν, Ἄλλον, δείκνυσιν αὐτοῦ τῆς ὑποστάσεως τὴν διαφοράν·
τῷ δὲ εἰπεῖν, Παράκλητον, τῆς οὐσίας τὴν συγγένειαν.

95. See p.31 above.

96. Thdr.Heracl. fr.Jo. 261 (TU 89,134), ἐξ ὧν δὲ λέγει αἰτεῖν τὸν
πατέρα, ἵνα ἄλλον παράκλητον πέμψῃ, σαφῶς τὰ τρία πρόσωπα τῆς μιᾶς

παρίστησι τριάδος· οὐδεὶς γὰρ λέγει, ὅτι ἑαυτόν τις αἰτεῖ καὶ ἑαυτὸν πέμπει ὅπερ φασὶν οἱ τὰς ὑποστάσεις συγχέοντες.

97. Thdr.Mops. Jo.Syr. on 14,16 (CSCO 115,272; trans. 116,194), *Alium autem dicit Paraclitum, id est, alium praeceptorem; paraclitum vocans, id est consolatorem, doctrinam in angustiis; quia Spiritus, sua gratia, leviora reddet quae illis ab hominibus inferentur mala, et, consolationis instar, per dona sua faciet illos leviter ferre mala, sicut de facto contigit. Nam quantum discipuli prius timebant mortem, tantum post descensum Spiritus gaudebant in tribulationibus suis.* Cf. Jo. 126 (ST 141,391), Ἄλλον δὲ παράκλητον λέγει ἀντὶ τοῦ ἄλλον διδάσκαλον, Παράκλητον λέγων τὴν ἐν τοῖς δεινοῖς διδασκαλίαν, ὡς ἂν τοῦ Πνεύματος τῇ οἰκείᾳ χάριτι μέλλοντος ἐπικουφίζειν αὐτοῖς τὰ παρὰ τῶν ἀνθρώπων ἐπαγόμενα καὶ ῥᾷον φέρειν παρασκευάζοντος· ὁ δὴ καὶ ἐπ' αὐτῶν ἐδείχθη τῶν πραγμάτων, τῶν μαθητῶν οὕτω μὲν πρότερον δεδιότων τὸν θάνατον, οὕτω δὲ μετὰ τὴν τοῦ Πνεύματος κάθοδον ἐφ' οἷς ἔπασχον ἡδομένων.

98. Thdr.Mops. hom. 10,7 (ST 145,256-257), *C'est elle qu'il appelle aussi Paraclet, c'est-à-dire 'consolateur', parce qu'il peut et est capable d'enseigner ce qu'il leur faut pour les consoler dans les épreuves multiples de ce monde.* Cf. (above n.97) *id est, alium praeceptorem* (Jo.Syr.) and ἀντὶ τοῦ ἄλλον διδάσκαλον (Jo.).

99. Didym. Spir. 25 (PG 39,1056), *Consolatorem autem venientem Spiritum sanctum dicit, ab operatione ei nomen imponens: quia non solum consolatur eos quos se dignos repererit, et ab omni tristitia et perturbatione reddit alienos . . . . Sempiterna quippe laetitia in eorum corde versatur, quorum Spiritus sanctus habitator est.*

100. Didym. Spir. 27 (PG 39,1058), *Quem alium paracletum nominavit, non juxta naturae differentiam, sed operationis diversitatem. Cum enim Salvator mediatoris et legati personam habeat . . . . Spiritus sanctus secundum aliam significantiam paracletus, ab eo quod consolatur in tristitia positos, nuncupatus est.*

101. Didym. Trin. 3,38 (PG 39,972-973), Ἀντὶ γὰρ τοῦ νοεῖν Παράκλητον, ἢ διὰ τὸ παρακαλεῖσθαι ὡς θεὸν παρὰ τῆς κτίσεως, ἢ διὰ τὸ παραμυθεῖσθαι αὐτὴν, καὶ θυμηδίαν καὶ εἰρήνην ἐμβάλλειν· συνώνυμοι γὰρ αἱ λέξεις τῆς παρακλήσεως καὶ παραμυθίας εἰσιν· . . . Οἱ δὲ ἀντὶ τοῦ οὕτω νοεῖν, λέγουσιν διὰ τὸ παρακαλεῖν ὑπὲρ αὐτῆς ὠνομάσθαι Παράκλητον· καὶ ἐπάγουσιν, ὅτι καὶ ἀποστέλλεται.

102. See, e.g., Eus. e.th. 3,5,11 (GCS 14,161); also Gr.Nyss. ref. Eun. 186 (Jaeger 2,391) who recognises both senses of the term but does not indicate which applies in the paraclete passages, leaving that to the judgment of the reader. This reticence on the part of Gr. plus the fact that so many writers recognise the dual meanings of the term παράκλητος even when wanting to stress only one of them may suggest that an understanding of *Paraclete* as *intercessor* was not only known but rather widespread in the Fourth and Fifth Century Church. This may be true despite the fact that there seems to be no extant writing which specifically teaches so.

103. Or μεθ' ὑμῶν ᾖ. Chrys. quotes the clause both ways in one paragraph. See on 14,16 in the Appendix.

104. Chrys. hom. 75,1 in Jo., Μεθ' ὑμῶν μένει. Τοῦτο δηλοῖ, ὅτι
οὐδὲ μετὰ τελευτὴν ἀφίσταται (PG 59,404); Τί ἐστι, Μεθ' ὑμῶν ᾖ; Ὁ
φησιν αὐτός, ὅτι Ἐγὼ μεθ' ὑμῶν εἰμι. Ἄλλως δὲ, καὶ ἕτερόν τι
αἰνίττεται, ὅτι Οὐ πείσεται ταῦτα ἅπερ ἐγώ, οὔτε ἀποφοιτήσει (PG
59,405).

105. Cyr. Jo. 9,1 (Pusey 2,467), Πνεῦμα γάρ ἐστιν αὐτοῦ. καὶ γοῦν
τῆς ἀληθείας αὐτὸ κατωνόμασε Πνεῦμα, καὶ διὰ τῶν προκειμένων ἑαυτὸν
εἶναι τὴν ἀλήθειαν λέγων. Following this analysis Cyr. argues at
some length for the deity of the Spirit and for his one essence
with Father and Son. It is a highly interesting passage which Cyr.
caps by suggesting that, if the Spirit is create, we should expect
Christ to say something other than that the world cannot receive
while the Apostles can and do.

106. Thdr.Mops. Jo. 126 (ST 141,391), Jo.Syr. on 14,17 (CSCO 115,
272), καὶ Πνεῦμα δὲ ἀληθείας ἐκάλεσεν, ὡς οὐδὲν ἕτερον ἢ τὴν ἀλήθειαν
διδάσκον τὸ μηδ' ἐπιδέχεσθαι τὴν εἰς τὸ ἐναντίον τροπήν. Cf. hom.
10,3 (ST 145,248-249).

107. Chrys. hom. 75,1 in Jo. (PG 59,404), Πνεῦμα δὲ ἀληθείας αὐτὸ
καλεῖ, διὰ τούτου τοὺς τύπους τοὺς ἐν τῇ Παλαιᾷ δηλῶν.

108. See e.g., Apoll. Jo. 104 (TU 89,42-43); Bas. Spir. 22,53
(Johnston 107-108; SCH 17,211-212); Nonn. par.Jo. (Scheindler 159);
Thdr.Heracl. fr.Jo. 262 (TU 89,134).

109. Cf. Apoll. Jo. 104 (TU 89,43) and Bas. Spir. 22,53 (Johnston
108-109; SCH 17,212).

110. Chrys. hom. 75,1 in Jo. (PG 59,404-405), Ἀλλ' ἐνταῦθα τὴν
γνῶσίν φησιν. Ἐπήγαγε γοῦν· Οὐδὲ γινώσκει αὐτό· οἶδε γὰρ καὶ ἐπὶ
τῆς ἀκριβοῦς γνώσεως θεωρίαν λέγειν. Ἐπειδὴ γὰρ τῶν αἰσθήσεων
τρανοτέρα ἐστὶν ἡ ὄψις, διὰ ταύτης ἀεὶ τὴν ἀκριβῆ παρίστησι γνῶσιν.
By κόσμος, adds Chrys., Jesus here means the wicked (τοὺς πονηρούς).

111. Cyr. Jo. 9,1 (Pusey 2,469).

112. Didym. Trin. 3,38 (PG 39,976), Τὸ δὲ γράφειν, . . . ἔδειξεν,
ὅτι οἱ μὲν κοσμικοὶ, τοῦτ' ἐστιν αἱρετικοὶ, οὐ δύνανται λαβεῖν
αὐτὸ, ὅτι οὐ θεωροῦσιν αὐτὸ τοῖς τῆς πίστεως ὀφθαλμοῖς, οὐδὲ γινώσκου-
σιν αὐτὸ, μὴ δοξάζοντες ὡς θεόν· οἱ δὲ ὁμολογοῦντες αὐτὸ εἶναι
θεόν, ἔχουσιν αὐτὸ μένον παρ' αὐτοῖς.

113. Thdr.Mops. Jo.Syr. on 14,17 (CSCO 115,273; trans. 116,195),
*Tam mirum est, inquit, donum Spiritus, quem accepturi estis per me, ut
mundus universus, etiam in unum coniuratus, nequeat sumere eum, nisi
sponte sua descendat super eos. Non enim dixit: quem non potest
accipere, sed: quem non potest sumere; id est, nemo potest detinere
eum, ne totus quidem mundus simul, nisi pergratiam suam super illum,
qui dignus est, descendat per voluntatem suam aut per voluntatem
Patris.* See also hom. 10,6 (ST 145,254-255).

114. Thdr.Mops. Jo.Syr. on 14,17 (CSCO 115,273-274; trans. 116,
195), *Quapropter confirmans verbum suum, dixit: quia non videt eum,
nec scit eum. Quod enim est supra visum et intellectum eorum, cuius
natura est abscondita et incomprehensibilis cogitationi creaturarum,
quomodo posset exprimi scientia eorum? Vos autem quod incomprehensibi-
le est cognoscetis et accipietis per me. Non dixit: etiam videbi-*

tis eum; hoc enim est impossibile. See also <u>hom</u>. 10,6 (ST 145,254-255).

115. See Chrys. hom. <u>75,1 in Jo.</u> (PG 59,405). Cf. Nonn. par.Jo. (Scheindler159-160), but contrast Thdr.Heracl. <u>fr</u>.Jo. 262 (TU 89, 134) who suggests that Jesus could speak the final two clauses of 14,17 because the disciples had already received the gift through baptism and were about to receive it through the Paraclete in a very short time.

116. Thdr.Heracl. <u>fr</u>.Jo. 271-272 (TU 89,136-137), for example, alone among the Greeks of this era uses the verses as part of his continuing anti-Montanist polemic. He combats the Montanist assertion that Montanus, Priscilla, and Maximilla are the first-fruits of the Spirit. The Lord, he says, promises in 14,26 that the Spirit will call things to memory. But it is impossible to call things to memory which are not already known. Therefore, since neither Montanus, Maximilla, nor Priscilla had seen and listened to the Lord, it is impossible that they had ever heard anything from him. How then can they be the first-fruits of the Spirit? No, says Thdr., this promise is principally applicable to the apostles, they who both heard the Lord and were later reminded by the Paraclete.

117. Cyr. <u>Jo.</u> 10 (Pusey 2,506.508).

118. Amph. <u>hom. on Jo. 14,28</u> (Moss 337; trans. 351).

119. Amph. <u>hom. on Jo. 14,28</u> (Moss 337; trans. 352).

120. Thdr.Mops. <u>Jo.Syr.</u> on 14,25-26 (CSCO 115,277; trans. 116,198), *Dum loquitur de emittendo super eos Spiritu, manifesto haud designat naturam Spiritus; non enim utpote extra mundum existens, tunc venturus est super homines. Sed ita designat Spiritus gratiam et operationem erga credentes, quae crescit et interdum extinguitur . . . . Non enim de natura Spiritus hoc dicebat, quia nequit humana iniquitas minuere naturam Spiritus.* It is, as will be seen below, typical of Thdr. to understand all such (anthropomorphic) statements in the paraclete passages in terms of the grace of the Spirit rather than of his nature.

121. Cyr. <u>Jo.</u> 10 (Pusey 2,506), τὴν δὲ τοῦ μυστηρίου τελειοτάτην καὶ ἀκριβεστάτην ἡμῖν ἀποκάλυψιν διὰ τοῦ παρκλήτου γενέσθαι λέγει, τουτέστι, τοῦ Ἁγίου Πνεύματος ἀποσταλέντος παρὰ τοῦ Πατρὸς ἐπὶ <u>τῷ ὀνόματι</u> αὐτοῦ, λέγω δὴ τοῦ Υἱοῦ.

122. Thdr.Mops. <u>Jo.Syr.</u> on 14,25-26 (CSCO 115,277; trans. 116,198), *Sed, inquit, haec locutus sum vobis, ut sciatis quid oporteat vos observare, quamdiu vobiscum sum. Cum enim ascendero in caelum ac vos receperitis gratiam Spiritus, tunc per operationem Spiritus multa nondum nota addiscetis.* Cf. <u>Jo.</u> 128 (ST 141,394).

123. Amph. hom. on Jo. 14,28 (Moss 338,trans. 353), "'*He therefore shall teach you everything, and he shall bring everything to your remembrance*'. He shall teach those things which I have not said; he shall bring to remembrance those things which I have said."

124. See Cyr. Jo. 10 (Pusey 2,506), ὡς γὰρ Χριστὸς ἐν ἡμῖν τὸ Πνεῦμα
αὐτοῦ· διὰ τοῦτό φησιν ὅτι ἐκεῖνος διδάξει ὑμᾶς πάντα ἃ εἶπον ὑμῖν
ἐγώ· ἐπειδὴ γάρ ἐστι Πνεῦμα Χριστοῦ καὶ νοῦς αὐτοῦ, κατὰ τὸ γεγραμ-
μένον, οὐχ ἕτερόν τι παρ' αὐτὸν ὄν, κατά γε τὸν ἐν ταυτότητι φυσικῇ
λόγον, καίτοι νοούμενόν τε καὶ ὑπάρχον ἰδίως, οἶδε πάντα τὰ ἐν αὐτῷ,
and Didym. Trin. 3,38 (PG 39,976), Τὸ δὲ, ''Εκεῖνος . . . ἃ εἶπον
ὑμῖν,' παράγγελμά ἐστιν μὴ ἀπιστῆσαι τῷ ἁγίῳ Πνεύματι . . . Οὐκ
ἀπᾴδουσα γάρ, φησίν, τῆς ἐμῆς γνώμης καὶ διδασκαλίας ἔσται ἡ αὐτοῦ·
ἐπειδὴ καὶ τῇ θεότητι ἡνωμένως καὶ ἐχομένως ἔχει· κοινὰ δὲ τῆς
ἁγίας Τριάδος τὰ διδάγματα, καὶ τὰ πρὸς σωτηρίαν δωρήματα.

125. Cyr. Jo. 10 (Pusey 2,506-507), οὐκοῦν, ὡς εἰδὸς τὰ ἐν τῇ
βουλήσει τοῦ Μονογενοῦς, πάντα ἡμῖν ἀναγγέλει, οὐκ ἐκ μαθήσεως ἔχον
τὴν εἴδησιν, ἵνα μὴ φαίνηται διακόνου τάξιν ἀποπληροῦν, καὶ τοὺς ἑτέρου
τυχὸν διαπορθμεύων λόγους, ἀλλ' ὡς Πνεῦμα αὐτοῦ, καθάπερ ἀρτίως
εἰρήκαμεν, καὶ εἰδὸς ἀδιδάκτως πάντα τὰ ἐξ οὗ καὶ ἐν ᾧπερ ἐστι, τὰ
θεῖα τοῖς ἁγίοις ἀποκαλύπτει μυστήρια.

126. See Thdr.Mops. hom. 10,7 (ST 145,256-257) and Mac.25.26 (PO
9,665-666).

127. Chrys. hom. 77,3 in Jo. (PG 59,417), 'Εκεῖνος ἀξιόπιστος ἔσται·
Πνεῦμα γὰρ ἀληθείας ἐστι. Διὰ τοῦτο οὐ Πνεῦμα ἅγιον, ἀλλ' ἀληθείας
αὐτὸ ἐκάλεσε.

128. Cyr. Jo. 10,2 (Pusey 2,607.609).

129. Thdr.Mops. hom. 10,8 (ST 145,256-257). But cf. Mac. 27 (PO
9,666-667) where, speaking of this title without specifying his source,
he suggests that the Paraclete is called Spirit of truth because he
conducts those who receive him into all truth (cf. Jo. 16,13) and
that he is the leader into all truth because he possesses exact
knowledge about everything.

130. Thdr.Mops. Jo.Syr. on 15,26-27 (CSCO 115,288; trans. 116,206),
Volens autem culpam augere ex persona huius qui testimonium perhibebit,
ait: qui a Patre procedit; id est, ille cuius essentia est ex natura
Patris. Nam nisi per vocabulum 'procedit' naturalem inde intellegeret
processionem, sed extrinsecam quamdam missionem, dubium esset de quo
loquatur . . .; Jo. 130 (ST 141,398), ["Οτι δὲ οὐ πρὸς χάριν εὕρηται
μαρτυρεῖ τὸ Πνεῦμα τοῖς λεγομένοις], ὃ ἐξ αὐτῆς τοῦ Πατρὸς τῆς οὐσίας
ἔχει τὴν ὕπαρξιν. Εἰ γὰρ μὴ τὴν φυσικὴν ἐκεῖθεν πρόοδον ἔλεγεν διὰ
τοῦ ἐκπορεύεται, ἀλλά τινα ἀποστολὴν ἔξωθεν γινομένην, ἄπορον περὶ
τίνος λέγει, . . . (The words in brackets are supplied by the editor
from John Chrysostom.) Cf. also hom. 10,8-10 (ST 145,256-261) where
Thdr. writes that this clause means that the Spirit is eternally with
God the Father and inseparable from him because he is eternally in
him.

131. Thdr.Heracl. fr.Jo. 302 (TU 89,144), δι' ὧν δὲ λέγει, διδάσκει,
ὅτι τὸ πνεῦμα ἐκ τῆς τοῦ πατρὸς οὐσίας ἐκπορεύεται διὰ τοῦ υἱοῦ
εἰς ἀνθρώπους καταπεμπόμενον. Note that Thdr. here expresses precisely
the Eastern doctrine of the procession of the Holy Spirit: the Spirit
proceeds from the Father through the Son.

132. Cyr. Jo. 10,2 (Pusey 2,607), 'Ιδοὺ γὰρ ἰδοὺ πνεῦμα τῆς ἀληθείας,
τουτέστιν ἑαυτοῦ, τὸν Παράκλητον εἰπών, παρὰ τοῦ Πατρὸς αὐτὸν

ἐκπορεύεσθαί φησιν. ὥσπερ γάρ ἐστιν ἴδιον Πνεῦμα τοῦ Υἱοῦ φυσικῶς, ἐν αὐτῷ τε ὑπάρχον καὶ δι' αὐτοῦ προϊόν, οὕτω καὶ τοῦ Πατρός· οἷς δὲ τὸ Πνεῦμα κοινόν, τούτοις εἴη δήπου πάντως ἂν καὶ τὰ τῆς οὐσίας οὐ διωρισμένα.

133. Cyr. Jo. 10,2 (Pusey 2,609), μαρτυρήσει δὲ πῶς; ἐνεργήσαν γὰρ ἐν ὑμῖν τε καὶ δι' ὑμῶν τὰ παράδοξα, μάρτυς ἔσεται δίκαιός τε καὶ ἀληθὴς τῆς ἐμῆς θεοπρεποῦς ἐξουσίας, καὶ τῆς ἐν δυνάμει μεγαλειότητος. Cf. Thdr.Mops. Jo. 130 (ST 141,399), Jo.Syr. on 15,26-27 (CSCO 115, 288). Thdr., with his usual concern to stress the incorporeality of the Spirit, says that 15,27 is added precisely that the disciples might not think the Spirit's witness is to be given in words.

134. See Chrys. hom. 77,3 in Jo. (PG 59,417); Cyr. Jo. 10,2 (Pusey 2,609); Nonn. par.Jo. (Scheindler 170); cf. Thdr.Mops. Jo.130 (ST 141,399).

135. Cyr. Jo. 10,2 (Pusey 2,615-616).

136. Cyr. Jo. 10,2 (Pusey 2,616), ἐξήρκει μὲν γὰρ συμπαρὼν αὐτοῖς ἔτι πρὸς τὸ ἀνασώζειν εὐκόλως, καὶ ἐκ παντὸς ῥύεσθαι πειρασμοῦ, καὶ τὴν ἐφ' ἄπασι τοῖς συμβαίνουσι καθηκόντως ποιεῖσθαι διδασκαλίαν τε καὶ ἐπανόρθωσιν.

137. Chrys. hom. 78,1 in Jo. (PG 59,421). Chrys. adds a reason the others do not. He suggests that Jesus did not say these things from the beginning so that no might say he was merely guessing from the ordinary course of events. He also considers the problem raised by passages like Mt. 10,17.18. Is it true, he says, that our Lord had not told them these things before? *In nuce* his answer is that, while Jesus had previously told them about scourging and coming before princes (e.g., in Mt. 10,17.18), he has hitherto not portrayed their death as a thing so desirable that it should even be considered a service to God, as he does here; he has not told them that they are to be judged as impious and corrupters, a thing suited above all others to terrify them; and he has before spoken only of gentile persecutions whereas now he foretells in a stronger way the acts of the Jews, as well, and announces that the event is at their very door.

138. Thdr.Mops. Jo.Syr. on 16,4b (CSCO 115,291; trans. 116,208), *Non erat necesse, inquit, ut prius haec dicerem vobis; non enim urgebat me tempus, cum vobiscum essem, ut singulatim de eventibus illis loquerer vobis, quia praesentia mea inter vos sufficiebat.*

139. See Cyr. Jo. 10,2 (Pusey 2,616-617). Jesus knew the ascent to the Father to be essential from the point of view of his human nature. But as God he also knew the overwhelming sorrow of the disciples at the realization that he would not always be with them. He sympathises with their suffering, as it proceeds from love, and with the speechlessness which kept them from asking the reason of his departure. See also Chrys. hom. 78,1 in Jo. (PG 59,421). According to Chrys. the disciples were despondent because of their anguish at being left by Jesus and because of their anguish in the face of the terrible things which they have just learned are to come to them. It is, says Chrys., a great comfort to them to learn (through these verses) that Jesus knows the excess (ὑπερβολή) of their despondency (ἀθυμία). Why, he asks, if Jesus were consoling

them by revealing that he knew the excess of their sorrow, did he
not go on to tell them they have been guaranteed the Spirit? It
is so that we might learn the great virtue of the disciples who
heard, as it were, the worst and yet did not flinch despite their
excessive sorrow and might consider what sort of men they were likely
to be after the gift of the Spirit if this is what they were before.

140. See Chrys. hom. 5,4 in I Cor. (Field 2,53; PG 61,45), ep.
3,4 (SCH 13,159-160; PG 52,576); Thdr.Heracl. fr.Jo. 309 (TU 89,
146); Thdr.Mops. Jo. 130 (ST 141,399), Jo.Syr. on 16,5-6 (CSCO 115,
292). Cyr. Jo. 10,2 (Pusey 2,616-617) may imply the same thing.

141. See Bas. moral. 5,5 (PG 31,709); Chrys. hom. 78,1 in Jo. (PG
59,421); Cyr. Jo. 10,2 (Pusey 2,617); Thdr.Mops Jo.130 (ST 141,400),
Jo.Syr. on 16,7 (CSCO 115,292). Bas. (loc.cit.) even goes so far as
to infer the principle or rule (ὅρος) ὅτι τὴν κατὰ Χριστὸν ἀγάπην
ὁ ἔχων ἔστιν ὅτε καὶ λυπεῖ πρὸς τὸ συμφέρον τὸν ἀγαπώμενον from
16,7 (and other verses).

142. Cyr. Jo. 10,2 (Pusey 2,617-620).

143. Cyr. Jo. 10,2 (Pusey 2,620).

144. Cyr. Jo. 10,2 (Pusey 2,620-621), οὐκοῦν ἀληθὴς τοῦ Σωτῆρος ὁ λόγος Συμφέρει ὑμῖν λέγοντος τὸ ἀποδημῆσαί με εἰς οὐρανούς· ἐκεῖνος
γὰρ ἦν ὁ καιρὸς τῆς καθόδου τοῦ Πνεύματος.

145. Chrys. hom. 78,1 in Jo. (PG 59,421), Τί λέγουσιν ἐνταῦθα οἱ
τὴν προσήκουσαν περὶ τοῦ Πνεύματος οὐκ ἔχοντες δόξαν; συμφέρει
Δεσπότην ἀπελθεῖν, καὶ δοῦλον παραγενέσθαι; Ὁρᾷς πῶς πολλὴ τοῦ
Πνεύματος ἡ ἀξία; Cf. hom. 1,5 in Ac. (PG 60,20).

146. Chrys. hom. 78,3 in Jo. (PG 59,423), Διατί δὲ οὐκ ἤρχετο πρὶν
ἢ αὐτὸν ἀπελθεῖν; Ὅτι οὔπω τῆς κατάρας ἀρθείσης, οὔπω τῆς ἁμαρτίας
λυθείσης, ἀλλ' ἔτι πάντων ὑπευθύνων ὄντων τῇ τιμωρίᾳ, οὐκ ἂν
παρεγένετο. Δεῖ οὖν, φησὶ, τὴν ἔχθραν λυθῆναι, καὶ καταλλαγῆναι
ὑμᾶς τῷ θεῷ, καὶ τότε δέξασθαι τὸ δῶρον ἐκεῖνο. Διατί δέ φησι,
Πέμψω αὐτόν; Τουτέστι, Προπαρασκευάσω ὑμᾶς πρὸς τὴν ὑποδοχήν. Πῶς
γὰρ τὸ πανταχοῦ ὂν πέμπεται;

147. Chrys. hom. 1,5 in Ac. (PG 60,20). In this context Chrys. maintains that the fulfillment of the promise of the Paraclete (he quotes
14,16 and 16,7) came on the day of Pentecost and explains that the
infusion of Jo. 20,22-23 was merely a preparing of the disciples to
receive the Spirit. In his earlier hom. 86,3 in Jo. (PG 59,491),
however, where he specifically seeks to reconcile 16,7 with 20,22-
23, he rejects this interpretation of the latter passage. Some
espouse it, he şays, on the ground that Jesus said not ἐλάβετε but
rather λάβετε Πνεῦμα ἅγιον. Chrys. here thinks it more likely that
the disciples did receive some spiritual power and grace at 20,22-
23, namely, the power to remit sins. The fuller miracle working
power came at Pentecost. Eus. e.th. 3,5,13-14 (GCS 14,161-162) agrees
with this almost exactly when he suggests that Jesus gave the disciples
at 20,22 a part of the gift of the Spirit, namely the ability to
forgive sins, but that the gift came in greater and more perfect
power and with completeness at Pentecost. Cyr.H. catech. 17,12
(Rupp 2,266; PG 33,984-985) is similar, but Cyr. H. maintains that

it is the fellowship of the Spirit which is bestowed in 20,22. He
also enters the caveat ὅτι πνεῦμα οὐ μεμέρισται, ἀλλ' ἡ δι' αὐτοῦ
χάρις. So for him, too, the Spirit is given to the apostles in
part before the ascension (Jo. 20,22) but fully at Pentecost. In
Alexandria Cyr. Jo. 12,1 (Pusey 3,131-141) takes the same line that
the disciples received at 20,22 the necessary first installment of
the promised gift which was more manifestly confirmed for them and
more generally given to the world on the day of Pentecost. He also
(Pusey 2,136) draws an interesting parallel between the infusion of
Jesus in 20,22 and God's breathing into man the breath of life in
Genesis.

148. Cyr. Jo. 10,2 (Pusey 2,621-622). Cf. Chrys. hom. 78,1 in Jo.
(PG 59,421-422) who also seems to see the Spirit's work delineated
here in 16,8(-11). His exegesis is that the Spirit is to bear witness to Jesus.

149. Cyr. Jo. 10,2 (Pusey 2,622), . . . τὸν κόσμον, τουτέστι, τοὺς
ἀπαιδεύτους τε καὶ ἀπίστους ἔτι καὶ ταῖς ἐν κόσμῳ φιληδονίαις
κεκρατημένους . . .

150. Cyr. Jo.10,2 (Pusey 2,623).

151. Cyr. Jo. 10,2 (Pusey 2,622), . . . τοῖς ἀγαπῶσι Χριστὸν, ὡς
ἀξίοις ἤδη καὶ πεπιστευκόσι γένηται . . .

152. Cyr. Jo. 10,2 (Pusey 2,622), . . . μόνοις δὲ τοῖς ἀξίοις
ἐγκατοικιεῖ τὸν Παράκλητον, οἳ διὰ πίστεως εἰλικρινοῦς ὡς θεὸν ὄντως
τετιμήκασι, καὶ τῶν ὅλων ὡμολόγησαν δημιουργὸν καὶ Κύριον.

153. See Apoll. Jo. 118-119 (TU 89,47-48); Chrys. hom. 78,2 in Jo.
(PG 59,422); cf. Thdr.Mops. Jo.Syr. on 16,9 (CSCO 115,293). See
also the citations in n.154.

154. Cyr. Jo. 10,2 (Pusey 2,622); Apoll. Jo.118 (TU 89,47).

155. See Apoll. Jo. 118-119 (TU 89,47-48); Cyr. Jo. 10,2 (Pusey 2,
622); Thdr.Mops. Jo.Syr.on 16,9 (CSCO 115,293).

156. Chrys. hom. 78,2 in Jo. (PG 59,422). The proof that Jesus'
abiding with the Father is continual and not merely transitory
Chrys. takes, interestingly enough, from the clause οὐκέτι θεωρεῖτέ
με. (See also Thdr.Mops. Jo.Syr. on 16,10 (CSCO 115,293) who also
sees the righteousness of Jesus in this verse, though the argument
of his exegesis is different, or rather, nonexistent.)

157. See Cyr. Jo. 10,2 (Pusey 2,622-623); Thdr.Heracl. fr.Jo.312
(TU 89,147); cf. Apoll Jo. 119 (TU 89,48).

158. See Apoll Jo. 119 (TU 89,48); Thdr.Heracl. fr.Jo. 311.313
(TU 89,146-147); Thdr.Mops. Jo.Syr.on 16,11 (CSCO 115,293); Cyr. Jo.
10,2 (Pusey 2,623). Thdr.Heracl. (loc.cit.) gives an interesting
exposition of the grounds of the Devil's condemnation: he who brought
death to men tries to squirm out of his culpability by pleading that
Adam died, not on his (i.e. Satan's) account, but because of his
(Adam's) own sin. But this pleading is in vain; the Ruler of this
world is justly judged because he unjustly incited the Jews to do

to death the sinless Christ, the second man. And it is on this account that Jesus speaks the condemnation of the Devil in 16,11. Thdr.
Mops. (loc. cit.) remarks that it is to be shown by the Spirit that
it was the passion of Christ which was efficacious for the condemnation of Satan.

159. Chrys. hom. 78,2 in Jo. (PG 59,422), Πάλιν ἐνταῦθα τὸν περὶ
δικαιοσύνης ἀνακινεῖ λόγον, ὅτι κατεπάλαισε τὸν ἀντίδικον. Οὐκ
ἂν δὲ ἁμαρτωλὸς ὢν κατεπάλαισεν· ὅπερ οὐδὲ δίκαιός τις ἀνθρώπων
ποιῆσαι ἴσχυσεν.

160. Cyr. Jo.10,2 (Pusey 2,623), προσμαρτυρήσει γὰρ τῇ δόξῃ τοῦ
Χριστοῦ, καὶ αὐτὸν ὄντως ἀποδείξας ὄντα τὸν τῶν ὅλων Κύριον, ἐλέγξει
τὸν κόσμον, ὡς πεπλανημένον, καὶ τὸν μὲν ἀληθῶς τε καὶ φύσει ἀφέντα
θεὸν, προσκυνήσαντα δὲ καὶ λελατρευκότα τῷ μὴ κατὰ φύσιν, τουτέστι,
τῷ σατανᾷ. See also 10,2 (Pusey 2,624-625).

161. Cyr. Jo. 10,2 (Pusey 2,623-624).

162. Cyr. Jo. 10,2 (Pusey 2,625), νόθον οὖν ἄρα τὸ τῆς ἀρχῆς ὄνομα
τῷ σατανᾷ φυσικῶς μὲν οὐ πρὸς τὸν θεὸν, ἐν δὲ τῇ τῶν πλανωμένων
βδελυρίᾳ διασωζόμενον.

163. See Chrys. hom. 78,2 in Jo. (PG 59,422) and 78,3 (PG 59,424).
Cf. hom. 1,5 in Ac. (PG 60,20) where Chrys., probably alluding to
Jo. 16,12-13, similarly and explicitly says, Εἰ δὲ ἔλαττον ἦν τὸ
Πνεῦμα, οὐκ ἦν ἀρκοῦσα ἡ παραμυθία. Πῶς δὲ καὶ ἔλεγε, Συμφέρει ὑμῖν;
Διὰ τοῦτο τὰ μείζονα αὐτῷ τετήρηται τῆς διδασκαλίας, ἵνα μὴ ἔλαττον αὐτὸ
νομίσωσι.

164. See Chrys. hom. 78,2 in Jo. (PG 59,422-423) and 78,3 (PG 59,
424).

165. Cyr. Jo. 10,2 (Pusey 2,625ff).

166. Thdr.Mops. Jo.Syr. (CSCO 115,294; trans. 116,210), Vos, inquit,
ceteris magis experiemini virtutem Spiritus. Illa enim quae nunc ne
audire quidem potestis, quia non possetis ea intellegere si vobis
dicerentur; illa, inquam, intellegetis quando receperitis donum
Spiritus, quia omnem veritatem recipietis ab eo; atque non solum
audire poteritis, sed intellegere omnia quae dicta sunt. Cf. Jo.
131 (ST 141,400).

167. See n.166.

168. See Cyr. Jo. 10,2 (Pusey 2,626.627); Didym. Spir. 33 (PG 39,
1063); Eus. e.th. 3,5,12 (GCS 14,161); Thdr.Heracl. fr.Jo. 314
(TU 89,148).

169. Or. Cels. 2,1 (GCS 2,128). See p.7 above.

170. Didym. Spir. 33 (PG 39,1062-1063), Ex his enim sacramentorum
verbis edocemur, quod cum multa docuisset discipulos suos Jesus,
dixerit: 'Adhuc habeo plurima dicere vobis,' quia verbum istud,
'adhuc multa habeo dicere vobis,' non ad novos quoslibet, et penitus
Dei gratia vacuos dirigitur: sed ad eos qui auditores verborum
ejus, necdem fuerant omnia consecuti. Quaecunque enim sufficere

porterant, tradens eis, in futurum tempus reliqua distulit. (In the
same place Didym. suggests that God answered the prayer of the
Psalmist at Ps. 24(25),5 by sending the Holy Spirit who directs into
all truth.)

171. Cf. the discussions on 16,12-13 in Chrys. hom. 5,5 in I Cor.
(Field 2,53; PG 61,45) and hom. 78,2 in Jo. (PG 59,423); Cyr. Jo.
10,2 (Pusey 2,626); Thdr.Heracl. fr.Jo.314 (TU 89,148); Thdr.Mops.
hom. 8,3 (ST 145,190-191) and Jo.Syr.on 16,13 (CSCO 115,294-295).

172. Thdr.Mops. Jo.Syr. on 16,13 (CSCO 115,294-295; trans. 116,
210-211), *Non autem sermone docebat Spiritus discipulos, sed inef-
fabili mysterio, doctrinae revelationem animis eorum communicabat,
et sensum veritatum profundiorum dabat eis; unde quae audierant ab
Unigenito et non intellexerant, praecipue quando loquebatur de sua
natura, cum facilitate magna intellegere valuerunt post Spiritus
adventum.*

173. Cyr. Jo. 10,2 (Pusey 2,628).

174. Cf. Chrys hom. 78,2 in Jo. (PG 59,422-423); Cyr. Jo. 10,2
(Pusey 2,629); Thdr.Mops. Jo.Syr. on 16,13 (CSCO 115,295-296).

175. Cf. esp. Chrys. hom. 78,3 in Jo. (PG 59,424) and Thdr.Mops.
Jo.Syr. on 16,13 (CSCO 115,295-296).

176. Cf. Chrys. hom. 78,3 in Jo. (PG 59, 424) and Thdr.Mops. Jo.Syr.
on 16,13 (CSCO 115,296).

177. See Cyr. Jo. 10,2 (Pusey 2,629), . . . μονονουχὶ λέγων Σημεῖον
τοῦτο ἔσται ὑμῖν, ὅτι δὴ πάντως ἐκ τῆς ἐμῆς οὐσίας τὸ Πνεῦμά ἐστι,
καὶ οἶον ἐμός ἐστι νοῦς, τὸ ἐρεῖν αὐτὸν τὰ ἐσόμενα, καθάπερ ἐγώ.
. . . οὐκ ἂν οὖν ἄρα καθάπερ ἐγὼ προερεῖ τὰ ἐσόμενα, μὴ οὐχὶ πάντως
ἐν ἐμοί τε ὑπάρχον καὶ δι' ἐμοῦ προϊόν, καὶ τῆς αὐτῆς οὐσίας ὑπάρχον
ἐμοί. For a brief examination of Cyril's doctrine of the procession
of the Spirit, reflected in this passage, see Swete, Procession, 148-
150.

178. See Cyr. Jo. 11,1 (Pusey 2,633-634), Ὡς ἀποκαλύπτειν μέλλοντος
τοῖς τούτου τυχεῖν ἀξίοις τοῦ Ἁγίου Πνεύματος τὸ ἐπὶ Χριστῷ μυστήριον,
καὶ παραδεικνύειν ἀκριβῶς τίς μέν ἐστι κατὰ φύσιν, πόση δὲ αὐτῷ
δύναμίς τε καὶ ἐξουσία, καὶ ὅτι πάντων βασιλεύει μετὰ Πατρὸς, ἀναγκαίως
φησιν ὅτι ἐκεῖνος ἐμὲ δοξάσει. ἀνωτέρω μὲν γὰρ ἵστησι φρονημάτων
Ἰουδαϊκῶν τὸν ἡμέτερον νοῦν . . .

179. Chrys. hom. 78,2 in Jo. (PG 59,423), Ἐκεῖνος ἐμὲ δοξάσει.
Πῶς; Ἐν τῷ ὀνόματι τῷ ἐμῷ δώσει τὰς ἐνεργείας.

180. See Cyr. Jo. 11,1 (Pusey 2,634-635). The essence of Cyr.'s
argument is contained in these words: Δοξάζει τοιγαροῦν τὸν Υἱὸν ὁ
Παράκλητος, τουτέστι, τὸ ἴδιον αὐτοῦ Πνεῦμα, πάντα ἰσχύον καὶ πάντα
εἰδός. δοξάζει δὲ πῶς; ἃ γὰρ οἶδε καὶ δύναται τὸ Πνεῦμα αὐτοῦ,
πῶς ἂν αὐτὸς οὐκ εἰδείη τυχόν, ἢ πῶς οὐκ ἂν δύναιτο; καὶ εἰ καθάπερ
αὐτός φησιν, ἐξ αὐτοῦ λαμβάνει τὸ Πνεῦμα, καίτοι πάντα ἰσχύον καὶ
κατορθοῦν, πῶς ἂν αὐτὸς οὐκ ἔχῃ τὸ ἐφ' ἅπασιν ἰσχυρόν;

181.   Thdr.Mops.   Jo.Syr. on 16,14 (CSCO 115,297-298), *Si enim pars, quae in vobis est, tam potens est, capax rapiendi omnes homines in admirationem, cogitate quaenam gloria mihi facta sit*(CSCO 115, 298; trans. 116,213).

182.   See Chrys. hom. 78,2 in Jo. (PG 59,422) and 78,3 (PG 59,424-425); Cyr. Jo. 11,1 (Pusey 2,636).

183.   Cf. Apoll. Jo. 120 (TU 89,48-49); Chrys. hom. 78,3 in Jo. (PG 59,424); Cyr. Jo. 11,1 (Pusey 2,635); Thdr.Heracl. fr.Jo.315 (TU 89,148), a tantalising fragment which says only, Τὸ γὰρ ἅγιον πνεῦμα μάρτυς γέγονε τῆς τοῦ μονογενοῦς θεότητος ἐκ τῆς οὐσίας αὐτοῦ ὂν καὶ τὴν οὐσίαν αὐτοῦ ἐξαγγέλλον.

184.   Cyr. Jo. 11,1 (Pusey 2,635), ἐπειδὴ δὲ ὁμοούσιόν τε ἐστι τῷ Υἱῷ, καὶ πρόεισι θεοπρεπῶς δι' αὐτοῦ, πᾶσαν αὐτοῦ τὴν ἐφ' ἅπασι τελειωτάτην ἔχον ἐνέργειάν τε καὶ δύναμιν, διὰ τοῦτό φησιν ᾿Ότι ἐκ τοῦ ἐμοῦ λήψεται.

185.   For the exposition of Thdr.Mops. on ἐκ τοῦ ἐμοῦ see below on 16,15b.

186.   Apoll. Jo. 120 (TU 89,48), τὸ δὲ παρ' ἐμοῦ λέγων δῆλον καὶ τὸ παρὰ τοῦ πατρός· ἐμὰ γάρ ἐστι τὰ πατρῷα.

187.   Eus. e.th. 3,5,18 (GCS 14,162-163), . . . 'ἐκ τοῦ ἐμοῦ λήψεται καὶ ἀναγγελεῖ ὑμῖν', ἐκ τοῦ ἐμοῦ δηλαδὴ θησαυροῦ· ἐν αὐτῷ γάρ 'εἰσιν πάντες οἱ θησαυροὶ τῆς σοφίας καὶ γνώσεως ἀπόκρυφοι'.

188.   Chrys. hom. 78,2 in Jo. (PG 59,423).

189.   The proposition of the whole of Cyr. Jo. 11,2, which comprises his discussion of 16,15-33, is ᾿Ότι φυσικῶς ἐν τῷ Υἱῷ καὶ ἐν τῇ οὐσίᾳ αὐτοῦ τὸ Πνεῦμα αὐτοῦ, τουτέστι τὸ ῞Αγιον, καθὰ καὶ ἐν τῇ οὐσίᾳ τοῦ Πατρός (Pusey 2,637).

190.   Cyr. Jo. 11,2 (Pusey 2,637-638.639) reasons further for the consubstantiality of the Spirit in an argument which reduces to this: Father and Son are consubstantial and have an identity of attributes in common (deduced from 16,15 and, in earlier books of Jo., from other passages). God the Father has the Spirit who is in him essen-tially and proceeds from him inseparably and indivisibly. Therefore, as the Son has been shown to be consubstantial with the Father, this same Spirit is also his distinct property, ἀλλ' ἴδιον γὰρ Πνεῦμα τοῦτό ἐστι καὶ τοῦ Μονογενοῦς, ὁμοούσιος γάρ ἐστι τῷ Πατρί.

191.   Cyr. Jo. 11,2 (Pusey 2,637-638) and 12,1 (Pusey 3,135-136).

192.   Cyr. Jo. 11,2 (Pusey 2,638-639).

193.   Thdr.Mops. Jo.Syr. on 16,15 (CSCO 115,298; trans. 116,213), *Om-nia quaecumque habet Pater, mea sunt. Nam etiam universalem dominati-onem accepi, inquit. Et nos credimus hoc ita esse. Particeps est enim omnium quae sunt Dei Verbi, propter suam coniunctionem cum eo.*

194.   Thdr.Mops. Jo.Syr. on 16,15 (CSCO 115,298-299); cf. on 16,14 (CSCO 115,297).

Chapter 3

LATIN EXEGESIS BETWEEN THE COUNCILS OF
NICAEA AND CHALCEDON

INTRODUCTION

In general, conditions in the Church in the West between
325 and 451 are identical to those which obtain in the East.[1] Under
the increasingly benign smile of the Empire, there is the same re-
lease to develop and defend Churchly dogma; there is the same liberty
to expound and interpret the Scriptures and to develop the exegetical sciences. The Latin Church does face its own squabbles and
heresies, chiefly the Donatist and Pelagian controversies. But these
have little bearing on the exegesis of paraclete passages. More
formative are the great Christological and Trinitarian controversies operative throughout the Church.

The paraclete exegeses of East and West are in broad outline
perfectly conformable. A commonality of direction and external
conditions, generally, and the need to defend and develop a common
rule of faith in the face of common enemies, specifically, combine
to make it so. Latin exegesis does not develop in total isolation;
certain lines of interpretation must have been hammered out in the
ecumenical debate on issues to which the paraclete passages are
not only germane but vital. And East touches West explicitly in
Ambrose of Milan who seems to have made a rather thorough study of
classics on the Holy Spirit by Athanasius, Basil, Didymus, and
others. Their arguments are digested and arranged and their exegeses

refined in his book De Spiritu Sancto.[2]

    But, though Greek and Latin treatments of paraclete passages
are so similar, there are also differences between them, most of
which relate more or less directly to that often remarked Latin
practicality which characterizes Western Christian writing. The
Western mind is more concerned with the problems of organising and
governing Churchly society and life than with inquiring into the
ultimate nature of the cosmos; there is intellectual speculation,
to be sure, but it tends to be ancillary to utilitarian purposes.
Consequently, the temper of paraclete passage usage in the literature of the West tends to be practical and pastoral rather than
merely intellectual, even though the basic issues are the same,
East and West. Perhaps this explains why the sole Latin commentary
on the Gospel of John, the Tractates of St. Augustine, is in homiletical form. Stated another way, Latin usage has more in common with
Antioch than Alexandria; nevertheless, its creative scope is narrower
than even that of the Antiochenes.

    As in the East, paraclete passages are invoked in two basic
literary genres, viz., those which concern themselves with doctrine
and those which deal directly with exegetical matters. We examine
each of these more or less separately, looking most closely at those
elements in each unique to the West.

DOGMATIC WRITINGS

    As in the Greek East, the paraclete passages are seen in the
West to have a special relevance to the dogmatic issues of the Fourth
and Fifth Centuries. Here as there they assume their greatest importance in the development of the doctrines of the Trinity, the
Christ, and the Holy Spirit. Here, as there, they are enlisted most

often by the catholic dogmatists in the defense against heresies which
go astray at just these points.

Nevertheless, it is characteristic of the Latin turn of mind
that dogmatic writers refer directly to our materials much less
frequently than their Greek counterparts. Indeed, though their extant
literatures are of comparable volume, the Greeks invoke the paraclete
passages roughly three times as often as the Latins.[3] This is in part
due, of course, to a difference in the subject matter of the respective literatures; a greater proportion of the Latin *corpus* is concerned with matters to which the paraclete passages are irrelevant.
But it is also due to a greater Latin reluctance to amass long lists
of proof-text quotations such as one finds, for example, in Didymus of
Alexandria.

It is also characteristic of the Latin mind that it shows
relatively greater concern with exegesis *per se*. When passages are
quoted in dogmatic writings they tend to be given more or less full
exposition. In consequence, dogma and exegesis are often more easily
distinguished here than in the Greek East. The exegesis itself tends
to be less speculative and more scientific, often conforming to what
we have come to regard as 'modern' interpretation.

To judge from frequency of citation, the paraclete passages
become increasingly important in the West up to the time of Augustine
who, though he leaves whole books without one mention of them, refers
to them more often than any other writer.[4] Immediately after Augustine
citations drop off dramatically.

As in Chapter 2 above, we consider the dogmatico-polemical
writers under the sub-categories Trinity, Christology, and Pneumatology.[5]

The Trinity

There is some effort in the West to support from the paraclete
passages the distinction of persons in the Godhead. Thus Ambrose infers from Jo. 14,16 that, while Spirit and Son possess in *paracletus*
an identity of name, the adjective *alius* both distinguishes them and,
therefore, prevents any Sabellian confusion of their persons.[6] Others
look to 14,26 and 15,26, insisting that there are three divine persons
to be distinguished in these verses: the one who sends, the one who
goes, and the one from whom he is sent.[7]

More often, however, our materials are invoked in support
of the unity and consubstantiality of the Trinity. Ambrose attempts
in one place to show the divine unity by inferring from Jo. 14,26 that
the three persons are possessed of a common name: the name of Son
and Spirit is one as the Spirit comes in the name of the Son (14,26).
But, since Son and Father have a common name (already established
from Jo. 5,43, et al.), the Spirit, in so doing, also comes in the
name of the Father. Therefore, the name of all three divine persons is
one.[8] Ambrose further infers the unity of the name of Son and Spirit
from the fact that both are called *paracletus*.[9]

A second approach seeks to demonstrate the divine unity by
showing that Father, Son, and Spirit are inseparable in will and
operation. What one wills and does the others will and do: from Jo.
16,13-15 it is inferred that what one member of the Trinity speaks
the others also speak.[10] 16,7-8 is invoked to show that it is in the
province of the Spirit to rebuke (*arguo*) just as in Scripture Father
and Son are shown to do.[11] The fathers also support the community
of action in the Trinity by showing from a juxtaposition of 16,7,
14,26, and 15,26 that the Spirit is sent inseparably by both Father
and Son[12] and from 14,16 that Son and Spirit both perform the work of

advocacy.[13] Augustine appeals further to *uobiscum manet et in uobis est*, 14,17, to show that the Spirit is one with Father and Son in their abiding with those who love them. He anticipates the objection that the Spirit leaves when Father and Son come by a reference to the final clause of 14,16, *ut uobiscum sit in aeternum*.[14] Father, Son, and Spirit are one, therefore, because their operation is one.

The Latin fathers also see the unity of the Godhead in Jo. 16, 15 (and context), though this insight does not seem ever to be used as a formal proof of the unity. In general, the three persons are shown to be perfectly equal and one because they possess all things (e.g., eternity) in common.[15] Specifically, all that the Son has he has received through unity of substance from the Father (16,15a), and all that the Spirit has he has through unity of substance from the Son without the medium of any organ of hearing and without receiving anything he did not already have (16,15b and context). In this common possession of all things is to be seen, therefore, the essential oneness of the Godhead; it also explains why neither Son nor Spirit can be said to speak anything from themselves.[16] Although the details differ, the appeals to paraclete passages to show community of name, action, and possession have their parallels among the Greeks.[17]

Christology

Paraclete passages also relate to the Christological controversies of this era in ways analogous to developments in the more prolific Greek East.[18] The Son is not inferior to the Father because, as Jo. 16,15 shows, he possesses all the things which the Father has.[19] This verse, on the contrary, shows clearly that the Son is both equal[20] and consubstantial[21] with the Father. Hilary, making a somewhat different approach, sees the unity of nature between

Father and Son in 16,15 on the ground that what the Spirit receives
from the Son (16,15b) he necessarily also receives from the Father
because of their community of possession (16,15a).[22] Not only is
the Son equal and consubstantial with the Father, but Ambrose shows
that he is good: the Spirit is good; since, therefore, he receives
of the Son's (16,15b), the Son must also be good.[23] And, finally,
because there is nothing of the Godhead lacking to the Son (16,15a),
he is himself God.[24]

From their writings we are also able to see rather clearly
how the Latin fathers understand the word *omnia* in 16,15. It refers,
not to anything created, i.e., not to anything Jesus might possess
external to himself, though it were the entire universe, but to
the properties and attributes of the divine nature. The Son possesses by nature all that the Father is.[25] This means that the Son
possesses (and *omnia* includes) in common with the Father such divine
properties as Godhead, eternity, sovereignty, omnipotence,[26] the
divine will,[27] the divine power,[28] and the divine life;[29] the two are
of one substance.[30] *Omnia* also includes the Father's knowledge and
particularly knowledge of the precise moment of the end; for Jo. 16,15
is enlisted to show that the Son cannot be ignorant of the day and
hour, as would seem to be suggested by Mt. 24,36 and Mk. 13,32.[31]

Pneumatology

The subordination of the Spirit to the Son (and the Son to the
Father) is a distinct feature of Arian dogma. According to the Arian
bishop Maximinus, whose verbatim debate with Augustine is extant, Arians
believe in one God the Father from whom all illumination descends by
steps to all. The Son receives from the Father; the Spirit, who gives
it to the apostles and saints, receives from the Son. Maximinus sup-

ports this scheme in part by a quotation of Jo. 16,12-14.[32] Augustine,
however, does not see any subordinationism in these verses. The Spirit
is to receive from the Son (as the Son from the Father) only in the
sense that the words *omnia quae habet pater mea sunt* are true. Therefore, what the Spirit receives is from the Father.[33] Nor is the
fact that the Spirit is to speak only what he hears indicative of
subordinationism; for it is because of his procession from the Father
that he is said not to speak from himself.[34] Furthermore, the Spirit
cannot be said to be inferior to Father and Son because he is said to
be sent (cf. Jo. 14,26; 15,26; 16,7) since this is said only with
respect to those corporeal signs which, like the dove and tongues of
fire, manifest themselves in time.[35] If the Spirit is not inferior
to the Son, neither is he superior, despite the fact that he descended
upon him at the baptism. The Spirit was upon Christ as Son of man,
but as God he is not over him but dwells in him. This the fathers
proof-text from Jo. 16,14-15.[36]

     So the Spirit, being neither superior nor inferior to Father
and Son, is equal to them. His oneness with them in nature and Godhead is also shown in various other ways: that the Spirit is one with
the Son in nature and substance is to be seen in the fact that both
are paracletes; in designating the Spirit *alius paracletus* in Jo. 14,16
the Lord shows himself to be a paraclete also, a thing made explicit
in 1 Jo. 2,1. It is also to be seen in the fact that both are shown
to be truth; the Lord is himself truth, as in Jo. 14,6, and the Spirit
is the Spirit of truth, as in 14,17.26; 16,13.[37] The Spirit is shown
from paraclete passages to be of one substance and deity with Father
and Son in that he shares in all their operations. Specifically, as
the Father bears testimony to the Son with men, so does, according to
15,26, the Spirit.[38] The Saviour further shows the Spirit's identity

with the Godhead in nature and substance when he says concerning him *a patre procedit* (15,26) and *de meo accipiet* (16,14.15). The exegesis of the former clause is rather straightforward: it means that the Spirit proceeds from and is one with the Father's substance.[39] The reasoning concerning the second clause is only slightly more convoluted: the Son, in saying *omnia quae patris sunt mea sunt* (16,15, cf. 17,10) signifies the Father's substance to be his own. When he adds *de meo accipiet* he shows that the Spirit, who proceeds from the Father, must also have (via the Son, it is implied) the Father's substance.[40]

Paraclete passages, especially Jo. 15,26, are used to support the doctrine of the procession.[41] Indeed, Augustine sees in them evidence for the doctrine of the procession of the Spirit from both Father and Son. That the Spirit is the Spirit of both Father and Son he maintains from (among other things) a juxtaposition of Christ's words *quem ego mitto uobis a patre* (15,26) and *quem mittet pater in nomine meo* (14,26). That he proceeds from both is shown by *de patre procedit* (15,26) with respect to the Father and from the insufflation of 20,22 with respect to the Son.[42] Ambrose makes two comments which are germane both to his exegesis of 15,26 and to his doctrine of the procession. First, he observes that when the Spirit proceeds from the Father and Son he is in no way separated from them; because all three persons are present in each, when the Spirit comes down so do Son and Father.[43] Similarly, he insists that we are not to infer from 15,26 that the Spirit's mission and procession actually involve movement from place to place. Such a conception would make Father, Son, and Spirit corporeal and locally circumscribed, both of which are inimical to what we already know to be true about God.[44]

Polemical writings

Montanism and Manichaeism are not isolated Greek phenomena. It becomes necessary, therefore, that catholic writers in the West counter their teachings, and especially (for our purposes here) their respective claims that the Lord's promise of the paraclete was fulfilled in Montanus and Manichaeus.[45] The main argument against this claim insists that Montanists and Manichaeans cannot apply the paraclete passages to themselves for the simple reason that the promises have already been fulfilled in apostolic times on the day of Pentecost.[46] This is identical to one of the arguments used by the Greek fathers.[47] Augustine offers a second rationale which does not seem to have any direct Eastern parallel. He points to the words of Jo. 16,13, *ipse uos inducet in omnem ueritatem*, and insists that the teaching of Manichaeus cannot be from the Paraclete on the ground that one cannot be led into all truth by one who claims that Christ is a deceiver, as he has shown that Manichaeus does.[48] There are other arguments against the Montanist and Manichaean claims, of course, but these are the two which arise out of and exhibit exegesis of paraclete passages.

EXEGETICAL WRITINGS

Strictly speaking, we possess no commentary on the Gospel of John from the Latin fathers who wrote between 325 and 451 A.D. We do have, however, an exposition of the whole Gospel in Augustine's 124 Tractates In Iohannis Euangelium composed in Hippo in the years ca. 413-418.[49] This is the work which, supplemented *passim* from other writings, forms the basis for our consideration of the more forthrightly exegetical Latin writing on the paraclete passages. As in Chapter 2 above, we organise our discussion according to the order of the Biblical materials.

<u>14,15-17</u>

Commenting on Rom. 8,38, Pelagius explores in a passing way the relationship between the love of Christ and the keeping of the commandments; for him Jo. 14,15 means that the loving consists of the keeping.[50] But the monk from Britain is virtually alone in even noticing those implications of Jo. 14,15 which Origen and the Greeks discuss at some length. [51] Slightly more attention is paid to the question of the identity of the Paraclete of 14,16, though the answer is widely assumed and therefore seldom commented on directly. According to the fathers, the Paraclete-Spirit of truth promised in these verses by Jesus is the same Spirit spoken of by others, writers such as Isaiah (57,16, implied), Moses (Num. 11,29), Joel (2,28), Zachariah (1,6; 12,10);[52] he is the same who spoke in the prophets and apostles and is elsewhere called the Spirit of God and Christ, Spirit of life, Holy Spirit, et al.;[53] he is that Holy Spirit of the Trinity which is consubstantial and coeternal with Father and Son.[54]

For Augustine Jo. 14,15-17 poses a conundrum not apparent to the mentality of the East. The disciples are here commanded to love Jesus and keep his commandments as a condition for receiving the Holy Spirit. But how are they to love and obey in order to receive him without whom they can do neither?[55] Is Jesus saying that the prior love of himself somehow makes us worthy to receive the Spirit who in turn enables us to love God the Father (a reference to Rom. 5,5)? Augustine rejects such an interpretation on the ground that it is impossible to love the Son truly without also loving the Father.[56] He further points out that the disciples manifestly loved Jesus in that they acknowledged him Lord, a thing which we know from 1 Cor. 12,3 no one can do who does not have the Holy Spirit.[57] Augustine resolves the puzzle this way: he who loves has the Holy Spirit already and by that merits a fuller possession so that, having more, he loves more. The

disciples both had and lacked in the sense that they already had the

Spirit in a limited, hidden way, but were yet to receive him in the

ampler, manifest way promised by the Lord. Indeed, the present pos-

session is necessary to the conscious knowledge of the fuller gift.[58]

Ambrosiaster faces a similar question in his book of Quaes-

tiones. His interlocutor wants to know whether the apostles pos-

sessed the Spirit while the Lord was yet with them because he is con-

fused by a juxtaposition of Jo. 7,39, 14,15-17, 20,22, and Ac. 2,1-4.

With respect to what appear to be multiple bestowals, Ambrosiaster sug-

gests that, while the Spirit is one, his gifts are many and that, when

Spiritus sanctus is read in these passages, we are to understand not

the person himself but his office.[59] Sorting out the seeming contra-

diction in Jo. 14,15-17 requires a different approach: what Jesus says

here about the Spirit is said, not of his person, but of his nature.

In nature he is indivisible from Christ and must be considered present

wherever he is. In this sense it is true that the Spirit is both

present with the disciples and about to come to them; for he is

present in Christ with whom he is consubstantial. It is in this sense,

then, that Jesus says, when he promises that the Spirit is about to

come, *uos uidetis eum, quia apud uos manet et uobiscum est.*[60]

Three individual items of exegesis arise out of specific

elements in these verses rather than from the passage as a whole.

From 14,16 the Latin fathers gather that not only is the Holy Spirit

a Paraclete but that Jesus is one, as well. This exegesis is based

primarily on the phrase *alium paracletum*; Jesus' designation of the

coming Paraclete as *alius* in this context is tantamount to a declara-

tion that he is himself a paraclete.[61] But it is also supported

from time to time by a reference to 1 Jo. 2,1 which specifically calls

Jesus our Paraclete with the Father.[62] This understanding is entirely
conformable to Greek exegesis of the same phrase.[63] Less conformable
is Augustine's understanding of the term *mundus* in 14,17 which he
takes to refer to those who love the world (in the sense of Rom 8,7)
with a love not of the Father and in direct opposition to the love of
God shed abroad in our hearts by the Holy Spirit. The world can
neither receive nor see nor know the Spirit, therefore, because worldly
love lacks those invisible eyes without which the Holy Spirit cannot
be seen.[64] The third item is Augustine's exegesis of *uos autem
cognoscetis eum, quia apud uos manebit, et in uobis erit,* concerning
which he makes two comments: firstly, he suggests that this must be
understood to mean that the Paraclete will be in (*in*) the disciples
in order to dwell with them, rather than vice-versa, because being
anywhere is prior to dwelling there.[65] Secondly, he explains that the
words *in uobis erit* are epexegetic upon *apud uos manebit* and are added lest we imagine the Spirit to be with us in any physical sense.[66]
He is, rather, seen in an invisible way and, as with a man's conscience, cannot be known unless he be in us. The difference, of
course, is that, while a man's conscience can only be within the man,
the Spirit may also be apart from us.[67]

14,25-26

The scanty exegesis on Jo. 14,25-26 may be arranged into three
sections, the first of which contains interpretations of the language
of location found in the passage. Augustine considers the Lord's
words in 14,25, especially *apud uos manens*, and contrasts the manner
of dwelling spoken of here with that promised in the verses preceding:
this dwelling is corporeal, temporary, outward, and visible; that is
future, spiritual, and inward. When Jesus says *haec locutus sum uobis,*

therefore, he is referring to those things spoken with the disciples while he was with them in the flesh.[68] Gaudentius of Brescia points out that these verses announce both Christ's return to the heavens after the passion and the coming of the Spirit from the same place. But he enters the caveat that such language is anthropomorphic and is not in any sense to be understood to imply that Father, Son, and Spirit are locally circumscribed.[69]

A second group of patristic passages relate 14,25-26 to Trinitarian doctrine. Augustine warns that we are not to infer from these verses any separation of role between Spirit and Son. It is not somehow Jesus' peculiar function to speak and the Spirit's to teach; for, as he concludes from a series of Scripture references, what one member of the Trinity does all do.[70] Rather, the members of the Godhead are introduced individually precisely so that we might recognise the Trinity of personality in the one nature.[71] Gaudentius interprets the text in the light of the catholic doctrine of the indivisible nature when he suggests that *in nomine meo* is equivalent to saying *in dei nomine*; the name of the Father is in the Son.[72] In a similar way he writes that the Son, in telling us that the fulness of his doctrine is to come through the Spirit, intends us to believe him his equal in omnipotence; for there is no division in the Trinity.[73]

Thirdly, we look at several items from the Aduersus Arium of C. Marius Victorinus. Three of them are from Ar. 1,12. At the beginning of this chapter Victorinus has arrived at the point in his argument where he asserts that, if God, Jesus, and the Spirit are all Spirit, then they are ὁμοούσιος.[74] In this context he reveals something of his exegesis of 14,26 when he quotes it to demonstrate that the Paraclete is from the Son; it also shows that God is in Christ

and Christ in the Spirit.[75] Victorinus goes on to suggest on the
strength of this verse, that the Spirit's message will be identical
with Christ's. The difference is that, whereas with Christ in the flesh
all things were hidden through parables and signs, with the Spirit all
things will be spoken openly to the spirits of men. It is on this account that Jesus said *ipse docebit uos*.[76] Further, Victorinus draws
attention to the future *dixero* and exegetes that it refers the Spirit's
coming not to the immediate future but to the time after Christ's
ascension.[77] Finally, in Ar. 3,15 he exegetes *in nomine meo* to mean
pro me.[78]

15,26-27

        The even scantier exegesis on Jo. 15,26-27 is essentially lim-
ited to one comment on each verse, both by the Bishop of Hippo. He
first explores the meaning of 15,26, placing it squarely within the
context of the preceding verse and bringing to it the illumination
of his high view of the atonement. For him the shed blood of Christ
was so efficacious that it could cover even the sin of shedding it. It
is in this light that he understands the words of Jesus in this passage to suggest that such will be the testimony of the Paraclete that
he will bring even those who hated the Lord and did him to death when
he lived among them to believe in him now that he is no longer visible
to sight. He sees this as having been preeminently fulfilled on the
day of Pentecost.[79] Augustine then turns to an exposition of 15,27:
as the Spirit, so shall the disciples witness to Christ. Indeed, they
are already capable of bearing testimony to him by virtue of having
been present with him in his earthly ministry. It is lack of courage
which stops their mouths at present, but when the Spirit comes he is
to give them the courage they need. Again, Augustine attributes to these
words of Jesus a prevision of the events of the day of Pentecost.[80]

16,4b-15

According to Augustine of Hippo, *haec* in Jo. 16,4b does not refer to the sufferings which Jesus has just said are coming to the disciples; for so to take it would be prejudicial to the credibility of the other Gospels, particularly St. Matthew. They show Jesus announcing the coming trials not only prior to the Last Supper on the eve of his passion (cf. Mt. 24,9; Mk. 13,9-13; Lc. 21,12-17) but in the very beginning of his ministry on the occasion of the commissioning of the Twelve (cf. Mt. 10,17). No, *haec* here refers to all Jesus says in this context about the coming of the Spirit to bear witness at the time when they would have such distress. He has not told them these things previously because, while he was with them, they, spiritual infants as they were, were comforted (*consolabantur*) through his bodily presence (*corporali praesentia*), the only thing they could comprehend (implied). Now that he is going away the Comforter or Advocate[81] has become necessary, and on the eve of his departure Jesus must speak with the disciples of the coming Spirit through whom they will be hardened to bear persecution and emboldened to witness to Christ.[82]

Augustine's interpretation of Jo. 16,5 is unique; for, rather than seeing in the verse an untimely, fear-induced muteness, he sees Jesus saying that his departure (into heaven) is to be of such a nature that the disciples will see and not this time need to ask *quo uadis* as they did when he announced it a short time before (cf. Jo. 13,36).[83] His exegesis of 16,6-7 is, however, conformable to exegesis found in Greek fathers.[84] In 16,6, he says, Jesus reveals that he is aware of the effect his words are having on the disciples. Not yet having in them the spiritual consolation they are later to have by the Spirit, and perceiving that they are about to lose what they possess in Jesus, they are understandably saddened. But Jesus has to speak,

for he knows what is better for them, namely, that inward vision to
be brought to their hearts by the Holy Spirit. If the disciples are
not weaned from their (spiritually) infantile dependency on the physical presence of Jesus, they will never learn to relish the solid
food requisite to spiritual maturity; they will never have room for
the Spirit.[85] For, in Augustine's exegesis, it is the meaning of
Jo. 16,7 (cf. 2 Cor. 5,16) that the disciples are incapable of receiving the Spirit so long as they know Christ in the flesh.[86] The
Bishop of Hippo goes on to note that it is not in place of Jesus that
the Spirit comes; though Jesus is physically to depart, he and the
Father are still with the disciples spiritually along with the Spirit
with whom they are coessential. Any disjunction in the Godhead apparent in this passage is not real but arises from the necessity of
presenting to notice the distinction of the three persons, though
there is no diversity of essence among them.[87]

    We discover when we come to Jo. 16,8-11 that those fathers
who do comment demonstrate a high degree of unanimity in their understanding of these verses and that their exegeses are generally quite
conformable to those found in the more highly speculative Greek
fathers.[88] The difference between the writings of East and West where
the exegesis on these verses is analogous is one of tone and detail
rather than of understanding. The comments of Augustine and Ambrosiaster on 16,8 itself do not overlap, but it is unlikely that they would
seriously disagree. Augustine maintains that *ille arguet mundum de
peccato, et de iustitia, et de iudicio* does not mean that Jesus himself does not also reprove the world;[89] rather, it is said because it
is the Holy Spirit who is going to put into the disciples' hearts the
love which casts out that fear which would have kept them from reproving the world.[90] Ambrosiaster, whose exegesis, always restrained

and insightful, is especially appealing with respect to these verses,
wonders what *arguere mundum* in 16,8 means; he decides it means showing
the world that those things it does not want to believe are true.[91]
And in what manner has the world been reproved by the Spirit since
his coming? In this way: in the name of the condemned Saviour many
miracles were accomplished by the disciples; healings, resuscitations,
exorcisms, and the like (he gives a long list).[92] But the Lord's
meaning in 16,8 is made more fully plain in the verses which follow;
for they are epexegetic upon it.[93]

The univocal exegesis of 16,9 is that the sin of which the
Spirit is to convict the world[94] is the sin of not believing on Jesus,
that sin which led it ultimately to do him to death.[95] But 16,9 does
not speak simply of believing that Jesus is the Christ; it does not
speak of a mere credendum. As the Bishop of Hippo points out, even
the devils believe that. Rather, this verse speaks of believing
on (*in*) Christ in faith, a thing quite different from mere intellectual assent. That man believes on Christ who both hopes in and loves
him; to such a man Christ comes and with him unites himself.[96] Jesus
singles out this sole sin for comment here because it is, as it were,
the fountainhead of all sins. In the sin of unbelief are all sins
retained; but through faith in Christ all are remitted.[97]

There are two basic interpretations of Jo. 16,10 and the
iustitia to which it refers. The first, the simpler and perhaps
more appealing of the two, belongs to the Quaestiones of Ambrosiaster.
According to it, it is the righteousness of Jesus concerning which the
Spirit is to convict the world. For one of the things the world did
not want to believe was that the Saviour came from God. But by
returning to God he proved that he came from there, since no one has
ascended to God save he who descended from God (Jo. 3,13). And it

is this return to God that the Spirit will use to demonstrate Jesus'
righteousness.[98] Similar reasoning is found in Victorinus[99] and in
St. Augustine.[100] This, it will be remembered, is essentially the
approach of John Chrysostom.[101]

But, although Augustine seems to share this exegesis of 16,10
in one passage, his main thrust seems to be in another direction: it
is his exegesis in, e.g., the Tractates on John that it is the righteousness of believers concerning which the world is to be reproved.[102]
It is manifestly not to be reproved of its own righteousness; for how
can the same man who has been reproved of sin also be convicted of
righteousness?[103] Nor is the *iustitia* of 16,10 to be identified with
any state of sinlessness: there is no one who is without sin, and
even the righteous are open to reproof.[104] Rather, the righteousness
of believers concerning which the world is to be reproved is the righteousness of faith in the unseen Jesus who we know is unseen because he
has returned to the Father.[105] If the Spirit is to reprove the world
of the vice of unfaith with respect to the Jesus it did see, he is
also to convict it of the virtue of faith, i.e., the righteousness, of
those who have faith though they are never again to see their Lord in
his humbled and earthly guise.[106] And, indeed, there is no faith by
which one lives except the one believed on is unseen.[107] This is in
essence the line taken by, among others, Cyril of Alexandria.[108]

As is usual in the ancient Christian world, the Latin fathers
agree in identifying the *princeps huius mundi* with, simply, the
Devil.[109] Augustine goes further to specify the sense in which the
title is true: the Devil is not the ruler of the physical *mundus*,
the universe and all that is in it. Rather, he is ruler of the same
mundus spoken of in Jo. 1,10, namely, the world of unbelieving men.[110]
The fathers also agree in seeing the Christ whom the world rejected

as both the agent of judgment and the judge who condemns the *princeps huius mundi* to judgment,[111] a condemnation to everlasting fire.[112] Augustine, again, adds an independent insight to patristic exegesis: for him, it is not solely of the judgment of its prince that the world is reproved. As believers are identified with the righteousness of Christ (see on 16,10 above), so also is there a similar solidarity between the Devil and his servants. For this reason, the world is also convinced that its own condemnation is imminent; for, in Satan's judgment is its own implicit.[113]

Unlike the Greek writers, Augustine refuses to discuss what the *multa* of Jo. 16,12 are which the disciples cannot yet bear, and unlike Tertullian, he makes no attempt to refer to this verse teachings with little support in the rest of Scripture. He simply refuses to speculate about things which he and his hearers might be as unready as the apostles to understand. What is clear from the Saviour's words, he says, is that the disciples were not yet able to bear the *multa* because they had not yet received the Spirit.[114] But, even granted that the Spirit has come and many can now bear what the apostles could not then bear, and though these things may now be common knowledge, it is impossible to identify even the profound truths of Scripture written after the Spirit's coming with the *multa* of 16,12 because nowhere in Scripture is such an identification made explicit.[115] But, though Augustine refuses to speculate on specifics, it is clear from his writing that he is in complete agreement with Greek teaching that the things, now deferred, which the Spirit will teach are the deep mysteries of the Christian faith.[116] He goes on to admonish his hearers to grow in that love given by the Spirit that they may receive his teaching[117] and to warn them against the many profane and ensnaring doctrines taught by those who appeal to 16,12 for justification.[118]

The Bishop of Hippo also draws two related ethical principles
from Jo. 16,12 which are quite unlike anything written, East or West,
before him. First, from the fact that Jesus himself is here seen
to conceal certain truths from the disciples, he concludes that it
is not always culpable to refrain from speaking what is true, especially if those who are to hear are unable to bear or will receive
harm in the hearing. (It is, however, always wrong to speak falsehood.)[119] Sometimes, then, it is more useful for truth to be kept
back because of the inability of those who hear to understand, just
as the Lord himself in 16,12 condescends to the weakness of the
disciples.[120] From this thinking Augustine develops, secondly, the
negative principle that truth must not be given out which is beyond
the ability of the hearers to receive[121] and the positive principle
that souls are, and (by implication) ought to be, taught according to
the level of their maturity.[122]

On 16,13 Augustine makes more than one comment. As with *multa*
of the previous verse, he does not usually discuss the specific content of *omnem ueritatem*, though he does at one point imply that the
term includes the secret things of God.[123] But he does stress that,
although the promise that we shall know *omnem ueritatem*, whatever
that may or may not include, cannot be completely fulfilled so long
as we inhabit these corruptible and soul-corrupting bodies, we nevertheless have during the present life the earnest, in the person of the
Spirit, of that full truth the Lord promises. For, though full revelation is reserved for the next life, he teaches believers in proportion to their capability of apprehending and growing in things
spiritual.[124]

What does Jesus mean by the words *non enim loquetur a semetipso,
sed quaecumque audiet loquetur*? When he spoke the similar words of

Jo. 5,30 he was speaking with reference to his own human nature. But
here he is speaking of the Holy Spirit who assumed no humanity, no
angelic nature, and no creaturely nature. How, then Augustine wonders,
are we to understand these words from Jo. 16,13?[125] They are to be
understood in this way: the Spirit speaks not of himself because he
is not of himself but of the Father, who alone has the property of
being from himself,[126] from whom he proceeds. The Spirit has both
his essence and his knowledge through his procession from the Father,
and it is in this sense of having his knowledge, as his being, from
the Father that he may anthropomorphically be said to hear.[127] Because the Spirit is a consubstantial member of the Trinity, his knowing, and therefore his hearing, are eternal; with him hearing is
identical with knowing and knowing with being. We are not, therefore,
to be disturbed by the future *audiet*. Any tense of the verb would
be correct.[128] The following clauses, *et quae uentura sunt, annuntiabit uobis*, Augustine says are clear and need no interpretation.[129]

    Augustine makes various comments on Jo. 16,14.15, and it is
with a summary of these several points that we close our look at
paraclete exegesis among the Latin fathers of this era. Concerning
ille me clarificabit he tells us we are to understand that the Spirit
is to show believers how it is that the Son, whom they had previously
known only in the flesh and considered to be mere man, is equal with
the Father, or (*uel*), at the least, that the Spirit is so to free them
from fear and fill them with love that they would themselves spread
Jesus' fame. For what they were to do the Spirit was also to do.[130]
Augustine also points out that the Greek word δοξάσει, from δόξα, is
here translated by some writers with *clarificabit* and by others with
glorificabit. But, as the idea of the Greek δόξα may be translated
by both *clarus* and *gloria*, this is both right and, since by *gloria*

one is made *clarus* and by *claritas gloriosus*, uncontradictory.[131] But

we are not to suppose that when the Spirit glorified Christ he did any-

thing great for Christ himself; rather, he brought in so doing great

benefit to the world.[132]

Finally, Augustine insists on interpreting the final words of

16,14 (and 16,15), *de meo accipiet, et annuntiabit uobis*, in a way

which is entirely consonant with catholic dogma. For these words must

not be understood, as they are with certain heretics, to suggest that

the Spirit is subordinate to the Son in any way. That there is no

subordinationism here Jesus makes plain by the words of 16,15; for,

if the things of the Father belong to the Son, then *omnia quae habet*

Pater mea sunt is tantamount to saying that the Spirit, who receives

of the Son's things, receives from the same Father.[133] In the

Trinity, all three persons are equal and consubstantial.

NOTES

1.   See pp.27-28 above.

2.   Ambr., indeed, seems to have been the first Latin writer to com-
pose an independent work of any magnitude on the Holy Spirit. There
does seem to be little truly original in the book, though surely
this is better attributed to the author's good sense and humility than
to a spirit of plagiarism. Ambr. does not cite the paraclete passages
as often as his sources, on the whole, but where he does his approach
is rather different. He is not so concerned to cast them up as proof-
texts but tends more to exegete and expound them, drawing out their
full significance for the doctrine of the Holy Spirit.

3.   Indeed, several major figures such as Gregory and Jerome, refer
to them either seldom or not at all.

4.   Certain of Augustine's writings, particularly Trin., are less fruitful for this study than would be expected from an acquaintance with
Greek works on the same subjects. The explanation is to be found,
perhaps, in the fact that (unlike Ambr.) Aug. was not in his lifetime
often called upon to defend the Godhead of Spirit and Son. It is at
these points that the paraclete passages are most often invoked in
dogmatic writing, and neither is seriously in question after the
triumph of the Nicene faith at Constantinople in 381 and Ambrose'

success in 385 against an imperial attempt to reintroduce Arianism into Milan. To Augustine fell the task, rather, of erecting on the Nicene base a theology with appeal to Western forms of thought. See
H.B. Swete, The Holy Spirit in the Ancient Church (London, 1912),
322-323.

5. As in Chapter 2, it will be unnecessary to summarise the broader
context of every patristic passage cited; in most cases we will go
directly to the elements important to paraclete exegesis. For example, the broad context of a given book, chapter, or paragraph may
be in support of the consubstantiality of the three divine persons.
But if in its immediate context a portion of our material is quoted
as, say, evidence of the deity of the Son, then it will usually be
convenient to ignore the wider context and concentrate on the immediate. Similarly, in working with homiletical materials like the
Tractates of Augustine, we shall deal only with those elements important to the actual exegesis of paraclete passages.

6. See Ambr. Spir. 1,13,136-137 (CSEL 79,73-74) and Lc. 2,13 on
1,30-32 (CCL 14,35-36); cf. Aug. fund. 6 (CSEL 25,199) and Vic. Ar.
3,14 (CSEL 83,1,214). Cf. on Tert. p.12 above. (For a summary of
Victorinus' peculiar doctrine of the consubstantiality and of his
double dyade understanding of the Trinity see SCH 68,77-83. These
doctrines are sometimes based in part on Victorinus' exegesis of
paraclete passages, but because they fulfill neither our criterion of
being representative nor that of being important to the later history
of exegesis (whether through imitation or reaction) we do not pursue
them here.)

7. See Eus.Ver. Trin. 4,8 (CCL 9,58), 4,28-29 (CCL 9,63); Isaac I.
f.i. 3 (CCL 9,342). This is probably also the understanding of Aug.
Trin. 15,28,51 (CCL 50A, 533-534).

8. Ambr. Spir. 1,13,134 (CSEL 79,73). Ambr. has already in 1,12,
132 sought to establish the unity of the name by quoting Mt. 28,19
and suggesting that the singular nomine there is in support of his
thesis.

9. Ambr. Spir. 1,13,135-139 (CSEL 79,73-75). On the commonality
of the name paracletus Ambr. juxtaposes Jo. 14,16 with 1 Jo. 2,1.
(Note: for the sake of uniformity we adopt the spelling paracletus
in this thesis except when quoting a text which employs alternative
orthography.)

10. See Ambr. fid. 5,11,134 (CSEL 78,265), Neque enim verborum hic
[i.e., Jo. 12,50] aliquem significat auditum, sed unitatem voluntatis
atque virtutis, quae et in patre est et in filio. Quam etiam in
spiritu sancto esse memoravit alio loco dicens: Non enim loquitur a
se, sed quae audit loquitur, ut adverteremus quia quidquid spiritus
loquitur, loquitur et filius, et quidquid loquitur filius, loquitur
et pater, quia una sententia et operatio trinitatis est. Cf. Didym.
Spir. 30 (PG 39,1060). See also Ambr. Spir. 3,16,115 (CSEL 79,199)
and Prisc. Trin. (PLS 2,1498). Cf. the intriguing argument of Aug.
serm.Ar. 23 (PL 42,700) which also seeks the unity of the divine persons in the inseparability of their speaking: Quod enim dictum est,
Non a se loquetur: non est dictum, Quaecumque a me audierit; sed,

*quaecumque audierit loquetur. Cur autem dictum sit, paulo ante jam
claruit ex ipsius quam commemoravi Domini expositione, ubi ait, Omnia
quae habet Pater, mea sunt; propterea dixi, De meo accipiet. Unde
autem accipiet, inde est procul dubio quod loquetur; quia inde audit,
unde procedit. Scit enim Dei Verbum, procedendo inde unde nascitur
Verbum, ita ut sit communiter Spiritus et Patris et Verbi.*

11. See Ambr. Spir. 3,6,35 (CSEL 79,164).

12. See Aug. serm.Ar. 4 (PL 42,686), *Nec a solo Filio missus est,
sicut scriptum est, Cum ego iero, mittam illum ad vos; sed a Patre
quoque, sicut scriptum est, Quem mittet Pater in nomine meo. Ubi
ostenditur quod nec Pater sine Filio, nec Filius sine Patre misit
Spiritum sanctum, sed eum pariter ambo miserunt. Inseparabilia quippe
sunt opera Trinitatis.* See also Ambr. Spir. 3,1,8 (CSEL 79,153);
Aug. Ps. 102,10 (CCL 40,1461), serm.Ar. 19 (PL 42,697), Trin. 1,12,
25 (CCL 50,64), 4,20,29 (CCL 50,200); and Vic. Ar. 1,13 (CSEL 83,1,72),
3,15 (CSEL 83,1,217); cf. Prisc. Trin. (PLS 2,1498). Note that in
these passages Aug. harmonises the apparent discrepancy between 14,
26, 15,26, and other paraclete passages with respect to who actually
sends the Paraclete by teaching that both Father and Son do so in
a community of action. Indeed, nowhere in his writing does Aug. seem
to recognise that there might in fact be any such discrepancy; his Nicene faith seems everywhere to colour his exegesis at this point.

13. See Aug. serm.Ar. 19 (PL 42,697), *Porro Scriptura sancta, quae
istos divinos actus non differentia potestatum, sed operum ineffabili-
tate metitur, advocatum nostrum etiam ipsum judicem novit, dicente
apostolo Joanne: Si quis peccaverit, advocatum habemus ad patrem,
Jesum Christum justum. Quod etiam ipse significat ubi dicit, Rogabo
Patrem, et alium advocatum dabit vobis. Neque enim esset Spiritus
sanctus advocatus alius, nisi hoc esset et Filius.*

14. Aug. Trin. 1,9,19 (CCL 50,55-56), *Non itaque ab hac mansione
separatus est de quo dictum est, uobiscum manet et in uobis est.
Nisi forte quisquam sic absurdus est ut arbitretur cum pater et filius
uenerint ut mansionem faciant apud dilectorem suum, discessurum
inde spiritum sanctum et tamquam locum daturum esse maioribus. Sed
et huic carnali cogitationi occurrit scriptura; paulo quippe superius
ait: Et ego rogabo patrem, et alium aduocatum dabit uobis ut uobiscum sit in aeternum. Non ergo discedet patre et filio uenientibus,
sed in eadem mansione cum ipsis erit in aeternum quia nec ille sine
ipsis uenit nec illi sine illo.*

15. See Leo tract. 75,3 (CCL 138A,467-468) who, after quoting Jo.
16,12-13.15, says, *Non ergo alia sunt Patris, alia Filii, alia Spiritus
sancti, sed omnia quae habet Pater, habet et Filius, habet et Spiritus
sanctus, nec umquam in illa unitate non fuit ista communio, quia
hoc est ibi omnia habere, quod semper existere.* Cf. tract. 77,6
(CCL 138A,492-493). Cf. also Ambr. i.d.s. 8,84 (CSEL 79,266) and
Ambrstr. Eph. 2,17 (PL 17,384).

16. See Ambr. Spir. 2,12,131-134 (CSEL 79,137-139), *Omnia patris
habet filius, quia iterum ait: Omnia, quae pater habet, mea sunt.
Et quae accepit ipse per unitatem naturae, ex ipso per eandem unitatem
naturae accepit et spiritus, sicut ipse dominus Iesus declarat de
spiritu suo dicens: Propterea dixi: de meo accipiet et adnuntiabit*

*vobis. Quod ergo loquitur spiritus, fili est, quod dedit filius,
patris est* (134 (CSEL 79,138-139)). See also Ambr. <u>Spir</u>. 2,11,118
(CSEL 79,132). Cf. Aug. <u>serm</u>.<u>Ar</u>. 23 (PL 42,700) who seems to understand Jo. 16,15 in much the same way.

17. See above pp.32 and 37-39.

18. See, e.g., pp.32-35 above.

19. See Ambr. <u>fid</u>. 5,18,224 (CSEL 78,302), *In quo enim minor,
qui <u>omnia</u> habet, <u>quae</u> <u>pater</u> <u>habet</u>?*

20. See Aug. <u>Max</u>.<u>haer</u>. 2,20,3 (PL 42,789) and <u>Trin</u>. 1,11,23 and
context (CCL 50,61).

21. See Ambrstr. <u>quaest</u>. 125,1 (CSEL 50,385); Hil. <u>Trin</u>. 9,73 (PL
10,339); Vic. <u>Ar</u>. 1,15 (CSEL 83,1,75), 1,19 (CSEL 83,1,85), 2,7
(CSEL 83,1,180-181); cf. Gaud. <u>tract</u>. 14,2 (CSEL 68,125).

22. Hil. <u>Trin</u>. 8,19-20 (PL 10,250-252). (Hil. <u>Trin</u>. 8,19 (PL 10,
250) also sees the unity in 15,26 in the fact that the *Spiritus
veritatis* who proceeds from the Father is also sent by the Son. His
meaning is not explicitly clear, but apparently Hil. sees unity of
nature here because he sees something like unity of action. Cf.
Ambr. <u>fid</u>. 2,9,76 (CSEL 78,83-84).)

23. Ambr. <u>Spir</u>. 1,5,70 (CSEL 79,45), *Unde et illud intellegitur,
quam amentes sint, qui bonum filium dei abnegant, cum bonum spiritum
Christi negare non possint, de quo ait dei filius:* <u>Propterea</u> <u>dixi</u>
'de <u>meo</u> <u>accipiet</u>'.

24. See Hil. <u>Trin</u>. 7,12 (PL 10,209) and 8,52 (PL 10,275).

25. See Ambr. <u>fid</u>. 2,4,38 (CSEL 78,69-70) and 3,16,134 (CSEL 78,155-
156); Hil. <u>Trin</u>. 9,31 (PL 10,305) and 9,73 (PL 10,339-340), cf. 2,7
(PL 10,57).

26. See Ambr. <u>fid</u>. 2,4,38 (CSEL 78,69-70), *Quae sunt omnia? Non
utique locutus est de creatis; haec enim facta per filium. Sed ea
quae <u>pater</u> <u>habet</u>, id est aeternitatem, maiestatem divinitatemque
nascendo possedit. Ergo eum, qui <u>omnia</u> habet, <u>quae</u> <u>pater</u> <u>habet</u> . . .
omnipotentem esse dubitare non possumus.*

27. See Ambr. <u>fid</u>. 2,6,51 (CSEL 78,74), *Quamquam cum dixerit:* <u>Omnia,</u>
<u>quae</u> <u>pater</u> <u>habet</u>, <u>mea</u> <u>sunt</u>, *sine dubio, quia nihil excipitur, quam
pater habet, eandem habet et filius voluntatem.*

28. See Eus.Ver. <u>Trin</u>. 11(8),37 (CCL 9,155), *Nam deus uerbum et
deus filius, qui est sapientia, uirtus, potestas et uoluntas patris,
omnem semper paternam habuit et habet potestatem, ipso dicente:* <u>Omnia</u>
<u>quaecumque</u> <u>habet</u> <u>pater</u> . . .

29. See Aug. <u>Max</u>.<u>haer</u>. 2,14,7 (PL 42,774), *Sed <u>vitam</u> <u>Filius</u>, inquit,
<u>accepit</u> <u>a</u> <u>Patre</u>. Accepit sicut genitus a gignente.* <u>Omnia</u>, *inquit,*
<u>quae</u> <u>habet</u> <u>Pater</u>, <u>mea</u> <u>sunt</u>.

30. See Ambr. fid. 3,14,109 (CSEL 78,147) who quotes 16,15 to support
the proposition *Quod unius sit Filius cum Patre substantiae* and shows
thereby that in his exegesis *omnia* includes the divine *substantia*.

31. See Ambrstr. Mt. (PLS 1,666) and Aug. serm.V.T. 16A,11 (CCL 41,
228). Ambr. Spir. 2,11,114-118 (CSEL 79,131-133) handles the problem implied for Nicene Christology by Mk. 13,32 somewhat differently
from Aug. and the Greek writers, at least insofar as the paraclete
materials are concerned. He infers from Jo. 16,13 that the Spirit
possesses all knowledge in common with Father and Son and is ignorant
of nothing (2,11,114-115): *Qui dicit 'omnem', nihil praeterit, non
diem non horam, non praeterita non futura.* Then, noticing that the
Spirit is left out of the Markan list of ignorants, he concludes that
the Spirit does know the day and hour of the end. He suggests that
the Son is included in the list with respect to his human nature
(2,11,116-117). But he also points out that what the Spirit knows
he has through consubstantiality with the Son just as the Son has it
of the Father; that is what Jo. 16,14-15 means. He concludes, therefore, that the Son is not ignorant of the time of the end as Son of
God, with respect, that is, to his divine nature (2,11,118). Cf.
Ambrstr. Mt. (PLS 1,666) also in this regard.

32. See Aug. Max. 5 (PL 42,711), *Nos enim unum auctorem Deum Patrem
cognoscimus, a quo illuminatio omnis per gradus descendit.*

33. See Aug. Max. 11 (PL 42,714), Parm. 2,15,34 (CSEL 51,88), Trin.
2,3,5 (CCL 50,85-86).

34. Aug. Trin. 2,3,5 (CCL 50,85-86).

35. See Aug. Trin. 2,5,7-2,7,12 (CCL 50,87-96).

36. See Ambr. Spir. 3,1,6 (CSEL 79,151), *Nam secundum divinitatem
non super Christum est spiritus, sed in Christo, quia sicut pater in
filio et filius in patre, ita dei spiritus et spiritus Christi et
in patre est et in filio, quia oris est spiritus. Manet enim in deo,
qui ex deo est, ... Et manet in Christo, quia a Christo accipit
et in Christo est, quia iterum scriptum est: Ille de meo accipiet
. . . ;* and Max.Tur. epiph. (JTS 16,166).

37. See Ambrstr. quaest. 97,15 (CSEL 50, 181-182) and 125,23 (CSEL 50
392); Leo ep.16,3 (PL 54,699-700).

38. See Pel. Trin. fragment 4 (PLS 1,1549-1550). Pel. attempts to
show through this part of the fragment *Quod autem eiusdem sit sanctus
spiritus cuius pater et filius substantiae, ex hoc absolutissime
perdocetur quod quaecumque pater uel filius, eadem etiam facere
spiritus sanctus ostenditur.* See also Aug. Script. 3 (CSEL 12,
320-321) who quotes Jo. 14,15-17.25-26; 15,26-27; 16,6-7.12-15 as
part of a great catena in support of this statement: *Item de Spiritu
sancto, quod cooperator sit Patris et Fili et quod unius cum Patre
et Filio Spiritus sanctus substantiae sit atque deitatis* (CSEL 12,315).

39. See Ambr. Spir. 2,5,42 (CSEL 79,102); Ambrstr. quaest. 125,6
(CSEL 50,386-387); Eus.Ver. Trin. 4,11 (CCL 9,59), 7,9 (CCL 9,95),
11(8),1 (CCL 9,149), 11(8),70-71 (CCL 9,160). (It is interesting to
note in the light of the uncertain authorship of the various parts of

Eus.Ver. Trin. that book 11 in particular, and all twelve books in
general, contain collections of proof-texts and text-juxtapositions in
support of its arguments which are more interesting than the usual
Latin collections and certainly as subtle as anything in the Greek
fathers.)

40. See Ambrstr. quaest. 125,5-6 (CSEL 50,386-387). Cf. Ambr. Spir.
3,19,152 (CSEL 79,214) and Eus.Ver. Trin. 4,11 (CCL 9,59).

41. Most often, writers merely quote the appropriate clause from
Jo. 15,26 as a proof-text without much exegetical explanation. See,
e.g., Bach. prof.fid. 3 (PL 20,1027), *Pater ingenitus, Filius genitus,
Spiritus sanctus a Patre procedens, Patri et Filio coaeternus; sed
ille nascitur, hic procedit, sicut in Evangelio beati Joannis legitur:
Spiritus qui a Patre procedit, ipse vobis annuntiabit omnia. Itaque
Spiritus sanctus, nec Pater esse ingenitus, nec Filius genitus,
aestimetur; sed Spiritus sanctus, qui a Patre procedit. Sed non est
aliud quod procedit, quam quod unde procedit.*

42. Aug. Trin. 15,26,45 (CCL 50A,525), *Et multis aliis diuinorum
eloquiorum testimoniis comprobatur patris et filii esse spiritum qui
proprie dicitur in trinitate spiritus sanctus, de quo item dicit ipse
filius: Quem ego mitto uobis a patre, et alio loco: Quem mittet
pater in nomine meo. De utroque autem procedere sic docetur quia
ipse filius ait: De patre procedit, et cum resurrexisset a mortuis et
apparuisset discipulis suis, insufflauit et ait: Accipite spiritum
sanctum, ut eum etiam de se procedere ostenderet* . . . . Though he
does not use the term here, this is clearly an expression of the
filioque, not strictly a double procession as Aug. teaches it throughout his work, but a single spiration from both Father and Son. Indeed,
the *filioque* as taught in the West almost necessarily follows from the
doctrine of the homoousion. See also Trin. 15,27,48 (CCL 50A,529-
530) where, quoting his own Jo. 99,8 (CCL 36,587), he exegetes that in
saying *de patre procedit* the Son does not deny that the Spirit also
proceeds from himself but is following his usual habit of referring
to the Father (with whom he is consubstantial) that which is also
his own. See J.N.D. Kelly, The Athanasian Creed (London, 1964), 87-
90,for a discussion of Hilary of Poitiers and Marius Victorinus (but
definitely not Ambrose) as forerunners of Augustine in the development
of the theology of the double procession.

43. Ambr. Spir. 1,11,120-125 (CSEL 79,66-68).

44. Ambr. Spir. 1,11,116-119 (CSEL 79,65-66).

45. An interesting exposition of the Manichaean point of view is
given in Aug. Fel. 1,9 (CSEL 25,2,811) in a speech by the Manichaean
Felix. It is, perhaps, worth quoting in full as it shows something of
Manichaean application of our materials: *Fel. dixit: Ego de ipso
ago, quia, si in ipso, et in omnes. et si in ipso - Paulus enim in
altera epistula dicit: ex parte scimus et ex parte prophetamus; cum
uenerit autem quod perfectum est, abolebuntur ea, quae ex parte dicta
sunt - nos audientes Paulum hoc dicere, uenit Manichaeus cum praedicati-
one sua, et suscepimus eum secundum quod Christus dixit: mitto uobis
spiritum sanctum. et Paulus uenit et dixit et ipse quia uenturus est,
et postea nemo uenit; ideo suscepimus Manichaeum. et quia uenit*

*Manichaeus et per suam praedicationem docuit nos initium, medium
et finem; docuit nos de fabrica mundi, quare facta est et unde facta
est, et qui fecerunt; docuit nos quare dies et quare nox; docuit nos
de cursu solis et lunae: quia hoc in Paulo non audiuimus nec in
ceterorum apostolorum scripturis, hoc credimus, quia ipse est paracletus.*

46.   Among anti-Montanist writings see Jer. ep. 120,9,16-17 (CSEL 55,
498-499), cf. 41,1 (CSEL 54,311-312); among anti-Manichaean writings
see Aug. Faust. 13,17 (CSEL 398-399) cf. 32,17 (CSEL 25,777), Fel.
1,2-5 (CSEL 25,802-807) and 1,10ff (CSEL 25,811ff).

47.   See p.39 above.

48.   See Aug. Faust. 32,16 (CSEL 25,1,776), *deinde paracletus sic est
promissus, ut diceretur: ipse uos inducet in omnem ueritatem. quomodo uos autem ille inducet in ueritatem, qui uos docet Christum
esse fallacem?*

49.   There seems to be some debate on the precise times and modes of
delivery of the Tractates. On this question see B. Altaner and A.
Stuiber, Patrologie (7. Aufl.; Freiburg, 1966), 431, and R. Willems,
CCL 36,vii.

50.   Pel. Rom. on 8,38 (PLS 1,1151), *Deum diligebat in Christo, cuius
dilectio consistit in custodia mandatorum, sicut ipse ait: 'Si
diligitis me, mandata mea seruate', qui imitationem amoris sui in
fraterna caritate constituit, dicens: 'in hoc cognoscent omnes
quia mei discipuli estis, si dilexeritis inuicem'.* Cf. Jer. ep.
148,4,3 (CSEL 56,332-333) which, in commenting on 2 Cor. 5,15, suggests that living is nothing else than the keeping of the commandments and quotes, among others, Jo. 14,15 in support: *uiuere autem
illi non aliud est quam eius praecepta seruare, quae nobis ille quasi
certum quoddam dilectionis suae pignus seruanda mandauit. si
diligitis, inquit, me . . .*

51.   See pp.8 and 40-41 above.

52.   See Jer. Is. 16,57,16 (CCL 73A,656), cf. 17,63,8/10 (CCL 73A,728).

53.   See Ambr. Spir. 1,4,58-59 and context (CSEL 79,39-40).

54.   See Aug. Jo. 74,1 (CCL 36,512), *Hic est utique in Trinitate
Spiritus sanctus, quem Patri et Filio consubstantialem et coaeternum
fides catholica confitetur.*

55.   Aug. Jo. 74,1 (CCL 36,512-513). Aug. quotes 14,15-16 and then
says, . . . *cum hoc dicat de Spiritu sancto, quem nisi habeamus, nec
diligere Deum possumus, nec eius mandata seruare? Quomodo diligimus
ut eum accipiamus, quem nisi habeamus, diligere non ualemus? Aut
quomodo mandata seruabimus ut eum accipiamus, quem nisi habeamus,
mandata seruare non possumus?*

56.   Aug. Jo. 74,1 (CCL 36,512-513), *An forte praecedit in nobis
caritas, qua diligimus Christum, ut diligendo Christum eiusque
mandata faciendo, mereamur accipere Spiritum sanctum, ut caritas
non Christi, quae iam praecesserat, sed Dei Patris diffundatur in*

*cordibus nostris per Spiritum sanctum qui datus est nobis? Peruersa
est ista sententia. Qui enim se Filium diligere credit, et Patrem
non diligit, profecto nec Filium diligit, sed quod sibi ipse confinxit.*

57. Aug. Jo. 74,1 (CCL 36,513), *Deinde apostolica uox est: Nemo
dicit: Dominus Iesus, nisi in Spiritu sancto; et quis Dominum Iesum,
nisi qui eum diligit, dicit, si eo modo dicit quo apostolus intellegi
uoluit? . . . et si eo modo dicebant, ut non ficte dicerent, ore
confitentes, corde et factis negantes; prorsus si ueraciter hoc dicebant, procul dubio diligebant. Quomodo igitur diligebant, nisi in
Spiritu sancto? Et tamen eis prius imperatur ut diligant eum, et
eius mandata conseruent, ut accipiant Spiritum sanctum, quem nisi
haberent, profecto diligere et mandata seruare non possent.*

58. Aug. Jo. 74,2 (CCL 36,513), *Restat ergo ut intellegamus Spiritum
sanctum habere qui diligit, et habendo mereri ut plus habeat, et plus
habendo plus diligat. Iam itaque habebant Spiritum discipuli, quem
Dominus promittebat, sine quo eum Dominum non dicebant; nec tamen eum
adhuc habebant, sicut eum Dominus promittebat. Et habebant ergo,
et non habebant, qui quantum habendus fuerat, nondum habebant.
Habebant itaque minus, dandus erat eis amplius. Habebant occulte,
accepturi fuerant manifeste; quia et hoc ad maius donum sancti Spiritus
pertinebat, ut eis innotesceret quod habebant.*

59. Ambrstr. quaest. 93,1 (CSEL 50,162-163), *. . . quia unus quidem
est spiritus, sed dona habet multa. cum ergo legitur spiritus
sanctus, intellegi debet et eius officium, in quo sit significatus.*
See Jer. ep. 120,9 (CSEL 55,492-500) who also answers a similar question by distinguishing the one Spirit from the diverse gifts. Cf.
this understanding with the frequent insistence by Thdr.Mops. that
passages which seem to speak of the giving or sending of the Spirit
refer not to his nature but to his grace and operation to believers.
Thdr. is, of course, not solving the same problem that Ambrstr.
faces but is interpreting paraclete (and other) materials in a way
which seems to him consonant with the divine nature of the Spirit.
See, for example, n.120 on p.73 above.

60. Ambrstr. quaest.93,1 (CSEL 50,163), *nam quia et cum eis erat et
uenturus erat, non est falsum, sed si non istud ad personam trahas,
sed ad naturam. alterum enim se uenturum a patre promisit Christus,
ut, quia indifferens est eorum diuinitas, in praesentia Christi non
absens putetur spiritus sanctus et in aduentu et in apparentia
spiritus sancti praesens aestimetur et Christus. ideo cum uenturum
eum promittat, dicit: uos uidetis eum, quia apud uos manet et uobiscum est.* Cf. Vic. Ar. 3,14 (CSEL 83,1,215-216), *Unde autem aut est
in illis, aut iam manet spiritus sanctus, si adhuc postea uenturus
est, et non iam per Christum apud illos esse coepit?*

61. See Aug. Jo. 74,4 (CCL 36,514), serm.Ar. 19 (PL 42,697);
Eus.Ver. Trin. 12(11),(39-)41 (CCL 9,173); Jer. ep. 120,9,17 (CSEL
55,499). This is apparently also the understanding of Vic. Ar.
1,11 (CSEL 83,1,69).

62. See Aug. Jo. 74,4 (CCL 36,514) and Eus.Ver. Trin. 12(11),41
(CCL 9,173). It is interesting to note that the Biblical text before
Aug. must have read *aduocatus* at 1 Jo. 2,1; for, before using it as
corroboration of his reading of *alium*, he is compelled to point out

that *paracletus* means *aduocatus: Paracletus enim latine dicitur
aduocatus; et dictum est de Christo: Aduocatum habemus ad Patrem,
Iesum Christum iustum*. Cf. serm.Ar. 19 (PL 42,697) and Trin. 1,8,18
(CCL 50,52-53) where *aduocatus* translates παράκλητος in the text
of Jo. 14,16.

63. See p.43 above.

64. Aug. Jo.74,4 (CCL 36,514-515), *Mundum quippe ait hoc loco, mundi
significans dilectores, quae dilectio non est a Patre . . . . Mundus
ergo eum accipere non potest, quia non uidet eum, neque scit eum.
Non enim habet inuisibiles oculos mundana dilectio, per quos uideri
Spiritus sanctus, nisi inuisibiliter non potest*. See also Aug.
Trin. 1,8,18 (CCL 50,52). This view has not a little in common with
the understanding of κόσμος in Cyr. Jo. 10,2 (Pusey 2,622-623), for
which see p.52 above.

65. Aug. Jo. 74,5 (CCL 36,515), *Erit in eis ut maneat, non manebit
ut sit; prius est enim esse alicubi, quam manere*.

66. Aug. Jo. 74,5 (CCL 36,515), *Sed ne putarent quod dictum est:
apud uos manebit, ita dictum quemadmodum apud hominem hospes uisibili-
ter manere consueuit; exposuit quid dixerit: apud uos manebit,
cum adiunxit et dixit: in uobis erit*.

67. Aug. Jo. 74,5 (CCL 36,515), *Ergo inuisibiliter uidetur; nec si
non sit in nobis, potest esse in nobis eius scientia. Sic enim a
nobis uidetur in nobis et nostra conscientia; nam faciem uidemus
alterius, nostram uidere non possumus; conscientiam uero nostram
uidemus, alterius non uidemus. Sed conscientia numquam est, nisi
in nobis; Spiritus autem sanctus potest esse etiam sine nobis; datur
quippe ut sit et in nobis*. Cf. Vic. Ar. 3,14 (CSEL 83,1,215).

68. Aug. Jo. 77,1 (CCL 36,520), *Illa itaque mansio alia est, quam
promisit futuram; haec uero alia, quam praesentem esse testatur.
Illa spiritalis est, atque intrinsecus mentibus redditur, haec
corporalis forinsecus oculis atque auribus exhibetur. Illa in
aeternum beatificat liberatos, haec in tempore uisitat liberandos.
Secundum illam Dominus a suis dilectoribus non recedit; secundum hanc
it et recedit. Haec, inquit, locutus sum uobis, apud uos manens,
utique praesentia corporali, qua cum illis uisibilis loquebatur*.

69. Gaud. tract. 14,4-5 (CSEL 68,125-126), *Praenuntiare quidem beatis
apostolis eloquio isto dignatus est et suum post incumbentem passionem
ad caelos regressum et sancti spiritus super eos de caelis adventum,
. . . . Sed neque spiritus sanctus in caelo erat solum et in terra
non erat, neque filius ita caelos ascensurus erat, ut terras re-
linqueret, neque pater tantum caelestem thronum possidet, ubi
remeare filius et unde sanctus venire spiritus perhibetur*.

70. Aug. Jo. 77,2 (CCL 36,520-521), *Numquidnam dicit Filius, et docet
Spiritus sanctus, ut dicente Filio uerba capiamus, docente autem
Spiritu sancto eadem uerba intellegamus? Quasi dicat Filius sine
Spiritu sancto, aut Spiritus sanctus doceat sine Filio; aut uero non
et Filius doceat et Spiritus sanctus dicat, et cum Deus aliquid dicit
et docet, Trinitas ipsa dicat et doceat?* Cf. Vic. Ar. 1,12 (CSEL 83,
1,70-71) and 3,14 (CSEL 83,1,216).

71. Aug. Jo. 77,2 (CCL 36,520-521), *Omnis igitur et dicit et docet Trinitas; sed nisi etiam singillatim commendaretur, eam nullo modo humana capere utique posset infirmitas. Cum ergo omnino sit inseparabilis, numquam Trinitas esse sciretur, si semper inseparabiliter diceretur.*

72. Gaud. tract. 14,19-21 (CSEL 68,129-130), *. . . divisionem non capit unitas deitatis. Ait denique ibi Christus de sancto spiritu: Quem mittit pater meus in nomine meo, id est in dei nomine, deum scilicet sicut filium profitendum.* Gaud. continues to show this through a discussion of the appropriate bits of text from Jo. 5,43 and Mt. 21,9. Then he continues, *Pater enim deus est et filius deus est et spiritus sanctus deus est, sicut sanctarum scripturarum testimoniis dilectioni vestrae saepius approbavi; ac propterea unum trinitatis est nomen, cuius una virtus atque divinitas permanet in omnia saecula.*

73. Gaud. tract. 14,19 (CSEL 68,129), *Quod vero plenitudinem doctrinae suae per sanctum pollicetur spiritum tribuendam, aequalem suae omnipotentiae eum credi voluit. Non est enim in trinitate dominus et servus, deus et angelus, creator et creatura, sed est aliud idem: aliud persona, idem natura; ac proinde non dii, sed deus, quia divisionem non capit unitas deitatis.*

74. Vic. Ar. 1,12 (CSEL 83,1,70-71). He goes on to explore this concept through a series of *quod* statements supported by various Scriptures, one of which is Jo. 14,26.

75. Vic. Ar. 1,12 (CSEL 83,1,70), *Quod a filio paraclitus: paraclitus autem sanctus spiritus, quem pater mittet in nomine meo, ille vos docebit omnia, quae ego dixero. Manifestum ex his, quod in Christo deus et in sancto spiritu Christus; primum paraclitus Christus, paraclitus sanctus spiritus.*

76. Vic. Ar. 1,12 (CSEL 83,1,70), *Quae locutus est Christus, ipsa loquitur sanctus spiritus. Sed Christus locutus est in parabolis et fecit signa; ergo in occulto omnia, quod ipse in carne erat; sicut ipse intus, sic et verum intus in parabolis et signis. Spiritus autem sanctus docet omnia; etenim sanctus spiritus loquitur spiritui hominum; ipsum quod est loquitur et quod est loquitur in nulla figura. Et ideo ipse docebit vos.*

77. Vic. Ar. 1,12 (CSEL 83,1,70), *Dixero de futuro est. De quo futuro? Non eo quod nunc, sed eo quod est post ascendere ad patrem. Et si istud, paraclitus veniens a deo in nomine Christi illa docet, quae dicit Iesus.* Does *dixero* translate an underlying ἂν εἴπω?

78. Vic. Ar. 3,15 (CSEL 83,1,217), *Denique sic ait: mittit pater in nomine meo, id est pro me, aut in nomine meo, quoniam spiritus Christus et ipse spiritus sanctus, aut in nomine meo, quia spiritus sanctus ipse de Christo testimonium ferret.*

79. Aug. Jo. 92,1 (CCL 36,555-556), *Christi enim sanguis sic in remissionem peccatorum omnium fusus est, ut ipsum etiam peccatum posset delere quo fusus est. Hoc ergo intuens Dominus dicebat: Odio habuerunt me gratis; cum autem uenerit Paracletus, ille testimonium perhibebit de me, tamquam diceret: Odio me habuerunt, et*

occiderunt uidentes; sed tale de me Paracletus testimonium perhibebit,
ut eos faciat in me credere non uidentes. Though details of exposition differ, the catholic writers of the West concur with the view
of Augustine expressed in this passage that the promise of the Paraclete is most abundantly fulfilled in the upper room on the day of
Pentecost. For other passages where this view is expressed see, e.g.,
Aug. Jo. 74,2 (CCL 36,513-514), which suggests that it is the same
Spirit who is given at Jo. 20,22 and in Ac. 2 and that perhaps the
two-fold bestowal takes place because of the two-fold commandment of
love to neighbour and to God. Nevertheless, the implication here
is that the Pentecost bestowal is the main fulfillment of the Paraclete promise. See also Aug. Trin. 2,15,26 (CCL 50,115). See Jer.
ep. 120,9 (CSEL 55,492ff) which resolves the apparent double bestowal
of Jo. 20,22 and Ac. 2 by distinguishing the one Spirit from the
diverse gifts (cf. above p.91 and n.59); see also Leo tract. 76,4
(CCL 138A,476-478) who suggests that, though the disciples had a
certain measure of the power of the Spirit given on the occasion
recorded in Lk. 10,19, and though the gift was renewed on the occasion
of Jo. 20,22-23, the perfection which was to be conferred on the
disciples required *maior gratia et abundantior inspiratio* that they
might be able to receive what they had not yet received and have
more excellently what they had already. This, Leo suggests, is
what the Lord promised at Jo. 16,12-14; the promise was fulfilled
on the day of Pentecost.

80. Aug. Jo. 92,2 (CCL 36,556-557).

81. Aug. Jo. 94,2 (CCL 36,562) indicates that the Greek *paracletus*
means both 'advocate' (to which he has already drawn attention in
Jo. 74,4; see n.62 above) and 'comforter': *Consolator ergo ille uel*
aduocatus (utrumque enim interpretatur quod est graece paracletus),
cf. Faust. 13,17 (CSEL 25,398-399), *paracletum, id est consolatorem*
uel aduocatum. Aug. nowhere seems to prefer one meaning over the
other; here in Jo. 94,2 elements of both concepts are present in the
description of what the Spirit will do. He does not usually translate the Greek word but uses the transliterated *paracletus* (consistently so in Jo. 74-100, but cf. again *aduocatus* at serm.Ar. 19
(PL 42,697), where he follows his text of Jo. 14,16). By contrast
Jer. Is. 11,40,1-2 (CCL 73,454), commenting on Is. 40,1-2 (*Consolamini,*
consolamini populum meum . . .), quotes from Jo. 14,16.26, 15,26, and
16,7 in turn, rendering παράκλητος in each case by *consolator*. When
he has done that he says, *Consolator est, cui et nunc praecipitur, ut*
consoletur populum Dei. Jer., at least in this passage, understands
paracletus to mean *consolator*. Aug. and Jer. seem to be the only
Latins to comment on the meaning of *paracletus*. Elsewhere, the
Greek term is in the majority of cases rendered by transliteration.
Where it is not, the translation *advocatus* occurs somewhat more
frequently than *consolator*. (In this light, it is a reasonable guess
that the Western fathers usually adopt the word which lies before
them in their Latin version. Cf. J. Behm, "παράκλητος," Theological
Dictionary of the New Testament, Vol.V, ed. G. Friedrich, trans. and
ed. G.W. Bromiley (Grand Rapids, 1973), 806, who says, "Of early NT
translations the Codd. of Vetus Latina, if they do not keep to the Gk.
forms *paracletus* or *paraclitus*, usually have *advocatus*, though also
consolator.")

82. Aug. Jo. 94,1-2 (CCL 36,561-563).

83. Aug. Jo. 94,3 (CCL 36,563), *Significat sic se iturum ut nullus interrogaret, quod palam fieri uisu corporis cernerent; . . . Nunc uero ita se promittit iturum, ut nullus eorum quo uadit interroget.*

84. Cf. pp.50-52 above.

85. Aug. Jo. 94,4 (CCL 36,563).

86. Aug. Jo. 94,4 (CCL 36,563-564), *Quid est ergo: Si non abiero, Paracletus non ueniet ad uos, nisi: non potestis capere Spiritum, quamdiu secundum carnem persistitis nosse Christum?*

87. Aug. Jo. 94,5 (CCL 36,564). This is Augustine's usual explanation for passages which appear to deny the consubstantiality of the Godhead. Vic. Ar. 1,13 (CSEL 83,1,72), taking a different tack, seems to suggest that it *is* in place of Christ in the flesh that the Spirit comes: *Quod duplex potentia* τοῦ λόγου *ad deum, una in manifesto, Christus in carne, alia in occulto, spiritus sanctus – in praesentia ergo cum erat* λόγος, *hoc est Christus, non poterat venire* λόγος *in occulto, hoc est spiritus sanctus –: etenim si non discedo, paraclitus non veniet ad vos.* Vic. goes on to draw his conclusions, suggesting that they are two, then, the one coming from the other, the Spirit from the Son just as the Son from the Father, and, in logical consequence, the Spirit from the Father. All of this is intended in support of the unity of the Three. Note that Vic.'s exegesis of 16,7 is diametrically opposed to Aug. Jo. 94,4 (CSEL 36,563) which maintains that 16,7 does *not* mean that Jesus was unable to send the Spirit while still here himself. Ironically, Vic.'s passage gives answer to the rhetorical question in Aug. Jo. 94,4 (CCL 36,563), *Numquid hic positus, eum non poterat mittere? Quis hoc dixerit?*

88. See pp.52-54 above.

89. Aug. Jo. 95,1 (CCL 36,564-565) rejects this interpretation on the grounds that there are many Scriptures which show Jesus reproving the world (cf. Jo. 15,19.22; 17,25; Mt. 25,41; Ac. 1,7.8); that, when the Spirit reproves the world through the disciples, Christ does it along with him (cf. 2 Cor. 13,3); and that the operations of the Trinity are inseparable, though it is necessary in this passage to distinguish the persons without confounding them together.

90. Aug. Jo. 95,1 (CCL 36,565), *Quos itaque arguit Spiritus sanctus, arguit itaque et Christus. Sed quantum mihi uidetur, quia per Spiritum sanctum diffundenda erat caritas in cordibus eorum, quae foras mittit timorem, quo impediri possent ne arguere mundum qui persecutionibus fremebat, auderent, propterea dixit: Ille arguet mundum, tamquam diceret: Ille diffundet in cordibus uestris caritatem; sic enim timore depulso, arguendi habebitis libertatem.*

91. Ambrstr. quaest. 89,1 (CSEL 50,149), *et hoc est 'arguere mundum', ostendere illi uera esse quae credere noluit.*

92. Ambrstr. quaest. 89,2 (CSEL 50,150), *hoc modo spiritus sanctus arguit mundum, quia in nomine saluatoris, qui reprobatus est a mundo, omnium curationum uirtutes operatus est.*

93. See Aug. Pel. 3,3,4 (CSEL 60,489), Ps. 109,8 (CCL 40,1608),

serm. 144,1 (PL 38,788). Other writers agree with this in substance though they may not say so directly.

94. Aug. serm. 144,2 (PL 38,788) gives the explanation that the unfaithful ones to be reproved, i.e., the *mundus* of 16,8, are those who love this world: *De peccato igitur arguuntur infideles, id est, dilectores mundi: nam ipsi significantur mundi nomine.* This is the understanding we have come to expect from Aug.; see on Jo. 14,17 Jo. 74,4 (CCL 36,514-515) and above p.92.

95. See Ambrstr. quaest. 89,1 (CSEL 50,150); Aug. Jo. 95,2 (CCL 36, 565), Pel.3,3,4 (CSEL 60,489), Ps. 77,14 (CCL 39,1078), 109,8 (CCL 40, 1608), serm. 143,2 (PL 38,785), 144,2 (PL 38,788); Vic. Ar. 3,15 (CSEL 83,1,218).

96. Aug. serm. 144,2 (PL 38,788), *Sed multum interest, utrum quisque credat ipsum Christum, et utrum credat in Christum. Nam ipsum esse Christum et daemones crediderunt, nec tamen in Christum daemones crediderunt. Ille enim credit in Christum, qui et sperat in Christum et diligit Christum. Nam si fidem habet sine spe ac sine dilectione, Christum esse credit, non in Christum credit. Qui ergo in Christum credit, credendo in Christum, venit in eum Christus, et quodam modo unitur in eum, et membrum in corpore ejus efficitur.* (Aug.'s usual expression for the sin of 16,9 is *credere* with the negative. A few times, however, as at Pel. 3,3,4 (CSEL 60,489) he uses other words, words like *infidelitas.*) Aug. is here very precise in separating credenda about Christ from faith in Christ; though Vic. is less discriminating, he probably would not disagree with the African Bishop when he says at Ar.3,15 (CSEL 83,1,218), *De peccato, inquit, quoniam in me non credunt, vel quod vita sit Christus vel quod dei filius et a deo missus et qui peccata dimittat.*

97. See Aug. serm. 143,2 (PL 38,785), *De hoc ergo uno peccato voluit mundum argui, quod non credunt in eum: videlicet quia in eum credendo cuncta peccata solvuntur, hoc unum imputari voluit, quo caetera colligantur,* and 144,2 (PL 38,788), *Cum enim dicitur, Arguet mundum de peccato; non alio quam quod non crediderunt in Christum. Hoc denique peccatum si non sit, nulla peccata remanebunt, quia justo ex fide vivente cuncta solvuntur.* Cf. Jo. 95,4 (CCL 36,568).

98. Ambrstr. quaest. 89,1 (CSEL 50,149), *et hoc est 'arguere mundum', ostendere illi uera esse quae credere noluit. credere enim noluit a deo uenisse saluatorem. saluator autem seruata iustitia non trepidauit reuerti ad eum qui se miserat, et per id quod regressus est, probauit se inde uenisse, quia nemo ascendit ad deum, nisi qui descendit a deo. uidentes ergo potestates ascendere eum confusae sunt, uidentes uerum esse quod uelut falsum spreuerant. itaque ista iustitia arguit eos, qua iustum probatum est, quia regressus est unde uenerat.*

99. See Vic. Ar. 3,16 (CSEL 83,1,219), where such an approach is, if nothing more, implied: *De iustitia autem, quod ad patrem vado. Et hoc potest esse de peccato, quod iniuste fecerunt qui eum in crucem sustulerunt, quia se filium dei dicebat. Et nunc pergit ad patrem. Quod item erit omnium, si in deum credant et faciant dei iussa, ut et ipsi ad patrem pergant. Iustificantur enim.* He goes on to give the example of Abraham. Cf. Ar. 3,15 (CSEL 83,1,218).

100.   Aug. serm. 144,3 (PL 38,788), *Quid enim de justitia recte argui possit? An de peccato quidem suo, de justitia vero Christi mundus arguitur? Non video quid aliud possit intelligi: quandoquidem, De peccato, inquit, quia non crediderunt in me; de justitia vero, quia ad Patrem vado. Illi non crediderunt, ipse ad Patrem vadit. Illorum ergo peccatum, ipsius autem justitia.*

101.   See p.53 above.

102.   See Aug. Jo. 95,2-3 (CCL 36,566-567), serm. 143,4 (PL 38,786-787), cf. pec. 32,52 (CSEL 60,122-123) and Ps. 109,8 (CCL 40,1608). It is interesting to note that Aug. takes this line in serm. 143,4, coming, as it does, in such close proximity in the collection to serm. 144,3 (see n.100 above) where he suggests that it is the righteousness of the vindicated Christ which is spoken of. See further serm. 144,6 (PL 38,790), *Et ideo nos non debemus ab illa justitia separatos putare, quam Dominus ipse commemorat, dicens: De justitia, quia ad Patrem vado. . . . Arguitur ergo mundus de peccato, in eis qui non credunt in Christum: et de justitia, in eis qui resurgunt in membris Christi. Unde dictum est: Ut nos simus justitia Dei in ipso. Si enim non in ipso, nullo modo justitia. Si autem in ipso, totus nobiscum vadit ad Patrem, et haec implebitur in nobis perfecta jusititia.*

103.   See Aug. Jo. 95,2 (CCL 36,565-566); but see also serm. 144,3 (PL 38,788) and the quotation from it in n.100 above.

104.   Aug. Jo. 95,2 (CCL 36,565-566), *Numquid enim si arguendus est peccator propterea quia peccator est, arguendum putabit quisquam et iustum propterea quia iustus est? Absit! Nam et si aliquando iustus arguitur, ideo recte arguitur, quia, sicut scriptum est: Non est iustus in terra qui faciet bonum, et non peccabit. Quocirca etiam cum iustus arguitur, de peccato arguitur, non de iustitia.*

105.   See Aug. Jo. 95,2 (CCL 36,566), *Quo pacto igitur mundus arguendus est de iustitia, nisi de iustitia credentium? Arguitur itaque de peccato, quia in Christum non credit; et arguitur de iustitia eorum qui credunt . . . . Quapropter mundus de peccato quidem suo, de iustitia uero arguitur aliena, ... Et quoniam ista uox infidelium esse consueuit: Quomodo credimus quod non uidemus? ideo credentium iustitiam sic oportuit definiri: Quia ad Patrem uado, et iam non uidebitis me. Beati enim qui non uident, et credunt.* See also Ps. 109,8 (CCL 40,1608).

106.   See Aug. Jo. 95,3 (CCL 36, 566-567), *Quid ergo est: Ad Patrem uado, et iam non uidebitis me, nisi, quomodo sum, cum uobiscum sum? Tunc enim adhuc erat mortalis in similitudine carnis peccati, qui esurire poterat ac sitire, fatigari atque dormire: hunc ergo Christum, id est talem Christum, cum transisset de hoc mundo ad Patrem, non erant iam uisure.* See also 101,1 (CCL 36,591), *quia ad Patrem uado, et iam non uidebitis me, quia scilicet mortalem Christum ulterius non uiderent.*

107.   See Aug. Ps. 109,8 (CCL 40,1608), *. . . ex fide nemo uiuit, nisi non uidendo quod credit, . . .*

108.   See p.53 above.

109. See Aug. Jo. 95,4 (CCL 36,567), serm. 144,6 (PL 38,790); Vic.
Ar. 3,17 (CSEL 83,1,222), cf. 3,15 (CSEL 83,1,218) where he suggests
that Jo. 16,11 indicates all the powers adverse to Christ: *Mysterio
enim crucis omnes adversae Christo ab eodem Christo triumphatae
sunt potestates.*

110. Aug. Jo. 95,4 (CCL 36,567), *Non enim caeli et terrae et omnium
quae in eis sunt, est diabolus princeps, qua significatione intellegitur mundus, ubi dictum est: Et mundus per eum factus est; sed
mundi est diabolus princeps, de quo mundo ibi continuo subiungit
atque ait: Et mundus eum non cognouit, hoc est homines infideles,
quibus toto orbe terrarum mundus est plenus.* Cf. serm. 144,6 (PL 38,
790).

111. See Ambrstr. quaest. 89,1 (CSEL 50,150); Aug. Jo. 95,4 (CCL 36,
567-568); Vic. Ar. 3,15 (CSEL 83,1,218). Ambrstr. (loc. cit) suggests
how it is that the world knows their ruler is adjudged: *de iudicio
uero sic eos corripuit, dum ostendit principem mundi reum factum et
conpressum ab eo, cuius fidei non communicarunt. uidentes enim
animas de inferis ire in caelos cognouerunt adiudicatum esse principem
huius mundi, ut reus factus in causa saluatoris quae tenebat amit-
teret.*

112. See Aug. Jo. 95,4 (CCL 36,568), *. . . princeps mundi huius de
quo alibi dicit: Nunc princeps mundi huius missus est foras,
utique iudicatus est: quoniam iudicio ignis aeterni irreuocabiliter
destinatus est.*

113. See Aug. Jo. 95,4 (CCL 36,568), *Et de hoc itaque iudicio quo
princeps iudicatus est mundi, arguitur a Spiritu sancto mundus;
quoniam cum suo principe iudicatur, quem superbus atque impius
imitatur,* and serm. 144,6 (PL 38,790), *Ergo quemadmodum nobiscum, id
est, cum corpore suo unus est Christus: sic cum omnibus impiis quibus
caput est, cum quodam corpore suo unus est diabolus. Quapropter
sicut nos non separamur a justitia, de qua Dominus dixit, Quia ad
Patrem vado: sic impii non separantur ab illo judicio, de quo dixit,
Quia princeps hujus mundi jam judicatus est.*

114. Aug. Jo. 96,1 (CCL 36,568-569), *Nunc ergo quae ista sint quae
apostoli tunc portare non poterant, uultis forsitan scire. Sed quis
nostrum audeat eorum se dicere iam capacem, quae illi capere non
ualebant? Ac per hoc nec a me exspectanda sunt ut dicantur, quae
forte non caperem, si mihi ab alio dicerentur, nec uos ea portare
possetis, etiamsi ego tantus essem, ut a me ista quae uobis altiora
sunt audiretis . . . atque ait: Cum autem uenerit ille Spiritus
ueritatis, docebit uos omnem ueritatem; sic utique demonstrans illos
ideo quae habebat dicere, portare non posse, quia nondum ad eos
uenerat Spiritus sanctus.*

115. Aug. Jo. 96,2 (CCL 36,569-570).

116. See, e.g., Aug. Jo. 96,4 (CCL 36,571-572); cf. p.56 above.

117. Aug. Jo. 96,4 (CCL 36,571-572), *Quapropter, carissimi, non a
nobis exspectetis audire quae tunc noluit Dominus discipulis dicere,
quia nondum poterant illa portare; sed potius in caritate proficite,
quae diffunditur in cordibus uestris per Spiritum sanctum qui datus*

est uobis, ut spiritu feruentes et spiritalia diligentes, spiritalem
lucem spiritalemque uocem, quam carnales homines ferre non possunt
. . . interiore conspectu et auditu nosse possitis.

118. Aug. Jo. 96,5 (CCL 36,572), *Quae cum ita sint, dilectissimi,*
moneo uos in caritate Christi, ut seductores caueatis impuros et
obscoenae turpitudinis sectas . . . ne cum horrendas immunditias
docere coeperint, quas humanae aures qualescumque sint, portare
non possunt, dicant ipsa esse quae Dominus ait: Adhuc multa habeo
uobis dicere, sed non potestis portare modo; et per Spiritum sanctum
asserant fieri ut possint illa immunda et nefanda portari. See also
97,2-5 (CCL 36,573-576). It is likely that Aug. refers at this point
to specifically heretical teaching. But it is just possible that
he would have included in his warning those who, as Tert. (see above
pp.26ff), would appeal to this passage as justification for harsh, but
catholic, disciplines.

119. See Aug. Ps. 5,7 (CCL 38,23), *Verum autem occultauit et Dominus,*
cum discipulis nondum idoneis dixit: Multa habeo uobis dicere, sed
nunc non potestis portare illa . . . . Vnde manifestum est non esse
culpandum, aliquando uerum tacere. Falsum autem dicere, non inuenitur
concessum esse perfectis, and serm.Mont. 2,20,67 (CCL 35,163), *Quia*
et dominus, quamuis nihil mentitus sit, uera tamen aliqua occultare se
ostendit dicens: Adhuc multa habeo uobis dicere, sed adhuc non potestis
illa portare.

120. See Aug. don.pers. 16,40 (PL 45,1017), ep.83,5 (CSEL 34,391),
cf. Jo. 98,8 (CCL 36,581). At ep. 166,9,28 (CSEL 44,584) Aug. suggests that he is ignorant of the origin of the human soul because,
as with the disciples and the *multa* in Jo. 16,12 (which he quotes),
he is unworthy of the knowledge in that he could not bear it at
the present time.

121. Aug. Ps. 36,1,1 (CCL 38,337), *Vnde intellegimus non omnia*
promenda esse, quae capere non possunt hi quibus promuntur. Dicit
enim alibi: Multa habeo uobis dicere, sed non potestis illa portare
modo.

122. Aug. quaest. 53,4 (OSA 10,152), *Et quod pro suis gradibus animae*
doceantur, et ipse Dominus demonstrat dicens: 'Multa habeo vobis
dicere; sed nunc non potestis portare illa'. It may be noted that
Leo tract. 76,5 (CCL 138A,478-479) also reads spiritual immaturity
in 16,12-14. According to Leo, these verses neither contradict passages like Jo. 15,15 nor indicate inferiority of Son to Spirit; the
Son is both *ueritas* and that *uerbum* without whom the Father cannot
speak nor the Spirit teach (which is what Jesus indicates when he says
de meo accipiet). We are not to understand from 16,12-14 that the
Spirit is to bring another truth. But we are to understand that he
is, among other things, to augment the capacity of those who are being
taught.

123. Aug. fid. 19 (CSEL 41,24), *et quia reconciliati et in amicitiam*
reuocati per caritatem poterimus omnia dei secreta cognoscere,
propterea de spiritu sancto dicitur: ipse uos inducet in omnem
ueritatem.

124. See Aug. Jo. 96,4 (CCL 36,572) and 97,1 (CCL 36,572). Phoeb. Ar.

11 (PL 20,20) also sees the Holy Spirit as the agent of revelation.
He suggests that Jesus, in saying *omnem ueritatem*, excepts nothing and
that through the Spirit we are able to find out whatever we seek (in
this life, it is implied).

125. Aug. Jo. 99,1-2 (CCL 36,581-583), *Cum igitur Spiritus sanctus*
nulla susceptione hominis sit homo factus, nulla susceptione angeli
sit angelus factus, nulla susceptione cuiusquam creaturae creatura
sit factus, quomodo de illo intellengendum est quod Dominus ait:
Non enim loquetur a semetipso, sed quaecumque audiet, loquetur?
(CCL 36,583).

126. Aug. Jo. 99,4 (CCL 36,584), *Pater quippe solus de alio non est.*

127. Aug. Jo. 99,4 (CCL 36,584-585), *Non ergo loquetur a semetipso,*
quia non est a semetipso. Sed quaecumque audiet, loquetur; ab
illo audiet a quo procedit. Audire illi scire est; scire uero
esse, sicut superius disputatum est. Quia ergo non est a semetipso,
sed ab illo a quo procedit, a quo illi est essentia, ab illo scientia;
ab illo igitur audientia, quod nihil est aliud quam scientia.

128. Aug. Jo. 99,5 (CCL 36,585), *Nec moueat quod uerbum futuri*
temporis positum est. Non enim dictum est: quaecumque audiuit, aut:
quaecumque audit, sed: quaecumque audiet, loquetur. Illa quippe
audientia sempiterna est, quia sempiterna scientia. In eo autem
quod sempiternum est, sine initio et sine fine, cuiuslibet temporis
uerbum ponatur, siue praeteriti, siue praesentis, siue futuri, non
mendaciter ponitur. Cf. serm.Ar. 24 (PL 42,700) on Jo. 16,14-15,
accipiet. One wonders how Aug. would expound the parallel time of
the verb *loquetur.* It is likely that he would differentiate them
by saying that *audiet* refers to the inner and eternal working of
the Trinity while *loquetur* refers to the Spirit's then future, temporal
activity among men.

129. Aug. Jo. 100,1 (CCL 36,588).

130. Aug. Jo. 100,1 (CCL 36,588), *Quod enim ait: Ille me clarifica-*
bit, potest intellegi, quia diffundendo in cordibus credentium carita-
tem, spiritalesque faciendo, declarauit eis quomodo Filius Patri
esset aequalis, quem secundum carnem prius tantummodo nouerant, et
hominem sicut homines cogitabant. Vel certe, quia per ipsam caritatem
fiducia repleti, et timore depulso, annuntiauerunt hominibus Christum,
ac sic fama eius diffusa est toto orbe terrarum. Vt sic dixerit:
Ille me clarificabit, tamquam diceret: Ille uobis auferet timorem,
et dabit amorem, quo me ardentius praedicantes, gloriae meae per
totum mundum dabitis odorem, commendabitis honorem. Quod enim
facturi fuerant in Spiritu sancto, hoc eumdem Spiritum dixit esse
facturum.

131. Aug. Jo. 100,1 (CCL 36,588), *Verbum quippe graecum quod est*
δοξάσει, *alius clarificabit, alius glorificabit, latini interpretes*
in sua quisque translatione posuerunt; quoniam ipsa quae graece
dicitur δόξα, *unde dictum est uerbum* δοξάσει, *et claritas interpreta-*
tur et gloria. Gloria namque fit quisque clarus, et claritate
gloriosus; ac per hoc quod utroque uerbo significatur, idipsum est.

132. Aug. Jo. 100,1 (CCL 36,588), *Quae cum est in hoc mundo facta*

*de Christo, non Christo credenda est magnum aliquid contulisse, sed
mundo. Bonum enim laudare, non laudato, sed laudantibus prodest.*

133. Aug. Jo. 100,4 (CCL 36,590), *Quod autem ait: De meo accipiet,
et annuntiabit uobis, catholicis audite auribus, catholicis percipite
mentibus. Non enim propterea, sicut quidam haeretici putauerunt,
minor est Filio Spiritus sanctus, quasi Filius accipiat a Patre, et
Spiritus sanctus a Filio quibusdam gradibus naturarum. . . . Denique
continuo soluit ipse quaestionem, et cur hoc dixerit, explanauit.
Omnia, inquit, quaecumque habet Pater, mea sunt; propterea dixi quia
de meo accipiet, et annuntiabit uobis. Quid uultis amplius? Ergo
de Patre accipit Spiritus sanctus, unde accipit Filius, quia in hac
Trinitate de Patre natus est Filius, de Patre procedit Spiritus
sanctus.* Cf. 107,2 (CCL 36,613-614).

Chapter 4

POST-CHALCEDONIAN EXEGESIS

THE GREEK FATHERS

The importance of the paraclete passages declines markedly in the Greek East after the Council of Chalcedon in 451. Symptomatic is the dramatic reduction in the number of citations in extant literature: beyond the commentary fragments of Ammonius of Alexandria, there are fewer than twenty fruitful citations in only six authors in the three centuries prior to the death of John of Damascus. These figures are especially significant when contrasted with the hundreds of citations in the literature of the decades between Nicaea and Chalcedon. Further, there is virtually nothing new after 451; such exposition as we do find follows the lines laid down during the earlier centuries and differs from earlier interpretation only in its lack of creative speculation. Paraclete exegesis has become refined and conventional.[1]

This decline is, of course, connected with the resolution of the great Trinitarian, Christological, and Pneumatological controversies of the Fourth and Fifth Centuries. During those years the paraclete passages had been important both because it was necessary to rescue them from the misappropriation of the heretics and because catholic writers rightly saw their significance for the development of orthodox dogma. With the Trinitarian question sorted out, however, the paraclete passages recede into the background, and, since they contain nothing particularly germane to the monophysite and

monothelete controversies, do not regain their earlier importance
in the new era. Greek writers do, of course, continue to reaffirm
the doctrine of the Trinity, but on lines which have now become
conventional; exposition of the paraclete passages almost of necessity
partakes of that conventionality. Even the one 'purely' exegetical
work, the commentary of Ammonius of Alexandria,[2] seems to do nothing
new but exhibits, in its paraphrastic way, the refinement and
culmination of earlier patristic exegesis.

We may illustrate post-Chalcedonian dependence on earlier
exegesis by looking briefly at a few specific passages. Maximus
Confessor seems to follow John Chrysostom in his exegeses of paraclete
passages. In the first place, he identifies the commandments of
Jesus at 14,15 (cf. 15,10 et al.) with the command of 15,12 that the
disciples love one another (ἀλλήλους);[3] at one point his words seem
to imply that the love of one another is synonymous with the love of
one's neighbour (πλήσιος).[4] Chrysostom, it will be remembered,
variously identified the command of 14,15 with the command to love
one another in 13,34 and with the two commandments of Mt. 22,34-40
(and parallels).[5] Anastasius Sinaita also seems to follow Chrysostom, among others,[6] when he, seeking to reconcile the promise of Jo.
16,7 with 20,22, suggests that the disciples were given the authority
and spiritual gift of releasing sins at the insufflation, but that
the grace of the Spirit's baptism and the power of signs came on
Pentecost day.[7] Similar dependence upon the earlier writers is
recognised when Anastasius of Antioch, the anti-Monophysite writer,
uses the 'truth' (ἀλήθεια, *veritas*) word group as evidence for the
consubstantiality of the three divine persons;[8] when he appeals to
the juxtaposition of Jo. 14,26 and 16,7 for evidence that both Father
and Son send the Paraclete;[9] and when he and others appeal to 15,26

as a proof-text for the eternal and consubstantial procession of the
Holy Spirit.[10]

    We have already said that there are no new lines of exegesis
in the post-Chalcedonian period. There are, however, two passages
which contain what seem to be novel applications of old themes. Isaias
Abbas, speaking of the kind of behaviour to be expected from those
Christians who possess the Spirit, reasons backwards from Jo. 14,15-
17 (and others) to teach that a man may, by his actions, be recognised to have or lack the Spirit.[11] John of Damascus in a dogmatic
work appeals to 16,15 for evidence that, while terms like δουλεία and
δεσποτεία may be significant of the relationship between Father and
Son, they do not apply to the essence (οὐσία) and nature (φύσις) of
God. If the Son is the servant of the Father, he reasons, then 16,15
cannot be true; for he certainly does not have himself as a servant.
The implied conclusion is that the Son is not, therefore, by essence
a servant.[12]

    As there is nothing new in the fragments on John by Ammonius
of Alexandria (the only extant commentary on the Gospel from this
period), it will suffice if we limit ourselves to these few observations. Ammonius was acquainted with and used the work of the great
exegetes in writing his commentary. Indeed, though he follows no
single writer exclusively, his exposition is heavily informed by
the interpretations of the fathers who precede him, especially
Apollinaris, Cyril of Alexandria, John Chrysostom, Theodore of Heraclea,
and Theodore of Mopsuestia.[13] His own contribution to the history
of exegesis comes not at the point of new insight into the text of
John but in his refinement and simplification of the old. In common
with his age, Ammonius lacks the creativity and exploring energy of
the great centuries; in few words he goes directly to the essence of

his text, an essence highly coloured by preceding exegesis and con-
troversy. In his perfection of the old lines of interpretation, in
his orthodoxy, and in his reluctance to use many words, Ammonius
epitomizes the characteristics of post-Chalcedonian paraclete exegesis.

THE LATIN FATHERS

The paraclete passages are relatively more important in the
West after Chalcedon than they are in the East. The amount of writing
on them is small, it is true, when compared with the volume of Latin
writing as a whole, but it is significantly greater than that left
us by Greek writers. This is in large measure due to their relevance
for the Latin Church in the face of continuing pressure from invad-
ing Arians and semi-Arians.

There is, nevertheless, a notable lack of innovation in
exegesis and application of paraclete passages after 451, indeed, after
Augustine. Rather than new developments, we find a honing and refin-
ing of ante-Chalcedonian thinking. As with their predecessors, the
fathers who write after Chalcedon are more interested in applying
our materials to the dogmatic issues raised by their Arian opposition
than in expounding them for their own sakes; there is little isolated exegesis. Nevertheless, although there is an element of conventionality in the paraclete exegesis of this period,[14] there is no
great feeling, on the whole, that the post-Chalcedonian fathers are
blindly following. The best of them, Faustus of Riez in Gaul and
(especially) his younger contemporary Fulgentius of Ruspe in Africa,
have internalized what they have learned from their teachers and re-
handle it as living material.[15]

There is, at one or two points, indication that the Latin writers after 451 are aware of and dependent upon Greek materials in

their handling of paraclete passages. Vigilius of Thapsus is a case
in point. In his Contra Arianos dialogus he depicts Arius exegeting
from Jo. 16,14 (among other paraclete passages) the subordination
of the Spirit.[16] In response Athanasius, who in the dialogue is made
to defend the coequality and coessentiality of Spirit with Father and
Son, reinterprets the verse in the light of catholic dogma. First
he establishes from Jo. 8,44 that the Spirit would be a liar were
he to speak his own things. Then he says that, on this principle,
the Spirit is shown by 16,14 to speak truly inasmuch as he does not
speak *de proprio*, but speaks the things which have to be said concerning Father and Son. (16,15 shows that what he receives from the
Son are also the things of God the Father.)[17] This reasoning is very
similar to that to be found in the writings of Origen and Didymus,[18]
but not quite like anything to be found in ante-Chalcedonian Latin
writing. Such exclusive connection with Greek exegetical thought
is the exception rather than the rule. Latin writers of this period
tend to be rather strongly related to their predecessors in the West
both in manner, approach, and content; one may usually explain their
paraclete exegesis independently of the Greek fathers, even where
East and West agree.

The lack of significant innovation makes it possible for us
to summarise the features of post-Chalcedonian Latin exegesis in
rather brief compass. With respect to the doctrine of the Trinity,
Jo. 14,15-17 is adduced to support the teaching that the divine
persons are three in number on the ground that, whether in name or
in action, three discrete persons are to be distinguished here.[19]
But the names *Pater*, *Filius*, and *Spiritus* in the paraclete passages
indicate, as elsewhere, a distinction not of nature but of person.
The Trinity is a trinity in person only; in nature it is single and

undivided. This is catholic dogma for which these fathers, as did
their predecessors, seek some support from our materials.[20] The com-
munion and coessentiality of the Godhead are shown in part from the
fact that its persons share its acts in common. And it is evident
from the paraclete passages that the Spirit joins Father and Son in
teaching (Jo. 14,26; 15,26; and 16,12-13),[21] in the work of rebuking
(*arguo*) the world (Jo. 16,8),[22] and in foreknowing all things (Jo.
16,13).[23] In Christological passages the fathers take Jo. 16,15 as
spoken by Christ in his divine, rather than in his human, nature.[24]
They also use it as a proof-text for the teaching that, without
division, Father and Son possess all things in common, including knowledge of the day and hour of the end time.[25]

There is a relatively greater volume of writing which relates
the paraclete passages to the catholic pneumatology, nearly all of
it by the semi-Pelagian Faustus of Riez and Fulgentius the Augustinian
of Ruspe. Again, because of the traditional and uninnovative nature
of this material we treat it rather summarily, glancing first at
those inferences concerning the person and nature of the Spirit
drawn from our materials.

For Faustus the Spirit is clearly and definitely God, an
equal and consubstantial member of the Trinity. He is certainly no
creature, for it is never at any time said of any creature that it is
sent into the world in the name of God as it is of the Spirit (in Jo.
14,26).[26] Rather, the Spirit who is destined to come in place of
God (i.e., the Son) to confirm his gifts (16,7)[27] and who both shall
and can be given to the whole world (14,16-17)[28] is also God. The
equality of the Spirit's deity is seen in Jo. 16,7[29] and 14,16[30] in
the fact that the Spirit shares with the Son both the name *paracletus*
and the divine work implied thereby. In the latter passage we see (in

alium paracletum) both distinction of person and equality of substance.[31] Faustus also sees the consubstantiality and essential deity
of the Spirit in his procession from the Father (15,26).[32]

    Fulgentius sees the equality of the Spirit with Father and
Son and his unity with the divine substance in Jo. 16,12-13.[33] He
takes as evidence the facts that the Spirit strengthens the disciples
to bear what they could not bear when the Saviour presented it *secundum carnem*[34] and that the same Saviour has reserved the full teaching
of truth (*plenam ueritatis doctrinam*) for the Spirit whose coessentiality with himself and the Father he was desiring to demonstrate.[35]
Indeed, Christ reserved the fuller teaching for the Spirit so that no
one might think him less than Father and Son and so that he might show
the one nature and power of the Trinity.[36] Fulgentius also finds
evidence from 16,13-15 for the Spirit's consubstantiality with Father
and Son in the fact that the three hold all things common: Jo. 16,13.
14 shows that the things of the Son belong to the Spirit, and in 16,15
we see that all the Son has belongs also to the Father.[37] The African
father goes on to apply the doctrine of the consubstantiality to the
interpretation of the language of hearing and receiving in 16,13.14.
And he follows Augustine in asserting that with the Spirit hearing,
knowing, and receiving are synonymous with being. The Spirit receives
nothing not already his own by nature; rather what he hears he hears
eternally through unity with the divine essence by virtue of the fact
that he proceeds from the Father and the Son.[38] Similarly, speaking
means communicating directly with the hearts of men through grace.[39]

    The origin of the Spirit is also sought in the paraclete pas-
sages: Jo. 15,26, *qui ex patre procedit*, shows that the Spirit proceeds eternally from the Father,[40] whose Spirit he is,[41] and is undoubtedly the prime source of the catholic doctrine of the procession.

But the Spirit is not from the Father alone; he is, as Jo. 14,26 shows, also sent from the Son. And these two texts are several times juxtaposed to show that the Spirit's mission[42] and even his procession[43] are from both Father and Son.

We come finally, at the very end of our account of patristic paraclete exegesis, to look briefly at a few miscellaneous bits of exegesis not strictly related to the major dogmatic themes we have just been considering. From Jo. 14,15 it is inferred, as it was by Origen so many years before, that those who keep Jesus' commandments are they who love him.[44] In 14,16 our Lord, by designating the Spirit *alterum paracletum*, shows that he himself is also a Paraclete.[45] The term *paracletus* itself is understood, as in both halves of the Church during earlier centuries, in more than one way:[46] Faustus, recognising that it may mean either *aduocatus* or *consolator*, suggests that it is the former meaning which applies to the Son at 1 Jo. 2,1 but the latter which applies to the Spirit in the paraclete passages (esp. 16,7).[47] Victor also recognises the dual possibility, but he prefers the translation *consolator*.[48] Isidor of Seville seems to waver, for in his Etymologiarum he first says that the Greek word *paracletus*, applied to both Spirit and Son, means *aduocatus* with no hint that it may ever mean anything else;[49] later, however, he states equally categorically that the Spirit is called Paraclete because of his work of consolation.[50] Fulgentius has left us three further miscellaneous exegeses: from 14,16.17 he infers that the Spirit will remain with the faithful, receding only from those whom the Father repels from his presence.[51] Concerning 16,5-6 he suggests that the disciples' sorrow and disquiet are not of the flesh (*non carni*) but of the spirit (*sed animae*).[52] And he asserts his understanding that these promises on Jesus' part that he would send the Paraclete were fulfilled on the day of Pentecost.[53]

NOTES

1. See, e.g., Is.Ab. or. 25,23 (PG 40,1189-1190) and Sev.Ant. hom.
92 (PO 25,1,43), 98 (PO 25,1,148), 123 (PO 29,1,149), 125 (PO 29,1,239),
Gram. 2,1 (CSCO 111,63) among Monophysite theologians. See Anast.Ant.
or. 1,11 (PG 89,1316), 1,13 (PG 89,1319), 1,22 (PG 89,1324-1325)
among anti-Monophysite writers. See Ant.Mon. hom. 1 (PG 89,1436) and
72 (PG 89,1642-1644) among ascetics. And see Max. ascet. 7 (PG 90,
917), carit. 1,16 (PG 90,964), 4,55 (PG 90,1060); Anast.S. qu.et resp.
148 (PG 89,802-804); and Jo.D. f.o. 65 (PTS 12,164), 91,3 (PTS 12,
216) among the anti-heretical writers.

2. According to B. Altaner and A. Stuiber, Patrologie (7.Aufl.;
Freiburg, 1966), 516-517, *Der Verfasser könnte jener A. sein, der 457
gegen Timotheus Aelurus Stellung nahm . . ., oder jener A., der nach
Anastasius Sinaita als Gegner der Monophysiten in der 1. Hälfte des
6. Jh. literarisch tätig war.* Cf. Joseph Reuss, TU 89,XXVIII.

3. Max. ascet. 7 (PG 90,917), Καὶ τίς ἐστιν ἡ ἐντολὴ ἣν τηρήσαντες,
αὐτὸν ἀγαπήσωμεν, αὐτοῦ ἄκουσον, λέγοντος· Αὕτη δὲ ἐστιν ἡ ἐντολὴ
ἡ ἐμή, ἵνα ἀγαπᾶτε ἀλλήλους.

4. Max. carit. 1,16 (PG 90,964), Ὁ ἀγαπῶν με, φησὶν ὁ Κύριος, τὰς
ἐντολάς μου τηρήσει· αὕτη δὲ ἐστιν ἡ ἐντολὴ ἡ ἐμή, ἵνα ἀγαπᾶτε
ἀλλήλους. Ὁ οὖν μὴ ἀγαπῶν τὸν πλησίον, τὴν ἐντολὴν οὐ τηρεῖ. Ὁ
δὲ τὴν ἐντολὴν μὴ τηρῶν, οὐδὲ τὸν Κύριον ἀγαπῆσαι δύναται.

5. See p.41 above.

6. See Ch.2 n.147 (pp.76-77) above. See also text and n.66 on p.39
above.

7. Anast.S. qu.et resp. 148 (PG 89,802-804). Signs such as effecting
cures which the disciples performed before the passion were not done,
suggests Anast., in the Spirit, but only through the authority and
command of Christ.

8. Anast.Ant. or. 1,13 (PG 89,1319). The Father is shown from Scripture to be true (*verus*) God, Jo. 17,3; the Son to be the truth (*veritas*), Jo. 14,6; and the Spirit to be the Spirit of truth (*Spiritus
veritatis*). Anast. extends somewhat the thought of earlier writers who
had taken the divine title πνεῦμα τῆς ἀληθείας to indicate the Spirit's
Godhead (see p.37 above) and his oneness with Christ (see p.38 above).
This extension is, however, already implicit in the work of earlier
writers and it may be an accident of history that we do not have extant
an ante-Chalcedonian example of it.

9. Anast.Ant. or. 1,22 (PG 89,1324-1325), *ac rursus Spiritus ex ipso
procedens, et missus non solum a Patre, sed a Filio, sicut ait ipse
Dominus: Paracletus autem quem mittet vobis Pater; et iterum: Si
abiero, mittam eum ad vos;* . . . Cf. Apoll. and Chrys. p.42 above
and Eus. p.61 n.15. It will be noticed that Anast. simply states
this as though it were one of the assured results of exegesis whereas
the earlier Greek writers are constrained to discuss both the problem
and its solution more fully. Cf. p.84 above.

10. Cf. Anast.Ant. or. 1,11 (PG 89,1316), 1,13 (PG 89,1319); Sev.Ant.

hom. 123 (PO 29,1,149), 125 (PO 29,1,239), and Gram. 2,1 (CSCO 111, 63) with pp.35-36 and 49 above. H.B. Swete, The Holy Spirit in the Ancient Church (London, 1912), p.275, observes that even in this matter of the doctrine of the procession there tended to be little advance beyond the Constantinopolitan Creed in the two centuries and a half after Chalcedon.

11. Is.Ab. or. 25,23 (PG 40,1189-1190), *Vides, frater, quomodo velit hominem sibi esse similem, ut anima ejus sit sponsa ipsius. Ex propriis igitur actionibus agnoscit anima cognitiones suas; nam si recte agit, Spiritus sanctus habitat in ea. Actiones bonae reddunt animam a perturbationibus liberam. Porro fieri non potest ut in ea quae talis est, non habitet Spiritus sanctus. Si me diligitis, inquit Dominus, mandata mea servate. Et ego rogabo Patrem, et mittet vobis paracletum Spiritum veritatis* . . . . Yet even this is not strictly new; for Or. (see p.8 above) prepared the way centuries earlier when he reasoned back from the text to teach that a man may be observed to have or lack love for the Lord in his keeping or ignoring of the commandments. Thdr.Heracl. hinted at Isaias' teaching (see pp.41-42 above) when he suggested that, as the disciples' actions demonstrated the love of the Lord, there could be no doubt that the Spirit had come upon them because Jesus himself had promised that it would be so.

12. Jo.D. f.o. 65 (PTS 12,164), Εἷς γὰρ ὢν ὁ Χριστὸς οὐ δύναται δοῦλος ἑαυτοῦ εἶναι κύριος ὤν· ταῦτα γὰρ οὐ τῶν ἁπλῶς λεγομένων εἰσίν, ἀλλὰ πρὸς ἕτερον. Τίνος οὖν ἔσται δοῦλος; Τοῦ πατρός; Οὐκοῦν οὐ πάντα, ὅσα ἔχει ὁ πατήρ, καὶ τοῦ υἱοῦ εἰσιν, εἴπερ τοῦ πατρός ἐστι δοῦλος, ἑαυτοῦ δὲ οὐδαμῶς.

13. See Ammon. Jo. 488-543 (TU 89,317-331). Here follows a table which is intended to suggest, though it does not spell out, certain relationships which seem to exist between Ammon. and his ante-Chalcedonian predecessors. All page and note references are to Chapter 2 above.

With Jo. 488 (TU 89,317-318) on 14,16(-17) cf. above on Cyr., Chrys., Thdr.Heracl. pp.43-44; on Chrys. p.42; on Cyr. pp.42-43; on Amph. p.47.
"   Jo. 489 (TU 89,318) on 14,16-17 cf. above on Chrys. p.45.
"   Jo. 490 (TU 89,318) on 14,17 cf. above p.45 and n.108.
"   Jo. 501 (TU 89,321) on 14,26 cf. above on Thdr.Heracl. n.116 p.73.
"   Jo. 502 (TU 89,321) on 14,26 cf. above on Amph. p.48.
"   Jo. 536 (TU 89,329) on 16,6 cf. above p.50 and n.140.
"   Jo. 537 (TU 89,329) on 16,7 cf. Chrys. on 14,16 above p.42. This understanding (that the withdrawal referred to in this verse signifies the passion) is first made explicit here though it seems to have been frequently assumed by Ammonius' predecessors. More often Jesus' words about going (in these passages) are interpreted to refer to the ascension.
"   Jo. 538 (TU 89,329) on 16,8-9 cf. above pp.52-53 and notes. Interestingly, the very language of Ammon. here is strongly reminiscent of the language of Thdr.Mops. Jo.Syr. on 16,8-11 (CSCO 115,293).
"   Jo. 539 (TU 89,329-330) on 16,11 cf. above on Thdr.Heracl. n.158 pp.77-78.

With Jo. 540 (TU 89,330) on 16,9 cf. above p.53 and notes.
"   Jo. 541 (TU 89,330) on 16,13 cf. above pp.56-57 and notes.
"   Jo. 542 (TU 89,330) on 16,13 cf. above on Chrys. p.55; also
     pp.55-56 and notes; also pp.31-32 and notes.
"   Jo. 543 (TU 89,331) on 16,14 cf. above p.58 and notes.

Joseph Reuss (TU 89,XXVI-XXX) confirms broadly what we have already
discovered in detail. In summing up he says, *Zusammenfassend können
wir sagen, dass Ammonius, der, wie schon betont wurde, die Johannes-
Erklärungen des Theodor von Heraclea, Apollinaris von Laodicea,
Didymus, Johannes Chrysostomus, Theodor von Mopsuestia und Cyrill von
Alexandrien kennt und sie weitgehend auch benutzt, in gewandter Weise
den Evangelien-Text erklärt und einen recht guten Kommentar zum 4.
Evangelium hinterlassen hat* (89,XXX).

14. The writings of Vigilius of Thapsus partake, perhaps, of something of this quality of conventionality. For examples of passages
which involve paraclete materials see Ar.2,12 (PL 62,176); 2,14 (PL
62,177); 2,32 (PL 62,218), which copies the speech of Arius in 2,12;
and 2,35 (PL 62,220).

15. Consider, for instance, Faust. Spir. 1,9-13 (CSEL 21,115-129)
or Fulg. Fab. 25,3-5 (CCL 91A,802-803), et al. (Faust. was apparently
in his time a well-known semi-Pelagian; see Altaner-Stuiber, 473.
Fulg., the Bishop of Ruspe from ca. 507, *ist wohl der bedeutendste
Theologe seiner Zeit, ein kraftvoller Bekämpfer des Arianismus und
Verteidiger der augustinischen Gnadenlehre gegen die Angriffe der
gallischen Semi-pelagianer* (Altaner-Stuiber, 489).)

16. Vig. Ar. 2,12 (PL 62,176), repeated at 2,32 (PL 62,218).

17. Vig. Ar. 2,35 (PL 62,220-221), *Et ideo hic verum loquitur,
quia non de proprio, id est non a seipso, sed de Patris et Filii, quae
loquenda sunt loquitur. De meo, inquit, accipiet, et annuntiabit
vobis. Et ut ostenderet hoc esse a se accipere, quod est etiam de
Patre sumpsisse, ait: Ideo dixi, De meo accipiet, quia omnia quae
habet Pater, mea sunt. Vides ergo Spiritum sanctum a Patre et Filio
non esse discretum, dum ea loquitur quae Patris et Filii propria
esse noscuntur.*

18. See above pp.4 and 37.

19. See Faust. Spir. 1,10 (CSEL 21,120); Fulg. ep.Don. 8,4 (CCL 91,
258-259), incarn. 20 (CCL 91,329-330); cf. Rust. aceph. (PL 67,1178-
1179). See also Haereticus in Rust. aceph. (PL 67,1226) who sees not
only three persons in these verses, but three paracletes and the
objector in Fulg. resp. (CCL 91,85) who maintains that, since
Father, Son, and Spirit are distinct, they are patently not of one
nature.

20. See, e.g., Fulg. resp. (CCL 91,71) who, with respect to Father
and Son proof-texts this from Jo. 16,15: *Non enim ipse est Pater qui
Filius, quoniam in utroque personarum proprietas reseruatur. Sed quod
Pater est, hoc est et Filius, quia de Deo Deus, de perfecto perfectus,
de immenso immensus, de omnipotente omnipotens, de aeterno Patre
natus est Filius coaeternus, eadem ueritate dicente: Omnia quae habet
Pater, mea sunt.*

21. See Fulg. <u>Fab</u>. 3,6-7 (CCL 91A,768-769). Fulg. begins by saying, *Ante suam quippe Dominus passionem, ad docendum uenturum discipulis Paracletum Spiritum eo loco praedixit, ubi a Patre simul et a Filio ipsum Paracletum mittendum esse promisit.* Then,after quoting 14,26, 15,26, and 16,12-13,he goes on to say, *Ubi ex ipsa similitudine operis ostensa est communio deitatis,* and to show from other Scripture passages Father and Son teaching, as well. (The context of this fragment is summarised in the words of the (editorial) margin: *Et angeli seu nuntii, et doctoris, et iudicis officia, Patri et Spiritui sancto communia sunt. Differt subministratio a ministerio.*

22. See Cass. <u>Ps</u>. 6,2 (CCL 97,73) who uses this argument in passing in support of the Trinity: *. . . Arguit etiam Spiritus sanctus, sicut scriptum est:* <u>*Cum uenerit Spiritus Paracletus, ipse arguet*</u> <u>*mundum de peccato*</u>. *Dicite nunc, peruersi, ubi est hic naturae potestatisque distantia, quando nec ipsa discrepant uerba? Conticescat Ariana nequitia, ne qui uolunt in sancta Trinitate sacrilegas diuisiones inferre, ipsi se a regno Domini probentur abscindere*; also Victor <u>hist</u>. 2,90 (CSEL 7,65).

23. See Victor <u>hist</u>. 2,85 (CSEL 7,62).

24. See Cass. <u>Ps</u>. 74,3 (CCL 98,686) and Faust. <u>ep</u>. 7 (CSEL 21,204).

25. See Cass. <u>Ps</u>. 2,9 (CCL 97,46), 9,39 (CCL 97,111), and 71,2 (CCL 98,649).

26. Faust. <u>Spir</u>. 1,10 (CSEL 21,118), *. . .* <u>*ille spiritus ueritatis,*</u> <u>*quem mittet pater in nomine meo*</u>. *mittet, inquit, pater in nomine meo, de trinitate euidenter. de qua hoc umquam creatura dictum uel legimus uel audiuimus, quod in hunc mundum in nomine dei uenerit?*

27. Faust. <u>Spir</u>. 1,10 (CSEL 21,118), *hic ergo, de quo Christus dominus deus dicit:* <u>*nisi ego iero, paracletus non ueniet ad uos,*</u> *deus absque dubio est, qui in locum dei ad confirmanda dei munera destinatur. in his duabus sententiis* [see also n.26 above] *sub distinctione trinitatis absolute persona etiam sancti spiritus declaratur.*

28. Faust. <u>Spir</u>. 1,10 (CSEL 21,120), *nam dum saluator loquitur per Iohannem:* <u>*et ego rogabo patrem et alium paracletum dabit uobis,*</u> <u>*spiritum ueritatis, quem hic mundus non potest accipere,*</u> *qui uniuerso mundo dari potest, manifeste deus est mundi.*

29. Faust. <u>Spir</u>. 1,10 (CSEL 21,118-119), *non inmerito itaque et hoc* [i.e., Jo. 16,7 as quoted in n.27] *ad diuinitatis aequalitatem refertur, quod sicut filius ita etiam spiritus sanctus in scripturis paracletus nuncupatur. et unde hoc adprobare poterimus? utique ex apostoli Iohannis auctoritate, cum dicit:* <u>*si quis, inquit, nostrum*</u> <u>*peccauerit, paracletum habemus apud patrem Iesum Christum et ipse*</u> <u>*est propitiatio pro peccatis nostris*</u>.

30. Faust. <u>Spir</u>. 1,10 (CSEL 21,119), *in Iohannis euangelio habemus:* <u>*et*</u> <u>*ego, inquit, rogabo patrem et alium paracletum dabit uobis*</u>. *alium paracletum, id est similis potentiae, paris gloriae eiusdemque naturae.*

31. Faust. <u>Spir</u>. 1,10 (CSEL 21,119), *et alium paracletum: duplici*

hic intellectu et personae distinctionem et aequalitatem cognosce
substantiae. (See Victor <u>hist</u>. 2,93-94 (CSEL 7,66-67) who clearly
also sees distinction of person when he says concerning 14,16, . . .
sine dubio, cum dicit <u>alterum paracletum</u>, se quoque paracletum mani-
festat.)

32. See Faust. <u>Spir</u>. 1,11 (CSEL 21,122) and 1,13 (CSEL 21,128).

33. See Fulg. <u>Fab</u>. 25,1-3 (CCL 91A,801-802).

34. Fulg. <u>Fab</u>. 25,1 (CCL 91A,801-802), *In illo autem loco euangelii,*
ubi eum putas minorem subiectumque monstrari, ibi agnoscitur Spiritus
sanctus ab unitate Patris et Filii non esse naturaliter alienus.
Vide enim quid dicat Christus: <u>Adhuc multa habeo</u> . . . <u>in omnem</u>
<u>ueritatem</u>. Hic primum uirtutem Spiritus sancti Saluator noster
dignatus est commendare, quando ea quae, ipso secundum carnem praesente
atque docente, discipuli portare non poterant, sancti Spiritus munere
confortati, essent sine dubio portaturi. Vbi utique non maiorem
uirtutem Spiritus sancti ostendit esse quam suam; sed unam uirtutem
esse Spiritus sancti demonstrauit et suam.

35. Fulg. <u>Fab</u>. 25,3 (CCL 91A,802), *Non est hic igitur aliquod*
indicium subiectionis, ubi manifestatur unitas naturalis; sed Christus,
qui est uera sapientia, illius aduentui plenam ueritatis inuenitur
reseruasse doctrinam, cuius unam secum et cum Patre uolebat demonstrare
substantiam. Quod subsequentibus uerbis ostendit, dicens: <u>Non enim</u>
<u>loquetur a semetipso</u>. . . . <u>Ille me clarificabit, quia de meo accipiet</u>
<u>et annuntiabit uobis</u>.

36. Fulg. <u>Fab</u>. 25,2 (CCL 91A,802), *Hoc ergo Christus fecit, non quia*
minus poterat dare quam quod dedit Spiritus sanctus (cum in omni
munere ita sit unum sanctae Trinitatis donum, sicut in omni opere
unum est sanctae Trinitatis officium); sed hoc fecit Deus Filius,
ad ostendendam sanctae Trinitatis unam naturam, unamque uirtutem;
ut eum a quo doceri apostolos in omnem ueritatem, ipso praedicante
Saluatore, constaret, nemo minorem Patre et Filio aliquatenus
aestimaret. Cf. also Faust. <u>serm</u>. 31 (CSEL 21,345-346) who, having
suggested that the Spirit's coming to teach the disciples (Jo.14,26;
15,26) is neither because Christ had not taught them nor because his
teaching was imperfect, goes on to say, *sed quia fides uestra in*
patre est et in filio et in spiritu sancto, hoc uoluit mittendo
spiritum sanctum saluator ostendere, quod ecclesias suas et uoluntas
dei patris aedificaret et passio filii redimeret et doctrina sancti
spiritus confirmaret.

37. Fulg. <u>Fab</u>. 25,3 (CCL 91A,802), . . . *<u>quia de meo accipiet et an-</u>*
<u>nuntiabit uobis</u>. Ecce primum ostendit non esse alia Spiritus sancti
quam quae sunt Filii. Deinde ut ostenderet omnia sua esse quae
Patris sunt, adiecit: <u>Omnia quaecumque habet Pater, mea sunt;</u>
<u>propterea dixi quia de meo accipiet et annuntiabit uobis</u>.

38. See Fulg. <u>Fab</u>. 25,3-5 (CCL 91A,802-803), *Illud igitur primitus*
attendamus, quod ait: <u>Non enim loquetur a semetipso, sed quaecumque</u>
<u>audiet loquetur</u>. Quis autem comprehendit qualis sit illius simplicis
naturae locutio, uel qualis auditio? Vbi sicut non est aliud sapere
uel scire quam esse, ita non est aliud audire quam esse. Audit
itaque Spiritus sanctus quaecumque Pater et Filius dicit, et haec

*eadem similiter dicit; sicut uidet Filius quae Pater facit, et haec
eadem similiter facit. In illa enim natura, ubi est summa et uera
simplicitas, in eo Filius uidet quod Pater facit, et Spiritus sanctus
audit quod cum Patre Filius dicit, quia communione naturalis essentiae
et Filius de Patre natus exstitit et Spiritus sanctus de Patre Filioque procedit. Hoc est igitur Spiritui sancto audire, quod est de
natura Patris Filiique procedere;* and 27,4-5 (CCL 91A,805-805), *Haec
est uox Filii, haec est locutio Spiritus sancti, hoc a Patre audiuit
et Filius et Spiritus sanctus; quia de natura Patris natus est Filius,
et exinde procedit Spiritus sanctus; hoc etiam a Patre et Filio
Spiritus sanctus audit, quia de Patre et Filio communis diuinitatis
aequalitate procedit. Non ergo Spiritus sanctus loquitur a seipso,
quia non est a seipso, sed de Patre et Filio habet naturalem locutionem,
unde naturaliter procedens habet originis ueritatem. Ad hoc utique
pertinet quod ait: Ille me clarificabit, quia de meo accipiet, et
annuntiabit uobis.* See on Aug. pp.87 and 100-101 above.

39. Fulg. Fab. 25,5 (CCL 91A,803), *. . . et hoc est loqui, quod est
per gratiam nostris cordibus ineffabiliter intimare.*

40. See Faust. Spir. 1,9 (CSEL 21,115),equals serm. 31 (CSEL 21,344),
and Isid. etym. 7,3,7 (PL 82,268). Av. div.Spir. (PL 59,385-386)
agrees with Isid. about the eternity of the procession, but explains
it from the tense of the verb in this clause: *Enimvero non dicendo
processit, sed procedit, non tempus procedentis docuit, sed praeterito
futuroque submoto, sub interminabilis aeternitate praesentiae virtutem
processionis ostendit.* (He goes on to affirm that the Spirit also
proceeds from the Son.)

41. See Faust. serm. 31 (CSEL 21,346), *Quod autem spiritus sanctus
patris spiritus sit, dominus et saluator noster dixit: spiritus,
inquit, qui a patre procedit.* (He continues to show from Ro. 8,9 that
the Spirit is also the Spirit of the Son.)

42. See Av. div.Spir. (PL 59,386); Fulg Mon. 2,6,4 (CCL 91,40), Fab.
27,6-7 (CCL 91A,805-806); Isid. ep. 6,8 (PL 83,904).

43. See Fulg. Fab. 27,6-7 (CCL 91A,805-806) who, having established
that both Father and Son send the Spirit, moves from the language of
mission to that of procession in summing up: *Mittit eum Pater in
nomine Filii, quia unus Spiritus est Patris et Filii; mittit eum
Filius a Patre, quia sic procedit a Filio sicut procedit a Patre;
idem quoque Spiritus Patris, qui Spiritus est ueritatis. De Filio
ergo accepit, et omnia quae habet Pater Filii sunt, quae Spiritus
sanctus accepit; quia non de solo Patre, nec de solo Filio, sed simul
de utroque procedit.* See also Isid. ep. 6,8 (PL 83,904) who establishes the procession from the Son from Jo. 20,22.

44. See Cass. Ps. 98,7 (CCL 98,886) who, discussing Ps. 99,7, says,
Reddit causas quare eos [Moses, Aaron, Samuel, et al.] *exaudire
Dominus dignaretur, quia ipse illum uere diligit, qui eius mandata
custodit, sicut ipse discipulis dicit: Si me diligitis, mandata
mea seruate.* Cf. p.8 above.

45. See Victor hist. 2,93 (CSEL 7,66), *Nam et ipse dominus cum
dicit ad apostolos: alterum paracletum mittet uobis pater, sine dubio
cum dicit alterum paracletum, se quoque paracletum manifestat.*

46. On former discussions of the meaning of παράκλητος see above
pp.4-5, 44, and 112 n.81.

47. Faust. Spir. 1,10 (CSEL 21,119) who, having just quoted 1 Jo. 2,1,
continues, *paracletum, id est aduocatum, quod ad personam filii
respicit, siue etiam consolatorem, quod ad sanctum spiritum pertinet,
una Graeci sermonis enuntiatio utrumque significat.*

48. Victor hist. 2,93 (CSEL 7,66), *Paracletus enim aduocatus est uel
potius consolator secundum Latinam linguam.* In this context Victor
is attempting to demonstrate the Trinity by showing all three persons
to be paracletes.

49. Isid. etym. 7,2,31 (PL 82,266), *Paracletus autem Graecum est,
quod Latine dicitur advocatus. Quod nomen et Filio, et Spiritui sancto ascribitur, juxta quod et Dominus in Evangelio ait: Rogabo Patrem,
et alium Paracletum dabit vobis.*

50. Isid. etym. 7,3,10 (PL 82,268), *Spiritus sanctus, quod dicitur
Paracletus, a consolatione dicitur; παράκλησις enim Graece, Latine
consolatio appellatur. Christus enim eum apostolis lugentibus misit,
postquam ab eorum oculis ipse in coelum ascendit.* The heretic in
Rust. aceph. (PL 67,1226) seems to read *paracletus* in a similar way
when, in trying to establish that the Father is also a paraclete, he
says, *Si propter consolationem Paracletus dictus est, et Pater
Paracletus est; consolatur etenim animas justorum, et mitigat dolores,
sicut scriptum est: Memor fui Dei, et consolatus sum.*

51. Fulg. Fab. 28,14 (CCL 91A,812), *Ecce Dominus Iesus fidelibus suis
dedit Spiritum sanctum, ut cum eis sit in aeternum et in eis maneat.
Quod si uerax est promissio Saluatoris, quod nemo Christianus dubitat,
necesse est ut Spiritus sanctus a fidelibus non recedat; qui non
nisi ab illis aufertur, quos Deus a facie sua proiecerit.*

52. Fulg. Tras. 3,21,3 (CCL 91,165), *Anima tristatur, ipsa turbatur.
Ideo et ipse Saluator, ut ostenderet perturbationem istam non carni,
sed animae deputandam, sic discipulos suos consolatur, cum de futuro
eius contristarentur abscessu: Non turbetur cor uestrum, neque
formidet. Ad eosdem denuo sic loquitur: Nunc uado ad eum qui me
misit, et nemo ex uobis interrogat me: Quo uadis? Sed quia haec
locutus sum uobis, tristitia impleuit cor uestrum.*

53. Fulg. Fab. 29,12 (CCL 91A,820), *Nam et die Pentecoste ipsum
sanctum Spiritum apostoli acceperunt quem eis promiserat Dominus,*
. . .

Chapter 5

THE FATHERS ON THE PARACLETE PASSAGES: ASSESSMENT

INTRODUCTION

We must now try to form some impression of the fathers'
success in arriving at a true interpretation of the paraclete passages. This requires a word of caution since in seeking to assess
we imply the assumption that *we* possess a true understanding. Yet
we, no less than they, are subject to the limitations of our generation. If we seek to judge, we can only do so in the knowledge that
we may ourselves be open to criticism, perhaps most where we least
suspect. This is not meant to suggest that objective interpretation
is impossible. If we are not to be entirely cynical, we must recognise some sense in which a given exegesis is right or wrong. But it
is well to remind ourselves at the outset that we,too, are creatures
of our times and that we ought to approach the abiding work of our
ancestors with a certain humility.

That we differ from the Church fathers in both concern and
approach no one would deny. It may be useful to ennumerate some of
the differences here. The fathers were men of faith seeking to comprehend the implications of the New Testament for life and doctrine;
they sought to understand themselves in the light of the text. Our
approach is quite different, as Professor Stuhlmacher has recently
reminded us.[1] Their questions were often coloured by their orienta-
tion to Greek philosophy and their need for system. Ours are similarly coloured, but the nature of our presuppositions is different. They
assumed the literal inspiration of the Scriptures;[2] for Origen the

very letters of the (Greek) text of the Old Testament carried meaning
hidden for the faithful exegete to discover. Such an understanding
is unthinkable for today's 'scientific' investigator. Whereas the
fathers assumed that the words of the Farewell Discourses are the
ipsissima verba of Jesus, we sometimes doubt whether they can be traced
so far back as the original author and draft of the Gospel. The
fathers were, of course, unfamiliar with the developments of the last
century-and-a-half; they were quite without the modern tools of
historico-critical research. Nonetheless, they frequently demonstrate a sympathy and feeling for the Johannine text not always
appreciated in the Twentieth Century.[3]

Let us make two or three further observations before beginning our more detailed assessment. We must, for one thing, recognise
that in a very real sense there is no single patristic interpretation
for a given text. On some points there seems to be almost as full
a range of interpretations as we boast today. Secondly, as is implied
above, we will want to resist the notion that an idea is wrong merely
because it has been left behind and is no longer fashionable. Thirdly,
while we can only assess the fathers by bringing to bear on them the
full insight of contemporary exegesis, we must not yield to the temp-
tation to engage in dialogue with our contemporaries. Our business is
with the Church fathers.

The approach in these pages is straightforward. The intimate
relationship between exegesis and theology in the fathers[4] makes it
necessary for us now to abandon the distinction convenient earlier in
setting out their approach to paraclete materials. For this reason,
we evaluate patristic interpretations of these passages as they appear in their canonical order, avoiding, for the sake of economy, discussion of the sayings irrelevant to the evaluation. In closing, we
make some attempt to summarise the results of our study.

ASSESSMENT OF PATRISTIC EXEGESIS

14,15-17

Interpretation of the paraclete passages depends to some extent on the investigator's understanding of their nature and their relationship to both the Farewell Discourses and the rest of the Gospel. The Church fathers considered them to be the words of Jesus correctly reported and properly placed within their context[5] by the Evangelist himself. The supposition that the Discourses are the *ipsissima verba* of Jesus can no longer be maintained.[6] Recent scholarship has, however, tended to uphold the paraclete passages as genuinely Johannine and integral to the Gospel as first published.[7]

The Greek fathers are therefore right to seek to tie 14,15 to its (preceding) context.[8] But it is not entirely correct to say, as they do, that 14,15 is added to 14,14 in order to give the qualifying condition for the asking, to show who it is that is qualified to ask and under what condition. In one of those frequent Johannine shifts of subject, Jesus has stopped talking of prayer in his name and has begun to talk of the keeping of the commandments and the coming of the Paraclete. It is true that this saying is of a piece with its context. It is not contrary to Johannine thought to insist that only those who love Jesus and keep his commandments (sc. believers) are worthy of the promise of 14,14, that loving (expressed by keeping the commandments) is prior to asking in Jesus' name. But there is nothing in these verses to support the view that 14,15 is added for the purpose of qualifying 14,14. One suspects that such an interpretation owes more to the demands of a prior view of the nature of Christ and his discourse than to the text itself.

The overall meaning of 14,15 is clear. Love for Jesus is more than sentiment, it is ethical and issues in obedience to him.[9] The fathers are justified in deducing from this that love goes beyond oral allegiance; loving Jesus consists in keeping his commandments.[10] That they are also justified in stating the converse, viz., that he who keeps loves,[11] is clear from 14,21. It is but a simple step to the quite reasonable inference (cf. v.16) that men demonstrate their possession[12] or lack[13] of the Spirit by whether or not they demonstrate love for Jesus.[14]

The identification by Chrysostom and Maximus of τὰς ἐντολὰς τὰς ἐμάς with the command to love one another[15] of 13,34; 15,12.17 (cf. 1 Jo. 3,23; 2 Jo. 5) rightly recognises the only command specifically referred to as Jesus' own and the natural referent in the context,[16] a reference strengthened by the proximity of 15,12 to 15,10. But it fails to take account of the tension between the plural here and the singular ἐντολή at 13,34 and 15,12.[17] It also fails to note the resumption of τηρεῖν τὰς ἐντολάς[18] by τηρεῖν τὸν λόγον μου, 14,23[19] (cf. 1 Jo. 2,7b) which seems to refer to receiving and responding to the revelation given in Jesus[20] and may be equivalent to 'believe'.[21] This tends to expand the thought of 14,15 to embrace the whole life of faith (including love for one another) and to exclude the idea of a specific code as a sort of Christian Law.[22] It also precludes identification of τὰς ἐντολάς with the summation of the Law in Mt.22, 37-39.[23] Cyril relates the fact that Jesus here speaks of *his* commandments (in contrast to 12,49; 14,10.24; et al.) to the consubstantiality of Father and Son.[24] Consubstantiality cannot, of course, be deduced from 14,15 alone (nor is Cyril trying to do so), but the verse is harmonious with John's portrayal of Jesus as equal to and one with God.[25] The commandments of Jesus are here given a divine preeminence.[26]

How can one love and obey in order to receive the Spirit

without whom he can do neither? In posing and resolving this issue,
Augustine[27] displays something of his insight into the psychology of
Christian experience. It is, nevertheless, exegetically a false
dilemma.[28] In the Fourth Gospel the Spirit is thought to be essential
to the fulfillment of the disciples' mission,[29] but 14,15 does not en-
visage the prior presence of the Spirit-Paraclete as the *sine qua non*
of obedient love.[30] Keeping the commandments is the result[31] of the
disciples' love for Jesus on their part; he for his part procures the
gift of the Paraclete.

For certain Greek fathers, the words of 14,16 conflict with
orthodox Christology and with other passages which portray Jesus himself as bestower of the Spirit. Wary of Arianism, they feel they
must explain the verse in such a way as to avoid any hint of subordinationism.[32] Some, with Cyril, suggest that Jesus speaks these words
entirely as a man and not at all in his divine person.[33] John Chrysostom has recourse to his doctrine of condescension; these are humble
words spoken to ensure credibility with minds not yet ready for the
fuller truth.[34] For Theodore, the words mean δι' ἐμοῦ δέξεσθε τὴν
χάριν, which is not wrong in itself; but he goes on to deny that Jesus
will in fact ask for the Spirit.[35] This is improper exegesis. Out of
dogmatic concern, each of these commentators over-simplifies to some
degree the complexities of Johannine thought.[36] In the Fourth Gospel,
Jesus does bestow the Paraclete (15,26; 16,7; cf. 20,22). This is consistent with the theme of his equality and unity with the Father.[37]
At the same time, the Son is subordinate to the Father.[38] 14,16, which
identifies the Father as the source of the Spirit's mission (cf. 14,26;
15,26 παρὰ τοῦ πατρός, ὃ παρὰ τοῦ πατρὸς ἐκπορεύεται) as he was of the
Son's, is harmonious with this theme. These are balancing halves of
the whole truth; the Evangelist intends no contradiction. We recall

that Eusebius gives a similar explanation of the apparent discrepancy between 14,16.26 and 15,26; 16,7.[39] Augustine and certain Latin fathers simply assert that Son and Father both send; this is perhaps due more to dogmatic than exegetical considerations.[40]

For Chrysostom, as we have seen (p.54), the tense of ἐρωτήσω[41] shows that the gift of the Spirit is as yet in the future. In hom. 75,1 in Jo. he places it at a time when Jesus' work on Calvary is complete and the disciples are preparing to carry on without him.[42] This is appropriate to the wider context; according to the Fourth Gospel, the Spirit is not given until after Jesus' glorification (7,39; cf. 16,7; 20,22). In this homily, however, it seems unlikely that Chrysostom has formed this judgment from his reading of the Gospel.[43] His further insight, that the Spirit was not given sooner because he was not needed while Jesus was with them, is consonant with our sayings as a whole. It is in the situation created by the Master's absence, the situation of the Church, that the aid of the Paraclete becomes necessary.

This raises the wider question: what did the Evangelist understand to be the fulfillment of the Paraclete promises? We infer from hom. 75,1 in Jo. that Chrysostom accepted Pentecost as the fulfillment;[44] other fathers make this explicit.[45] Yet others (including, elsewhere, Chrysostom) are troubled by the fact that Jo. 20,22 and the account in Acts 2 seem mutually exclusive and seek to reconcile them. One approach interprets the insufflation as merely a preparation to receive the fuller gift at Pentecost.[46] Another accepts that it is a partial gift which, some specify, bestows the authority to remit sins; the full measure is then granted as portrayed in Acts 2.[47] It is in fact difficult to accomodate the two passages; it is also difficult to conceive the Evangelist ignorant of a tradition so widespread as that in Acts 2 seems to have been. Given the tradition and

their view that Scripture must not contradict Scripture, it is under-

standable that the fathers should interpret any promise of the Spirit

in the light of Pentecost and also understandable that they should

attempt to reconcile the Johannine and Lukan accounts. It is to be

granted that nothing in the Fourth Gospel repudiates Pentecost. At

the same time, there can be no doubt that the event recorded in Jo. 20,

21-23 is John's portrayal of the bestowal of the Spirit-Paraclete and

that the disciples are after this fully equipped for their mission.[48]

We must note in this regard that the instinct of the early theologians

with regard to enthusiastic sects is sound, whether in their view the

Spirit was given on resurrection Sunday or not until fifty days after

the ascension. If there were those, as the fathers believed, who felt

that the Paraclete first appeared in Montanus (or Manes or anyone

else), the first line of criticism is to show in Biblical terms that,

on the contrary, he came as promised upon the completion of Jesus'

earthly work.[49]

Παράκλητος is the *crux interpretum* of the paraclete passages.

Its use in the ancient world outside the New Testament shows it to be

a forensic term designating one who is summoned as a legal advisor, an

intercessor, an advocate.[50] This creates a problem; for, while this

meaning fits παράκλητος as it is used in 1 Jo. 2,1, it does not seem

suitable in the context of the Farewell Discourses. Here the Paraclete

is not portrayed as an intercessor but is, in the words of O. Betz,

ein prophetischer[51] *Lehrer, der Jesu Offenbarung bewahrt, ergänzt und*

vollendet.[52] How, then, shall we understand παράκλητος? Semasio-

logical study only exposes the problem, it does not solve it. It is

this which has driven scholars to seek both an explanation of the term

and a model for the figure of the Paraclete in the thought-world sur-

rounding the New Testament.[53] This search, while it brings illumination at several points, has hitherto been only partially successful;
we are left with a figure for whom there is no satisfactory model and
a term which we cannot with precision define.[54] We shall need to bear
this in mind as we assess the Church fathers.

They also experienced some discomfort over παράκλητος as it is
used in the Fourth Gospel. This is not evident, of course, in the
passages where it is taken to mean, simply, 'advocate'[55] or 'comforter'.[56] But it is quite plain wherever an acceptance that both
meanings are possible leads to ambivalence.[57] Three writers, Origen,
Didymus, and Faustus of Riez, go further. Comparing 1 Jo. 2,1 with
the paraclete passages, they understand παράκλητος to carry its
etymological sense (*deprecator, advocatus*) in the former and to mean
'comforter' (*consolator*) in the latter.[58]

How are we to assess the fathers on this?[59] Obviously, there
are real differences between their approach and ours. They do not do
semasiological studies, nor do they seek the *religionsgeschichtlich*
backgrounds of the word and the concept. For the former they cannot
be faulted, as they lacked the necessary access to a range of literature
and the full lexical aids available in our technological age; but the
latter is precluded by their presuppositions, even supposing they had
the equipment to do it. They assumed that these words are the exact
record of a new revelation of Jesus;[60] in this they are children of
their times. Given their assumptions and theological preoccupations,
it is unlikely that they would have appreciated the need for the comparative studies which occupy us. Turning to specifics, we are able to
say something positive about each approach. Those who take παράκλητος
to mean 'intercessor, advocate' have the merit of interpreting it in
its generally accepted sense.[61] Some of them, particularly the Latins,

may have known of no other possibility.[62] Those who understand the

Paraclete to be the comforter have rightly recognised the context of

consolation in the Discourses[63] and drawn attention to the inevitable

psychological result of the Paraclete's working.[64] The ambivalent are

quite understandably cautious about what is a difficult problem and

in some instances may be acknowledging that they lack full enough

information for a decision. We may commend Origen, Didymus, and

Faustus; for, whether or not the Fourth Evangelist understood παράκ-

λητος to mean 'comforter', they have rightly observed that the usual

forensic sense, appropriate at 1 Jo. 2,1, does not easily fit the con-

text of the Gospel. They have called attention to an issue which con-

tinues to exercise scholars today. Nonetheless, we must bring this

general criticism against the fathers: few recognise the problem of

the Paraclete; of those who do, none seems to understand its full

magnitude.[65]

14,16 promises, however, not simply τόν but ἄλλον παράκλη-

τον.[66] It is possible that ἄλλος is pleonastic,[67] but it is hardly

likely. Both context[68] and Johannine usage[69] suggest that the phrase

most naturally means 'another Paraclete' and strongly implies that

Jesus is in his earthly life[70] himself a paraclete.[71] With this the

fathers compare most favourably; it is their univocal understanding.[72]

The same interpretation is visible where they see in ἄλλος the dis-

tinction of persons in the Godhead.[73] If the theologians sometimes

verge on dogmatic eisegesis here,[74] they nevertheless clearly see that

14,16 is not susceptible of a Sabellian interpretation.[75] ἄλλος does

distinguish Jesus from the 'other Paraclete'. Further, as they rightly

point out, this verse plainly speaks of three distinct persons, him who

asks, him who sends, and him who is sent.[76] Similar arguments applied

to 14,26, 15,26, and 16,7.14 are equally valid.[77]

Άλλον παράκλητον is resumed and more closely identified in v.17 by the appositive τὸ πνεῦμα τῆς ἀληθείας,[78] an expression repeated at 15,26 and 16,13.[79] Of the two interpretations of this phrase in the fathers, we may with confidence reject that of Cyril[80] and Theodoret[81] who understand it to mean that the Paraclete is the Spirit of Jesus, the truth (14,6).[82] Theodore's judgment is more acceptable.[83] ἀληθείας is here neither a possessive nor a defining genitive; the Paraclete is designated τὸ πνεῦμα τῆς ἀληθείας because he communicates truth, particularly all the truth about Jesus. This is especially evident where τὸ πνεῦμα τῆς ἀληθείας gives true (it is implied) testimony concerning Jesus, 15,26, and leads the disciples ἐν τῇ ἀληθείᾳ πάσῃ; but it is also clear at 14,26 and 16,8-11 where the phrase τὸ πνεῦμα τῆς ἀληθείας does not appear.[84] In each case the Spirit of truth is seen to communicate some aspect of the truth about Jesus. The appropriateness of precisely this phrase as a designation for the Paraclete is underscored by the fact that in the Fourth Gospel ἀλήθεια characteristically refers to the revelation brought by and revealed in Jesus.[85]

Ὃ ὁ κόσμος οὐ δύναται λαβεῖν. The Spirit of truth is to be given to the disciples, but the world cannot receive him. κόσμος is an important word in the Fourth Gospel. While it occasionally does designate the created order (11,9; 17,5.24; 21,25), it generally stands for the realm of men and human affairs.[86] It is the world which God loved (3,16) and for which Jesus came to be light (1,9; 3,19-21; 8,12; 9,5; 12,46), salvation (1,29; 3,16.17.18; 4,42; 12,47), and the bread of life (6,33-35.51). Used pejoratively, κόσμος is the human and earthly as opposed to the eternal and heavenly; its use thus involves an element of dualism (1,9-10; 8,23; 12,25; 13,1). In this sense it is especially the world of unbelieving men and is as such at enmity

with Jesus and his disciples (7,7; 15,18-25). The believing disciple
no longer belongs to the world (14,22; 15,18-25; 16,20; 17,6.9.15-16.
18.20-21.23.25). The antithesis between disciple and world in 14,17
makes it clear that here ὁ κόσμος is the world of unbelieving men. It
carries the same meaning at 16,8.11, cf. 16,9. To their credit, the
fathers see this;[87] that their manner of expression varies depends
partly on the context here and partly on their several purposes.[88]

As a verb of receiving, λαβεῖν is the counterpart of δώσει.
From the context it is clear that the Paraclete is not offered to the
world; the world does not love Jesus and keep his commandments, it
hates him. But, if that is implied, the stress here is on the world's
radical inability to receive. The κόσμος is by definition antipathetic
to the things of God; the world and the Spirit of truth are antitheti-
cal by nature. It is not that the unbeliever cannot become a believer, but that the world cannot receive the Spirit while it remains the
world. As we have seen, the believer is somehow no longer part of
the world.[89]

At first glance the clause ὅτι οὐ θεωρεῖ αὐτὸ οὐδὲ γινώσκει
might seem to explain why the world cannot receive. In fact, ὅτι is
not causal here, as the reversal of the elements in the antithesis
makes plain. In Bengel's pithy phrase, *est quasi epanodos. Mundus
non accipit quia non novit: vos nostis quia habetis. Itaque "nosse"
et "habere" ita sunt coniuncta, ut non nosse sit causa non habendi, et
habere sit causa noscendi*.[90] Thus receiving on the one hand and seeing and knowing on the other describe the same process. It is difficult to know how the fathers understood the ὅτι-clause as they do
not directly comment on this aspect of the verse. But in general,
we may say that those who, like Theodore of Heraclea, take it to be
causal[91] have missed the point.

In the Fourth Gospel θεωρεῖν is used both simply, of physical sight (6,19; 9,8; 10,12; 20,6.12.14) and metaphorically, of mental or spiritual perception (4,19; 12,19).   In certain places it refers pregnantly to the perception of supersensual realities behind, or revealed in, the sensible (6,40; 12,45; cf. 6,62); its meaning then is closely related to that of πιστεύειν. What shall we make of it here? Apollinaris and Theodore of Heraclea understand it to refer to sight; the κόσμος is materialistic and is unable to accept what it cannot see with its eyes.[92] This exegesis is hardly correct. For one thing, it takes no account of the reproach implied. The world neither 'sees' nor 'knows', but it might have done so.   The disciples cannot be said to 'see' in this sense, yet they are open to the Spirit. The objection that θεωρεῖν is not used with regard to the disciples,[93] fails to recognise that the one word γινώσκετε provides the antithesis for both οὐ θεωρεῖ and οὐδὲ γινώσκει.[94] Furthermore, there is nothing in the context to suggest that θεωρεῖν must be sensual. On the contrary, the parousia of the Paraclete is incorporeal (cf. 20,22; 14,22-23), as Apollinaris and Theodore rightly recognise. It is best therefore to understand θεωρεῖν to refer to spiritual perception. Jesus here enunciates the general truth (the present tense is gnomic) that the world cannot perceive the Spirit at all. This is true whether he is to be perceived inwardly[95] or through historical persons and events.[96] If the world had perceived the Spirit of truth at work in Jesus, it would be open both to perceiving him at work in the disciples and to his operation in themselves. Augustine and others are right, therefore, when they interpret θεωρεῖν here in terms of spiritual sight.[97]

For confirmation that θεωρεῖ is not to be understood corporeally, John Chrysostom points to οὐδὲ γινώσκει. The Evangelist habit-

ually speaks of knowledge (γνῶσις) as sight (θεωρία), the most vivid
of the senses.[98] Leaving aside the question of the meaning of γινώσ-
κειν/γνῶσις in his thought, he is right at least in this: θεωρεῖν and
γινώσκειν are not here to be distinguished (cf. the similar use of
γινώσκειν with ὁρᾶν in 14,7). This is shown by the fact that the antithesis which follows resumes both expressions with the one word γινώσκετε. (These verbs do overlap in the Fourth Gospel; γινώσκειν more
than once bears the meaning 'recognise' (1,10, cf. 1 Jo. 4,2) or 'perceive (see 5,6; 6,15; 10,38; 13,35).[99])

     To recapitulate, the world is excluded from the gift of the
Spirit of truth by its radical inability either to receive or perceive
him. Worldly men cannot perceive the Spirit with physical sight, because his parousia is incorporeal. But (what is the issue here)
neither have they the eyes of faith necessary to discern him spiritually, whether at work behind mundane realities or, in some sense,
directly.[100] If the Church fathers sometimes misinterpret οὐ
θεωρεῖ[101] or fail to appreciate the precise nuance of ὅτι, they do
understand the overall significance of these clauses. They see clearly
that the κόσμος is the world of men who are in opposition to the things
of God and that, culpably blind, it can take no account of spiritual
realities. Furthermore, even when they interpret ὅτι causally and
θεωρεῖν corporeally, they understand that the Spirit of truth can only
be perceived spiritually, that is, by the man whose eyes have been
opened to heavenly things.

     By contrast,[102] the disciples are alert to the Spirit of
truth; he remains with them and is in them. The present tense (γινώσκετε . . . μένει . . . ἐστιν[103]), the natural tense to follow θεωρεῖ
and γινώσκει, is proleptic. Jesus here speaks of a future gift, the
coming of which is in fact contingent upon his own departure (16,7, cf.

7,39). The prolepsis continues in vv.18 and 19. Thus,Ambrosiaster[104]

and Theodore of Heraclea[105] to the contrary, this verse does not sug-

gest that the Spirit is already present with the disciples during the

period of Jesus' earthly ministry.[106] For them his parousia is yet

to come. Accordingly, both Ambrosiaster's appeal to consubstantiality

and Theodore's appeal to the baptism ἐν πνεύματι ἁγίῳ[107] are unnec-

essary.

Μένει stresses the enduring nature of the Spirit's presence

with the disciples. Taken with v.16, παρ' ὑμῖν μένει means that the

Paraclete is to remain with the Church perpetually (εἰς τὸν αἰῶνα).

Ammonius and Fulgentius rightly observe, therefore, that the Spirit's

presence with the faithful is permanent, not to be withdrawn.[108] Ful-

gentius may be thinking only of the period of the Church. Ammonius,

quoting John Chrysostom on 14,16, projects the μένειν beyond death

into the next life.[109] This is understandable if εἰς τὸν αἰῶνα[110]

is considered independently of context. But the Farewell Discourses

are concerned largely with the life of those left behind after Jesus'

departure; and the paraclete passages themselves treat of the aid to

be expected of the Paraclete temporally. In this light, it is better

to accept that these phrases speak of the presence of the Spirit of

truth with the disciples in this life and that they are not directly

concerned with the life to come.

If παρ' ὑμῖν μένει suggests the presence of the Spirit in the

Church, ἐν ὑμῖν ἐστιν pertains to his indwelling in the believer.[111]

Thus Chrysostom, in his paraphrase of these words, explains that the

Spirit is not to be with the disciples physically as Jesus has been

but will indwell their souls.[112] Augustine's remarks are fuller:

in uobis erit describes the manner of the Spirit's abode; it prevents

the disciples thinking that *apud uos manebit* means that he will be physically present among them.[113] This interpretation is in its es-

sential feature correct. While it is not very likely that the words

ἐν ὑμῖν ἐστιν were included by the Evangelist *for the purpose* of show-

ing that the Spirit's μένειν is an interior one, they do show that,

nonetheless.[114] These verses are spoken to the disciples as a group,

but they implicate the individual Christian. For the Spirit's pres-

ence with the disciples (μεθ' ὑμῶν, παρ' ὑμῖν) is effected and be-

comes known by his dwelling in them (ἐν ὑμῖν).[115] As both Apollinaris

and Augustine point out, the disciples discern the Spirit in the only

way he can be discerned, through direct experience of him.[116]

14,25-26

In 14,25, Jesus speaks of his own ministry to the disciples,

in 14,26 of the Paraclete's. The words παρ' ὑμῖν μένων have as their

referent Jesus' earthly sojourn, now about to end; the fathers have

no difficulty with this.[117] They experience discomfort, however,

over the phrase ὃ πέμψει ὁ πατήρ because it seems to conflict with

a Pneumatology in which the omnipresent and co-equal Spirit cannot be

sent. Thus they explain that it is not the divine Spirit himself who

is here in view but rather the visible symbols of his presence (Augus-

tine)[118] or his grace soon to be poured out upon the believer (Theo-

dore).[119] (Cf. Gaudentius who simply does not take πέμψει serious-

ly.)[120] The point to note is that these interpretations are ex-

pedients for explaining tensions imposed on the Gospel and not peculiar

to it; in forcing the text to conform to a fifth century Pneumatology

they fail to do it justice. Amphilochius, while he shares the same

dogmatic bias, nevertheless seems to be on firmer ground when he

tells us that these words show the Father's role in the dispensation

of the Spirit.[121] That is exactly what they do. Jesus has described

the impending presence and mission of the Paraclete. Now in this phrase

he reiterates (cf. 14,16; 15,26) that the Paraclete is not self-moti-
vating but receives his mission from the Father. As he sent Jesus,
so he sends the Paraclete in Jesus' name.

The precise meaning of ἐν τῷ ὀνόματί μου is somewhat uncertain.
It may suggest Jesus' part in sending the Paraclete (cf. 14,16; 15,26;
16,7). It may on the other hand recall that the Paraclete is the
ἄλλος who comes to act for Jesus and in his place just as Jesus himself acted for the Father (ἐν τῷ ὀνόματι τοῦ πατρός μου, 5,43; 10,
25), on his authority and as his representative. By way of interpretation, Barrett suggests "perhaps, 'because I ask', or 'to act in
relation to me, in my place, with my authority'."[122] Victorinus may
be on the right track, therefore, when he takes *in nomine meo* to mean
pro me.[123] Gaudentius, who says *in nomine meo, id est in dei nomine*,
is not; this in him is eisegesis on dogmatic grounds.[124]

The role assigned to the Paraclete in this passage is a
didactic one: ἐκεῖνος ὑμᾶς διδάξει πάντα καὶ ὑπομνήσει ὑμᾶς πάντα
ἃ εἶπον ὑμῖν (ἐγώ). In contrast with Jesus, whose teaching was
necessarily limited,[125] the Paraclete will teach the disciples all
things. But we must not overdraw the contrast. The Paraclete brings
no revelation independent of that given in Jesus, as the wider context shows.[126] Teaching and reminding are not separate functions;
ὑπομνήσει ὑμᾶς is epexegetic of ὑμᾶς διδάξει and shows wherein the
teaching consists. The Paraclete teaches all things by bringing to
the disciples' minds all that Jesus has said. He continues the revelation brought by Jesus by elucidating and applying it.[127]

It is not always possible to know exactly how the fathers
interpret this material. Their observations are often too brief or
obscured by theological concerns. Did Didymus,[128] for example, conclude that the Spirit's teaching will be the same as (οὐκ ἀπᾴδουσα)

Jesus' on exegetical grounds or out of concern to expound catholic

Trinitarian theology? Victorinus[129] is susceptible of similar ques-

tions. Theodore notes the distinction between the teaching of the

earthly Jesus, which is adequate for the disciples so long as he is

with them, and the fuller teaching to be expected of the Spirit, but

he neither explains nor expands.[130] Cyril[131] quite satisfactorily

points out that Jesus' revelation is incomplete and that the most

perfect revelation τοῦ μυστηρίου is to come through the Paraclete.

But he continues with an explanation that is dogmatic rather than

exegetical. The most straight-forward exposition is the terse ob-

servation by Amphilochius[132] that the Paraclete teaches the things

that Jesus did not say and brings to mind the things that he did say.

This is unacceptable; ὑπομιμνῄσκειν and διδάσκειν are not separate

tasks but complementary aspects of the same task.[133] In general,

therefore, we must say that patristic exegesis of this part of 14,26

(and, indeed, of the whole of these two verses) leaves something to be

desired. The fathers sometimes contain what seem to be valid in-

sights; but, partly through brevity and theological preoccupation, they

fall short of adequate exposition.

Theodore of Heraclea also reveals a faulty exegesis of ὑπομ-

νήσει ὑμᾶς πάντα ἃ εἶπον ὑμῖν. He argues, it will be recalled, that

Montanus and his circle cannot represent the fulfillment of the promise

of the Paraclete because it is impossible for the Spirit to remind any-

one of words of Jesus which they never heard him utter.[134] He is fol-

lowed and quoted by Ammonius of Alexandria.[135] Theodore is right, of

course, to insist that the promise was fulfilled in apostolic times;[136]

in the context of the Discourses the gift is as imminent as the

departure of Jesus (cf. 16,7).[137] But he limits the ὑπομιμνῄσκειν to

a simple reminiscence of actual words of Jesus. In fact, as we sug-

gest above, it is much more than that; it is a living, creative exposition and application of the Gospel. Furthermore, he verges on
restricting the Paraclete to the apostles, as Hegemonius does explicitly in his anti-Manichaean exposition of Jo. 16,14.[138] But this,
too, is false exegesis. Jesus' promise is made to the disciples, it
is true, but to the disciples as representatives of the later community. The Paraclete remains εἰς τὸν αἰῶνα; he is active during
the whole time of the Church. In Theodore's exegesis, he is too
narrowly circumscribed.

15,26-27

The clause ὁ παρὰ τοῦ πατρὸς ἐκπορεύεται[139] turns up rather
frequently in the fathers. This is hardly surprising as it is the
foundation upon which they build the doctrine of the eternal procession of the Spirit.[140] But their interpretation is plausible only so
long as these words are read in isolation. The context requires a
different understanding. The Evangelist is not here speculating on
the inner life of the Godhead; he is concerned with the disciples in
the world and the temporal mission of the Paraclete as witness. That
ὁ παρὰ τοῦ πατρὸς ἐκπορεύεται is harmonious with its context is evident from the parallelism between (a) ὁ παράκλητος ὃν ἐγὼ πέμψω ὑμῖν
παρὰ τοῦ πατρός and (b) τὸ πνεῦμα τῆς ἀληθείας ὃ παρὰ τοῦ πατρὸς
ἐκπορεύεται.[141] As the first element refers to the mission, it is difficult to conceive that the second does not. In this light, παρὰ τοῦ
πατρός (b) does not mean 'from the Father's substance' or 'inmost
being';[142] ἐκπορεύεται is not a technical term for procession; the
present tense does not suggest, as Avitus thought, the timelessness
of the eternal present.[143] The words ὁ παρὰ τοῦ πατρὸς ἐκπορεύεται
serve to reiterate the Father's role in the dispensation of the
Paraclete (cf. 14,16.26).[144] It is not insignificant that Jesus' own

mission is described in the Gospel in similar terms and with a similar turn of phrase.[145] Jesus' work in the world was validated by its
origin in the Father; so also is that of the Paraclete.

If the early theologians misconstrue ὃ παρὰ τοῦ πατρὸς ἐκπορεύεται,[146] they do rather better at explaining the apparent contradiction between ὃν ἐγὼ πέμψω in this verse and ὃ πέμψει ὁ πατήρ
in 14,26.[147] In their view these statements, far from conflicting,
illustrate the unity of the Father and the Son. That is why they
can juxtapose 14,26 and 15,26[148] (or, similarly, 14,26 and 16,7[149])
as proof that the Spirit is sent by neither acting alone but by both
together. Although some fathers mistakenly apply this interpretation
to the doctrine of the double procession[150] and some are susceptible to
the suspicion that it is not exegesis that has informed their doctrine
but rather the contrary,[151] the basic insight is valid. These seemingly contradictory declarations about the mission of the Paraclete do
illustrate the Johannine theme that the Son and the Father are one.
That the Father gives or sends the Paraclete is established in 14,16.
26. Now in 15,26 we see that the Son also has a part to play, a part
so active that he too may be said to send. This is, of course, nothing
more than a new formulation of a motif already voiced (ἐρωτήσω, 14,16;
ἐν τῷ ὀνόματί μου, 14,26). In fact, the dual dispensation of the
Paraclete is visible in each of the first two paraclete passages; on
our reading, it is also present in 15,26, though this is not apparent
to the fathers.[152] But, in addition to unity, 15,26 also reflects
the theme of the subordination of the Son to the Father.[153] For,
while Jesus shares in the sending of the Paraclete, the Father is
the ultimate source of the mission (παρὰ τοῦ πατρός, ὃ παρὰ τοῦ πατρὸς
ἐκπορεύεται). Cf. 14,16 (the Father bestows, Jesus only requests) and
14,26 (the Father has the primary role, that of Jesus is no more than
hinted).[154] On the whole, the fathers fail to recognise this theme

here,[155] and it is undoubtedly their dogmatic bias which has blinded
them.[156]

The principal affirmation of the present passage comes at the
end of v.26 and the beginning of v.27. Without warrant the world has
hated Jesus and will on his account persecute the disciples.[157] But
the world does not have the final word; for over against it is set
the Paraclete, who will, when he has come, bear decisive witness to
Jesus (cf. 16,8-11), and the disciples, who also bear witness. The
precise relationship between his testimony and theirs is left un-
specified; but clearly, his work must be mediated to the world which
cannot receive him (14,17) by the proclamation of those who alone
can (cf. 17,20). His testimony comes to the world through theirs.[158]
John places the witness of the disciples alongside that of the Paraclete because the two are interdependent. This fact does not escape
the patristic exegetes. It is most fully expounded by Augustine,[159]
but Theodore[160] and Cyril[161] make note of it, as well. They also
rightly understand the ὅτι-clause of v.27: the disciples are
qualified to bear witness to Jesus because they are eye-witnesses
of his ministry.[162]

16,4b-7

The fourth paraclete passage begins with a reference to the
material immediately preceding it. Jesus has just for the first time
given warning of the persecutions inevitably to come upon the disciples when he is gone (15,18-16,4a). 16,4b explains that it was unnecessary to broach this subject so long as he was with them. Until
now (ἐξ ἀρχῆς) he has been their sufficiency; but he is on the eve
of departure to the Father and must prepare them for what is to come.
The ancient commentators understand this well.[163] That includes John
Chrysostom, although his additional observation that 'these things'

were withheld in the beginning so that no one might accuse Jesus of
merely making an educated guess is without foundation.[164] It is plainly to be inferred from their writings that the fathers also rightly
identify as the antecedent of ταῦτα what has just been said about
persecution.[165] Augustine is the notable exception. So to interpret
16,4b would cause it to conflict with Matthew 10,17-18 (and parallels),
which is for him unthinkable on *a priori* grounds. That is why he
refers the demonstrative to 15,26 and the coming of the Spirit to
bear witness at the time of trial.[166] This neglects the sense of the
verse in its context. *Haec autem uobis ab initio non dixi* may be intended to include the content of 15,26-27, but the primary referent is
the teaching on persecution. That is clearly the antecedent of ταῦτα
in 16,1.4a; there is no good reason why it should have a different
antecedent in v.4b.[167]

Augustine is even less successful with his exegesis of 16,5.
In his view, it will be recalled, *at nunc uado ad eum qui me misit*
speaks of the visible ascension of Jesus εἰς τὸν οὐρανόν (Acts 1,9-11,
cf. Lk. 24,50-51). When Jesus returns to the Father, the disciples
will not need to ask *quo uadis* because they will see for themselves.[168]
At base Augustine misses the mark because he has not understood the
significance for John of Jesus' ὑπάγειν; it covers not only the return
to the glory of the Father but also his departure in death (cf. 13,3.
33.36-37; 14,28; 16,17-22).[169] This verse points to an imminent (νῦν)
event to take place in the wake of Judas' betrayal. And it speaks of
the disciples' immediate reaction to what Jesus has told them. They
are so filled with grief that they do not enquire concerning his destination and thus find comfort. As Barrett points out, it is necessary
here to give the present tense of ἐρωτᾷ its full value.[170] It is
neither historical, which would conflict with 13,36 and 14,5, nor,

Augustine to the contrary, proleptic. In their sorrow the disciples
are *now* neglecting to ask Jesus ποῦ ὑπάγεις - now when they have most
need of the answer. It would seem that this understanding of ἐρωτᾷ
is shared by the Greeks.[171]

The overall meaning of vv.5-6 can hardly be missed: the
disciples are paralysed through their anguish at what Jesus has told
them. Thus the Greek commentators;[172] but Chrysostom and Cyril add
the observation that Jesus here comforts his followers by showing
that he is aware of their despondency and sympathising with it.[173]
Undoubtedly there is comfort in the context, but it lies in the pro-
jection of the Paraclete into the midst of their trials, not here.
These verses rebuke the disciples for failing to appropriate the consolation they might have had through knowing Jesus' destination.
Chrysostom goes even further astray with his perplexing suggestion
that Jesus at this point withholds from his followers the promise of
the Spirit to help them so that we might observe their unflinching
steadfastness.[174] One wonders if he has really read the text in its
setting. Does he not see that Jesus resumes the teaching on the Paraclete just one verse later in 16,7 (not to mention 15,26-27)? Where
does the Evangelist offer such an idealised portrait of disciples who
have not as yet received the Spirit? Certainly not here.

Fulgentius is also open to criticism on these verses. It is
not clear precisely what he means when he says *Saluator, ut ostenderet
perturbationem istam non carni, sed animae deputandam, sic discipulos
suos consolatur.*[175] Perhaps he means to say that their perturbation is
not carnal, that is, not sinful, or perhaps that it is not physical,
that is, that they are not in fear for their lives. In any case, the
distinction is exegetically groundless and invests *cor* with meaning that
the context will not bear.[176] Fulgentius has misread the motivation

for vv.5-6, and, like the Greek fathers, he mistakes rebuke for consolation.

According to v.7, Jesus' departure, grievous as it may seem to
the disciples now, is really to their advantage; for it is both the
occasion and the prerequisite for the mission of the Paraclete. The
underlying thought is the same as that of 7,39: the coming of the
Spirit is dependent upon the prior completion of the work of Jesus.
Much of the ancient commentary on 16,7 centres in the idea of expedi-
ency expressed in the verb συμφέρει. Such is the self-apparent observation that, despite their dismay at his words, Jesus persists in
telling the disciples what they for their own good need to know.[177]
Granted the assumption that Jesus is the model for Christian practice,
it then follows ὅτι τὴν κατὰ Χριστὸν ἀγάπην ὁ ἔχων ἔστιν ὅτε καὶ λυπεῖ
πρὸς τὸ συμφέρον τὸν ἀγαπώμενον.[178] All this, while not brilliant, is
tolerable. Cyril's explanation that the departure is advantageous
to the disciples because the Lord had still to go into the Father's
presence to complete his work on our behalf is, however, unacceptable.[179] Although it is superficially coincidental with Johannine
thinking, it is based, not on exegesis of 16,7 or even of the Fourth
Gospel, but on theological ideas supported by quotations from Hebrews
and the epistles of St. Paul. But Cyril has not entirely missed the
point, as he shows when he goes on at some length to say that Jesus'
departure is expedient because it is the occasion of the descent of
the Spirit who strengthens the disciples in the face of opposition.[180]
Chrysostom infers the equality of Spirit and Son from this verse on
the assumption that it cannot be said to be expedient for a master to
depart in order that his servant might come.[181] His deduction fails
because his premise is faulty.

Why did the Spirit not come before Jesus' departure? Chrysos-

tom offers two different answers. In his homily on 16,4b-15, he maintains it is because the Spirit could not come until sin had been con-
quered and man reconciled to God.[182] Here he does seem to have

grasped the significance of ἐὰν γὰρ μὴ ἀπέλθω, ὁ παράκλητος οὐκ ἐλεύσεται πρὸς ὑμᾶς. He has not, however, properly understood πέμψω αὐτὸν
πρὸς ὑμᾶς which he takes to mean προπαρασκευάσω ὑμᾶς πρὸς τὴν ὑποδοχήν. He arrives at this interpretation not on the basis of sound
exegetical principle but because any more usual reading of πέμψω
seems inimical to the doctrine of the omnipresence of the Spirit. In
his homily on the opening verses of Acts, Chrysostom asserts that
the Lord withheld the Spirit for a time in order to create such a
longing in the disciples that the consolation of his coming might be
sufficiently great. He further assumes the equality of the Spirit with
the Son, as the disciples will be sufficiently consoled only if the
void left by Jesus in their lives is filled by a presence commensurate
with his.[183] This explanation of the timing of the Spirit's advent is
speculation for which there is no foundation in the text of John.

Augustine offers an interpretation which is, if not so speculative, not entirely dissimilar. For him, *si non abiero Paracletus
non ueniet ad uos* means that the disciples must be weaned of Jesus'
physical presence; so long as they know him *secundum carnem* they will
have no room for the Spirit, no appetite for the solid food of the
Gospel.[184] Whatever there may be of psychological, perhaps even
theological, merit in this approach, it will not do as exegesis
because there is nothing in the verse to substantiate it. Augustine
errs here, it would seem, because he characteristically misunderstands
the significance for the Evangelist of Jesus' departure.[185] While
departure undoubtedly includes Jesus' disappearance from the earthly
scene (cf. 16,10), the point of v.7 is that the successful completion
of his ministry, with all that that means, is the precondition for

the coming of the Spirit. Accordingly, Augustine is also wrong to
deny (probably for dogmatic reasons) that this verse implies that
Jesus was unable to send the Spirit before his departure. He does
rather better when he points out on the basis of 14,16.23 (he also
quotes Mt. 28,20) that the Spirit does not simply replace Jesus but
that he is present together with him and the Father in the disciples.[186] It is perhaps understandable in a theologian of his epoch
and convictions that in expounding this insight he goes too far and
gives exegesis a dogmatic overlay; but even that does not destroy
the validity of the basic exegesis. (This is not to say that Faustus
and Victorinus are wrong to deduce from v.7 that the Paraclete does
replace (the earthly) Jesus.[187] Our passages teach this and they
take them at face value. They simply do not match Augustine's concern for the nuances required by the wider context.)

16,8-11

Καὶ ἐλθὼν ἐκεῖνος ἐλέγξει τὸν κόσμον περὶ ἁμαρτίας καὶ περὶ
δικαιοσύνης καὶ περὶ κρίσεως. In the coming conflict, the Paraclete
will take the offensive against the world. In particular, he will
convict it of sin, of righteousness, and of judgment (see further on
vv.9-11 below). The world will undoubtedly not submit willingly, but
he will compel it to recognise and admit these facts.[188] Thus Ambrosiaster rightly says, *hoc est 'arguere mundum', ostendere illi*
uera esse quae credere noluit.[189] How will the Paraclete convict the
world? We are not told; but, as we have already seen (p.154), his
work vis-a-vis the world (which cannot receive him) must be mediated
through that of the Church. There are various things in patristic
exegesis of 16,8 with which we must be uncomfortable. According to
Augustine, for example, *ille arguet mundum* is meant to convey that the
Spirit will cast out the fear which keeps the disciples from reproving

the world.[190] And for Ambrosiaster the Spirit has since his coming
effected his ἐλέγχειν by performing public miracles in Jesus' name
through the disciples.[191] Neither of these observations can be derived from the text before us. Yet both imply the more valuable insight that the Paraclete accomplishes his operation on the world not
directly but through the disciples.[192] We have met this idea explicitly stated in Augustine before now (see p.154).

   V.8 is explained in what follows. The Paraclete will, first
of all, convict the world περὶ ἁμαρτίας . . . ὅτι οὐ πιστεύουσιν εἰς
ἐμέ (v.9). That is, he will prove that it is in its rejection of
Jesus guilty of sin. We can have no quarrel with the patristic
writers on this verse; for, speaking generally, they seem to have
a firm grasp of its meaning.[193] There is, to be sure, a difference
between the expositions of East and West, but it is a difference of
emphasis, not one of disagreement. If the Greek fathers concentrate
on the fact that the world is to be condemned by the Paraclete on
account of its sin, they are not unaware of the nature of that sin.[194]
If the Latin fathers make more of the offence itself, the sin of unbelief,[195] and observe that, while this is not the only sin, it is
singled out for mention because it is the archetypal sin,[196] they do
not overlook the Paraclete's work of conviction. Granted, Augustine is
the only one to point out in this connexion the difference between
believing certain facts about Jesus and believing on him in the sense
of faith.[197] But even here there would have been no dissentient
voice. He does no more than bring to expression what for others is
axiomatic. Despite differences of tone and emphasis, the ancients are
pretty well united in a true understanding of 16,9.

   Secondly, the Paraclete will convict the world περὶ δικαιοσύνης
. . . ὅτι πρὸς τὸν πατέρα ὑπάγω καὶ οὐκέτι θεωρεῖτέ με (v.10). But,

as Augustine observes,[198] he cannot convict it of its own righteousness, since it cannot at the same time be both righteous and sinful.[199] So far the fathers are in tacit agreement: the sin of which
the world is convicted is its own, the righteousness is another's.
But whose? That is the question which divides them. Some take it to
be the righteousness of the believers, those who continue to have
faith in Jesus though he is no longer visible to sight.[200] But this
cannot be right. For, in the first place, it misconstrues the significance of οὐκέτι θεωρεῖτέ με, where the reference is not to the
blessedness of those who believe without having seen (cf. 20,29) but
to the disappearance of Jesus in the departure which is at once his
death and his exaltation. And, in the second place, it misapprehends
the contrast of vv.9-10, which sets the world in opposition to Jesus
rather than to the disciples.[201] The better approach is found in
those fathers who teach that it is the righteousness of Jesus which
is here in view.[202] Although the world deemed Jesus to be a sinner
and refused to believe that he came from God, he was in fact blameless; his mission from God is proved by his return to God (cf. 3,13).
The Paraclete thus completely overturns the world's verdict. He
convicts it of sin (in men) where it had assumed righteousness and of
righteousness (in Jesus) where it had thought to find sin. It may be
inferred that the disciples are also righteous, but only in a derived
sense.[203]

     Thirdly, the world is to be convicted περὶ δὲ κρίσεως, ὅτι ὁ
ἄρχων τοῦ κόσμου τούτου κέκριται (v.11). ὁ ἄρχων τοῦ κόσμου τούτου -
in this precise form the expression is peculiar to the Fourth Gospel
(cf. 12,31 and 14,30) - is universally in the early Church identified as Satan, the devil.[204] Nowhere does the Evangelist make the
identification explicit, but there can hardly be any doubt that the

Church is right. In 8,44 the opponents of Jesus are said to be children of the devil, and, while the metaphor is different, the thought
of that passage is identical to the idea implied by this. The son
is dominated by the will of the father, the world is under the sway
of its prince. Furthermore, if the world's sin is the rejection of
Jesus, it is Satan who motivates that sin and is responsible for bringing it to its ultimate expression in the crucifixion: the world seeks
to kill Jesus because that is the desire of its father, the devil (8,
40-41.44); it is the devil or Satan (the terms are interchangeable)
who possesses Judas to betray his Lord (13,2.27). And yet responsibility for the events of the passion is also assigned to ὁ τοῦ κόσμου
ἄρχων (14,30). Since there is no reason to suspect that John had two
separate figures in mind, we are free to accept that the ἄρχων of
16,11 is the devil. We may also remark in the light of all this that
Ammonius and Theodore of Heraclea are not out of harmony with the
wider context of the Gospel when they comment that the world's prince
is condemned for inciting the Jews to do Jesus to death,[205] though
that cannot be inferred from 16,11 and the immediate context alone.
What is not clear, however, is to what degree their exposition here is
actually based on a reading of the Gospel itself.

Augustine rightly calls attention to the fact that the κόσμος
the ἄρχων rules is the world of unbelieving men (see above pp.144-
145).[206] That Cyril is correct to say that Satan merits this title
not by right but because he has usurped the place of God, that he is
a pretender to the throne and continues to rule only by holding the
world in thrall,[207] cannot, of course, be deduced from this passage.
But it is not inconsistent with the thought of the Gospel as a whole.
The rightful ruler of men is he who made them (cf. 1,10-12). Until
now, Satan has had them in subjection; but his tyranny is ended, he

will be put out of office and they will be freed. The cross represents for Jesus not defeat but glorification, for Satan not the hour
(as it seems) of his triumph but his downfall (12,31-32).[208] Here-
after he stands under judgment, ὅτι ὁ ἄρχων τοῦ κόσμου τούτου κέκριται.
But the matter, as Augustine remarks, does not end there. For, just
as the disciple partakes of the righteousness of Jesus, the world is
included in and shares the condemnation of its prince.[209] This is
implied in 16,8-11; it comes to expression in 12,31 where the judgment
of the world and the expulsion of Satan are placed side by side. The
converse, voiced by John Chrysostom, that in the condemnation of the
ἄρχων is inherent the vindication of Jesus and his disciples[210] is
also valid. It must be so because the radical opposition here between Jesus and the world allows no middle ground. If Jesus is righteous, the world is sinful; if the prince who put Jesus on the cross
comes under judgment, Jesus is thereby vindicated.

        Cyril's portrayal of the form the Paraclete's third reproof
will take - he will show that the world has strayed from God and
taken up the worship of Satan[211] - we cannot accept as it reads too
much into the passage. The same is true of the assumption by Ammonius
and Theodore that the condemnation of the ἄρχων is demonstrated in
the miraculous works of the disciples.[212] That may well be to John's
mind part of the Paraclete's method, but there is nothing here to
indicate that it is so (cf. above p.160).

16,12-15

        16,12-13 returns to the theme, formerly sounded in 14,25-26,
of the Paraclete as teacher and guide of the Church. Here again are
clearly delineated the two stages of revelation. Jesus represents the
first and central stage. He has been the teacher until now. But his
ministry is (necessarily) incomplete; there are may things which he

has had to leave unsaid. By contrast, the Spirit of truth who comes after will not share the constraints which have limited Jesus. He will, so the disciples are told, ὁδηγήσει ὑμᾶς ἐν τῇ ἀληθείᾳ πάσῃ,[213] with emphasis on πάσῃ. For John, God reveals himself in Jesus, but it requires the presence and operation of the Spirit of truth to make that revelation complete.

Patristic exposition of vv.12-13a is, on the whole, not very successful.[214] The general drift, namely, that Jesus cannot say all he would but that the Paraclete will complete his revelation, is to the ancient exegetes more or less self-evident. Their concerns lie elsewhere. In the first place, they are very quick to speculate on the nature of the πολλά which Jesus defers to the fuller revelation of the Spirit. The usual approach is to identify particular types of truth or information, such as the spiritual exegesis of the Law[215] or, more generally, the deeper truths and mysteries of the faith for which the renewing work of the Spirit is pre-requisite.[216] The latter, variously specified but quite often with Trinitarian over-tones, obviously reflect the preoccupations of the writers. Augustine refuses to speculate about what Jesus' *multa* might include, though it is clear he too assumes that it has to do with the deeper mysteries of the faith.[217] All this, of course, implies that the Paraclete has additional, in the sense of novel, revelations to impart, an interpretation made explicit in Didymus[218] and, more radically, in Phoebadius.[219]

It is, in fact, just here that a basic flaw in the patristic approach to these verses becomes visible. It is true that Jesus, whose teaching is limited, is contrasted with the Spirit of truth, who will not share his limitations; but, as at 14,26, it is possible to exaggerate the contrast. The Paraclete, when he comes, will guide the

disciples in the realm of all truth, but not by bringing completely
fresh revelation.[220] He is tied to the revelation already given in
Jesus, as is made plain in vv.13-15 (cf. 14,26). It will be his task
to illuminate that revelation and make it perennially relevant in the
Church. ἀλήθεια thus retains its usual Johannine sense (Jesus is the
truth, 14,6) and πνεῦμα τῆς ἀληθείας its appropriateness in this context (see p.144). To his credit, Leo seems to have a clear understanding of the connexion between Jesus and the Spirit's ὁδηγεῖν.[221]
But the rest are fundamentally amiss. It is not just that their
pronouncements concerning what it is that Jesus has left for the
Spirit to reveal are purely speculative, but is at once less simple
and more basic. They fail to see, on the one hand, that the Spirit is
to bring no independent truth and that, on the other, we are told what
the content of his revelation will be. If they had understood that,
they would have had no need to speculate (or refuse to speculate)
concerning what new doctrines it would be the task of the Spirit to
reveal. As it is, they tend to read their own preoccupations into the
text.

A second concern is to establish exactly why the disciples are
unable to bear the Lord's further revelation. The predominant explanation involves their Jewishness. Because of their background and
training they are not yet, not (some specify) until the resurrection
and coming of the Spirit have created a new openness, ready for the
whole Christian message.[222] This, of course, is conjecture, though it
is not unlikely that the disciples did at times know some such limi-
tation. Theodore explains simply that the disciples are unable to bear
Jesus' further teaching because, until they know the guidance of the
Spirit, it is beyond their understanding.[223] Both interpretations
imply a fair grasp of the essential meaning. Jesus withholds from the

disciples what yet remains because at the moment it exceeds their capacity. Certain aspects of the truth will only become meaningful
after the completion of his ministry (cf. 12,16), others only in the
light of what the future brings (v.13b). Such things are beyond the
disciples now, but under the guidance of the Paraclete they will come
to full understanding. Cyril interprets οὐ δύνασθε βαστάζειν in terms
of the despondency mentioned in v.6: Jesus has further predictions of
coming persecution which he refrains from sharing so as not to dispirit the disciples further.[224] But it seems clear from vv.13-15
that neither specific predictions concerning the world's hostility nor
the despondency of the disciples is primarily in view.

Vv.12-13a are also the subject of practical application in the
early Church. Augustine draws from v.12 the ethical principle, which
he expresses in various ways, that it is not always necessary or even
helpful to tell the whole truth, especially if telling it would bring
the hearer injury or is beyond his ability to bear.[225] On the assum-
tion that the example of Jesus is the model for all Christian practice, this is quite allowable. The pastoral applications, which
Augustine begins to explore, are wide-ranging.

Tertullian's earliest interest in this passage is apologetic.
Against those who reject the *regula fidei* with the argument that the
apostles were not omniscient and cannot therefore have delivered a
complete faith, he urges from v.13 that there is nothing they did not
know after the advent of the Spirit.[226] It will be apparent from this
that his exegesis, such of it as we can infer from his argument, is
heavily coloured by his prejudices. He implies that *ipse uos deducet
in omnem ueritatem* means that the apostles (!) will be provided with a
complete and static deposit of doctrine, the *regula fidei* of the
Church, to be preserved for all time. In fact his instinct is sound:

the paraclete is the guarantor that truth will prevail in the Church.
But his exegesis goes wide of the mark; for the Spirit of truth is
portrayed here not as one who simply drops parcelled truth once and for
all into the minds of the apostles but as one who keeps the revelation
of Jesus perpetually alive and understood. His mission extends beyond
the apostles to the whole time of the Church (cf. 14,16, but also the
entire context of our passages).

    This static concept of leading in all truth is displaced in
Tertullian's later moralizing writings by the idea that the Paraclete
is perpetually at work to develop Church discipline.[227] But there is
nothing either in 16,13 or elsewhere in the paraclete passages to
indicate that the Spirit's role of elucidating the revelation given
in Jesus and bringing it home to the Church includes giving specific
instruction about Church discipline. Even if such a case could be
made out, we would be left with the feeling that Tertullian is interested in this passage only as a proof-text to justify his own teaching. The shortcomings of his exegesis appear most plainly when he
defends his stringent demands by appealing to 16,12-13 to prove that
the Paraclete's teaching will be both novel and burdensome.[228] With
the notion of novelty we have already dealt. On the second point,
v.12 implies, not (as Tertullian seems to think) that the Paraclete
will bring burdensome revelation, but that the things which cannot now
be borne because the disciples are not ready for them will be no longer
unbearable under the leading of the Paraclete. Tertullian's applications of these verses, aside from being exegetically faulty, are
tendentious and reflect his own prejudices.

    V.13b begins a section which, continuing to the end of the
passage, delimits the Paraclete's ὁδηγεῖν. First of all, οὐ γὰρ
λαλήσει ἀφ' ἑαυτοῦ, ἀλλ' ὅσα ἀκούσει λαλήσει. As in the case of Jesus

(cf. 7,16-17; 8,28; 12,49; 14,10), the Spirit brings no autonomous revelation. His teaching originates in the Father; the truth he declares is God's truth. This is the guarantee of his trustworthiness.[229] On the essential point, the Greek fathers are correct.[230] If they tend to stress the accord between the revelation of the Spirit and that of Jesus, that is fully justified by the context. The difficulty is the overlay of Trinitarian theology which obscures the meaning of the text. John is not here concerned to expose the consubstantial equality of the Spirit with the Father and the Son as they seem to think. He speaks, rather, of the Spirit's mission of revelation in the Church and makes the point that his revelation is not independent but is the very word of God. The fathers, however, verge on treating this whole section as though it were a tract of Trinitarian orthodoxy, with the result that the theology of a later time tends to become the hermeneutical principle by which the Gospel is understood.[231]

In the West, Augustine and Fulgentius carry this tendency to its limit. Their sole concern with v.13b is to reconcile the words *quaecumque audiet* with the concept of an eternally omniscient Spirit. The Lord's words, they explain, must be understood in the light of the fact that the Spirit is not self-existent. As he receives his being, so also he receives his knowledge, that is, he hears, through the eternal procession from the Father and (thus Fulgentius) the Son.[232] This being so, Augustine adds, the future tense of the verb *audiet* need not disturb us. Where hearing is eternal, any tense of the verb would be correct.[223] The shortcoming of this approach is obvious: it completely sacrifices exegesis to theology.

Fulgentius extends this treatment to the rest of the passage. Vv.12-13a, for example, and the role there reserved for the Spirit he

takes as evidence that the Spirit is equal to the Father and the Son
and of one substance with them.[234] Here again he forces his theology
upon the text. As a result, he ascribes to the passage (and to Jesus)
a motive that cannot be deduced from it and renders himself insen-
sitive to all but the features which suit his purpose. This is false
methodology, and that, rather than any individual detail of interpretation, must be our primary quarrel with it. The point is important beyond Fulgentius, for the fault is not uniquely his. It is
repeated by the fathers to one degree or another wherever doctrine
colours their understanding of, or is their principal motive for
coming to, the text. It is wrong method - and here we touch the heart
of the present matter - that limits their success in interpreting
v.13b; wrong method also underlies the distortion in their expositions
of vv.14-15, as we shall want to bear in mind. This is neither meant
to reflect on the validity of their doctrines[235] nor to suggest that
16,12-15 has no value for theology or, indeed, for the doctrine of
the Trinity. But our concern is with exegesis, and exegesis must be
prior to theology. If the text, once its meaning has been ascertained,
contributes to theology, well and good. But it is intolerable that
doctrine should impose upon the text a predetermined meaning.

     For the Greek fathers, the final clause of v.13, καὶ τὰ
ἐρχόμενα ἀναγγελεῖ ὑμῖν, is also intended to convey dogmatic truth.[236]
Cyril says it is added to what precedes to underscore the consubstantiality of the Spirit with Jesus, who also foretold the future.[237] According to John Chrysostom, Jesus shows by these words the Spirit's
divine dignity, since foretelling things to come is especially the
property of God.[238] Here again the fathers, taking as their starting
point not exegesis but doctrine, attribute to the text an intention
which is foreign to it. In consequence they prove too much from it.

Furthermore, it is unlikely that these words, coming as they do in a
context which emphasizes the connexion between the Spirit's ὁδηγεῖν
and the revelation of God in Jesus, have to do with simple predictive
prophecy. As we have pointed out, the Paraclete is not (here or
elsewhere) presented as a source of new revelation. His is the task
of elucidating the revelation already given, of bringing full understanding of the divine truth set forth in Jesus. In view of this, it
would seem that τὰ ἐρχόμενα ἀναγγελεῖ ὑμῖν is best understood to
refer not to the prediction of future events but to the illumination
of the future itself in the light of that truth. The Paraclete
exercises his ὁδηγεῖν throughout the life of the Church. Whatever
comes, he will be at work in every generation to make clear the
significance of the Christian revelation for the contemporary situation.[239]

The preoccupation of the early Church fathers with theology
is particularly pronounced in their exposition of vv.14-15. They
write few lines that are unaffected by it. Yet it is possible to
discern some features of the way they interpret or fail to interpret
the details of the underlying text. In v.14 we are told, as part of
the continuing description of the Paraclete's task in the Church,
that he will give glory to Jesus. How he will do this is explained
in the ὅτι-clause. At first glance it might seem that the fathers
understand the verse reasonably well when they explain that the Spirit
glorifies Jesus by revealing to believers the fact that he is very
God.[240] At least, so it might be said, they have rightly identified
the method by which he works, whether or not they are entirely right
about what it is he will reveal. But two things suggest that they
formed their understanding of the manner in which the Spirit will
glorify Jesus on some basis other than exegesis of v.14: a) Nowhere in

the explanation of v.14a do they appeal to v.14b. In fact, their

treatment of the latter (see below) seems to be quite separate. b)

When they do raise the question of the Spirit's *modus operandi*, they

answer it in other terms. He will glorify Jesus, they variously say,

by performing miraculous works through the disciples,[241] by filling

them with boldness that they might proclaim Christ,[242] by being om-

nipotent and omniscient himself, which suggests that the Christ from

whom he receives must also have those attributes.[243] Whatever may be

the merits of these suggestions in other ways, they fail to do the

one necessary thing, that is, to take account of the Evangelist's own

explanation of ἐκεῖνος ἐμὲ δοξάσει: ὅτι ἐκ τοῦ ἐμοῦ λήμψεται καὶ ἀναγ-

γελεῖ ὑμῖν. In the light of these facts and the nature of the ex-

position, it seems probable that the origin of patristic interpreta-

tion of v.14a is theological rather than exegetical.

Exposition of v.14b is similarly coloured. Cyril, concerned

to defend the doctrine of consubstantiality, understands these words

to mean that the Spirit will speak in language identical to that of

Jesus and in complete accord with his will and purpose.[244] Chrysostom,

stressing the equality of Jesus and the Spirit, interprets that what-

ever Jesus has told the disciples the Spirit will also tell them.[245]

Neither of these interpretations is completely amiss. It cannot be

wrong in the context to understand from vv.14b.15b that the Spirit's

revelation will be in harmony with that of Jesus. But neither are

they entirely correct, for they fail to deal adequately with ἐκ τοῦ

ἐμοῦ. The meaning of the phrase is determined by the content of the

foregoing material. It is the truth not only of the teaching - though

that is included (16,12f; 14,26) - but also the mission and being of

Jesus (16,8-11; 15,26) that the Paraclete declares to the disciples

and through them to the world. Cyril, who is thinking not of the his-

torical revelation and mission of Jesus but of the consubstantial unity of the Spirit with the divine Son, misunderstands ἐκ τοῦ ἐμοῦ almost completely. Chrysostom displays partial understanding here. But
his subsequent explanation, this time stressing the unity of knowledge between the Spirit and Jesus, that ἐκ τοῦ ἐμοῦ means ἐξ ὧν ἐγὼ
οἶδα, ἐκ τῆς ἐμῆς γνώσεως[246] is less adequate. Theodore goes more
radically wrong. He understands ἐκ τοῦ ἐμοῦ λαμβάνει (v.15) to refer
to the grace which, entire in Jesus, is also partially to be bestowed
upon the disciples.[247] This interpretation not only fails to take
account of the wider context, it is also, unlike the interpretations
of Cyril and Chrysostom, incompatible with ἀναγγελεῖ ὑμῖν. Apollinaris and Vigilius make a quite different observation. They both
rightly point out that, in the light of v.15a, ἐκ τοῦ ἐμοῦ λήμψεται
(λαμβάνει) is equivalent to receiving from the Father.[248]

     We may briefly mention three further points with regard to
v.14. Firstly, several fathers infer from the verse and its context
that the true Spirit, and therefore the true teacher, may be distinguished by the fact that he speaks the things of, and gives glory
to, Jesus.[249] This criterion, used against the claims of Montanus
and others, is a valid deduction from the text. The Evangelist would
agree that he who is possessed of the Spirit of truth will neither
detract from the glory of Jesus nor contradict his revelation. Secondly, the Spirit's λαμβάνειν of v.14b creates the same problem for the
fathers and receives the same explanation from them as did his ἀκούειν
of v.13b (see above p.168).[250] Here, as there, they are guilty of
dogmatic eisegesis. Thirdly, we note the argument that ἐκ τοῦ ἐμοῦ
λήμψεται proves the deity of Jesus: if he were mere man, he would
receive revelation from the Spirit; that the Spirit, on the contrary,
receives of him shows that he is no creature.[251] The argument is care-

fully thought out, but fails in that neither the conclusion nor the
assumptions which lie behind it rest upon an exegesis of the passage.
John is here concerned to establish, not the divine nature of Jesus,
but the centrality of the revelation of Jesus for the mission of the
Spirit.

Finally, πάντα ὅσα ἔχει ὁ πατὴρ ἐμά ἐστιν. The fathers appeal to this clause very freely and in ways as varied as their several purposes. But their purposes are always at base Trinitarian,
and they share a common exegesis. For them, v.15a means that Jesus
possesses in himself the divine nature in its entirety and shows his
perfect equality and consubstantial oneness with the Father. That
the Spirit shares the same substance and deity becomes plain from the
second half of the verse.[252] Taken in isolation, the clause does indeed seem susceptible of a metaphysical explanation. But the context demands a different interpretation. From the preceding verses,
it is clear that John is not thinking of the divine nature; he is
thinking, as R.E. Brown rightly says, of "revelation to be communicated
to men".[253] The Spirit of truth, we have been told, does not speak
ἀφ' ἑαυτοῦ. The origin of his message is specified in v.15. When
he speaks, when he takes of the things of Jesus and expounds them,
he is propagating the very revelation of God. The fathers fail here,
as so often before, perhaps partly through an approach to exegesis
which takes insufficient account of the context, but fundamentally because they have allowed the needs and presuppositions of their theology
to override their sensitivity to what the text in itself says.

Summary

The paraclete passages have attracted the attention of exposi-
tors throughout the whole of Church history, but never more so than in
the patristic age when they were of special importance in the formation

of the foundation doctrines of the Trinity. It has been our purpose
in this study to describe and evaluate the interpretations given them
by the Church fathers. Having done so in detail, it is now time to
draw our discoveries together into a summary statement.

The fathers belonged to the pre-critical era of Biblical interpretation. In particular they lacked the insights, so familiar to us,
of the historico-critical method. And not the insights only; they
also in great measure lacked the tools of research and communication
that would have enabled them to apply the method had they been so in-
clined. All this, as we might have expected, imposes limits on their
understanding and means there is that about the text which they can
grasp only dimly, if at all.

This is not to say that they have no understanding of the passages; quite the contrary. They make up for their lack of critical
methodology by an acuteness of observation and attention to detail
that has been equalled but not often surpassed. Granted, they do not
stop to examine every detail of the text in quite the way we should
like them to; but they miss nothing which is, in their eyes, of importance. If their understanding of what is important sometimes differs from ours, that is partly a reflection of the times in which
they lived, and it must not be allowed to obscure one important fact:
their conscious aim and consistent purpose is to interpret the message of the Bible. Though they do so imperfectly, they frequently dis-
play a sound instinct for the essential meaning of the text which,
despite the lack of 'scientific' methodology, nevertheless penetrates
to its heart. It is a mark of their achievement that their best insights have become the point of departure for all since who would
give a true exposition of the paraclete passages.

But the fathers are also prey to weaknesses which seriously mar their exegesis. These may be summed up in the following three points.

a) They have an uncritical understanding of the formation and purposes

of the Gospel, with two results. They are often led to attribute to

Jesus' words an intention and motivation - invariably that of under-

girding their own prejudices - not in the mind of the author. They

also frequently interpret verses, clauses, and even phrases in isola-

tion from the control of their contexts. Under this treatment, the

words of the text come to mean anything that suits the inclination of

the expositor and even sometimes, as in the case of the homilists,

different things within the scope of the same paragraph. b) They

frequently lack the element of judgment necessary to distinguish

the difference in exposition between speculation on the one hand

and theological insight based on sound exegesis on the other. c) They

attempt to expound the passages too narrowly within the limited con-

fines of their own ways of thinking. This tendency becomes progres-

sively more pronounced as the perimeters of orthodoxy are more clearly

defined until the paraclete passages are in some cases little more than

proof-texts and exegesis is swallowed up in theology.

NOTES

1. P. Stuhlmacher, "Adolf Schlatter's Interpretation of Scripture,"
New Testament Studies 24,4 (July, 1978), 433-446.

2. This is not to imply that there were no differences among the
fathers on the question of inspiration. It is well known that there
were. For a brief discussion (with bibliography) see J.N.D. Kelly,
Early Christian Doctrines (5th ed.; London, 1977), 52-79.

3. The words of M.F. Wiles, The Spiritual Gospel (Cambridge, 1960), 1,
are instructive here: "There are some books of the Bible whose interpretation has been so completely revolutionised by modern critical
methods that the exegesis of earlier centuries is unlikely to add much
of value to our understanding of them. There is probably no book of
which this is less true than the Fourth Gospel. It is of such a nature that it seems to reveal its secrets not so much to the skilful

probings of the analyst as to a certain intuitive sympathy of understanding. We need not, therefore, despair of finding amongst such
early interpreters [i.e., the Church fathers] significant examples of
a true insight into the meaning of the Gospel."

4.   In the ancient world exegesis and theology were more intimately
related than they are today. According to S.G. Papadopoulos (Σ.Γ.
Παπαδοπούλου, ΠΑΤΕΡΕΣ. ΑΥΞΗΣΙΣ ΤΗΣ ΕΚΚΛΗΣΙΑΣ. ΑΓΙΟΝ ΠΝΕΥΜΑ
(Αθῆναι, 1970), 5), exegetical and systematic theology have become
distinct poles, each claiming an absolute, even exclusive authority.
In patristic writing there is no disjunction; we speak not of patristic exegetical or dogmatic theology, only of patristic thought.

5.   This is amply evident from the way they approach and handle the
sayings. They do on occasion recognise tensions between a saying and
its setting or between it and other portions of the NT. Aug. Jo. 94,1
(CCL 36,561-562), for example, seeks to resolve the tension between
16,4b and the Synoptic account by identifying the antecedent of *haec*
as he does (see p.95 above). (See Wiles, 13-21, for a discussion of
how the fathers view the relationship between the FG and the Synop-
tics.)

6.   This will in some measure affect our understanding of the fathers'
achievement, but not so greatly as might at first be suspected. We
recognise in them an uncritical approach to Gospel formation that
undoubtedly colours their applications of our materials in debate
about, say, inspiration of Scripture or the Trinity. It does not in
itself deprive the exegete of a sympathetic understanding of the meaning of the words of the text.

7.   H. Windisch, "Die fünf johanneischen Parakletsprüche," Festgabe
für Adolf Jülicher zum 70. Geburtstag 26 Januar 1927 (Tübingen, 1927),
110-137, and S. Schulz, Untersuchungen zur Menschensohn-Christologie
im Johannesevangelium (Göttingen, 1957), 143-149, (cf. I. de la Potterie, La vérité dans Saint Jean, T.1 Le Christ et la vérité, L'Esprit
et la vérité, Analecta Biblica, investigationes scientificae in res
Biblicas 73 (Rome, 1977), 339-341), among others, have argued that the
paraclete passages are secondary insertions which interrupt their contexts. Many scholars, however, rightly reject this and accept the
sayings as a genuine part of the Discourses. There seems, in fact,
to be no basis for considering them to be secondary. There is no
textual evidence for dislocation or original absence; linguistic,
stylistic, literary, and theological studies of the Gospel suggest
that they were formed by the Evangelist himself; no one seems to
have come up with a convincing explanation of how and why they might
have been inserted into already existing texts. (This says nothing,
of course, about the source(s), if any, from which the Evangelist may
have taken this material.) See the discussions (and literature cited)
in C.K. Barrett, The Gospel According to St John, 2nd.ed. (London,
1978), 89-90; O. Betz, Der Paraklet. Fürsprecher im häretischen
Spätjudentum, im Johannes-Evangelium und in neu gefundenen gnostischen
Schriften, Arbeiten zur Geschichte des Spätjudentums und Urchristen-
tums 2 (Leiden, 1963), 210-211; G. Bornkamm, "Der Paraklet im Johannes-
Evangelium," Geschichte und Glaube,1.Teil (= Gesammelte Aufsätze, Bd.
III), Beiträge zur evangelischen Theologie, Bd.48, hrsg. v. E. Wolf
(München, 1968), 68-69; R. Bultmann, The Gospel of John, trans. by G.R.
Beasley-Murray from the 1964 printing of Das Evangelium Johannes with

the supplement of 1966 (Oxford, 1971), 552 n.1; G. Johnston, The
Spirit-Paraclete in the Gospel of John, Society for New Testament
Studies Monograph Series No. 12, ed. M. Black (Cambridge, 1970), 61-
79; M. Miguéns, El Paráclito (Jn 14-16), Studii Biblici Franciscani
Analecta,2 (Jerusalem, 1963), 27-44; U.B. Müller, "Die Parakleten-
vorstellung im Johannesevangelium," Zeitschrift für Theologie und
Kirche 71 (1974), 40-43 (Jo. 14,14-15 Müller ascribes der Überarbeitung
des ursprünglichen Evangeliums, n.37); F. Mußner, "Die johanneischen
Parakletsprüche und die apostolische Tradition," Biblische Zeitschrift n.F. 5 (1961), 56-59; R. Schnackenburg, Das Johannesevangelium, 3.Teil, Herders theologischer Kommentar zum Neuen Testament,
Bd.IV (Freiburg, 1975), 160-163.

8.   Chrys. hom. 75,1 in Jo. (PG 59,403); Cyr. Jo. 9,1 (Pusey 2,463);
Thdr.Mops. Jo. 126 (ST 141,391), Jo.Syr. on 14,15 (CSCO 115,271-272).
See p.40 above.

9.   It has for its model the love of Jesus for the Father, 15,10.

10. Apoll. Jo. 103 (TU 89,42); Chrys. hom. 75,1 in Jo. (PG 59,403);
Cyr. Jo. 9,1 (Pusey 2,464-465); Or. sel. in Ps. on 118(119),45 (PG 12,
1596), cf. Cant. 1 (GCS 33,112); Pel. Rom. on 8,38 (PLS 1,1151). See
pp.8, 40-41, and 90 above.

11. Cass. Ps. 98,7 (CCL 98,886); see p.127 above.

12. Thdr.Heracl. fr.Jo. 260-261 (TU 89,133-134); see pp.41-42 above.

13. Is.Ab. or. 25,23 (PG 40,1189-1190); see p.122 above.

14. Such an inference is understandable in comparison with Gal. 5,
16-25 and similar texts.

15. Chrys. hom. 75,1 in Jo. (PG 59,403) (see above p.41) and Max.
ascet.7 (PG 90,917), cf. carit. 1,16 (PG 90,964) (see above p.121).
Cf. J.N. Sanders and B.A. Mastin, A Commentary on the Gospel According
to St. John, Black's New Testament Commentaries (London, 1968), 325-
326, and F. Tillmann, Das Johannesevangelium, Die heilige Schrift des
Neuen Testamentes, 3.Bd. (4.Aufl.; Bonn, 1931), 266.

16. Glimpses of other commandments of Jesus in the supper context
may perhaps be found at 13,14; 15,4.9.20, and other places. None
is so suitable a referent as the love command.

17. D.W. Brandt, Das ewige Wort. Eine Einführung in das Evangelium
nach Johannes (3. Aufl.; Berlin, 1940), 199, and H. Strathmann, Das
Evangelium nach Johannes, Das Neue Testament Deutsch, Teilband 4
(Göttingen, 1963), 201, take 14,15 to refer to the love command
diffracted in experience into an inexhaustible multiplicity.

18. This is a Johannine phrase; cf. 14,21; 15,10; 1 Jo. 2,3.4; 3,22.
24; 5,2.3.

19. This is not to suggest that the parallelism makes τὰς ἐντολάς
synonymous with the wider term τὸν λόγον; it is closer in meaning
to the plural τοὺς λόγους in v.24. (On the contrast τὸν λόγον . . .
τοὺς λόγους see Barrett, 467, 505.)

20. See 8,51; cf. 17,6 and, particularly, 15,20b where the application of the same phrase to the disciples confirms this understanding.

21. Thus Bultmann, 614. We recall Cyr. Jo. 9,1 (Pusey 2,464-465)
who defines τῶν θείων ἐντολῶν ἡ φυλακή not only as ἀπόδειξις τῆς
ἀγάπης but also as τελεώτατος τῆς πίστεως ὅρος. Cf. 1 Jo. 3,23.

22. *Pace* W. Bauer, Das Johannesevangelium, Handbuch zum Neuen Testament, 6 (3. Aufl.; Tübingen, 1933), 182, who sees in this saying *die
Gesetzlichkeit der werdenden katholischen Kirche*. Several commentators share the view adopted here, notably R.E. Brown, The Gospel According to John, The Anchor Bible, Vol. 29A (London, 1971), 638;
Bultmann, 612, 614; A. Schlatter, Der Evangelist Johannes (Stuttgart,
1948), 296-297; Schnackenburg, 83-84; A. Wikenhauser, Das Evangelium
nach Johannes, Regensburger neues Testament, 4. Bd. (Regensburg, 1961),
268; cf. M.-J. Lagrange, Évangile selon Saint Jean, Études Bibliques
(septième édition; Paris, 1948), 380-381.

23. Against Chrys. hom. 71,1 in Mt. (PG 58,661), see p.41 above; cf.
Max. carit. 1,16 (PG 90,964), p.121 above. Chrys. fails to note the
contrast between τὰς ἐμάς and the context of Mt. 22,34-40 where Jesus
is answering the question ποία ἐντολὴ μεγάλη ἐν τῷ νόμῳ; Max., it
seems, simply equates πλήσιος with ἀλλήλους which here refers to the
disciples.

24. Cyr. Jo. 9,1 (Pusey 2,465), see above p.41.

25. Cf. 1,10; 10,30; 20,28.31. So close is the relationship that to
see Jesus is to have seen the Father, 14,9, cf. 12,45; to honour the
Son is to honour the Father, 5,22-23.

26. On the one hand, the authority behind Jesus' words is divine,
14,10.24.31; on the other, it is the observation of his commandments
(not the fulfilling of the Law) that pleases the Father, 14,21.23b cf.
16,27, and procures the gift of the Paraclete.

27. Aug. Jo. 74,1-2 (CCL 36,512-513), cf. Lagrange, 381. See above
pp.90-91.

28. It arises from a desire to reconcile this verse with certain
other NT passages, e.g., Rom. 5,5 and 1 Cor. 12,3.

29. See Barrett, 89. The paraclete passages make it clear that the
Spirit-Paraclete is essential to the disciples' understanding (14,26;
16,13), witness (15,26.27), and conflict with the world (16,8-11).

30. Cf. Windisch, 115. The Paraclete-Spirit is not *eigentlich die
Kraft, die zu sittlicher Tat befähigt, darstellt: denn er wird ja erst
gegeben, wenn der Gehorsam geleistet ist.*

31. This accepts τηρήσετε which is well attested and best fits the
context, cf. especially vv.23.24 where there is no doubt about the
tense. τηρήσατε, also well attested, is less natural to the construction with ἐάν which nowhere else in the FG takes the aorist
imperative in the apodosis. τηρήσητε would continue the protasis, but
the lack of a conjunction would also make this unusual Greek. Tran-
scriptional considerations are inconclusive. The fathers are not to

be criticised for not making as much as we do of the variant readings
in our passages. Textual criticism as we know it presupposes the wide
accessibility of manuscripts. (Bultmann, 612, says that keeping the
commandments defines the love rather than stating its result. Cf.
Or. sel.in Ps. 118(119),45 (PG 12,1596), Ἡ ἀγάπη δὲ πρὸς τὸν θεὸν
ἡ τῶν ἐντολῶν αὐτοῦ ζήτησις καὶ κατόρθωσις.)

32. See Wiles, 121-124, for a discussion of the exegesis of Johannine texts of a subordinationist nature in this period; also T.E. Pol-
lard, Johannine Christology and the Early Church, Society for New
Testament Studies Monograph Series No. 13, ed. M. Black (Cambridge,
1970), passim. On the Johannine Christology see C.K. Barrett, "'The
Father is greater than I' (Jo 14,28): Subordinationist Christology
in the New Testament," Neues Testament und Kirche. Für Rudolf
Schnackenburg, hrsg. v. J. Gnilka (Freiburg, 1974), 144-159; cf. his
"Christocentric or Theocentric? Observations on the Theological
Method of the Fourth Gospel," La Notion biblique de Dieu, Le Dieu
de la Bible et le Dieu des philosophes, ed. par J. Coppens,
Bibliotheca Ephemeridum Theologicarum Lovaniensium, 41 (Leuven, 1976),
361-376.

33. Cyr. Jo. 9,1 (Pusey 2,466-467), see above pp.42-43; so also Ammon.
Jo. 488 (TU 89,317-318). Cyr. has already said that in these verses
Jesus λαλεῖ τοιγαροῦν ὡς θεός τε ὁμοῦ καὶ ἄνθρωπος. Jesus does speak
here as the incarnate Son of the Father, with all that means in this
Gospel. To choose this one phrase and attribute it to the man Jesus
does less than justice to the subtleties of its thought as a whole.
This two-nature exegesis is, of course, typical of Cyril. In adopting
it, he has allowed his fear of Arianism to obscure his sensitivity to
the text.

34. Chrys. hom. 75,1 in Jo. (PG 59,403-404), see above p.42.

35. Thdr.Mops. Jo. 126 (ST 141,392), Jo.Syr. on 14,16 (CSCO 115,
272), above p.43. The Spirit has already been promised (he cites
Acts 1,4); asking would be superfluous. Note the implicit concern
that the Christ not be underestimated.

36. Both the two-nature exegesis and the doctrine of condescension are
fairly freely used in exegesis of the FG from the second half of the
Fourth Century. Where we encounter them in connexion with our passages (see, e.g., on 14,25-26 Cyr. Jo. 10 (Pusey 2,506.508) and Amph.
hom. on Jo. 14,28 (Moss 337; trans. 351), above p.47), they are open
to criticism similar to that given here.

37. For references see n.25.

38. See 14,28. It is a subordination of obedience, 5,30 (cf. vv.19-
20); 7,16-18; 8,28; 12,49; 14,10.24.31; 15,10.

39. Eus. e.th. 3,5,11 (GCS 14,161), above p.61 n.15. With regard to
Johannine texts of a subordinationist nature, Eus. writes without
some of the dogmatic trammels of later fathers.

40. See Aug. serm.Ar. 4 (PL 42,686) and Ambr. Spir. 3,1,8 (CSEL 79,
153); cf. further p.104 n.12. Thus also Anast.Ant. or. 1,22 (PG 89,
1324-1325), above p.121.

41. The future is the expected tense after v.15. ἐρωτήσω continues
the apodosis.

42. Chrys. hom. 75,1 in Jo. (PG 59,404), cf. Ammon. Jo. 488 (TU 89,
317-318).

43. The fact that Chrys. is thinking of Pentecost rather than the
insufflation as the fulfillment of the promise suggests this, as does
his lack of any cross-referencing. For him the Spirit comes only
after the ascension. (Is he inconsistent here? Note his earlier
quotation of Jo. 20,22 in the same section.) Ammon. (see n.42) seems
to accept the crucifixion as the only prerequisite, but this may
be due to the highly condensed nature of his commentary. Cf. Vic.
Ar. 1,12 (CSEL 83,1,70), above p.111 n.77, who also speaks vaguely
of the time after the ascension as the time of the fulfillment of
the promise.

44. Cf. Ath. syn. 24,4 (Opitz 2,1,250), above p.67 n.66, and Tert.
haer. 22,10 (CCL 1,204), above p.13, who imply the same thing when
they refer the fulfillment simply to Acts.

45. See Aug. Faust. 13,17 (CSEL 25,1,398-399), Fel. 1,2-5 (CSEL 25,
802-807), 1,10ff (CSEL 25,811ff), Jo. 92,1 (CCL 36,555-556), cf. Jo.
74,2 (CCL 36,513-514), 92,2 (CCL 36,556-557), Trin. 2,15,26 (CCL 50,
115); Epiph. haer. 66,19,3 (GCS 37,43), 66,61,5-6 (GCS 37,98-99);
Fulg. Fab. 29,12 (CCL 91A,820); Gr.Naz. or. 41,12 (PG 36,445); Jer.
ep. 120,9,16-17 (CSEL 55,498-499), 41,1 (CSEL 54,311-312); above pp.
39,89,94, and 127.

46. Thus Chrys. hom. 1,5 in Ac. (PG 60,20), above p.76 n.147. See
E.C. Hoskyns, The Fourth Gospel, ed. F.N. Davey (London, 1967), 547,
who takes a similar line.

47. See Anast.S. qu.et resp. 148 (PG 89,802-804); Chrys. hom. 86,3
in Jo. (PG 59,491), contrast hom. 1,5 in Ac. (PG 60,20); Cyr. Jo.
12,1 (Pusey 3,131-141); Cyr.H. catech. 17,12 (Rupp 2,266; PG 33,984-
985); Eus. e.th. 3,5,13-14 (GCS 14,161-162); Leo tract. 76,4 (CCL
138A,476-478); above pp.76-77 n.147, 111-112 n.79, and 142. (Ambrstr.
quaest. 93,1 (CSEL 50,162-163) and Jer. ep. 120,9 (CSEL 55,492-500),
above p.91, seek to resolve the tension between Jo. 20,22 and Ac. 2
by distinguishing the one Spirit from the diverse gifts; it is not the
Spirit but his gifts that are given. This ignores the plain sense of
both passages.) Cf. Hoskyns, 547, who says that "the authority to
remit and retain sins is not a particular gift, but rather defines the
whole work of salvation, and is the characteristic function of the
Church in its complete activity."

48. Thus J.H. Bernard, A Critical and Exegetical Commentary on the
Gospel According to St. John, Vol.II, The International Critical
Commentary, ed. A.H. McNeile (Edinburgh, 1963), 677-678, and Barrett,
Gospel, 570. (Is this what Didym. Trin. 3,41,2 (PG 39,988) means
when he says Οὐδὲ γὰρ ἀτελές τι ἐποίει ὁ Δεσπότης, ἐμφυσῶν μετὰ τὴν
ἀνάστασιν εἰς πρόσωπα τῶν ἀποστόλων, καὶ λέγων· Λάβετε Πνεῦμα ἅγιον?
Whether it is or not, it is difficult to know how Didym. relates
Jo. 20,22 and Ac. 2; the lines which follow do not make this clear.)
Cf. Betz, 164-170.

49. Thus Aug. Faust. 13,17 (CSEL 25,1,398-399), Fel. 1,2-5 (CSEL 25,
802-807), 1,10ff (CSEL 25,811ff); Didym. Trin. 3,41,2 (PG 39,985.988);
Jer. ep. 41,1 (CSEL 54,311-312), 120,9,16-17 (CSEL 55,498-499); above
pp.39 and 89.   Cf. Thdr.Heracl. fr.Jo. 260-261 (TU 89,133-134) who
also seeks to show that the Paraclete first came in apostolic times,
but by another method (see pp.41-42 above). His inference (from the
quality of the disciples' lives, from the trustworthiness of the
Lord's promise) is quite logical, but it is an inference. It lacks
the force of the argument from history.

50. The evidence is concisely set out in J. Behm, "παράκλητος,"
Theological Dictionary of the New Testament, Vol.V, ed. G. Friedrich,
trans. and ed. G.W. Bromiley (Grand Rapids, 1973), 800-814. There are
other semasiological studies, though none so comprehensive. See, e.g.,
C.K. Barrett, "The Holy Spirit in the Fourth Gospel," The Journal of
Theological Studies N.S.1 (1950), 8-12; Bernard, 496-498; Lagrange,
381-383; P. della Madre di Dio, "Lo Spirito Santo nel Quarto Vangelo,"
Ephemerides Carmeliticae 7 (1956), 430-436; Schlatter, 297-298. For
παράκλητος as a loanword in rabbinic literature (in the form פרקליט,
פרקליטא), see H.L. Strack u. P. Billerbeck, Kommentar zum Neuen Testament aus Talmud und Midrasch, 2. Bd., Das Evangelium nach Markus,
Lukas und Johannes und die Apostelgeschichte (München, 1974), 560-562.

51. The connexion of the Paraclete with Christian prophetism is often
pointed out. See Johnston, 137-141, and the recent article by M.E.
Boring, "The Influence of Christian Prophecy on the Johannine Portrayal of the Paraclete and Jesus," New Testament Studies 25 (1978-1979),
113-120. Cf. Barrett, Gospel, 462-463, Holy Spirit, 12-15.

52. Betz, 2.

53. Since H. Sasse ("Der Paraklet im Johannesevangelium," Zeitschrift
für die neutestamentliche Wissenschaft und die Kunde der älteren Kirche,
24 (1925), 260) deplored den Mangel einer eingehenden theologischen
Untersuchung des Parakletproblems in 1925, scholars have devoted con-
siderable attention to the paraclete question. While it would be un-
helpful to mention all the literature on the Paraclete here, we may
summarise the more important contributions as follows:
        1) Literary-critical analyses: Sasse, 260-277; Windisch, 110-
137.
        2) Religionsgeschichtlich investigations which explain the
passages in terms of a) The helper figures of Mandaean myth: Bultmann,
566-572, cf. Bauer, 182, 184-185, who prepares the way for this explanation by his reference to the Mandaean Jawar and the translation
of παράκλητος by Helfer, and Windisch, 136, who refers to these
parallels as kräftige Analogien. Important objections are raised by
Behm, 807-809, and W. Michaelis, "Zur Herkunft des johanneischen
Paraklet-Titels," Coniectanea Neotestamentica 11 (1947), 147-162;
b) Development of the Vorläufer-Vollender idea of Judaism: Bornkamm,
68-89; c) Relationship to the spätjudische Menschensohnerwartung:
Schulz, Untersuchungen, 142-158, 177-179 (Schulz here develops his own
themageschichtliche Methode) and Das Evangelium nach Johannes, Das
Neue Testament Deutsch, Teilband 4 (Göttingen, 1972), 188-189; cf.
Bornkamm, 81-85, who also looks to the Son of Man as a Vorbild of the
Paraclete; d) Jewish Fürsprecher-Vorstellungen: N. Johansson, Parakletoi. Vorstellungen von Fürsprechern für die Menschen vor Gott in
der alttestamentlichen Religion, im Spätjudentum und Urchristentum

(Lund, 1940); S. Mowinckel, "Die Vorstellungen des Spätjudentums vom heiligen Geist als Fürsprecher und der johanneische Paraklet," Zeitschrift für die neutestamentliche Wissenschaft und die Kunde der älteren Kirche 32 (1933), 97-130; cf. Behm, 809-814; e) The ideas of the Qumran community: Betz, cf. A.R.C. Leany, "The Johannine Paraclete and the Qumran Scrolls," John and Qumran, ed. J.H. Charlesworth (London, 1972), 38-61; f) The Abschiedsrede Gattung: Müller, 31-77.

3) Explanations from the Sitz im Leben of the FG: Barrett, Gospel, 89-91, 462-463, and Holy Spirit, 1-15 ("The Paraclete is the Spirit of Christian paraclesis"; cf. Johnston, passim but especially 119-148, and J.L. Martyn, History and Theology in the Fourth Gospel (New York, 1968), 135-142); Brown, Gospel, 1135-1144, and the somewhat fuller article "The Paraclete in the Fourth Gospel," New Testament Studies 13 (1966-1967), 113-132; Johnston; Mußner, 56-70; and Schnackenburg, 156-173.

4) Elucidation from early Christian tradition, patristic usage, and the OT: Miguéns. He seeks through an examination of the passages (152-212) and their context (45-103), comparison with primitive Christian traditions concerning the Spirit (104-151), and patristic usage (213-238) to show that παράκλητος bears its usual forensic sense in the FG. The Paraclete is a creation of primitive Christianity whose forensic role has its sole background in certain functions attributed to Yahweh in the OT (239-270).

5) Linguistic attraction to certain uses of παρακαλεῖν/παράκλησις in the LXX (a) and the influence of ideas from apocalyptic Abschiedsreden (b) to give the sense 'comforter' (παράκλητος = παρακαλῶν): a) J.G. Davies, "The Primary Meaning of ΠΑΡΑΚΛΗΤΟΣ," The Journal of Theological Studies N.S. 4 (1953), 35-38; H. Riesenfeld, "A Probable Background to the Johannine Paraclete," Ex orbe religionum. studia Geo Widengren oblata, Vol.I,Studies in the History of Religions (Supplements to Numen), 21 (Leiden, 1972),266-274; cf. N.H. Snaith, "The Meaning of 'The Paraclete'," The Expository Times 57 (1945-1946), 47-50 (who argues similarly but for the translation 'convincer'), and Hoskyns, 465-470; b) Müller, 60-65 (Der 'Geist der Wahrheit' hieße in Joh 14 also Paraklet, weil er als παρακαλῶν entsprechend den jüdischen Texten gedacht werden muß (60).   Reference to early Christian usage of the cognate words shows the specific content of the work of the παράκλητος so that the term is best translated Verkündiger, Prediger (63-65); cf. Barrett, Gospel, 462, and Holy Spirit, 12-14.).

Useful summaries (and criticisms) of most of this literature may be found in Betz, 4-35; Brown, "Paraclete," 115-126; Johnston, 80-118; Müller, 31-40; and Schnackenburg, 163-169.

54. For many the Paraclete is the result of Johannine creativity. If we accept that the Evangelist or his circle received the expression παράκλητος from earlier Christian tradition and gave it new content, then we must acknowledge with Schnackenburg that we cannot expect to find an unequivocal derivation for the term (167); neither is it necessary that all the functions ascribed to the Paraclete be anchored to the term itself (159). Likewise, whatever the influence of Jewish conceptions may have been, it seems unlikely that an entirely suitable model for the Paraclete will ever be found (169). This is not to say that Jewish conceptions had no part to play in the formation of the Paraclete. The search for analogies (see n.53 above) has developed illuminating points of contact with certain figures and ideas of both orthodox and heterodox Judaism.

55. See Isid. etym. 7,2,31 (PL 82,266), above p.127, cf. Aug. serm.
Ar. 19 (PL 42,697).

56. See Jer. Is. 11,40,1-2 (CCL 73,454), above p.112 n.81, and Thdr.
Mops. Jo.Syr. on 14,16 (CSCO 115,272), above p.44. Cf. Didym. Trin.
3,38 (PG 39,972-973), Eus. e.th. 3,5,11 (GCS 14,161), Isid. etym.
7,3,10 (PL 82,268), and Rust. aceph. (PL 67,1226), above p.44 and n.
102, p.127 and n.50. Note that Didym. and Isid. appeal to the cognate
παράκλησις.

57. See Aug. Faust. 13,17 (CSEL 25, 398-399), Jo. 94,2 (CCL 36,562);
Gr.Nyss. ref.Eun. 186 (Jaeger 2,391); Victor hist. 2,93 (CSEL 7,66);
cf. Isid. etym. 7,2,31 and 7,3,10 (n.55 and n.56 above); above p.71
n.102, p.112 n.81, and p.127. Aug. simply indicates that *paracletus*
means either *consolator* or *advocatus*; Gr.Nyss. leaves it untranslated,
as the choice of meanings does not affect his argument; Victor prefers *consolator* (*Paracletus enim aduocatus est uel potius consolator*).

58. See Didym. Spir. 27 (PG 39,1058), Faust. Spir. 1,10 (CSEL 21,
119), Or. princ. 2,7,4 (GCS 22,151-152); above pp.4-5, 44, and 127.
Or. gives the fullest exposition of the three. Didym. does not actually translate, but his understanding is clear.

59. We are here concerned with their exegesis, not simply with their
wider use of the term παράκλητος/*paracletus*.

60. See Behm, 813, and Johansson, 265-267, who argue "that the idea
of a Paraclete in the earthly life of the disciples goes back ultimately to Jesus Himself" (Behm) and that Jesus is probably responsible
for the Spirit's designation as Paraclete (Johansson). Notice how
they differ from the fathers: Behm and Johansson seek to trace these
ideas to Jesus; the fathers assume without question that the passages
are an exact dominical quotation.

61. Miguéns, 213-238, rightly argues that παράκλητος retains its
usual forensic sense throughout the early period of the Church. It
is only in exegesis of the paraclete passages that oscillation begins.
(At the same time, his insistence on the etymological form and meaning of the term leads him to undervalue the contradictory evidence in
the fathers.)

62. Aug. and Jer. (see above nn.56.57) are the only pre-Chalcedonian
Latins explicitly to recognise any meaning other than *advocatus*. On
the whole, the Western fathers seem to have followed the text before
them, usually the transliterated *paracletus*, though sometimes *advocatus*
and, less frequently, *consolator*.

63. See, e.g., 14,1-4.18-23.27; 16,6-7.20-24.

64. Whether or not they actually did know a meaning of παράκλητος
equivalent to παρακαλῶν which would have been available to the Evangelist is very difficult to say. Or., the earliest of the fathers to
take this line, is a sensitive exegete; it is always dangerous to
ignore him. On the other hand, even if he did know such a meaning,
it need not have developed until after the writing of the FG. Later
writers may have been influenced by his exegesis, directly or indirectly.

65. The preoccupations of the patristic age gave the fathers other, more pressing matters to pursue.

66. Cf. ὁ παράκλητος, 14,26; 15,26; 16,7.

67. Thus Michaelis, 153. The Father will give *einen Anderen und zwar als Parakleten (oder: einen Anderen, nämlich den Parakleten)*.

68. The paraclete passages strongly suggest continuity between the offices of Jesus and the other Paraclete. Like Jesus, the Paraclete will be present with the disciples, 14,16-17 (unlike Jesus, he will remain εἰς τὸν αἰῶνα, cf. 13,33; 14,25; 16,4-5.7; 17,11; also Chrys. hom.75,1 in Jo. (PG 59,405),above p.45); he replaces him, 16,7. The Paraclete continues, and points back to, Jesus' teaching, 14,25-26; 16,12-13. He continues the witness to Jesus, 15,26, cf. 8,13-14.18. He convicts the world of sin, 16,8-9, cf. 7,7 and 15,22-24, also 3, 18-19; 5,22.27.30; 8,16.26; 9,39. (Parallels between the two figures are discussed by Bornkamm, 69; Brown, "Paraclete," 126-127; Bultmann, 566-567; and de la Potterie, 343.)

69. The adjectival use of ἄλλος is normal in the FG. See 10,16; 18, 15; 20,30; cf. 18,16; 20,2.3.4.8.25; 21,8. (It is also normal in the rest of the NT. F. Blass and A. Debrunner, A Greek Grammar of the New Testament and Other Early Christian Literature, trans. and ed. R.W. Funk (Chicago, 1967), § 306,5, lists no certain examples of 'pleonastic' ἄλλος (the reference to Jo. 14,16 does not occur in editions of the grammar prior to the article by Michaelis, q.v. n.11) and only one of pleonastic ἕτερος, Lk. 23,32.)

70. It is the earthly Jesus, not the heavenly intercessor of 1 Jo. 2, 1, who is the first Paraclete. This is clear from the fact that the ἄλλος παράκλητος functions here in the world and continues Jesus' earthly work. It is also suggested by the context of departure; the first Paraclete is leaving to return to the Father, but the 'other' Paraclete will remain εἰς τὸν αἰῶνα. See de la Potterie, 342-343, and Schnackenburg, 84-85.

71. Most scholars accept the translation 'another Paraclete' and the inference that Jesus is the first Paraclete. See, e.g., Barrett, Gospel, 461-462; Behm, 800; Betz, 127; Bernard, 545; Brandt, 199; Brown, Gospel, 638-639; Bultmann, 567 and n.1; Hoskyns, 458; Lagrange, 383; Lemonnyer (A. Lemonnyer, "L'Esprit-Saint Paraclet," Revue des sciences philosophiques et théologiques 16 (1927)), 297; Locher (G.W. Locher, "Der Geist als Paraclet. Eine exegetischdogmatische Besinnung," Evangelische Theologie n.F. 21 (1966)), 569; Loisy (A. Loisy, Le quatrième Évangile. Les épîtres dites de Jean (deuxième édition refondue; Paris, 1921)), 409-410; Miguéns, 152; Morris (L. Morris, The Gospel According to John, The New International Commentary on the New Testament, ed. F.F. Bruce (London, 1971)), 648-649 and n.42; Müller, 41-42; de la Potterie, 342-344; Schnackenburg, 84-85; Schulz, Evangelium, 187; Wikenhauser, 269; Windisch, 114.

72. For references see p.70 n.90, p.106 n.37, p.109 n.61, and p.133 n.45.

73. See Ambr. Spir. 1,13,136-137 (CSEL 79,73-74) and Lc. 2,13 on 1,30-32 (CCL 14,35-36), above p.84; Ammon. Jo. 488 (TU 89,317-318),

above p.129 n.13; Chrys. hom.75,1 in Jo. (PG 59,403), above pp.43-44;
Cyr. Jo. 9,1 (Pusey 2,467), above p.43; Eus. e.th. 3,5,1 and 3,5,6
(GCS 14,160), above p.31; Faust. Spir. 1,10 (CSEL 21,119), above pp.
125-126; Tert. Prax. 9,3 (CCL 2,1168-1169), above p.12; cf. Or. hom.
12,1 in Num. (GCS 30,95), above p.4.   See also Didym. Spir. 27 (PG
39,1058), above p.44, who stresses not distinction of persons but
distinction of functions. (The former is, of course, implied in the
latter.) Cf. Wikenhauser, 271.

74. It is, e.g., fanciful to see in the one word παράκλητος the unity
of substance as does Chrys. hom.75,1 in Jo. (PG 59,403), above p.43;
cf. Faust. Spir. 1,10 (CSEL 21,119), above pp.125-126.

75. They assume, of course, that the ἄλλος παράκλητος is intended
by the Evangelist to be a divine figure.

76. Thus Faust. Spir. 1,10 (CSEL 21,120), above p.124, and Thdr.
Heracl. fr.Jo. 261 (TU 89,134), above p.44.

77. See Aug. Jo. 77,2 (CCL 36,520-521), above p.93; Eus. e.th.
3,4,9 (GCS 14,159), 3,5,4-6.8.9 (GCS 14,160-161), above p.31; Eus.
Ver. Trin. 4,8 (CCL 9,58), 4,28-29 (CCL 9,63), above p.84; Epiph.
anc. 81,9 (GCS 25,102) and haer. 57,4,1 (GCS 31,348), above p.61
n.15; Isaac I. f.i. 3 (CCL 9,342), above p.84; cf. Tert. Prax. 25,1
(CCL 2,1195), above p.12.

78. The phrase is appositional. Johnston, 84, takes ἄλλον παράκλητον to be pleonastic and translates, 'and he will give to you as
another paraclete . . . the spirit of truth'. But, as Schnackenburg,
85 n.87, rightly points out, the interposition of the ἵνα-clause
makes this proposition unconvincing. (It need hardly be pointed out
that 'prolonged examination', Johnston's justification for this
exegesis, is not in itself sufficient.)

79. In each case it is appositional to παράκλητος, directly at
15,26 and indirectly (through ἐκεῖνος) at 16,13; cf. 14,26.

80. See Cyr. Jo. 9,1 (Pusey 2,467) on 14,17, above p.45; 10,2 (Pusey
2,607.609) on 15,26, above p.49; and 10,2 (Pusey 2,628) on 16,13,
above p.56. Cf. Jo. 2,1 (Pusey 1,188) and ep. 17 (ACO 1,1,1,39),
above p.38.

81. See Thdt. exp.fid. 5 (CAC 4,20), above p.38.

82. Gr.Nyss. rejects such an understanding at ref.Eun. 187-188
(Jaeger 2,391-392), above p.65 n.52.

83. See Thdr.Mops. Jo. 126 (ST 141,391) and Jo.Syr. on 14,17 (CSCO
115,272) on 14,17, above p.45; cf. Mac. 27 (PO 9,666-667), above p.
74 n.129. Cf. hom. 10,8 (ST 145,256-257) and Chrys. hom.77,3 in Jo.
(PG 59,417) which imply the same interpretation.

84. Cf. 1 Jo. 4,6; 5,6. Parallels sometimes adduced from the
Pseudepigrapha (T. Judah 20,1.5) and literature of Qumran (1QS 3,18-19.
20; 4,12.23) are not relevant, as Barrett, Gospel, 463, shows.

85. Thus de la Potterie in recapitulating his exhaustive study of the

idea of truth in the Johannine writings: *La vérité, pour Jean, est une réalité historique: la révélation définitive apportée par Jésus Christ et présente en lui* (1010); on ἀλήθεια see further Barrett, Gospel, 167, and the literature there cited. For a summary of his detailed work on the Spirit of truth, see de la Potterie, 466-471; the Spirit of truth is the Spirit *qui nous donne et nous communique la vérité de Jésus* (471).

86.   In this sense it occurs as a synonym for 'everyone' at 7,4; 12,19; 18,20.

87.   On κόσμος in 14,17 see Ammon. Jo. 490 (TU 89,318); Apoll Jo. 104 (TU 89,42-43); Aug. Jo. 74,4 (CCL 36,514-515) and Trin. 1,8,18 (CCL 50,52); Bas. Spir. 22,53 (Johnston 107-108; SCH 17,211-212); Chrys. hom.75,1 in Jo. (PG 59,404-405); Cyr. Jo. 9,1 (Pusey 2,469); Didym. Trin. 3,38 (PG 39,976); Thdr.Heracl. fr.Jo. 262 (TU 89,134); above pp.45-46, 92, 129 n.13. On κόσμος in 16,8.11 see Aug. Jo. 95,4 (CCL 36,567) and serm. 144,2 (PL 38,788); Cyr. Jo. 10,2 (Pusey 2,622-623); above pp.52-53, 114 n.94, 98.

88.   Thus, for example, several writers explain κόσμος at 14,17 in terms coloured by ὅτι οὐ θεωρεῖ αὐτό. The world comprises those who do not accept what lies beyond physical sight (Ammon., Apoll., Bas., Thdr.Heracl.), who cannot perceive with the eyes of faith (Aug., Didym.). Contrast Aug. on 16,11, *mundus . . . hoc est homines infideles* (cf. 16,9, ὅτι οὐ πιστεύουσιν εἰς ἐμέ). See further on θεωρεῖν below.

89.   λαβεῖν here is passive, 'accept, receive'; the gift is *given* (δώσει, cf. 20,22) to the believer. Contrast Thdr.Mops. Jo.Syr.on 14,17 (CSCO 115,273; trans. 116,195), above p.46, who stresses *Non enim dixit: quem non potest accipere, sed: quem non potest sumere*.

90.   Quoted with approbation in Bultmann, 617.   Brown, Gospel, 639, also accepts this interpretation.

91.   Thdr.Heracl. fr.Jo. 262 (TU 89,134).   Thus possibly also Aug. Jo. 74,4 (CCL 36,514-515); Didym. Trin. 3,38 (PG 39,976); Thdr.Mops. Jo.Syr. on 14,17 (CSCO 115,273).   Does Ammon. Jo. 490 (TU 89,318) get it right when he says λαβεῖν εἶπεν, ὅ ἐστιν οὔτε θεωρῆσαι οὔτε οὔτω γνῶναι δύνανται?

92.   For references see n.87.   Cf. Thdr.Mops. Jo.Syr. on 14,17 (CSCO 115,273-274; trans. 116,195), quoted above pp.72-73 n.114.

93.   Thus Bernard, 546. His argument from the analogy of 14,19 is inadequate; for, as he himself points out in his comment *ad loc.*, θεωρεῖν is 'used here of any kind of vision'. When Jesus is no longer physically present, the world will no longer perceive him. By contrast the disciples will perceive him. This may involve but cannot be limited to the resurrection appearances, cf. vv.22-23; 7,33-34. In v.19, therefore, θεωρεῖν is used precisely as it is in v.17. Since the world is limited to what is tangible, it cannot perceive the spiritual. In contrast with the disciples, it will no longer perceive Jesus when his presence in the world is no longer physical.

94.   See below on γινώσκειν.

95. See on ἐν ὑμῖν ἐστιν below.

96. I. de la Potterie, 347-352, accepts that θεωρεῖν here refers to
the spiritual discernment of faith but limits it to the discernment
of spiritual realities behind sensible events. The world is re-
proached for not having perceived the Spirit in Jesus' own mission.
In this he goes too far. His appeal to Johannine usage (348-350) is
unconvincing, as it is context which indicates when spiritual perception is mediated by the visible; there is no such indication here.
Furthermore, he misinterprets the tenses of the verbs in the verse
(350-352). They do not reflect the two stages of revelation, θεωρεῖ
and γινώσκει are gnomic presents. It is a general truth that the
Spirit of truth is excluded from the world. This is not true, by
contrast, of the disciples. (See further on γινώσκετε/μένει/ἐστιν
and, regarding the method of the Paraclete's operation vis-à-vis
the world, on 15,26-27 below.)

97. Aug. (Jo.74,4), Bas., Chrys., Cyr., Didym.; for references see
on 14,17 n.87 above.

98. Chrys. hom.75,1 in Jo. (PG 59,404-405). This passage is quoted
above p.72 n.110.

99. The precise nuance can be difficult to determine. 5,6 and 6,15,
for example, may refer to supernatural knowledge rather than to inference from observation. Brown, Gospel, 639, renders θεωρεῖν and
γινώσκειν in 14,17 as 'see' and 'recognise' respectively.

100. It is a Johannine theme that the world is characteristically
incapable of apprehending spiritual realities. It does not perceive
them behind the words and work of Jesus (cf. 1,10; 5,37-38; 7,28;
8,47; 10,25-26), although the Father sent him that it might do so
(6,40, cf. 3,16-21; 12,44-50; 15,21-24). We recall for example the
conversation with Nicodemus in Ch. 3 (see particularly vv.11-12).

101. They have a vested interest in underscoring the incorporeality
of the Holy Spirit of dogma.

102. ὑμεῖς reinforces the contrast.

103. Of the variae lectiones, ἔσται is probably a correction; ἐστιν
is to be preferred as the lectio difficilior.

104. Ambrstr. quaest. 93,1 (CSEL 50,163), above p.91. The text he
quotes is unmistakably from the Vetus Latina. The argument for prolepsis is as valid for this Latin version as for the Greek original.

105. Thdr.Heracl. fr.Jo. 262 (TU 89,134).

106. The Spirit was present in Jesus during the earthly ministry (1,
32-33; 3,34), but that presence is not here in view.

107. The promised baptism ἐν πνεύματι ἁγίῳ (Jo. 1,33; Mt. 3,11; Mk.
1,8; Lk. 3,16; cf. Acts 1,5 and 11,16) is irrelevant. It is difficult
to understand why Thdr. should have made reference to it here.

108. Ammon. Jo. 489 (TU 89,318), above p.129 n.13; Fulg. Fab. 28,14
(CCL 91A,812), above p.127.

109. Ammon., Εἰπὼν τὸ μένει ἐδίδαξεν, ὅτι οὐδὲ μετὰ τελευτὴν ἀφίσταται τὸ πνεῦμα; Chrys. hom.75,1 in Jo. (PG 59,404), Μεθ' ὑμῶν μένει. Τοῦτο δηλοῖ, ὅτι οὐδὲ μετὰ τελευτὴν ἀφίσταται, above p.45. It would seem from its position in the context that Chrysostom's comment pertains to 14,16 (on the form of the quotation see further the Table of Variants *ad loc.*). Reuss (TU 89,318) is very likely right to give Ammonius' fragment (q.v.) the heading 'Jo 14,17', but it is possible that this, too, comments on v.16 or even on both verses taken together.

110. This phrase always refers to unlimited duration in the FG. It is not without an eschatological colouring, cf. 4,14; 6,51.58; 8,51; 10,28; 11,26.

111. For other passages which portray or hint at the inner working of the Spirit in the believer, see 3,5-8; 6,63; 7,37-39; cf. 4,23-24.

112. Chrys. hom.75,1 in Jo. (PG 59,405), above p.46. Among others who imply the same understanding, see Ammon. Jo. 489 (TU 89,318), above p.129 n.13; Apoll. Jo. 104 (TU 89,43), above p.45; also Fulg. Fab. 28,14 (CCL 91A,812), above p.127.

113. Aug. Jo. 74,5 (CCL 36,515), above p.92. The time of the Spirit's coming to the disciples is for Aug. clearly future; it seems probable that this is a direct result of his use of the Vulgate (*apud vos manebit et in vobis erit*).

114. The future presence of Jesus with the believer is portrayed in similar terms in this chapter. He, together with the Father, makes his μονὴν παρ' αὐτῷ (v.23), but it is now a mystical μονή (v.20b, cf. 15,4; 17,23.26; also 6,56). This is true even if vv.19-20 refer in the first instance to the resurrection appearances because they also point beyond them to the whole of subsequent Christian history.

115. Cf. Boring, 114 and n.1, whose case to the contrary is unconvincing.

116. Apoll. Jo. 104 (TU 89,43), above p.45, αἰσθάνονται δὲ αὐτοῦ παρόντος οἱ μετέχειν δυνάμενοι. οὗτοι τὴν κρείσσονα αἰσθήσεως οὐσίαν ἐκ τῆς μετουσίας ἐπιγινώσκουσιν; Aug. Jo. 74,5 (CCL 36,515), above p. 92.

117. See Amph. hom. on Jo. 14,28 (Moss 337; trans. 351); Aug. Jo. 77,1 (CCL 36,520), above pp.92-93; and Cyr. Jo. 10 (Pusey 2,506), above p.47. Amph. and Cyr. apply two-nature exegesis to this passage; see above p.139 and n.36 for general assessment.

118. Aug. Trin. 2,5,7 - 2,7,12 (CCL 50,87-96), above p.87. Aug. is trying to rescue the Spirit from the charge that he is inferior to the Father and the Son because he is sent by them. For that purpose this exegesis is insufficient.

119. Thdr.Mops. Jo.Syr. on 14,25-26 (CSCO 115,277; trans. 116,198), above p.47. Thdr. applies this exegesis to the opening words of 15,26 at hom. 10,7 (ST 145,256-257) and Mac. 25.26 (PO 9,665-666), above pp.48-49. The same criticism applies there as here.

120. Gaud.tract. 14,4-5 (CSEL 68,125-126), above p.93. This

says nothing about the validity of his theology but only that, in his concern to preserve the immensity of the deity, he is so busy telling us what the text cannot mean that he neglects to tell us what it does mean; by implication he verges on explaining it away. Cf. the similar concern to support the doctrine of omnipresence in relation to our passages in Ambr. Spir. 1,11,116-119 (CSEL 79,65-66), above p.88, who comments on 15,26; Chrys. hom.78,3 in Jo. (PG 59,423), above p.52, who comments on 16,7; and Or. or. 23,1 (GCS 3,349-350), above p.8, who comments on 16,5 et al.

121. Amph. hom. on Jo. 14,28 (Moss 337; trans. 352), above p.47.

122. Barrett, Gospel, 467. Cf. further Bernard, 552-553; Brown, Gospel, 653; de la Potterie, 364-367; Schnackenburg, 95-96.

123. Vic. Ar. 3,15 (CSEL 83,1,217), above p.94.   Vic. offers two brief explanations, the second of which reads *in nomine meo, quia spiritus sanctus ipse de Christo testimonium ferret*.

124. Gaud. tract. 14,19-21 (CSEL 68,129-130), above p.93; cf. Faust. Spir. 1,10 (CSEL 21,118), above p.125. Faustus' argument from this phrase for the deity of the Spirit is based on faulty exegesis.

125. It was limited by time (context) and the disciples' capacity to receive it (16,12). The Paraclete, it is implied, will be free of these limitations.

126. The Paraclete focuses on the revelation in Jesus in his confrontation with the world (15,26; 16,8-11). His guidance of the Church ἐν τῇ ἀληθείᾳ πάσῃ is limited to bringing deeper understanding and application of that revelation (16,13-15).

127. On this interpretation, see further the discussions in Barrett, Gospel, 467-468, and 'Christocentric', 365-366; Brown, Gospel, 650-651; Bultmann, 626-627; Hoskyns, 461; de la Potterie, 367-378; Schnackenburg, 94-95; Schulz, Evangelium, 192; cf. Lagrange, 391-392.

128. Didym. Trin. 3,38 (PG 39,976), above p.74 n.124.

129. Vic. Ar. 1,12 (CSEL 83,1,70), above p.94.

130. Thdr.Mops. Jo.Syr. on 14,25-26 (CSCO 115,277; trans. 116,198), above p.48. Thdr. goes straight on to his explanation that it is not the nature (*natura*) of the Spirit that is sent (see above p.176).

131. Cyr. Jo. 10 (Pusey 2,506), above pp.47-48.

132. Amph. hom. on Jo. 14,28 (Moss 338; trans. 353), above p.48; cf. Ammon. Jo. 502 (TU 89,321), above p.129 n.13, ὅταν ἔλθῃ τὸ πνεῦμα, πολλὰ καὶ ἃ οὐκ ἴστε μαθήσεσθε καὶ ἃ εἶπον ἐπαναμιμνῄσκει.

133. In his discussion of 14,26, de la Potterie, 368-369, argues that διδάξει and ὑπομνήσει have but a single object; πάντα is repeated for light emphasis and rhythmic balance. This may well be so, it fits the overall sense of the passage.

134. Thdr.Heracl. fr.Jo. 271-272 (TU 89,136-137), above p.73 n.116.

135. Ammon. Jo. 501 (TU 89,321), above p.129 n.13.

136. Cf. Thdr.Heracl. fr.Jo. 260-261 (TU 89,133-134), above pp.41-42 and above n.49.

137. See above pp.140-141.

138. Hegem. Arch. 38(34),5-6 (GCS 16,55-56), above p.67 n.69. Cf. Mußner, 67-68, who, while acknowledging that John recognises a Spirit which all the faithful receive (he cites 7,39 and 4,14), limits the special activity of the Paraclete to the apostolic witnesses (15,27).

139. On exegesis of τὸ πνεῦμα τῆς ἀληθείας see above p.144. On the view (Thdr.Mops.) that 15,26 promises not the Spirit himself but his grace to believers, see above p.149 and n.119.

140. They both adduce it as a proof-text for, and expound it in a manner consistent with, the doctrine of the procession. For references see above pp.35-36, 49, 88, 121-122, 126, 126-127, and the relevant notes. Cf. Or. Cant. Prologus (GCS 33,74), above p.4.

141. Cf. de la Potterie, 386-389, who discusses this parallelism in some detail, and also Brown, Gospel, 689, and Schnackenburg, 135.

142. It was pointed out by Westcott (B.F. Westcott, The Gospel According to St John (London, 1887), 225) and again by de la Potterie, 386 n.159, that the creeds and Greek fathers ordinarily use not παρά but ἐκ with ἐκπορεύεσθαι to express the eternal procession of the Spirit. For Westcott this underscores his assertion that παρά here refers ἐκπορεύεται rather to the mission than the procession.

143. Av. div.Spir. (PL 59,385-386), above p.133 n.40, cf. Thdt. haer. 5,3 (PG 83,453-456), above p.36. Bultmann, 553 n.3, takes ἐκπορεύεται to be an atemporal present. De la Potterie, 388-389, argues that it is an imminent future (cf. adveniet, Vic. Ar. 1,13 (CSEL 83,1,72), above p.104 n.12).

144. See above pp.139 and 149-150.

145. See 16,28 (ἐξῆλθον παρὰ τοῦ πατρός) and 17,8 (παρὰ σοῦ ἐξῆλθον), cf. 7,29 (παρ' αὐτοῦ εἰμι), 8,42 (ἐκ τοῦ θεοῦ ἐξῆλθον), and 13,3 (ἀπὸ θεοῦ ἐξῆλθεν). Note the fluctuation between παρά and ἐκ with the verb of motion (cf. n.142). ἐκπορεύεσθαι is no more than a stylistic alternative for ἐξέρχεσθαι.

146. Certain of the passages considered above which use this clause also defend the procession of the Spirit from the Son. For references see p.107 n.42 and p.133 nn.40 (Av.) and 43. Consideration of this doctrine lies beyond our scope.

147. On what follows see also above pp.139-140.

148. See Ambr. Spir. 3,1,8 (CSEL 79,153), Aug. Ps. 102,10 (CCL 40, 1461), and Aug. Trin. 4,20,29 (CCL 50,200), above p.104 n.12; Aug. Trin. 15,26,45 (CSEL 50A,525), above p.88; Av. div.Spir. (PL 59,386), Fulg.

Fab. 27,6-7 (CCL 91A,805-806), Fulg. Mon. 2,6,4 (CCL 91,40), and Isid.
ep. 6,8 (PL 83,904), above pp.126-127; Vic. Ar. 3,15 (CSEL 83,1,217),
above p.104 n.12. It is not always made explicit that a writer has
ὃν ἐγὼ πέμψω in view when he cites 15,26, but this is the only natural inference from the context. Cf. the passages cited in n.149.

149. See Anast.Ant. or. 1,22 (PG 89,1324-1325), above p.121; also
Aug. serm.Ar. 4 (PL 42,686), 19 (PL 42,697), Trin. 1,12,25 (CCL 50,
64), above p.104 n.12.

150. This is inferred from the individual context. See, for example,
Aug. Trin. 4,20,29 (CCL 50,200), above p.104 n.12, and Trin. 15,26,45
(CCL 50A,525), above p.88 ; also Fulg. Fab. 27,6-7 (CCL 91A,805-806)
and Isid. ep.6,8 (PL 83,904), above p.133 n.43.

151. On this point, Eus. e.th. 3,5,11 (GCS 14,161), above p.61 n.15,
is less open to suspicion than some of the Latin exegetes. He at
least seeks to establish the mutual working of Father and Son from
elsewhere in the FG (5,19.30) as the basis for his interpretation.

152. Is Vic. Ar. 1,13 (CSEL 83,1,72), above p.104 n.12, perhaps an
exception? He supports his assertion *quod paraclitus a deo et a
Christo* by quoting 15,26 alone.

153. On these two themes in the FG and their relationship to each
other, see Barrett, "The Father is Greater than I". The essay includes an examination of patristic approaches to subordinationist passages.

154. Only in 16,7 does Jesus appear to be alone responsible for the
sending of the Paraclete. But even there the mission is contingent
upon his return to the Father (cf. 16,5.10).

155. Aug. Trin. 4,20,29 (CCL 50,200), above p.104 n.12, does seem to
recognise it. On the basis of *quem ego mittam uobis a patre*, with
which he contrasts the *quem mittet pater in nomine meo* (he stresses
that it does not say *a meo*) of 14,26, he infers that *totius . . .
deitatis principium pater est*. But he understands this in terms of
the (double) procession.

156. As we have seen (see above pp.139-140), they do feel the subordinationism implied in 14,16. But recognition of the true force of this
theme in the Gospel is for orthodox theologians precluded after about
the middle of the Fourth Century. Partly in reaction to radical
Arianism and partly in the light of the developments of Trinitarian
theology, they feel compelled to explain the subordinationism of such
passages as not veritable but apparent only. It is this circumstance
which gives rise to such expedients as the 'doctrine' of condescension
and the two-nature exegesis.

157. Aug. Jo. 92,1 (CCL 36,555-556), above p.94 , is rightly careful
to place 15,26-27 squarely within the context of persecution.

158. Cf. Mt. 10,19-20 and parallels.

159. Aug. Jo. 93,1 (CCL 36,558), *utique quia ille perhibebit etiam
uos perhibebitis: ille in cordibus uestris, uos in uocibus uestris;*

ille inspirando, uos sonando. This Aug. illustrates from the story of
Peter. His account in Jo. 92,1-2 (CCL 36,555-557), above p.94 , of
the effects of the Paraclete's witness - the disciples are given
courage, the world is converted - is also drawn largely from the life
of Peter. But it reflects the sensitive inference from this passage
and its context that as a result of the working of the Paraclete the
verdict of the world will be overturned (cf. 16,8-11) and the disciples
will become witnesses to the truth (contrast 18,15-18.25-27).

160. Thdr.Mops. Jo. 130 (ST 141,399), Jo.Syr. on 15,26-27 (CSCO 115,
288), above p.49. His description of the Paraclete's *modus operandi*
is based not on this passage but on 1 Cor. 2,4.

161. Cyr. Jo. 10,2 (Pusey 2,609), above p.49. Cyr. offers no support
for his account of the method of the Spirit's witness.

162. See Aug. Jo. 92,2 (CCL 36,556-557), above p.94; also Chrys.
hom.77,3 in Jo. (PG 59,417), Cyr. Jo. 10,2 (Pusey 2,609), cf. Thdr.
Mops. Jo. 130 (ST 141,399) and Jo.Syr. on 15,26-27 (CSCO 115,288),
above pp.49-51. ἀπ' ἀρχῆς refers to the election of the disciples
at the beginning of Jesus' public ministry. It is clear that the
fathers understand this though they do not say so explicitly.

163. See Aug. Jo. 94,2 (CCL 36,562-563), above p.95; also Cyr. Jo.
10,2 (Pusey 2,615-616) and Thdr.Mops. Jo.Syr. on 16,4b (CSCO 115,
291), above p.50.

164. Chrys. hom.78,1 in Jo. (PG 59,421), above p.50. In this passage
Chrys. visibly seeks to preserve Jesus' divine dignity and to protect
him from any hint of nescience.

165. See Chrys. hom. 78,1 in Jo. (PG 59,421), cf. hom.5,4 in I Cor.
(Field 2,53; PG 61,45) and ep. 3,4 (SCH 13,159-160; PG 52,576); Cyr.
Jo. 10,2 (Pusey 2,615-616); cf. Thdr.Heracl. fr.Jo. 309 (TU 89,146) and
Thdr.Mops. Jo.Syr. on 16,4b (CSCO 115,291); above p.50.

166. Aug. Jo. 94,1-2 (CCL 36,561-563), above p.95. His exegesis is
here influenced by his doctrine of Scripture.

167. Chrys. hom.78,1 in Jo. (PG 59,421), above p.75 n.137, as we have
seen, rightly identifies the antecedent of ταῦτα; but his attempt to
resolve the conflict by contrasting the contents of the Johannine and
Matthean accounts is no more convincing than is Augustine's approach.

168. Aug. Jo. 94,3 (CCL 36,563), above p.95.

169. John, of course, gives no account of the ascension as an ob-
servable phenomenon. Cf. 6,62 and 20,17.

170. Barrett, Gospel, 485.

171. See Chrys. ep. 3,4 (SCH 13,159-160; PG 52,576), hom.5,4 in I Cor.
(Field 2,53; PG 61,45); Thdr.Heracl. fr.Jo. 309 (TU 89,146); Thdr.Mops.
Jo. 130 (ST 141,399), Jo.Syr. on 16,5-6 (CSCO 115,292).

172. See Ammon. Jo. 536 (TU 89,329), above p.129 n.13; also Chrys.
ep. 3,4 (SCH 13,159-160;PG 52,576), hom.78,1 in Jo. (PG 59,421), hom.

5,4 in I Cor. (Field 2,53; PG 61,45); Cyr. Jo. 10,2 (Pusey 2,616-617);
Thdr.Heracl. fr.Jo. 309 (TU 89,146); and Thdr.Mops. Jo. 130 (ST 141,
399), Jo.Syr. on 16,5-6 (CSCO 115,292), above p.50.

173. See Chrys. hom.78,1 in Jo. (PG 59,421) and Cyr. Jo. 10,2 (Pusey
2,616-617), above p.50. But contrast the opening paragraph of the
same hom.78,1 in Jo. where Chrys. takes a much more acceptable line.
He is often inconsistent just as his exposition frequently suffers
because he does not pay due regard to the context of a given phrase or
verse.

174. Chrys. hom. 78,1 in Jo. (PG 59,421), above p.50. Note the
suggestion that Jesus speaks with the future readers of the FG as
well as the disciples in view. This is typical of Chrys. and of the
patristic age in general. It reflects something of both his Christology and his doctrine of Scripture.

175. Fulg. Tras. 3,21,3 (CCL 91,165), above p.127.

176. Jo. 14,1, the other verse adduced by Fulg., is equally uncon-
genial to this exegesis.

177. See Aug. Jo. 94,4 (CCL 36,563), above pp.95-96;   also Chrys.
hom. 78,1 in Jo. (PG 59,421), Cyr. Jo. 10,2 (Pusey 2,617), Thdr.Mops.
Jo. 130 (ST 141,400) and Jo.Syr. on 16,7 (CSCO 115,292), above p.50.
Thdr. seems to have a good grasp of the fact that 'going away' involves the passion. So does Ammon. Jo. 537 (TU 89,329), above p.129
n.13, ἐὰν μὴ πάθω, οὐκ ἐπιφοιτᾷ ὑμῖν τὸ πνεῦμα τὸ πάσης δόσεως
ἀγαθῆς αἴτιον.

178. See Bas. moral. 5,5 (PG 31,709), from whom the quotation is
taken; Chrys. hom. 78,1 in Jo. (PG 59,421); cf. Cyr. Jo. 10,2 (Pusey
2,617); above p.50.

179. Cyr. Jo. 10,2 (Pusey 2,618-620), above p.51.

180. Cyr. Jo. 10,2 (Pusey 2,620-621), above p.51. We must not linger
here to consider the details of the exposition, not all of which are
germane to 16,7 or our study. It is the main point that is to be
sustained.

181. Chrys. hom. 78,1 in Jo. (PG 59,421), above p.51. Cf. Didym.
Trin. 2,17 (PG 39,725), above p.39, also Faust. Spir. 1,10 (CSEL 21,
118), above p.125.

182. Chrys. hom. 78,3 in Jo. (PG 59,423), above pp.51-52, cf. hom.
1,5 in Ac. (PG 60,20).

183. Chrys. hom. 1,5 in Ac. (PG 60,20), above p.52.

184. Aug. Jo. 94,4 (CCL 36,563-564), above pp.95-96.

185. See above p.155. Cf. Vic. Ar. 1,13 (CSEL 83,1,72), above p.113
n.87, who seemingly labours under a similar misunderstanding.

186. Aug. Jo. 94,5 (CCL 36,564), above p.96. He probably does not
mean to imply that there is *no* sense in which the Spirit replaces Jesus.

187. Faust. Spir. 1,10 (CSEL 21,118), above p.125 and Vic. Ar.1,13 (CSEL 83,1,72), above p.113 n.87. We neglect their theologizing in these passages as it does not concern us here.

188. ἐλέγχειν περὶ we take to mean 'convict of' on the analogy of 8,46 (the only other instance of the expression in the FG) which can only mean 'Which of you convicts me of sin?'

189. Ambrstr. quaest. 89,1 (CSEL 50,149), above pp.96-97.

190. Aug. Jo. 95,1 (CCL 36,565), above p.96.   His attempt (CCL 36, 564-565) to show that 16,8 cannot mean that Jesus does not also reprove the world is dogmatically rather than exegetically motivated.

191. Ambrstr. quaest. 89,2 (CSEL 50,150), above p.97.   He of course intends this to be an historical observation. Cf. Ammon. Jo. 539 (TU 89,330), above p.129 n.13, and Chrys. hom. 78,1 in Jo. (PG 59, 421-422); also the passages cited in nn.160.161 on 15,27 above.

192. Cf. Apoll. Jo. 118 (TU 89,47) who on 16,9 remarks καὶ φαινόμενον ἐν τοῖς πιστεύουσι τὸ πνεῦμα κατάκρισις ἦν τῶν ἀπιστούντων.

193. This is not to suggest that we agree in every particular with every writer. The important thing here is that they all perceive the central meaning of the verse. For our purposes everything else is negligible.

194. See Ammon. Jo. 538 (TU 89,329), above p.129 n.13; Apoll. Jo. 118-119 (TU 89,47-48), Chrys hom. 78,1-2 in Jo. (PG 59,421-422), Cyr. Jo. 10,2 (Pusey 2,622), Thdr.Mops. Jo.Syr. on 16,9 (CSCO 115, 293), above p.53.

195. For references see above p.114 n.95.

196. For references see above p.114 n.97.

197. Aug. serm. 144,2 (PL 38,788), above p.97.

198. Aug. Jo. 95,2 (CCL 36,565-566) and serm. 144,3 (PL 38,788), above p.98.   This observation occurs in both passages, but the interpretation of 16,10 differs. We have already remarked (p.98) that Aug. is inconsistent here. He espouses quite different exegeses with equal conviction. Cf. nn.200-202 below.

199. A righteous world would in any case be for John a contradiction in terms (see pp.144-145).

200. See Apoll. Jo. 119 (TU 89,48); Aug. Jo. 95,2-3. (CCL 36,566-567), Ps. 109,8 (CCL 40,1608), serm. 143,4 (PL 38,786-787); Cyr. Jo. 10,2 (Pusey 2,622-623); Thdr.Heracl. fr.Jo. 312 (TU 89,147); above pp.53 and 98.

201. Cf. M.-F. Berrouard, "Le Paraclet, défenseur du Christ devant la conscience du croyant (Jo. XVI,8-11)," Revue des sciences philosophiques et théologiques 33 (1949), 382. Aug. rightly evaluates the contrast (and therefore rightly interprets the verse; see below) in serm. 144,3 (PL 38,788), quoted above p.115 n.100. It is his failure to do so elsewhere that leads him astray.

202. See Ambrstr. quaest. 89,1 (CSEL 50,149); Aug. serm. 144,3 (PL
38,788); Chrys. hom. 78,2 in Jo. (PG 59,422); Thdr.Mops. Jo.Syr. on
16,10 (CSCO 115,293); Vic. Ar. 3,16 (CSEL 83,1,219); above pp.53 and
97-98.

203. It is apparently in this derived sense that Aug. speaks of the
righteousness of believers in serm. 144,6 (PL 38,790), quoted above p.
115 n.102, the sermon where he identifies the righteousness spoken
of in 16,10 as that of Christ.

204. For references see above p.22 n.40 (cf. nn.38-39), p.77 n.158,
and p.116 n.109.

205. Ammon. Jo. 539 (TU 89,329-330), above p.129 n.13, and Thdr.
Heracl. fr.Jo. 311.313 (TU 89,146-147), above p.53.

206. Aug. Jo. 95,4 (CCL 36,567) and serm. 144,6 (PL 38,790), above
p.98.

207. Cyr. Jo. 10,2 (Pusey 2,625), above p.54. Here as elsewhere in
Cyr., accurate assessment requires careful thought. This is partly
due to his manner of expression, partly to the fact that he is not
always careful to indicate the source of his ideas.

208. The fathers have no difficulty recognising this. Cf., for
example, Thdr.Mops. Jo.Syr. on 16,11 (CSCO 115,293); also Vic. Ar.
3,15 (CSEL 83,1,218), above p.116 n.109.

209. Aug. Jo. 95,4 (CCL 36,568) and serm. 144,6 (PL 38,790), above
p.99.

210. Chrys. hom. 78,2 in Jo. (PG 59,422), above pp.53-54, cf. Thdr.
Mops. Jo.Syr. on 16,11 (CSCO 115,293).

211. Cyr. Jo. 10,2 (Pusey 2,623), above p.54. Cyr. does not, it
would seem, misunderstand the verse. He is just (typically) not
careful enough to tie his exposition to the text.

212. Ammon. Jo. 539 (TU 89,330), above p.129 n.13; Thdr.Mops. Jo.
Syr. on 16,11 (CSCO 115,293); cf. Cyr. Jo. 10,2 (Pusey 2,623-624).

213. Of the *variae lectiones*, ἐν τῇ ἀληθείᾳ πάσῃ has the best at-
testation and is probably to be preferred. We pursue the matter no
further here as the fathers do not comment directly on this clause.

214. The same is true in various ways of the whole of vv.12-15. This
is perhaps largely because patristic interest in these verses, and
particularly vv.14-15, is more dogmatic than exegetical. Frequently
the fathers cite them, not to interpret them, but to explain them in
a manner consistent with Trinitarian theology or to use them as a
mine for Trinitarian proof-texts. Consequently, while citations are
relatively more numerous than for the passages considered above, the
amount of careful exegesis is relatively smaller. This will place
some constraints on our analysis. Fortunately, it will not be necessary to undergo the tedium of examining each citation individually. We
shall lump together what can be treated together and deal with what is
representative, but that means we shall also have to be more general
at points than heretofore.

215. See Or. Cels. 2,2 (GCS 2,128-129), above p.7; cf. Didym. Spir. 33 (PG 39,1063), Eus. e.th. 3,5,12 (GCS 14,161), and Thdr.Heracl. fr. Jo. 314 (TU 89,148), above pp.55-56.

216. See Or. princ. 1,3,4 (GCS 22,53-54), 2,7,3 (GCS 22,150), hom. 3,2 in Josh. (GCS 30,303), above pp.5-7; Cyr. Jo. 10,2 (Pusey 2, 626.627), Eus. e.th. 3,5,12 (GCS 14,161), Thdr.Heracl. fr.Jo. 314 (TU 89,148), Thdr.Mops. hom. 8,3 (ST 145,190-191) and Jo.Syr. on 16,13 (CSCO 115,294-295), cf. Chrys. hom. 5,5 in I Cor. (Field 2,53; PG 61,45) and Didym. Spir. 33 (PG 39,1062-1063), above p.56; cf. Ammon. Jo. 542 (TU 89,330), above p.130 n.13, Aug. fid. 19 (CSEL 41, 24), above p.100, and Tert. Prax. 30,5 (CCL 2,1204), above p.10.

217. Aug. Jo. 96,1-2 (CCL 36,568-570), above p.99.

218. Didym. Spir. 33 (PG 39,1062-1063), above p.56.

219. Pheob. Ar. 11 (PL 20,20), above pp.117-118 n.124.

220. On the question whether or not John allows fresh revelation from the Paraclete, see E. Bammel, "Jesus und der Paraklet in Johannes 16," Christ and Spirit in the New Testament, ed. B. Lindars and S.S. Smalley in Honour of Charles Francis Digby Moule (Cambridge, 1973), 199-217.

221. Leo tract. 76,5 (CCL 138A,478-479), above p.117 n.122; cf. Thdr. Mops. Jo.Syr. on 16,12-13 (CSCO 115,294-295), above pp.55.56.

222. See Or. Cels. 2,2 (GCS 2,129), above p.7; also Cyr. Jo. 10,2 (Pusey 2,626), Didym. Spir. 33 (PG 39,1063), cf. Thdr.Heracl. fr.Jo. 314 (TU 89,148), above pp.55-56; cf. Ammon. Jo. 542 (TU 89,330), above p.130 n.13.

223. Thdr.Mops. Jo.Syr. on 16,12-13 (CSCO 115,294), above p.55. Cf. Cyr. Jo. 10,2 (Pusey 2,625-626) who says very much the same thing, if more loquaciously, almost as directly.

224. Cyr. Jo. 10,2 (Pusey 2,625).

225. For references see above p.117 nn.119-122.

226. Tert. haer. 22,8-10 (CCL 1,204), cf. haer. 8,14-15 (CCL 1,194) and 28,1 (CCL 1,209), above p.13.

227. See Tert. uirg. 1,4-5.7 (CCL 2,1209-1210), above p.14.

228. Tert. mon. 2,2.4 (CCL 2,1230), above p.15.

229. The Evangelist makes a similar point in stressing the divine origin of the mission itself. See above pp.152-153.

230. See Chrys. hom. 78,2 in Jo. (PG 59,422-423), Cyr. Jo. 10,2 (Pusey 2,629), and Thdr.Mops. Jo.Syr. on 16,13 (CSCO 115,295-296), above pp.56-57.

231. Among the Greeks, Thdr.Mops. is perhaps the prime example as regards this part of this verse. But the tendency is ubiquitous; it

is neither limited to the Greek fathers, as we shall see, nor to commentary on v.13b.

232. Aug. Jo. 99,4 (CCL 36,584-585), above p.101; Fulg Fab. 25,3-5 (CCL 91A,802-803), 27,4-5 (CCL 91A,804-805), above p.126. Fulg. refines Augustine's explanation and extends it to include v.14b., as well. Cf. Ambr. Spir. 2,12,131-133 (CSEL 79,137-138).

233. Aug. Jo. 99,5 (CCL 36,585), above p.101.

234. Fulg. Fab. 25,1-3 (CCL 91A,801-802), above p.126.

235. Such reflections lie in any case beyond the scope of our consideration.

236. See Chrys. hom. 78,2.3 in Jo. (PG 59,423.424), Cyr. Jo. 10,2 (Pusey 2,629), Thdr.Mops. Jo.Syr. on 16,13 (CSCO 115,296), above p.57.

237. Cyr. Jo. 10,2 (Pusey 2,629), above p.57.

238. Chrys. hom. 78,3 in Jo. (PG 59,424), cf. Thdr.Mops. Jo.Syr. on 16,13 (CSCO 115,296), above p.57.

239. On the significance of this clause, see further the discussions in Barrett, Gospel, 490; Brown, Gospel, 708.715-716; Bultmann, 575; de la Potterie, 445-453; and Schnackenburg, 154.

240. See Aug. Jo. 100,1 (CCL 36,588), above p.101; Cyr. Jo. 11,1 (Pusey 2,633-634), above p.57, cf. Jo. 4,1 (Pusey 1,509); cf. Thdr. Mops. Jo.Syr. on 16,14 (CSCO 115,297).

241. See Chrys. hom. 78,2 in Jo. (PG 59,423), above p.57; Thdr.Mops. Jo.Syr. on 16,14 (CSCO 115,297-298), above pp.57-58.

242. See Aug. Jo. 100,1 (CCL 26,588), above p.101.

243. See Cyr. Jo. 11,1 (Pusey 2,634-635), above p.57.

244. Cyr. Jo. 11,1 (Pusey 2,636), above p.58.

245. Chrys. hom. 78,2 in Jo. (PG 59,422), above p.58.

246. Chrys. hom. 78,2 in Jo. (PG 59,423), cf. Eus. e.th. 3,5,18 (GCS 14,162-163), above p.58; and Thdr.Heracl. fr.Jo.316 (TU 89,148) who similarly refer the phrase to knowledge or wisdom.

247. Thdr.Mops. Jo.Syr. on 16,15 (CSCO 115,298-299) cf. on 16,14 (CSCO 115,297), above p.59. Thdr. does rightly perceive the force of the partitive.

248. Apoll. Jo. 120 (TU 89,48), above p.58; Vig. Ar. 2,35 (PL 62, 220-221), above p.124.

249. See Epiph. haer. 48,11,5-10 (GCS 31,234-235), Ign.‡Eph. 9 (PG 5,740), above p.39; Or. Jo. 20,29 on 8,44 (GCS 10,366; Brooke 2,80), above p.4; cf. the similar arguments from v.13 et al. in Aug. Faust. 32,16 (CSEL 25,1,776), above p.89, and Didym. Trin. 3,19 (PG 38,889-892).

250. See Apoll. Jo. 120 (TU 89,48-49), Cyr. Jo. 11,1 (Pusey 2,635), above p.58, Fulg. Fab. 27,4-5 (CCL 91A,804-805) cf. 25,3-5 (CCL 91A, 802-803), above p.126; cf. Ambr. Spir. 3,16,115 (CSEL 79,199), above p.84. Details of the exposition differ slightly from father to father. Fulg., for example, accepts the double procession of the Spirit from Father and Son whereas Cyr. speaks in terms of the procession of the Spirit through the Son. But the argument is at base the same.

251. See Ath. Ar. 1,15 (PG 26,44), Cyr. thes. 4 (PG 75,45), above p.32; Nov. Trin. 16,2-3 (CCL 4,40), above p.11; cf. Ambr. Spir. 1,5,70 (CSEL 79,45), above p.86, where the same argument is used against those who deny that the Son of God is good.

252. For representative passages see above p.24 n.53, pp.62-64 nn.23.26-38, p.80 n.191, pp.104-106 nn.15-16.19-31, p.107 n.40, p.131 n.25.

253. Brown, Gospel, 709.

APPENDIX

VARIANT READINGS ATTESTED BY THE GREEK FATHERS

VARIANT READINGS ATTESTED BY THE GREEK FATHERS

INTRODUCTION

This appendix assembles evidence for the text of the paraclete passages from the Greek fathers, Origen to John of Damascus
inclusive. Before Origen there do not seem to be any quotations of
the passages extant, and after John of Damascus one is no longer
dealing with patristic materials. Because the text of the NT was for
all practical purposes established by the beginning of the Fifth
Century, it was at first proposed to gather no variant readings from
writings later than the Council of Chalcedon. But, for the sake of
completeness, collection has been carried to the end of the era of
the fathers.

The *modus operandi* for the search led to an examination of
all the writings listed in the standard patrologies (especially Quasten[1]), using the best critical editions wherever possible. But this
appendix almost surely includes less than all the evidence to be
found in the Greek fathers. Many things limit its completeness;
here are three. First, the patrologies used as guides, while generally accurate and very useful, are occasionally dated and, in places,
less than comprehensive. Secondly, the search for quotations has had
to rely heavily on indices, footnotes, and parenthetical references in
columns of print which have sometimes proved to contain significant
inaccuracies. And finally, the human researcher himself, however care-

---

[1]
J. Quasten, Patrology, 3 vols. (Utrecht, 1950-1960).

ful, is almost certain to overlook some things in a quest spanning
more than ten months and requiring the scanning of thousands of columns of print. There can be, therefore, no claim that the material
assembled here is complete. But it is as complete and accurate as it
could be made within limits imposed by time and the pressures of the
main line of research.

The appendix includes, then, with reasonable thoroughness,
readings from the Greek fathers to John of Damascus. It does not
include readings found in Syrian, Armenian, Coptic, Georgian, and
other writings. This is both because there seem to be no ante-
Nicene quotations in these literatures and because the scope of the
research for this book includes only Greek and Latin post-Nicene
writers. Neither does it include variants taken from the Latin
fathers; all the textual evidence from the Latin fathers is being assembled by the members of the Vetus Latina Institute in the Monastery
in Beuron, Germany where it is published from time to time in fas-
cicles by Biblical book. As their work may be consulted at the
Institute[2] and as the work of many will surely be more thorough than
that of one, evidence from the Latin fathers collected for this book
would be otiose and is not included here.

An attempt has been made to exclude insignificant variations

---

[2]
     This information is confirmed by the former director of the
Vetus Latina Institute, P.B. Fischer, in a letter of 16 January 1975
to Professor C.K. Barrett. The pertinent sentences from the letter are
these: *In Beuron ist das gesamte Material zu den lateinischen Kirchen-
vätern gesammelt und in einer Kartei nach den Bibelversen geordnet;
man kann es im Institut einsehen und benützen. Eine Bearbeitung dieses
Materials und die Vorbereitung für den Druck kann nur nach und nach
und jeweils nur für einzelne Bücher der Bibel erfolgen. Für die Evan-
gelien ist eine solche Bearbeitung noch nicht begonnen worden und auch
für die nächsten Jahre nicht in Aussicht genommen, da zunächst die
Paulusbriefe, Sapientia, Sirach, Judith bearbeitet werden.*

from the NT text by taking as normative the *sigla*, selection of variants, and apparatus of Nestle-Aland (NA) as found in the fifth edition
of Aland's <u>Synopsis</u>.[3] Slips have been made, therefore, for patristic
readings only at those places corresponding to the Nestle-Aland *sigla*.
Excluded variants are generally of little importance; most may be
recovered by referring to other readings which are collected here.
For example, evidence for the reading πατήρ μου in Jo. 14,26 has not
been listed because no variation is indicated at that point in NA. But
nearly all of the evidence for or against this reading may be recovered
by referring to writings cited here for, say, 14,26[T]. Although only
readings which occur in *places* marked by NA are recorded, specific
readings are included which are not found in the NA apparatus. For
example, NA at 16,7[f] reads οὐ μὴ ἔλθη and has οὐκ ἐλεύσεται in the apparatus. Certain fathers show other variants, as well, viz., οὐκ
ἔρχεται and οὐ μὴ ἔρχεται. These additional readings are included.

Only quotations close enough to the NT to indicate the probable
reading in the text used by any given father are cited (e.g., see on
16,15[□] below Gr.Naz. <u>ep</u>. 168 (PG 37,277)). But evidence is not included from mere allusions, however clear (e.g., see with respect to
16,15[□] Gr.Nyss. <u>ep</u>. 24,12 (Jaeger 8,2,78)). This is especially important with respect to 16,15[□] since any mere allusion to 16,15 could
also be an allusion to 17,10; the two verses are often juxtaposed.

For present purposes the data have been recorded precisely as
found in the editions with no discussion of their nature and implications. There may, for instance, be very good reasons why a given quotation of 14,26 excludes the reading [O]ἐγώ which have nothing to do with

---

[3]
        K. Aland (ed.), <u>Synopsis Quattuor Evangeliorum</u> (editio quin-
ta; Stuttgart, 1968).

the text of the NT. Such considerations have had to be left to one
side.

As will be patent, Syriac and Latin versions of the Greek
fathers do not at every point reveal the Greek readings behind them.
Jerome's Latin version of Didym. Spir. cannot distinguish, for instance, between κἀγώ and καὶ ἐγώ in 14,16. Syriac versions cannot
adequately distinguish between readings such as ἅ and ὅσα or εἶπον and
ἂν εἴπω in 14,26. Only those readings from Syriac and Latin versions
which are capable of indicating the probable nature of the Greek
original are dealt with here; the rest are ignored. Similarly, it
is possible to draw conclusions from Nonnus for only some of the variants which lay in the Biblical text before him. Only those readings
have been included, therefore, which seem fairly surely indicated by
his paraphrase.

Three items present special difficulties. The clause ὃ παρὰ
τοῦ πατρὸς (μου) ἐκπορεύεται from 15,26 passed early into the creeds
and thence into the language of the Church. It is now often difficult
to know whether its isolated presence in a writing represents quotation of the NT or use of a liturgical formula (which may itself preserve a reading from the text(s) used by the framers of the creeds).
Nevertheless, readings have been taken from the clause wherever it
occurs. Again, the omission or inclusion of the final two clauses in
16,7 (*siglum* ⌐) would seem to be little more than a quarrel between
the first and the correcting hands of p[66]. And the question of inclusion or omission of all of 16,15 is of such a nature that, except
in quotations which span 16,14-16 (none seem to occur), it is not possible to know when the text used by a given writer omitted it. One
cannot always be sure, therefore, of the value of given patristic evidence for either of these latter situations. But again, in the hope

that what evidence there is may be useful, all instances of the inclusion of 16,15 and the final two clauses of 16,7 are presented here.

The disposition of the table of readings is straightforward.
Materials are arranged by NT chapter and verse; they are subdivided
according to the order in which specific variants appear in NA. Readings from 14,15, therefore, precede those from 14,26 or 16,7; readings
under 15,26 $\ulcorner$ precede those under 15,26$\urcorner^{\shortmid}$; and evidence for τηρήσετε
(14,15) precedes evidence for τηρήσατε. Fathers and writings are
arranged in the alphabetical order of their abbreviations, with
authentic writings anteceding those which are disputed or spurious.
The title of each writing is given only once at each point in the table; multiple references to the same work are separated by commas.

Where (in Chrys. and Cyr.) a distinction must be made between
a text quoted at the head of a section of commentary and a quotation
interior to the exposition, the former is indicated by a raised *txt*
and the latter by a raised *com*. Cyr. Jo. 10,2^{txt} and 10,2^{com} are a
case in point. Both *txt* and *com* are omitted where no confusion would
result.

When necessary, the degree of certainty with which a given
reading is attested is indicated by *prob.* for *probably* or *pos.* for
possibly. Any fuller discussion required is put into footnotes
(given, to avoid confusion, as raised, lower-case letters of the alpha-
bet). Citations not accompanied by *prob.* or *pos.* contain evidence
which is more or less certain. Doubtful witnesses are not generally
included.

For a few writings two editions are cited. Such double
references are given only where no single edition is substantially
superior or where the best critical edition may not be readily available. Where editions with differing chapter and paragraph divisions

are cited for a writing, the one appearing first supplies the divisions used here.

Marginal readings are indicated by placing *mg* (not raised)
after the edition. There is no attempt to record the support for such
a variant, as this information is easily recovered from the editions
themselves. Only marginal readings with manuscript support are included.

Various Greek and Latin words appear from time to time. Those
set off by commas and italicized give the precise words of a reading
noteworthy because of some slight peculiarity, e.g., word order. The
unitalicized words *bis*, *ter*, and *quater* following a reference mean
that the particular reading under discussion appears two, three, or
four times, respectively, in that place.

An example may be helpful:

John 16,7 ^T

ἐγώ

    Didym. Eun. 5 (PG 29,764); Trin. 2,11, ἐγώ post μή (PG 39,661),
      2,17, ἐγώ post μή (PG 39,725).

This excerpt reveals that the reading ἐγώ for 16,7 occurs three times
in Didymus, once in Adversus Eunomium 5 (pseudo-Basil), once at De
Trinitate 2,11, and once at De Trinitate 2,17. The position of ἐγώ
in De Trinitate differs slightly from its position in NA; the order of
words here is ἐὰν γὰρ μὴ ἐγὼ ἀπέλθω. The abbreviation PG and the numbers which follow it give the volume and column of Migne's Patrologia
Graeca where each of the three quotations may be found.

Many questions were raised in compiling these lists which must
be held in abeyance. One such question closes this already lengthy
introduction. In a few places where the consensus of recent opinion
seems to assign authorship of a disputed or pseudonymous work to a

given known author (e.g., to Didym. Eun. 4-5), the text traditions of
the assigned works appear to be different in the paraclete passages
from those of the known works of the father to whom they are assigned.
Is it possible, therefore, that comparisons of text traditions ought
to play a more prominent part than they do in deciding questions of
disputed authorship?

TABLE OF VARIANT READINGS

John 14,15 ⌐

τηρήσετε

> Chrys. hom. 75,1 in Jo. (PG 59,403), 76,2 (PG 59,412).
> Cyr. Jo. 9,1com (Pusey 2,465).
> Epiph. haer. 74,13,4 (GCS 37,331).
> Eus. e.th. 3,5,1 (GCS 14,160).
> Thdr.Heracl. fr.Jo. 260 (TU 89,133).

τηρήσατε

> Ant.Mon hom. 72 (PG 89,1644).
> Apophth.Patr.v.s. 43,1 (PL 73,1058).
> Bas. reg.br. 213 (PG 31,1224); reg.fus. 5,2 (PG 31,921); †bapt.
> 1,24 (PG 31,1565).
> Chrys. hom. 24,3 in Heb. (Field 7,277; PG 63,171); hom. 75 in
> Jo.txt (PG 59,403).
> Cyr. Jo. 9,1txt (Pusey 2,462).
> Didym. Trin. 2,3 (PG 39,473), 2,6,2 (PG 39,509), 3,38 bis (PG
> 39,973.976).
> Eus. Ps. on 56,8ff (57,7ff) (PG 23,512).
> Hegem. Arch. 38(34),10 (GCS 16,56).
> Is.Ab. or. 25,23 (PG 40,1190).
> Mac.Aeg. hom. 19,2 (PG 34,644).
> Nonn. par.Jo. (Scheindler 159).
> Or. Cant. 1 (GCS 33,112); sel.in Ps. 118(119),45 (PG 12,1596).
> Thdr.Mops. hom. 10,3 (ST 145,248); Jo.Syr. on 14,15 (CSCO 115,
> 271).

τηρήσητε

> Ant.Mon. hom. 118 (PG 89,1804).
> Cyr. Jo. 2,1 (Pusey 1,188).

John 14,16 ⌐

κἀγώ

> Cyr. Jo. 2,1 (Pusey 1,188), 9,1txt (Pusey 2,466), 11,10 bis
> (Pusey 2,718.719).

Cyr.H. catech. 17,11 (Rupp,2,264).
Didym. Trin. 2,3 (PG 39,473), 2,6,2 (PG 39,509), 3,38 bis, (PG 39,973.976).
Epiph. anc. 69,8 (GCS 25,86); haer. 74,6,8 (GCS 37,322), 74,13,4 (GCS 37,331, mg ἐγώ).
Thdr.Mops. Jo. 132 (ST 141,402).

καὶ ἐγώ

Chrys. hom. 75 in Jo.txt (PG 59,403); pent. 1,1 (PG 50,454).
Eus. e.th. 3,5,1 (GCS 14,160), 3,5,6 pos. (GCS 14,160); Ps. on 56,8ff (57,7ff) (PG 23,512).

John 14,16

ἣ μεθ' ὑμῶν εἰς τὸν αἰῶνα

Cyr. Jo. 9,1txt (Pusey 2,466).
Didym. Spir. 27, sit vobiscum in aeternum (PG 39,1057); Trin. 2,3 (PG 39,473), 2,6,2, omits εἰς τὸν αἰῶνα (PG 39,509).
Eus. e.th. 3,5,1 (GCS 14,160); Is. on 40,1-2, εἴη for ἣ (PG 24, 364); Ps. on 56,8ff (57,7ff) (PG 23,512).
Thdr.Mops. hom. 10,3 (ST 145,248); Jo.Syr. on 14,16 (CSCO 115, 271).

μεθ' ὑμῶν ἣ εἰς τὸν αἰῶνα

Chrys. hom. 75,1 in Jo., omits εἰς τὸν αἰῶνα, bis (PG 59,404. 405).
Cyr.H. catech. 17,11 (Rupp 2,264).
Eus. e.th. 3,5,6 (GCS 14,160).

μένῃ μεθ' ὑμῶν εἰς τὸν αἰῶνα

Anast.S. hex. 8, maneat vobiscum in aeternum (PG 89,983).
Chrys. hom. 1,4 in Ac., omits εἰς τὸν αἰῶνα (PG 60,20); hom. 75 in Jo.txt (PG 59,403); pent. 1,1 (PG 50,454).
Cyr.H. catech. 17,11 (Rupp 2,264 mg n.8).
Didym. Trin. 3,38 (PG 39,973).

μεθ' ὑμῶν μένῃ εἰς τὸν αἰῶνα

Chrys. hom. 75,1 in Jo., omits εἰς τὸν αἰῶνα, pos.[a] (PG 59,404).
Cyr.H. catech. 17,4 (Rupp 2,254).

---

a
μεθ' ὑμῶν μένει. If it has been transmitted faithfully, this most probably represents a free quotation of μένῃ μεθ' ὑμῶν εἰς αἰῶνα (hom. 75 in Jo.txt), although a conflation of μένῃ μεθ' ὑμῶν (v.16) with παρ' ὑμῖν μένει (v.17) in the author's mind is not ruled out. But it may suggest that Chrys. was familiar with a tradition in which the order of words was μεθ' ὑμῶν μένῃ εἰς (τὸν) αἰῶνα.

John 14,17ᵀ

αὐτό

    Bas. Spir. 22,53 (Johnston 107; SCH 17,211).
    Chrys. hom. 34,3 in Heb. (Field 7,381; PG 63,235); hom. 75 in
        Jo.txt (PG 59,403), 75,1 (PG 59,405).
    Cyr. Jo. 9,1txt (Pusey 2,466).
    Cyr.H. catech. 17,11 (Rupp 2,264).
    Didym. Trin. 1,20 (PG 39,372), 2,6,2 (PG 39,509), 3,38 bis (PG
        39,973.976).
    Thdr.Mops. Jo.Syr. on 14,17 bis (CSCO 115,273).

John 14,17͞ᴦ

omit

    Cyr. Jo. 9,1txt (Pusey 2,466).
    Thdr.Mops. hom. 10,6 (ST 145,254).

δέ

    Bas. Spir. 22,53 bis (Johnston 107.108; SCH 17,211.212).
    Cyr.H. catech. 17,11 (Rupp 2,264).
    Didym. Trin. 1,20 (PG 39,372), 2,6,2 (PG 39,509), 3,38 bis (PG
        39,973.976).
    Thdr.Mops. Jo.Syr. on 14,17(CSCO 115,273).

John 14,17 ᴦ

μένει

    Apoll. Rom. on 5,1-6 (Staab 63).
    Bas. Spir. 22,53 bis (Johnston 107.108; SCH 17,211.212).
    Chrys. hom. 75,1 in Jo. (PG 59,405), 75,3 (PG 59,407), 75,4 (PG
        59,409).
    Cyr. Jo. 9,1txt (Pusey 2,466).
    Cyr.H. catech. 17,11 (Rupp 2,264).
    Didym. Trin. 1,20 (PG 39,372), 2,6,2 (PG 39,512), 3,38 bis (PG
        39,973.976), 3,41,2 (PG 39,985).
    Thdr.Heracl. fr.Jo. 262 (TU 89,134).
    Thdr.Mops. hom. 10,6[b] (ST 145,254); Jo.Syr. on 14,17 (CSCO 115,
        273).

μενεῖ

    Nonn. ·par.Jo. (Scheindler 160).

---

    b
    If the Syriac represents the original faithfully, then the
elements of the last part of 14,17 were inverted in the Greek so
that παρ' ὑμῖν went with the copula and ἐν ὑμῖν took μένει. The
witness is to μένει in any event.

John 14,17 Γ

ἔσται

> Apoll. Rom. on 5,1-6 (Staab 63).
> Chrys. hom. 75,1 in Jo. (PG 59,404).
> Cyr. Jo. 9,1txt (Pusey 2,466).
> Cyr.H. catech. 17,11 (Rupp 2,264).
> Didym. Trin. 1,20 (PG 39,372), 2,6,2 (PG 39,512), 3,38 bis (PG 39,973.976).
> Nonn. par.Jo. (Scheindler 160).
> Thdr.Heracl. fr.Jo. 262 (TU 89,134).

ἐστιν

> Chrys. hom. 75,4 in Jo. (PG 59,409).
> Didym. Trin. 3,41,2 (PG 39,985).
> Thdr.Mops. hom. 10,6c (ST 145,254); Jo.Syr. on 14,17 (CSCO 115, 273).

John 14,26 Γ

τὸ ἅγιον

> Amph. hom. on Jo. 14,28 bis (Moss 337).
> Ath. Ar. 4,29 (PG 26,513); ep.Serap. 1,6 (PG 26,541), 1,20 (PG 26,580), 4,3 (PG 26,641).
> Bas. Eun. 3,4 (PG 29,664).
> Cyr. Jo. 10txt (Pusey 2,506); thes. 34 (PG 75,581).
> Cyr.H. catech. 17,4 (Rupp 2,254), 17,11 (Rupp 2,264).
> Didym. Spir. 27 (PG 39,1057), 30 (PG 39,1060); Trin. 2,17 pos.d (PG 39,725), 3,38 (PG 39,972).
> Eus. e.th. 3,5,5 (GCS 14,160), 3,5,6 (GCS 14,160); Is. on 40,1-2 (PG 24,365); Ps. on 56,8ff (57,7ff) (PG 23,512).
> Thdr.Mops. Jo.Syr. on 14,26 (CSCO 115,276).

John 14,26 Τ

omit

> Amph. hom. on Jo. 14,28 bis (Moss 337).
> Ath. Ar. 4,29 (PG 26,513); ep.Serap. 1,6 (PG 26,541), 1,20 (PG 26,580), 4,3 (PG 26,641).
> Bas. Eun. 3,4 (PG 29,664).
> Chrys. hom. 75,3 in Jo. (PG 59,407).

---

[c]See n.b above.

[d]
    The quotation from the paraclete passages here, a confla-
tion, reads ὅταν ἔλθῃ τὸ πνεῦμα τὸ ἅγιον, ἐκεῖνο ὑμᾶς διδάξει καὶ
ἀναμνήσει πάντα, ἃ εἶπον ὑμῖν.

Cyr. thes. 34 (PG 75,581).
Cyr.H. catech. 17,11 (Rupp 2,264).
Didym. Spir. 27 (PG 39,1057), 30 (PG 39,1060); Trin. 2,19 (PG
    39,733), 3,38 (PG 39,972), 3,41,1 (PG 39,984).
Eus. e.th. 3,5,5 (GCS 14,160), 3,5,6 (GCS 14,160); Is. on 40,1-2
    (PG 24,365); Ps. on 56,8ff (57,7ff) (PG. 23,512).
Thdr.Mops. Jo.Syr. on 14,26 (CSCO 115,276).

ὑμῖν

Cyr. Jo. 10txt (Pusey 2,506).

John 14,26⌐

  ἅ

Bas. reg.br. 205 (PG 31,1217); †bapt. 1,20 (PG 31,1561).
Cyr. Jo. 10txt (Pusey 2,506), 10com (Pusey 2,506).
Cyr.H. catech. 17,11 (Rupp 2,264).
Didym. Trin. 2,17 (PG 39,725), 3,38 bis (PG 39,972.976).
Or. princ. 1,3,4 (GCS 22,53).

  ὅσα

Bas. reg.br. 205 (PG 31,1217 mg).
Cyr. thes. 34 (PG 75,581).
Cyr.H. catech. 16,14 (Rupp 2,222), 17,11 (Rupp 2,264 mg n.11).
Eus. e.th. 3,5,5 (GCS 14,160), 3,5,6 (GCS 14,161).
Nonn. par.Jo. (Scheindler 162).
Or. comm.in Mt. 15,30 (GCS 40,441).

John 14,26⌐

  εἶπον

Bas. †bapt. 1,20 (PG 31,1561).
Cyr. Jo. 10txt (Pusey 2,506), 10com (Pusey 2,506); thes. 34
    (PG 75,581).
Cyr.H. catech. 16,14 (Rupp 2,222), 17,11 (Rupp 2,264).
Didym. Trin. 2,17 (PG 39,725), 3,38 bis (PG 39,972.976).
Eus. e.th. 3,5,5 (GCS 14,160), 3,5,6 (GCS 14,161).
Nonn. par.Jo. (Scheindler 162).
Or. comm.in Mt. 15,30 (GCS 40,441); princ. 1,3,4, dixi (GCS 22,53).

  ἂν εἶπω

Bas. reg.br. 205 (PG 31,1217).

  λέγω

Amph. hom. on Jo. 14,28 (Moss 337).

John 14,26⁰

ἐγώ

    Amph. hom. on Jo. 14,28 (Moss 337).
    Cyr. Jo. 10^{txt} (Pusey 2,506), 10^{com} (Pusey 2,506).

omit

    Bas. reg.br. 205 (PG 31,1217); †bapt. 1,20 (PG 31,1561).
    Cyr. thes. 34 (PG 75,581).
    Cyr.H. catech. 16,14 (Rupp 2,222), 17,11 (Rupp 2,264).
    Didym. Trin. 2,17 (PG 39,725), 3,38 bis (PG 39,972.976).
    Eus. e.th. 3,5,5 (GCS 14,160).
    Or. comm.in Mt. 15,30 (GCS 40,441); princ. 1,3,4 (GCS 22,53).

John 15,26 ^{T}

omit

    Ath. ep.Serap. 1,6^e (PG 26,541), 3,1 (PG 26,625).
    Bas. †calumn.Trin. (PG 31,1492); Spir. 19,49 prob.^{f} (Johnston
        100; SCH 17,202).
    Chrys. hom. 77,3 in Jo. (PG 59,417).
    Didym. Spir. 25 (PG 39,1056); Trin. 3,19 (PG 39,889), 3,38 (PG
        39,972).
    Epiph. anc. 72,9 (GCS 25,91); haer. 74,9,9 (GCS 37,326).
    Thdr.Mops. hom. 10,7 bis (ST 145,256); Mac. 25 (PO 9,5,665), 26
        (PO 9,5,666).

δέ

    Ant.Mon. hom. 1 (PG 89,1436).
    Cyr. dial.Trin. 6 (PG 75,1012), 7 (PG 75,1104); Jo. 10,2^{txt} (Pusey
        2,606); thes. 34 bis (PG 75,581.617).
    Cyr.H. catech. 17,4 (Rupp 2,254), 17,11 (Rupp 2,264).
    Didym. Spir. 27 (PG 39,1058), 30 (PG 39,1060).
    Eus. e.th. 3,5,8 (GCS 14,161); Is. on 40,1-2 (PG 24,364).
    Hesych.H. Ps.tit. 93 (PG 27,1033).
    Nonn. par.Jo. (Scheindler 170).

---

       e
    According to Migne's note (PG 26,541 n.25), some mss and an
edition omit this part of the verse from ὅταν ἔλθῃ to παρὰ τοῦ πατρός.

       f
    The presence of παράκλητος suggests that this quotation is
to be read as taken from 15,26, most likely by memory, and by memory
conflated with 14,26 and 16,12. It may, however, witness to 16,13⁰
or contain no text critical value at all.

Or. princ. 1,3,4 pos.[g] (GCS 22,53).
Thdr.Mops. Jo.Syr. on 15,26 (CSCO 115,287).
Thdt. haer. 5,3 (PG 83,456).

οὖν

Cyr. Jo. 10,2[txt] (Pusey 2,606 mg).

John 15,26⸀

πέμψω

Anast.S hod. 3 (PG 89,89).
Ant.Mon. hom. 1 (PG 89,1436).
Ath. ep.Serap. 1,6[h] (PG 26,541), 1,33 (PG 26,608), 3,1 (PG 26,625).
Bas. †hom.Spir. pos. (PG 31,1433).
Chrys. hom. 77,3 in Jo. bis (PG 59,417).
Cyr. dial.Trin. 6 (PG 75,1012), 7 (PG 75,1104); Jo. 10,2[txt] (Pusey 2,606); thes. 34 bis (PG 75,581).
Cyr.H. catech. 17,4 (Rupp 2,254), 17,11 (Rupp 2,264).
Didym. Spir. 25 (PG 39,1056), 27 (PG 39,1058); Trin. 3,38 bis (PG 39,972).
Epiph. anc. 72,9 (GCS 25,91); haer. 74,9,9 (GCS 37,326).
Eus. e.th. 3,5,8 (GCS 14,161).
Thdr.Mops. hom. 10,7 (ST 145,256).

πέμπω

Epiph. haer. 74,9,9 (GCS 37,326 mg).
Nonn. par.Jo. (Scheindler 170).
Thdr.Mops. hom. 10,7 (ST 145,256); Jo.Syr. on 15,26 (CSCO 115, 287); Mac. 25 (PO 9,5,665), 26 (PO 9,5,666).

John 15,26⸆

omit

Ant.Mon. hom. 1 (PG 89,1436).
Ath. ep.Serap. 1,6[h] (PG 26,541), 3,1 (PG 26,625).

---

[g] It is impossible to say whether these are the opening words of 16,13 or of 15,26. They follow an exact quotation of 16,12, but the presence of *paracletus* and *qui ex patre procedit* suggests that one might include δέ here under 15,26. The exact words are *cum autem venerit paracletus spiritus sanctus, qui ex patre procedit*; they are followed immediately by words from the last part of 14,26.

[h] See n.[e] above.

Cyr. <u>dial</u>.<u>Trin</u>. 6 (PG 75,1012), 7 (PG 75,1104); <u>Jo</u>. 10,2^{txt}
(Pusey 2,606); <u>thes</u>. 34 bis (PG 75,581).
Cyr.H. <u>catech</u>. 17,4 (Rupp 2,254), 17,11 (Rupp 2,264).
Didym. <u>Spir</u>. 27 (PG 39,1058).
Eus. <u>e.th</u>. 3,5,8 (GCS 14,161).
Nonn. <u>par.Jo</u>. (Scheindler 170).

μου

Didym. <u>Trin</u>. 3,38 bis (PG 39,972.976).
Thdr.Mops. <u>Jo.Syr</u>. on 15,26 (CSCO 115,287); <u>Mac</u>. 25 (PO 9,5,
665).

John 15,26 T¹

omit

Anast.Ant. <u>serm</u>. 1,10 (PG 89,1316), 1,11 (PG 89,1316).
Anast.S. <u>hex</u>. 8 (PG 89,983).
Ant.Mon. <u>hom</u>. 1 bis (PG 89,1436).
Ath. <u>ep.Serap</u>. 1,6[i] (PG 26,541) 1,11 (PG 26,560), 1,33 (PG 26,
608), 3,1 (PG 26,625).
Chrys. hom. 77,3 in Jo. bis (PG 59,417).
Cyr. <u>dial.Trin</u>. 6 (PG 75,1012), 7 (PG 75,1104); <u>Jo</u>.10,2^{txt} (Pusey
2,606), 10,2^{com} bis (Pusey 2,609); <u>thes</u>. 4 (PG 75,45), 34 bis
(PG 75,581.589).
Cyr.H. <u>catech</u>. 17,11 (Rupp 2,264).
Didym. <u>Eun</u>. 5 (PG 29,764); <u>Spir</u>. 25 (PG 39,1056); <u>Trin</u>. 1,9 (PG
39,280), 2,2 (PG 39,460), 2,5 (PG 39,496), 2,11 (PG 39,661),
3,19 (PG 39,892), 3,38 bis (PG 39,972.976).
Dion.Ar. <u>d.n</u>. 2,1 (PG 3,637).
Epiph. <u>anc</u>. 67,1 (GCS 25,81), 72,9 (GCS 25,91); <u>haer</u>. 69,56,10
(GCS 37,204), 69,63,8 pos (GCS 37,213), 70,5,6 pos. (GCS 37,
254), 74,1,4 pos. (GCS 37,314), 74,4,1 (GCS 37,318), 74,9,9
(GCS 37,327).
Eus. <u>e.th</u>. 3,5,8 (GCS 14,161).
Gr.Naz. <u>or</u>. 31,8 (Mason 154; PG 36,141).
Gr.Nyss. <u>ref.Eun</u>. 188 (Jaeger 2,392).
Jo.D. <u>hom</u>. 4,36 (PG 96,641).
Or. <u>Cant</u>. Prologus (GCS 33,112); <u>hom</u>. 3,2 in Jos. (GCS 30,303);
<u>princ</u>. 1,3,4 (GCS 22,53), 3,5,8 (GCS 22,279).
Sev.Ant. <u>Gram</u>. 2,1 (CSCO 111,63); <u>hom</u>. 123 (PO 29,1,148), 125
(PO 29,1,238).
Thdr.Mops. <u>hom</u>. 10,7 bis (ST 145,254.256), 10,8 (ST 145,256),
10,9 (ST 145,258); <u>Jo.Syr</u>. on 15,26 bis (CSCO 115,288); <u>Mac</u>.
27 (PO 9,5,667).
Thdt. <u>exp.fid</u>. 5 (CAC 4,20); <u>haer</u>. 5,3 bis (PG 83,456); <u>repr</u>.
(ACO 1,1,6,134).

---

i
See n.^e above.

μου

Cyr. thes. 34 (PG 75,617).
Thdr.Mops. Jo.Syr. on 15,26 (CSCO 115,287); Mac. 25 (PO 9,5,
665).

John 15,27°

δέ

Chrys. hom. 77,3 in Jo. (PG 59,417).
Cyr. Jo. 10,2^{txt} (Pusey 2,606).
Thdr.Mops. Jo. 130 (ST 141,399).

omit

Chrys. hom. 1,2 in Ac. (PG 60,17).
Thdr.Mops. Jo.Syr. on 15,27 (CSCO 115,288).

John 16,4b ⌠·

post εἶπον

Chrys. hom. 78 in Jo.^{txt} (PG 59,419), 78,1 bis (PG 59,421).
Cyr. Jo. 10,2^{txt} (Pusey 2,615), 10,2^{com} (Pusey 2,616).
Thdr.Mops. Jo.Syr. on 16,4b (CSCO 115,291).

John 16,5⌐

omit

Bas. moral. 5,5 (PG 31,709).
Chrys. hom. 78 in Jo.^{txt} (PG 59,419), 78,1 bis (PG 59,421).
Cyr. Jo. 10,2^{txt} (Pusey 2,615).
Or. or. 23,1 (GCS 3,350).
Thdr.Mops. Jo.Syr. on 16,5 (CSCO 115,291).

John 16,6°

ἀλλ'

Bas. moral. 5,5 (PG 31,709).
Chrys. ascens. 5 (PG 50,449); ep. 3,4, ἀλλά (PG 52,576; SCH 13,
160); hom. 5,4 in I Cor. (Field 2,53; PG 61,45); hom. 72,3
in Jo. (PG 59,393), 78^{txt} (PG 59,419), 78,1 bis (PG 59,421).
Cyr. Jo. 10,2^{txt} (Pusey 2,615).
Nonn. par.Jo. (Scheindler 171).

omit

Thdr.Mops. Jo.Syr. on 16,6 prob. (CSCO 115,292).

John 16,6 $^{\Gamma}$

πεπλήρωκεν

    Bas. moral. 5,5 (PG 31,709).
    Chrys. ascens. 5, πεπλήρωσεν (PG 50,449); ep. 3,4 (PG 52,576;
        SCH 13,160); hom. 5,4 in I Cor. (Field 2,53; PG 61,45);
        hom. 72,3 in Jo. (PG 59,393), 78^{txt}(PG 59,419), 78,1 bis
        (PG 59,421); hom. 33,1 in Mt. (PG 57,388).
    Cyr. Jo. 10,2^{txt} (Pusey 2,615), 10,2^{com} (Pusey 2,625).
    Nonn. par.Jo. (Scheindler 171).
    Thdr.Mops. Jo.Syr. on 16,6 (CSCO 115,292).

John 16,7 $^{\top}$

omit

    Anast.S. qu.et resp. 148 (PG 89,801).
    Bas. moral. 5,5 (PG 31,709).
    Chrys. hom. 86,3 in Jo. (PG 59,471).
    Cyr. Jo. 10,2^{txt} (Pusey 2,617), 10,2^{com} (Pusey 2,620), 11,10
        (Pusey 2,719), 12 (Pusey 3,119), 12,1 (Pusey 3,134); Lc.
        7,28 (PG 72,620); resp. (Pusey 3,578); schol.inc. 25 (ACO
        1,5,204).
    Eus. e.th. 3,5,9 (GCS 14,161).
    Tit.Bost. fr.Lc. on 3,16 prob. (TU 21,1,154).

ἐγώ

    Chrys. hom. 1,4 in Ac. (PG 60,20); hom. 78,1 in Jo. (PG 59,
        421); pent. 1,3 bis (PG 50,457).
    Cyr. Ag. on 2,4-5 (Pusey proph. 2,263); Am. 4 (Pusey proph. 1,
        535); Jo. 9 (Pusey 2,392).
    Cyr.H. catech. 17,4 (Rupp 2,254), 17,11 (Rupp 2,264).
    Didym. Eun. 5 (PG 29,764); Trin. 2,11, ἐγώ post μή (PG 39,661),
        2,17, ἐγώ post μή (PG 39,725).
    Epiph. anc. 81,9 (GCS 25,102).
    Eus.Em. disc. 3,21 (Buytaert 1,91), 13,1,29 bis (Buytaert 1,312).
    Thdr.Mops. Jo.Syr. on 16,7 (CSCO 115,292), on 16,15 (CSCO 115,
        299).
    Thdt. haer. 5,3 (PG 83,456).

John 16,7 $^{\Gamma}$

οὐ μὴ ἔλθῃ

    Chrys.˙ hom. 78,1 in Jo. (PG 59,421), 86,3 (PG 59,471); pent.
        1,3 bis (PG 50,457).
    Cyr. Ag. on 2,4-5 (Pusey proph. 2,263); Am. 4 (Pusey proph. 1,
        535); Jo. 9 (Pusey 2,392), 10,2^{txt} (Pusey 2,617), 10,2^{com}
        (Pusey 2,620), 11,10 (Pusey 2,719), 12 (Pusey 3,119), 12,1
        (Pusey 3,134).
    Cyr.H. catech. 17,4 (Rupp 2,254).
    Thdr.Mops. Jo.Syr.on 16,7 prob. (CSCO 115,292), on 16,15 prob.
        (CSCO 115,299).
    Tit.Bost. fr.Lc. on 3,16 (TU 21,1,154).

οὐκ ἐλεύσεται

    Anast.S. qu.et resp. 148 (PG 89,801).
    Bas. moral. 5,5 (PG 31,709).
    Chrys. hom. 1,4 in Ac. (PG 60,20).
    Cyr. Am. 4 (Pusey proph. 1,535 mg); Lc. 7,28 (PG 72,620); resp.
       (Pusey 3,578); schol.inc. 25 (ACO 1,5,204).
    Didym. Eun. 5 (PG 29,764).
    Eus.Em. disc. 3,21 (Buytaert 1,91), 13,1,29 (Buytaert (1,312).

οὐ μὴ ἔρχεται

    Cyr.H. catech. 17,4 (Rupp 2,254 mg n.1), 17,11 (Rupp 2,264).

οὐκ ἔρχεται

    Cyr.H. catech. 17,4 (Rupp 2,254 mg n.1), 17,11 (Rupp 2,265 mg
       n.12).
    Didym. Trin. 2,11 (PG 39,661), 2,17 (PG 39,725).
    Epiph. anc. 81,9 (GCS 25,102).
    Eus. e.th. 3,5,9 (GCS 14,161).
    Thdt. haer. 5,3 (PG 83,456).

John 16,7 ⸌

ἐὰν δὲ πορευθῶ, πέμψω αὐτὸν πρὸς ὑμᾶς

    Cyr.H. catech. 17,11 (Rupp 2,264).
    Eus. e.th. 3,5,9 (GCS 14,161).
    Thdr.Mops. Jo.Syr. on 16,7 (CSCO 115,292).

ἐὰν δὲ ἀπέλθω, πέμψω αὐτὸν πρὸς ὑμᾶς

    Chrys. hom. 78,1 in Jo. (PG 59,421).
    Cyr. Ag. on 2,4-5 (Pusey proph. 2,263); Jo. 12 (Pusey 3,119).

ἐὰν γὰρ ἀπέλθω, πέμψω ὑμῖν τὸν παράκλητον

    Tit.Bost. fr.Lc. on 3,16 (TU 21,1,154).

ὅταν δὲ ἀπέλθω, πέμψω αὐτὸν πρὸς ὑμᾶς

    Cyr. Am. 4 (Pusey proph. 1,535); Jo. 11,10 (Pusey 2,719), 12,1
       (Pusey 3,134).

John 16,10 ⸀

omit

    Chrys. hom. 78,2 in Jo. (PG 59,422).
    Cyr. Jo. 10,2[txt] (Pusey 2,621), 10,2[com] (Pusey 2,622).
    Jo.D. f.o. 91,3 (PTS 12,216).

μου

Jo.D. f.o. 91,3 (PTS 12,216 mg).
Thdr.Mops. Jo.Syr. on 16,10 (CSCO 115,292).

John 16,12 ˢ

ὑμῖν λέγειν

Cyr. dial.Trin. 6 (PG 75,1072); Jo. 10,2^{txt}, ὑμῖν ἔχω λέγειν
(Pusey 2,625), 11,10, ὑμῖν ἔχω λέγειν (Pusey 2,718).
Didym. Spir. 32, *vobis dicere* (PG 39,1062), 33, *vobis dicere*
(PG 39,1063).
Or. Cels. 2,2 (GCS 1,129); princ. 1,3,4, *vobis dicere* (GCS 22,
53 mg).

λέγειν ὑμῖν

Bas. fid. 2 (PG 31,684).
Bas.Sel. or. 25 bis (PG 85,289.293).
Chrys. hom. 1,2 in Ac. (PG 60,16); hom. 5,5 in I Cor. (Field
2,53; PG 61,45); hom. 77,1 in Jo. (PG 59,415), 78,2 (PG 59,
422); hom. 30,4 in Mt. (PG 57,368), 54,3 bis (PG 58,535.
536); hom. 2 in Rom. (Field 1,12; PG 60,398); virg. 12,2
(SCH 125,128).
Cyr. dial.Trin. 6 (PG 75,1009); Jo. 4,1 (Pusey 1,509 mg).
Cyr.H. catech. 17,11 (Rupp 2,264).
Didym. Spir. 33 (PG 39,1062); Trin. 3,41,2 (PG 39,985).
Eus. e.th. 3,5,15 (GCS 14,162); Ps. on 56,8ff (57,7ff) (PG 23,
512).
Max. ambig.(PG 91,1256).
Or. Cels. 2,2 (GCS 1,128).
Thdr.Mops. Jo.Syr. on 16,12 (CSCO 115,293).
Thdt. qu.et resp. 112 (CAC 5,182).

John 16,12 ᵀ

omit

Bas fid. 2 (PG 31,684).
Bas.Sel. or. 25 bis (PG 85,289.293).
Chrys. hom. 1,2 in Ac. (PG 60,16); hom. 5,5 in I Cor. (Field
2,53; PG 61,45); hom. 77,1 in Jo. (PG 59,415), 78,2 bis
(PG 59,422); hom. 30,4 in Mt. (PG 57,368), 54,3 bis (PG 58,
535.536); hom. 2 in Rom. (Field 1,12; PG 60,398); virg.
12,2 (SCH 125,128).
Cyr. dial.Trin. 6 bis (PG 75,1009.1072); Jo. 4,1 (Pusey 1,509),
10,2^{txt} (Pusey 2,625), 11,10 (Pusey 2,718).
Cyr.H. catech. 17,11 (Rupp 2,264).
Didym. Trin. 3,41,2 (PG 39,985).
Epiph. anc. 72,9 (GCS 25,91); haer. 74,9,9 (GCS 37,327).
Eus. e.th. 3,5,15 (GCS 14,162); Ps. on 56,8ff (57,7ff) (PG 23,
512).
Max. ambig. (PG 91,1256).
Or. Cels. 2,2 bis (GCS 1,128.129).

Thdr.Mops. hom. 8,3 (ST 145,190); Jo.Syr. on 16,12 (CSCO 115,
    293); Zach. on 1,7-10 (PG 66,505).
Thdt. qu.et resp. 112 (CAC 5,182).

αὐτά

Didym. Spir. 32 (PG 39,1062), 33 (PG 39,1063).
Or. hom. 3,2 in Jos. (GCS 30,303); princ. 1,3,4 (GCS 22,53).

John 16,13°

δέ

Ant.Mon. hom. 1 (PG 89,1436).
Chrys. hom. 2 in Rom. (Field 1,12; PG 60,398).
Cyr. dial.Trin. 6 bis (PG 75,1009.1072); Jo. 4,1 (Pusey 1,509),
    10,2^{txt} (Pusey 2,625), 11,10 (Pusey 2,718).
Cyr.H. catech. 17,4 (Rupp 2,252), 17,11 (Rupp 2,264).
Didym. Spir. 32 (PG 39,1062), 33 (PG 39,1063); Trin. 1,18 (PG
    39,360), 3,41,2 (PG 39,985).
Epiph. anc. 72,9 (GCS 25,91 mg).
Eus. e.th. 3,5,15 (GCS 14,162); Ps. on 56,8ff (57,7ff) (PG 23,
    512).
Max. ambig. (PG 91,1256).
Nonn. par.Jo. (Scheindler 173).
Or. Cels. 2,2 (GCS 1,128); hom. 3,2 in Jos. (GCS 30,303).
Thdr.Mops. hom. 8,3 (ST 145,190); Jo.Syr. on 16,13 (CSCO 115,
    293); Zach. on 1,7-10 (PG 66,505).
Thdt. qu.et resp. 112 (CAC 5,182).

omit

Cyr.H. catech. 16,24 (Rupp 2,236).
Didym. Trin. 2,15 (PG 39,717), 3,41,2 (PG 39,985).
Epiph. anc. 72,9 (GCS 25,91); haer. 74,9,9 (GCS 1,91).
Nest. fr. 2 pos. (Loofs 2,227; ACO 1,1,2,49 and 1,1,7,110).
Or. Cels. 2,2 (GCS 1,129).

John 16,13ʳ

ὁδηγήσει ὑμᾶς

Anast.S. hod. 3, ὑμᾶς ὁδηγήσει (PG 89,89).
Ant.Mon. hom.1(PG 89,1436).
Bas. reg.br. 1, ὑμᾶς ὁδηγήσει (PG 31,1081 mg); Spir. 19,49,
    omits ὑμᾶς (Johnston 100; SCH 17,202).
Chrys. hom. 78,2 in Jo., omits ὑμᾶς, ter (PG 59,422.423); hom. 2
    in Rom. (Field 1,12; PG 60,398).
Cyr. dial.Trin. 6 bis (PG 75,1009.1072); Jo. 4,1 (Pusey 1,509),
    10,2^{txt} (Pusey 2,625), 10,2^{com} (Pusey 2,628), 11,10 (Pusey
    2,718).
Cyr.H. catech. 17,11 (Rupp 2,265 mg n.14).
Didym. Spir. 32 (PG 39,1062), 33 bis (PG 39,1063); Trin. 1,18
    (PG 39,360), 2,15 (PG 39,717), 3,19 (PG 39,892), 3,39, omits
    ὑμᾶς (PG 39,980), 3,41,2 (PG 39,985).

Epiph. anc. 72,9 (GCS 25,91); haer. 74,9,9 (GCS 37,327).
Max. ambig. (PG 91,1256).
Nonn. par.Jo. (Scheindler 173).
Or. Cels. 2,2 bis (GCS 1,128.129).
Thdr.Mops. Zach. on 1,7-10 (PG 66,505).
Thdt. haer. 5,3 (PG 83,456); qu.et resp. 112 (CAC 5,182).

ἐκεῖνος ὑμᾶς ὁδηγήσει

Sev.Ant. hom. 92 (PO 25,1,42).
Thdr.Mops. Jo.Syr. on 16,13 bis (CSCO 115,294).

διηγήσεται ὑμῖν

Cyr.H. catech. 17,11 (Rupp 2,264).
Eus. e.th. 3,5,15 (GCS 14,162); Ps. on 56,8ff (57,7ff) (PG 23,
   512).

ἀναγγελεῖ ὑμῖν

Cyr.H. catech. 17,11 (Rupp 2,265 mg n.14).

John 16,13 ⌐

εἰς τὴν ἀλήθειαν πᾶσαν

Cyr. Jo. 10,2com (Pusey 2,628), 11,10 (Pusey 2,718).
Didym. Trin. 1,18 (PG 39,360).
Epiph. anc. 72,9 (GCS 25,91 mg).
Or. Cels. 2,2 ter (GCS 1,128.129).
Thdr.Mops. Jo.Syr. on 16,13 bis (CSCO 115,294).

εἰς πᾶσαν τὴν ἀλήθειαν

Chrys. hom. 78,2 in Jo. ter (PG 59,422.423); hom. 2 in Rom.
   (Field 1,12; PG 60,398).
Cyr. dial.Trin. 6 (PG 75,1072); Jo. 10,2txt (Pusey 2,625).
Didym. Trin. 2,15 (PG 39,717), 3,41,2 (PG 39,985).
Epiph. anc. 72,9 (GCS 25,91); haer. 74,9,9 (GCS 37,327).
Thdr.Mops. Zach. on 1,7-10 (PG 66,505).

εἰς πᾶσαν ἀλήθειαν

Anast.S. hod. 3 (PG 89,89).
Bas. reg.br. 1 (PG 31,1081 mg).
Chrys. hom. 2 in Rom. (Field 1,12 mg).
Didym. Trin. 3,39 (PG 39,980).

in omnem veritatem

Didym. Spir. 32 (PG 39,1062), 33 bis (PG 39,1063).

ἐπὶ τὴν ἀλήθειαν

Cyr.H. catech. 17,11 (Rupp 2,265 mg n.14).

πρὸς πᾶσαν τὴν ἀλήθειαν

Bas. Spir. 19,49, 2 mss omit τήν (Johnston 100 and mg; SCH 17, 202).
Didym. Trin. 3,19 (PG 39,892).
Thdt. haer. 5,3 (PG 83,456); qu.et resp. 112 (CAC 5,182).

πᾶσαν τὴν ἀλήθειαν

Cyr.H. catech. 17,11 (Rupp 2,265 mg n.14).

τὴν ἀλήθειαν πᾶσαν

Cyr.H. catech. 17,11 (Rupp 2,264).
Eus. e.th. 3,5,15 (GCS 14,162).

τὴν ἀλήθειαν

Eus. Ps. on 56,8ff (57,7ff) (PG 23,512).

ἐν τῇ ἀληθείᾳ πάσῃ

Ant.Mon. hom. 1, ἁπάσῃ (PG 89,1436).
Cyr. dial.Trin. 6 (PG 75,1009-1012); Jo. 4,1 (Pusey 1,509).
Max. ambig. (PG 91,1256).
Nonn. par.Jo. (Scheindler 173).
Sev.Ant. hom. 92 (PO 25,1,42).

John 16,13 [T]

omit

Ath. Ar. 1,50 (PG 26,116); ep.Serap. 3,1 (PG 26,625); ‡dial.Trin. 1,22 (PG 28,1149); ‡Maced.dial. 1,16 (PG 28,1317).
Bas. fid. 4 (PG 31,685 mg).
Cyr. dial.Trin. 6 (PG 75,1072), 7 (PG 75,1121); Jo. 4,1 (Pusey 1,509); thes. 34 (PG 75,584).
Cyr.H. catech. 17,11 (Rupp 2,265 mg n.15).
Didym. Spir. 32 prob. (PG 39,1062).
Epiph. anc. 72,9 (GCS 25,91); haer. 74,9,9 (GCS 37,327).
Eus. e.th. 3,5,16 (GCS 14,162), 3,5,18 (GCS 14,162).
Marcell. fr. 67 (GCS 14,197 (and 158)).
Or. Cels. 2,2 (GCS 1,128).

ἄν

Anast.S. qu.et resp. 6 (PG 89,377).
Bas. fid. 1 (PG 31,677), 4 (PG 31,685); reg.br. 1 (PG 31,1081), 205 (PG 31,1217).
Chrys. hom. 78,2 in Jo. (PG 59,422), 78,3 (PG 59,424).
Cyr. dial.Trin. 6 (PG 75,1012); Jo. 10,2 [txt] (Pusey 2,625).
Cyr.H. catech. 17,11 (Rupp 2,264 (see n.15)).
Didym. Eun. 5 (PG 29,765).
Ign. ‡Eph. 9 (PG 5,740).

Sev.Ant. <u>hom</u>. 98 pos.^j (PO 25,1,158).

<u>John 16,13</u> Γ

ἀκούει

    Ammon. <u>Jo</u>. 542 prob. (TU 89,330).
    Ath. <u>Ar</u>. 1,50 (PG 26,116).
    Bas. <u>fid</u>. 4 (PG 31,685 mg).
    Cyr. <u>Jo</u>. 4,1 (Pusey 1,509).
    Nonn. <u>par.Jo</u>. (Scheindler 173).

ἀκούσει

    Ath. <u>ep.Serap</u>. 3,1 (PG 26,625); ‡<u>dial.Trin</u>. 1,22 (PG 28,1149).
    Cyr. <u>dial.Trin</u>. 6 (PG 75,1072), 7 (PG 75,1121); <u>thes</u>. 34 (PG 75,
       584).
    Cyr.H. <u>catech</u>. 17,11 (Rupp 2,265 mg n.15).
    Didym. <u>Spir</u>. 32 (PG 39,1062), 36 (PG 39,1065).
    Epiph. <u>anc</u>. 72,9 (GCS 25,91); <u>haer</u>. 74,9,9 (GCS 37,327).
    Eus. <u>e.th</u>. 3,5,16 (GCS 14,162), 3,5,18 (GCS 14,162).
    Marcell. <u>fr</u>. 67 (GCS 14,197 (and 158)).
    Or. <u>Cels</u>. 2,2 (GCS 1,128).
    Thdr.Mops. <u>Jo.Syr</u>. on 16,13 bis (CSCO 115,295).

ἀκούσῃ

    Anast.S. <u>qu.et resp</u>. 6 (PG 89,377).
    Ath. ‡<u>Maced.dial</u>. 1,16 (PG 28,1317).
    Bas. <u>fid</u>. 1 (PG 31,677); <u>reg.br</u>. 1 (PG 31,1081), 205 (PG 31,1217).
    Chrys. <u>hom</u>. 78,2 in Jo. (PG 59,422), 78,3 (PG 59,424).
    Cyr. <u>dial.Trin</u>. 6 (PG 75,1012); <u>Jo</u>. 10,2^{txt} (Pusey 2,625).
    Cyr.H. <u>catech</u>. 17,11 (Rupp 2,264, see n.15).
    Didym. <u>Eun</u>. 5 (PG 29,765).
    Ign. ‡<u>Eph</u>. 9 (PG 5,740).
    Sev.Ant. <u>hom</u>. 98 pos.^k (PO 25,1,158).

ἀκούη (sic)

    Bas. <u>fid</u>. 4^l (PG 31,685).

---

j
    Syriac has, of course, neither subjunctive nor the equivalent
of ἄν. But the awkward construction with 'if' here makes it at least
possible that the translator was attempting to render ἄν ἀκούσῃ or
ἀκούσῃ from the Greek before him.

k
    See n.^j above.

l
    Thus Migne's text. Is this original in Bas.? Is it a mis-
print (for ἀκούσῃ or ἀκούη or ἀκούει)?

John 16,15 □

Include

Amph. <u>hom</u>. 1 (PG 39,104).
Ant.Mon. <u>hom</u>. 1 (PG 89,1436).
Ath. <u>Ar. 1</u>,61 in Sev.Ant. <u>Gram</u>. 3,33 (CSCO 101,148), 1,61 (PG
  2<del>6,</del>140), 2,24 (PG 26,1<del>97</del>), 3,4 (PG 26,329); <u>ep</u>.Afr. 8 (PG
  26,1041); <u>ep</u>.<u>Serap</u>. 2,2 (PG 26,609), 2,5 (PG <del>26,6</del>16) 3,1 (PG
  26,625), 4,<del>3</del> (PG 26,641); <u>syn</u>. 49,2 (Opitz 2,1,273); ‡<u>dial</u>.
  <u>Trin</u>. 2,25 (PG 28,1196), 3,<del>3</del> (PG 28,1205); ‡<u>Maced</u>.<u>dial</u>. 1,
  <del>16</del> (PG 28,1317).
Bas. <u>ep</u>. 236,2 (Johnston 170); <u>hom</u>. 15,2 (PG 31,468).
Bas.Sel. <u>or</u>. 24 (PG 85,284).
Chrys. <u>comm</u>. <u>in</u> Gal. 1,5 (Field 4,13; PG 61,620); <u>hom</u>. 5,3 <u>in</u> Jo.
  (PG <del>59,58</del>), <del>78</del>,2 bis (PG 59,422.423).
Cyr. <u>dial</u>.<u>Trin</u>. 6 bis (PG 75,1012); <u>ep</u>.Euopt. (ACO 1,1,6,135);
  <u>Jo</u>. 1,<del>3</del> (Pusey 1,42), 1,4 (Pusey 1,<del>55</del>), 2,7 (Pusey 1,333),
  <del>11</del>,2^{txt} (Pusey 2,637), 11,2^{com} bis (Pusey 2,637.639), 12,1
  (Pusey 3,136); <u>Juln</u>. 9 (PG 76,952); <u>Lc</u>. 3,21 (PG 72,524),
  11,1 (PG 72,68<del>5</del>); <u>thes</u>. 11 (PG 75,15<del>6</del>), 12 (PG 75,184), 14
  (PG 75,240), 16 (P<del>G 75</del>,301), 20 (PG 75,353), 21(PG 75,357),
  32 bis (PG 75,557.560).
Cyr.H. <u>catech</u>. 17,11 (Rupp 2,264).
Didym. <u>Eun</u>. 4 (PG 29,696); <u>Spir</u>. 32 (PG 39,1062), 38 ter (PG 39,
  106<del>6</del>.1067); <u>Trin</u>. 1,26 <del>bis</del> (PG 39,384.388), 3,2,23 (PG 39,
  796).
Dion.Ar. <u>d</u>.<u>n</u>. 2,1 (PG 3,637).
Epiph. <u>anc</u>. 16,3 (GCS 25,24), 72,9 prob.^m (GCS 25,91); <u>haer</u>. 74,
  9,9 prob.^m (GCS 37,327).
Gr.Naz. <u>ep</u>. 168 (PG 37,277); <u>or</u>. 30,11 (Mason 123; PG 36,116).
Gr.Nyss. <u>Eun</u>. 1,594 (Jaeger 1,<del>197</del>), 1,683 (Jaeger 1,222); <u>ref</u>.
  <u>Eun</u>. <del>45</del> (Jaeger 2,330), 121 (Jaeger 2,364).
Hesych.H. <u>qu</u>.<u>ev</u>. 22 (PG 93,1412).
Jo.D. <u>f</u>.<u>o</u>. <del>65</del> (PTS 12,164); <u>Man</u>. 2 (PG 96,1324).
Leont.<del>H</del>. <del>Nest</del>. 5,19 (PG 86,1<del>741</del>).
Marcell. <u>fr</u>. 73 (GCS 14,198), 74 quater (GCS 14,199).
Nil. <u>epp</u>. <del>116</del> (PG 79,133), 323 (PG 79,357).
Nonn. <u>par</u>.<u>Jo</u>. (Scheindler 173).
Thdr.Mops. <u>Jo</u>.<u>Syr</u>. on 16,15 (CSCO 115,298).
Thdt. <u>eran</u>.<u>suppl</u>. (PG 89,329); <u>ep</u>. 151 (PG 83,1433); <u>haer</u>. 5,2
  (P<del>G</del> 83,45<del>3</del>).

John 16,15 ^T

omit

Ant.Mon. <u>hom</u>. 1 (PG 89,1436).

---

^m
    Epiph. ends his quotation of 16,12-14 here with πάντα,
which probably indicates that the copy of the NT he knew or was using
included the passage now referred to as John 16,15.

Ath. ‡Maced.dial. 1,16 (PG 28,1317).
Didym. Spir. 38 (PG 39,1066).

ὑμῖν

    Cyr. dial.Trin. 6 bis (PG 75,1012); ep.Euopt. (ACO 1,1,6,135);
       Jo. 11,2^{txt} (Pusey 2,637), 11,2^{com} (Pusey 2,639).
    Cyr.H. catech. 17,11 (Rupp 2,264).
    Didym. Spir. 32 (PG 39,1062).
    Nonn. par.Jo. (Scheindler 173).
    Thdr.Mops. Jo.Syr. on 16,15 (CSCO 115,298).

BIBLIOGRAPHY

BIBLIOGRAPHY

The Bibliography is limited to the relevant material which
has been consulted and found useful; no attempt is made to include
the many books and articles also consulted but not found useful.
Excluded is any reference to the works of individual Church fathers.
For these the reader is directed to the notes.

Editors (or, where these are lacking, directing societies)
cited for continuing collections of patristic texts are those given
in current issues of the series. The same is true of places of publication shown for all series and periodicals.

Full subtitles for a few major works, such as PG and PL, are
omitted as being too cumbersome and, for our purposes, unnecessary.

REFERENCE AIDS

Aland, K. (ed.). Synopsis Quattuor Evangeliorum, locis parallelis
    evangeliorum apocryphorum et patrum adhibitis. Editio quinta.
    Stuttgart, 1968.

Altaner, B. and A. Stuiber. Patrologie: Leben, Schriften und Lehre
    der Kirchenväter. Siebte, völlig neubearbeitete Auflage. Frei-
    burg, 1966.

Blass, F. and Debrunner, A. A Greek Grammar of the New Testament and
    Other Early Christian Literature, trans. and ed. R.W. Funk.
    Chicago, 1967.

Lampe, G.W.H. (ed.). A Patristic Greek Lexicon. Oxford, 1972.

Quasten, J. Patrology. 3 vol. Utrecht, 1950-1960.

COLLECTIONS OF PATRISTIC TEXTS

Acta conciliorum oecumenicorum, ed. E. Schwarz. 4 vol. Berolini,
    1914-1971.

Corpus apologetarum Christianorum saeculi secundi, ed. I.C.T. Otto.
    9 vol. in 7. Wiesbaden, 1969.

Corpus Christianorum, series Latina. Turnholti, 1953-.

Corpus scriptorum Christianorum orientalium, editum consilio Universi-
    tatis Catholicae Americae et Universitatis Catholicae Louvaniensis.
    Louvain, 1903-.

Corpus scriptorum ecclesiasticorum Latinorum, editum consilio et im-
    pensis Academiae Scientiarum Austriacae. Vindobonae, 1866-.

Die griechischen christlichen Schriftsteller der ersten drei Jahr-
    hunderte, hrsg. v. der Kommission für spätantike Religionsgeschich-
    te der deutschen Akademie der Wissenschaften zu Berlin. Berlin,
    1897-.

Johannes-Kommentare aus der griechischen Kirche, hrsg. v. J. Reuss.
    TU 89. Berlin, 1966.

Patrologiae cursus completus, series Graeca, ed. J.P. Migne. 161 vol.
    Paris, 1857-1866.

Patrologiae cursus completus, series Latina, ed. J.P. Migne. 221
    vol. Paris, 1844-1855.

Patrologiae cursus completus, series Latina, supplementum, ed. A.
    Hamman. 5 vol. Paris, 1958-1974.

Patrologia orientalis, ed. F. Graffin. Tournhout, 1903-.

Patristische Texte und Studien, hrsg. v. K. Aland u. W. Schneemelcher.
    Berlin, 1964-.

Pauluskommentare aus der griechischen Kirche, hrsg. v. K. Staab.
    Neutestamentliche Abhandlungen, Bd. 15. Münster i.W., 1933.

Sources Chrétiennes, director C. Mondésert. Paris, 1955-.

                  EDITIONS OF INDIVIDUAL PATRISTIC WRITERS

Amphilochius of Iconium. "S. Amphilochius of Iconium on John 14,28:
    'the Father who sent me is greater than I'," ed. and trans. C.
    Moss, Le Muséon 43 (1930) 317-364.

Athanasius. Athanasius Werke, hrsg. v. H.-G. Opitz. 3 Bde. Berlin,
    1934-1941.

Augustine. Oeuvres de Saint Augustin. Bibliothèque Augustinienne,
    publiée sous la direction des Études Augustiniennes. Paris, 1939-.

Basil of Caesarea. The Book of Saint Basil the Great Bishop of
    Caesarea in Cappadocia on the Holy Spirit written to Amphilochius,
    Bishop of Iconium, against the Pneumatomachi, ed. C.F.H. Johnston.
    Oxford, 1892.

Cyril of Alexandria. Sancti Patris nostri Cyrilli Archiepiscopi
    Alexandrini in D. Joannis Evangelium accedunt fragmenta varia
    necnon tractatus ad Tiberium Diaconum duo, ed. P.E. Pusey.
    3 vol. Oxonii, 1872.

    _____ . Sancti Patris nostri Cyrilli Archiepiscopi Alexandrini in
    XII Prophetas, ed. P.E. Pusey. 2 vol. Oxonii, 1868.

Cyril of Jerusalem. S. Patris nostri Cyrilli Hierosolymorum Archi-
    episcopi opera quae supersunt omnia, ed. G.C. Reischl (Vol. I)
    et J. Rupp (Vol. II). 2 vol. Monaci, 1848,1860.

Eusebius of Emesa. Eusèbe d'Émèse. Discours conservés en Latin:
    textes en partie inédits, ed. É.M. Buytaert. 2 vol. Louvain,
    1953, 1957.

Gregory of Nazianzus. The Five Theological Orations of Gregory of
    Nazianzus, ed. A.J. Mason. Cambridge, 1899.

Gregory of Nyssa. Gregorii Nysseni opera, auxilio aliorum virorum
    doctorum edenda curavit W. Jaeger. Leiden, 1952-.

John Chrysostom. Sancti Patris nostri Johannis Chrysostomi Archi-
    episcopi Constantinopolitani interpretatio omnium Epistolarum
    Paulinarum per homilias facta, ed. F. Field. 7 vol., editio nova.
    Bibliotheca patrum Ecclesiae Catholicae qui ante orientis et
    occidentis schisma floruerunt. Oxonii, 1845-1862.

Maximus of Turin. "An Ancient Homiliary," ed. A. Spagnolo and C.H.
    Turner, JTS 16 (1914-1915) 161-176, 314-322; 17 (1915-1916)
    321-337; 20 (1918-1919) 289-310.

Nestorius. Nestoriana: die Fragmenta des Nestorius, hrsg. v. F.Loofs.
    Halle a.S., 1905.

Nonnus of Panopolis. Nonni Panopolitani paraphrasis S. Evangelii
    Ioannei, ed. A. Scheindler. Leipzig, 1881.

Origen. The Commentary of Origen on S. John's Gospel, ed. A.E.
    Brooke. 2 vol. Cambridge, 1896.

Theodore of Mopsuestia. Essai sur Théodore de Mopsueste, R. Devréese.
    ST 141. Città del Vaticano, 1948.

_____. Les Homélies Catéchétiques de Théodore de Mopsueste:
    Reproduction phototypique du Ms. Mingana Syr. 561, ed. R. Tonneau
    en collaboration avec R. Devréese. ST 145. Città del Vaticano,
    1949.

Titus of Bostra. Titus von Bostra: Studien zu dessen Lukashomilien,
    hrsg. v. J. Sickenberger. TU 21,1. Leipzig, 1901.

                CONTEMPORARY LITERATURE ON THE FATHERS

Bardy, G. "Commentaires Patristiques de la Bible," Dictionnaire
    de la Bible Supplément II (Paris, 1934), 73-103.

Comeau, M. Saint Augustin, exégète du Quatrième Évangile. Paris, 1930.

Kelly, J.N.D. The Athanasian Creed: The Paddock Lectures for 1962-3.
    London, 1964.

Loewenich, W. von. Das Johannes-Verständnis im zweiten Jahrhundert.
    Beihefte zur Zeitschrift für die neutestamentliche Wissenschaft
    und die Kunde der älteren Kirche, Beih. 13, hrsg. v. Prof. D.
    Hans Lietzmann. Berlin, 1932.

Moingt, J. Théologie trinitaire de Tertullien. 4 vol. Paris, 1966-
    1969.

Mumm, H.J. "A Critical Appreciation of Origen as an Exegete of the
    Fourth Gospel." Unpublished Doctor's dissertation, Hartford
    Seminary Foundation, Hartford, Connecticut, 1952.

Oxford Society of Historical Theology. The New Testament in the
    Apostolic Fathers. Oxford, 1905.

Pagels, E.H. The Johannine Gospel in Gnostic Exegesis: Heracleon's
    Commentary on John. Society of Biblical Literature Monograph
    Series No. 17, ed. L. Keck. Nashville, 1973.

Pollard, T.E. Johannine Christology and the Early Church. Society
    for New Testament Studies Monograph Series No. 13, ed. M. Black.
    Cambridge, 1970.

Sanders, J.N. The Fourth Gospel in the Early Church: Its Origin
    and Influence on Christian Theology up to Irenaeus. Cambridge,
    1943.

Seeberg, R. Lehrbuch der Dogmengeschichte. 4 Bde. in 5; 5. Aufl.
    (Bd. 4,1, 6.Aufl.), unveränderter photomechanischer Nachdruck
    der 3.Aufl.(der 4.Aufl. Bd.4,1). Stuttgart, 1960.

Swete, H.B. The Holy Spirit in the Ancient Church: A Study of
    Christian Teaching in the Age of the Fathers. London, 1912.

_____. On the History of the Doctrine of the Procession of the
    Holy Spirit from the Apostolic Age to the Death of Charlemagne.
    Cambridge, 1876.

Warfield, B.B. Studies in Tertullian and Augustine. New York, 1930.

Wiles, M.F. The Spiritual Gospel: The Interpretation of the Fourth
    Gospel in the Early Church. Cambridge, 1960.

                    COMMENTARIES ON THE FOURTH GOSPEL

Barrett, C.K. The Gospel According to St John: An Introduction With
    Commentary and Notes on the Greek Text. 2d. ed. London, 1978.

Bauer, W. Das Johannesevangelium. Handbuch zum Neuen Testament 6.
    3.Aufl. Tübingen, 1933.

Bernard, J.H. A Critical and Exegetical Commentary on the Gospel
    According to St. John. 2 vols. The International Critical Com-
    mentary. Edinburgh, 1969.

Brandt, D.W. Das ewige Wort. Eine Einführung in das Evangelium nach
    Johannes. 3.Aufl. Berlin, 1940.

Brown, R.E. The Gospel According to John. 2 vols. The Anchor Bible.
    London, 1971.

Bultmann, R. The Gospel of John: A Commentary, trans. by G.R.
    Beasley-Murray from the 1964 printing of Das Evangelium des
    Johannes with the supplement of 1966. Oxford, 1971.

Hoskyns, E.C. The Fourth Gospel, ed. F.N. Davey. London, 1967.

Lagrange, M.-J. Évangile selon Saint Jean. Septième édition. Paris,
    1948.

Lightfoot, R.H. St. John's Gospel: A Commentary, ed. C.F. Evans.
    Oxford, 1969.

Lindars, B. The Gospel of John. New Century Bible, eds. R.E. Clements
    and M. Black. London, 1977.

Loisy, A. Le quatrième Évangile. Les épitres dites de Jean. Deuxième
    édition refondue. Paris, 1921.

Morris, L. The Gospel According to John: The English Text With
    Introduction, Exposition and Notes. The New International Com-
    mentary on the New Testament, ed. F.F. Bruce. London, 1971.

Sanders, J.N. A Commentary on the Gospel According to St. John,
    ed. and completed by B.A. Mastin. Black's New Testament Commen-
    taries, ed. H. Chadwick. London, 1968.

Schlatter, A. Der Evangelist Johannes. Wie er spricht, denkt und
    glaubt. Stuttgart, 1948.

Schnackenburg, R. Das Johannesevangelium. 3 Teile. Herders theol-
    ogischer Kommentar zum Neuen Testament, Bd. 4, Teile 1-3, hrsg.
    v. A. Wikenhauser, A. Vögtle, u. R. Schnackenburg. Freiburg,
    1972-1975.

Schulz, S. Das Evangelium nach Johannes. Das Neue Testament Deutsch
    4, hrsg. v. G. Friedrich. Göttingen, 1972.

Strack, H.L. and Billerbeck, P. Kommentar zum Neuen Testament aus
    Talmud und Midrasch. 6 Bde. München, 1974.

Strathmann, H. Das Evangelium nach Johannes. 10.Aufl. Das Neue
    Testament Deutsch, hrsg. v. P. Althaus u. G. Friedrich. Göttingen,
    1963.

Tillmann, F. Das Johannesevangelium. 4.Aufl. Die heilige Schrift
    des Neuen Testamentes 3, hrsg. v. F. Tillmann. Bonn, 1931.

Westcott, B.F. The Gospel According to St John: The Authorised
    Version with Introduction and Notes. London, 1887.

Wikenhauser, A. Das Evangelium nach Johannes. Regensburger Neues Tes-
    tament 4, hrsg. v. A. Wikenhauser u. O. Kuss. Regensburg, 1961.

OTHER BOOKS ON JOHN AND THE PARACLETE

Betz, O. Der Paraklet. Fürsprecher im häretischen Spätjudentum, im
    Johannes-Evangelium und in neu gefundenen gnostischen Schriften.
    Arbeiten zur Geschichte des Spätjudentums und Urchristentums 2.
    Leiden, 1963.

Johansson, N. Parakletoi. Vorstellungen von Fürsprechern für die
    Menschen vor Gott in der alttestamentlichen Religion, im Spät-
    judentum und Urchristentum. Lund, 1940.

Johnston, G. The Spirit-Paraclete in the Gospel of John. Society
    for New Testament Studies Monograph Series 12, ed. M. Black.
    Cambridge, 1970.

Martyn, J.L. History and Theology in the Fourth Gospel. New York,
    1968.

Miguéns, M. El Paráclito (Jn 14-16). Studii Biblici Franciscani
    Analecta 2. Jerusalem, 1963.

Παπαδοπούλου, Σ.Γ. ΠΑΤΕΡΕΣ. ΑΥΞΗΣΙΣ ΤΗΣ ΕΚΚΛΗΣΙΑΣ. ΑΓΙΟΝ ΠΝΕΥΜΑ.
    Αθῆναι, 1970.

Potterie, I. de la. La vérité dans Saint Jean. T.1, Le Christ et la
    vérité. L'Esprit et la vérité. T.2, Le croyant et la vérité.
    Analecta Biblica, investigationes scientificae in res Biblicas
    73-74. Rome, 1977.

Schulz, S. Untersuchungen zur Menschensohn-Christologie im Johannes-
    evangelium. Göttingen, 1957.

                              ARTICLES

Bammel, E. "Jesus und der Paraklet in Johannes 16," Christ and
    Spirit in the New Testament, ed. B. Lindars and S.S. Smalley in
    honour of C.F.D. Moule (Cambridge, 1973), 199-217.

Barrett, C.K. "Christocentric or Theocentric? Observations on the
    Theological Method of the Fourth Gospel," La Notion biblique
    de Dieu. Le Dieu de la Bible et le Dieu des philosophes, ed.
    par J. Coppens, Bibliotheca Ephemeridum Theologicarum Lovaniensium
    41 (Leuven, 1976), 361-376.

_____. "'The Father is Greater than I' (Jo 14,28): Subordination-
    ist Christology in the New Testament," Neues Testament und Kirche.
    Für Rudolf Schnackenburg, hrsg. v. J. Gnilka (Freiburg, 1974),
    144-159.

_____. "The Holy Spirit in the Fourth Gospel," JTS N.S.1 (1950),
    1-15.

Behm, J. "παράκλητος," Theological Dictionary of the New Testament
    5, ed. G. Friedrich, trans. and ed. G.W. Bromiley (Grand Rapids,
    1973), 800-814.

Berrouard, M.-F. "Le Paraclet, defenseur du Christ devant la con-
    science du croyant (Jo. XVI,8-11)," Revue des sciences philoso-
    phiques et théologiques 33 (1949), 361-389.

Boring, M.E. "The Influence of Christian Prophecy on the Johannine
    Portrayal of the Paraclete and Jesus," New Testament Studies 25
    (1978-1979), 113-123.

Bornkamm, G. "Der Paraklet im Johannes-Evangelium," Geschichte und
    Glaube, 1.Tl. (= Gesammelte Aufsätze, Bd.3), Beiträge zur evan-
    gelischen Theologie 48, hrsg. v. E. Wolf (München, 1968), 68-89.

Brown, R.E. "The Paraclete in the Fourth Gospel," New Testament
    Studies 13 (1966-1967), 113-132.

Davies, J.G. "The Primary Meaning of ΠΑΡΑΚΛΗΤΟΣ," JTS N.S.4
    (1953), 35-38.

Leany, A.R.C. "The Johannine Paraclete and the Qumran Scrolls,"
    John and Qumran, ed. J.H. Charlesworth (London, 1972), 38-61.

Lemonnyer, A. "L'Esprit-Saint Paraclet," Revue des sciences philoso-
    phiques et théologiques 16 (1927), 293-307.

Locher, G.W. "Der Geist als Paraklet. Eine exegetisch-dogmatische
    Besinnung," Evangelische Theologie 26 (1966), 565-579.

Michaelis, W. "Zur Herkunft des johanneischen Paraklet-Titels,"
    Coniectanea Neotestamentica 11 (1947), 147-162.

Mowinckel, S. "Die Vorstellungen des Spätjudentums vom heiligen Geist
    als Fürsprecher und der johanneische Paraklet," Zeitschrift für
    die neutestamentliche Wissenschaft und die Kunde der älteren
    Kirche 32 (1933), 97-130.

Müller, U.B. "Die Parakletenvorstellung im Johannesevangelium,"
    Zeitschrift für Theologie und Kirche 71 (1974), 31-77.

Mußner, F. "Die johanneischen Parakletsprüche und die apostolische
    Tradition," Biblische Zeitschrift n.F. 5 (1961), 56-70.

Pietro della Madre di Dio. "Lo Spirito Santo nel Quarto Vangelo,"
    Ephemerides Carmeliticae 7 (1956), 401-527.

Riesenfeld, H. "A Probable Background to the Johannine Paraclete,"
    Ex orbe religionum. Studia Geo Widengren oblata, Vol. 1, Studies
    in the History of Religions (Supplements to Numen) 21 (Leiden,
    1972), 266-274.

Sasse, H. "Der Paraklet im Johannesevangelium," Zeitschrift für die
    neutestamentliche Wissenschaft und die Kunde der älteren Kirche
    24 (1925), 260-277.

Snaith, N.H. "The Meaning of 'The Paraclete'," The Expository Times
    57 (1945-1946), 47-50.

Stuhlmacher, P. "Adolf Schlatter's Interpretation of Scripture,"
New Testament Studies 24 (1977-1978), 433-446.

Windisch, H. "Die fünf johanneischen Parakletsprüche," Festgabe für
Adolf Jülicher zum 70. Geburtstag 26. Januar 1927 (Tübingen,
1927), 110-137.

UNPUBLISHED CORRESPONDENCE

Fischer, P.B. Personal correspondence between P.B. Fischer, some-
time Director of the Vetus Latina Institute, and the Rev. Prof.
C.K. Barrett. 16 January 1975.

ADDITIONAL BIBLIOGRAPHY

Becker, J. Das Evangelium nach Johannes. Bd.2, Kapitel 11-21.
Ökumenischer Taschenbuchkommentar zum Neuen Testament 4/2, hrsg.
v. E. Gräßer u. K. Kertelge. Gütersloh, 1981.

Carson, D.A. "The Function of the Paraclete in John 16:7-11," Journal
of Biblical Literature 98 (1979), 547-566.

Durand, M.-G. de. "Pentecôte johannique et Pentecôte lucanienne chez
certains Pères," Bulletin de Littérature Ecclésiastique 79
(1978), 97-126.

Grayston, K. "The Meaning of PARACLĒTOS," Journal for the Study of
The New Testament 13 (1981), 67-82.

Haenchen, E. Das Johannesevangelium. Ein Kommentar aus den nach-
gelassenen Manuscripten, hrsg. v. U. Busse. Tübingen, 1980.

Painter, J. "The Farewell Discourses and the History of Johannine
Christianity," New Testament Studies 27 (1980-1981), 525-543.

Shafaat, A. "Geber of the Qumran Scrolls and the Spirit-Paraclete of
The Gospel of John," New Testament Studies 27 (1980-1981), 263-
269.

Stenger, W. "ΔΙΚΑΙΟΣΥΝΗ in Jo. XVI 8.10," Novum Testamentum 21
(1979), 2-12.

Wilckens, U. "Der Paraklet und die Kirche," Kirche, Festschrift für
Günther Bornkamm zum 75. Geburtstag, hrsg. v. D. Lührmann u. G.
Strecker (Tübingen, 1980), 185-203.

INDEXES

INDEXES

1. OLD TESTAMENT

2. NEW TESTAMENT

2 John
5   138

3. LITERATURE OF POST-BIBLICAL JUDAISM

Testament of the Twelve Pa-
  triarchs
  T. Judah
    20,1   185n
    5   185n

Community Rule (1QS)
    3,18-19   185n
    20   185n
    4,12   185n
    23   185n

4. EARLY CHRISTIAN LITERATURE

Ambrose   x, 81-82, 84,
                       86, 88, 102-
                       103nn, 107n
De Fide   x
  2,4,38   105nn
  2,6,51   105n
  2,9,76   105n
  3,14,109   106n
  3,16,134   105n
  5,11,134   103n
  5,18,224   105n
De incarnationis dominicae
  sacramento   x
  8,84   104n
De Spiritu sancto
                     x, 82
  1,4,58-59   108n
  1,5,70   105n, 198n
  1,11,116-119   107n, 189n
  1,11,120-125   107n
  1,12,132   103n
  1,13,134   103n
  1,13,135-139   103n
  1,13,136-137   103n, 184n
  2,5,42   106n
  2,11,114-118   106n
  2,11,118   105n
  2,12,131-133   197n
  2,12,131-134   104n
  2,12,134   104-105n
  3,1,6   106n
  3,1,8   104n, 179n,
                     190n
  3,6,35   104n

Ambrose (cont.)
  De Spiritu sancto (cont.)
    3,16,115   103n, 198n
    3,19,152   107n
  Expositio Evangelii secundum
    Lucam   x
    2,13   103n, 184n

Ambrosiaster   x, 96-97, 148,
                      159, 160
  Commentaria in Epistolam ad
    Ephesios   x
    2,17   104n
  In Matthaeum   x, 106n
  Quaestiones   x, 91, 97-98
    89,1   113n, 114nn,
                     116n, 194n
                     195n
    89,2   113n, 194n
    93,1   109nn, 180n,
                     187n
    97,15   106n
    125,1   105n
    125,5-6   107n
    125,6   106n
    125,23   106n

Ammonius   148, 151, 162,
                      163
  Fragmenta in Jo.
                      120-123

5.   MODERN AUTHORS, BOOKS, AND PERIODICALS

6. SUBJECTS